D1527638

Creation

Creation

Biblical Theologies in the Context of the Ancient Near East

Othmar Keel & Silvia Schroer

Translated by
Peter T. Daniels

Winona Lake, Indiana
Eisenbrauns
2015

www.eisenbrauns.com

Library of Congress Cataloging-in-Publication Data

Keel, Othmar, author.
    [Schöpfung. English]
    Creation : biblical theologies in the context of the ancient Near East /
    Othmar Keel & Silvia Schroer ; translated by Peter T. Daniels.
        pages   cm
    Includes bibliographical references and index.
    ISBN 978-1-57506-093-4 (hardback : alk. paper)
        1. Creation—Biblical teaching.   2. Egyptian literature—Relation to
    the Old Testament.   3. Assyro-Babylonian literature—Relation to the
    Old Testament.   I. Schroer, Silvia, 1958– author.   II. Daniels, Peter T.,
    translator.   III. Title.   IV. Title: Biblical theologies in the context of the
    ancient Near East.
        BS651.K3913 2015
        231.7′65—dc23
                                                                    2015009119

The paper used in this publication meets the minimum requirements of the American National
Standard for Information Sciences—Permanence of Paper for Printed Library Materials, ANSI
Z39.48–1984.♾™

Contents

Foreword

This book deals with some crucial moments in the Bible's attempts to comprehend the world as a felicitous and consecrated creation. This is no light undertaking in view of its complexity and opacity, and therefore it is also no wonder that very different models compete, alternating with and supplementing each other, over and over bringing new aspects to the foreground.

Once more, the Freiburg School has produced a collaborative volume. Both authors are responsible for every chapter. The essence and some of the substance of the book go back to many lectures and preliminary studies by both Othmar Keel, who has been interested since the 1960s in ancient Near Eastern and biblical depictions of creation, and Silvia Schroer, who since the 1980s has worked especially on feminist theological perspectives on the topic. The work reached its present form over a long process of lectures (in Berlin, Berne, Freiburg, and Zurich), addresses, writing, and frequent revisions, expansions, contractions, and extensions, during which the editorial pen was wielded by Schroer. Trying out the ideas on students at Protestant institutions in lectures on this topic was a stimulating and rewarding challenge.

The result, shaped by a laborious compositional process that occurred in several phases, is a quite compact creation theology spanning two theological generations, represented by the teacher and his student. It is suggestive to describe the coming into being of this book as a cosmogony writ small, for which several ancient Near Eastern models of coming into being—typically blended—can be invoked. Straight off, the process of origin can be described biologically, according to which the book grew organically, with a gestation period longer than an elephant's. It must remain an open question, however, who did the begetting, carrying, laboring, and birthing. Perhaps *in vitro* techniques would provide a better metaphor! The craftsman gods of the ancient Near East used to fiddle around with world eggs and children in the womb. The filing down of an ever-growing text, the preparation of a number of new drawings, and so on might as well be understood as this sort of manufacture. The creation process was a battle only in the sense that Schroer had to protect the existing manuscript—the cosmos—from chaos in the form of a never-abating flood of alterations and expansions. The work that came into the world cannot help exhibiting many traces of its complex evolution. We hope that—in the womb or on the potter's wheel of the reader and user—it will develop further and provide many with an impetus, perhaps even making them "battle-ready," for transformation of study and research, collegial collaboration, the teaching of religion, and so on, as well as for important dialogue with philosophers, scientists, and legal scholars.[1]

The illustrations for this book originated in large part as drawings of original pieces from the important collections of the Department of Biblical Studies in Freiburg. Within a few years, these collections will be made available to the

---

1. For the benefit of the wider reading public, we have not used Hebrew or Greek type and have opted for a simplified form of transliteration. Biblical passages and references are cited according to the *SBL Handbook of Style*, and Classical works according to the fourth edition of *RGG* (1998). "P" stands for "Priestly writings." The nonbiblical ancient sources are cited, where possible, from easily available editions and translations.

public in a Museum of Bible and Orient. We hope that through both the Freiburg publications and the museum the great contribution of ancient Near Eastern civilization and of the Bible to Western civilization will be made evident.

We thank Inés Haselbach, Hildi Keel-Leu, Julia Müller-Clemm, and Ulrike Zurkinden for their drawings; and Sabine Müller, Irène Schwyn, and Thomas Staubli for the careful reading of the manuscript in various stages of its development.

We dedicate the book to Dominique Barthélemy, who celebrated his eightieth birthday in 2001.[2] His services to the fields of textual history and criticism are recognized worldwide. His work will be continued in Freiburg by Adrian Schenker and Yohanan Goldman. For us, he is important as a representative of the older generation of theologians because of the friendly encouragment he gave his younger colleagues. His openness to the effect of the French Revolution, which is not all that common in French Catholicism, led him to found an Institute with a democratic and egalitarian structure more than thirty years ago. This headless organism is based on mutual listening, openness to the new, respect for the other, and cooperation. The present book arose in this spirit. It was also Dominique Barthélemy who nearly thirty years ago, with his—as it happens, collaborative (with Otto Rickenbacher)—*Konkordanz zum hebräischen Sirach,* inaugurated the happy and long-lasting collaboration between the University Press of Freiburg and the publisher Vandenhoeck and Ruprecht (Göttingen), which has developed primarily through the copublication of the series OBO and NTOA.

Freiburg and Berne, June 2001
Othmar Keel and Silvia Schroer

---

2. Sadly, Fr. Barthélemy passed away on February 10, 2002.

Preface
to the English Translation

The original edition of this book was published in 2002, and a slightly corrected edition, with some additional references, was published in 2008. We are very pleased that, with the appearance of an English translation, the circle of readers will once more be greatly expanded. During the past ten years, a veritable flood of literature has been published in the field of biblical anthropology, although no bestseller on the theme of creation has appeared; some specific texts (e.g., Ps 104) and topics (e.g., blessing) have received significant in-depth study.

In German-speaking countries, but also beyond, this book was well received by biblical scholars and especially by religious educators. The history of religion approach and the clear presentation of images from the ancient Near Eastern background were praised as helpful and illuminating in many individual book reviews and through feedback from individuals. Our contributions to the biblical theology of creation from various perspectives (ecology, feminist theology) were met with approval. On the other hand, more critical voices were heard from those working in systematic theology, primarily in the Reformed environment.

We were trying to embed our exegetical and historical work both theologically and in the history of research, as well as making explicit the implications of our work in concrete situations, we were aware that we were only sketching an outline and providing only selected examples. However, some readers expected a profound examination of all theological approaches and environmental discourses in the global context, especially in the World Council of Churches. It is not surprising that they were disappointed, because we actually had no intention of being exhaustive. In some cases, we barely mention the most important representatives of relevant positions. The book was planned as, and turned out to be, in the first place, a presentation of the Old Testament creation traditions, a discussion of their contexts and the connections of these contexts. If it should turn out that the primacy of the Exodus for the origin and self-determination of Israel is questioned, or if it is discovered that the sources point to the idea of the numinosity of creation, these are important observations for the history of research and for the history of monotheism.

The thesis we presented of the forgotten divinity of creation was not clearly understood by reviewers—insofar as the responses we have seen—despite a more detailed elaboration and exploration in two more recent articles that we have published.[1] These perspectives are widely ignored, because they do not fit into the traditional model of monotheism in which God and the world are diametrically opposed to each other, a model that prevails in Protestant more than in Catholic circles. This model is deeply lodged in systematic theology such that it

---

1. Silvia Schroer, "The Forgotten Divinity of Creation: Suggestions for a Revision of Old Testament Creation Theology in the 21st Century," in André Lemaire (ed.), *Congress Volume Ljubljana 2007* (VTSup 133; Leiden, 2008), 321–37; Silvia Schroer and Othmar Keel, "Die vergessene Göttlichkeit der Schöpfung: Ansätze zu einer Revision alttestamentlicher Schöpfungstheologie im 21. Jahrhundert," in Bernd Janowski and Kathrin Liess (eds.), *Der Mensch im Alten Israel: Neue Forschungen zur alttestamentlichen Anthropologie* (HBS 59; Freiburg i.Br., 2009) 537–90.

is no longer questioned and is an immovable dogma, thus affecting work in the fields of exegesis and biblical theology. One reviewer[2] said that the idea of the numinosity of creation and our discussion of the artwork of creation is obsolete, but this perspective ignores the fact that global political and environmental practices demonstrate every day how completely nature is viewed as an object targeted merely for exploitation. If this reviewer's ideas were accurate, a critical review of and dialogue with the biblical texts and the concomitant attempt to correct the dominant conceptions of the relationship between God and the world would be at best naive and romantic or in any case a waste of time. This, however, would surely stand as an example of putting the biblical texts aside whenever they are considered obsolete for some reason or appear incompatible with modern sensibilities. However, to encounter the full force of facts with a full capitulation and to do so without a historically or biblically based rebuttal would be completely irresponsible.

The present translation is based on the second edition of the German edition. We have, so as not to distort the historical snapshot that a book such as this must be, decided only to add a selection of recent literature as an additions to the bibliography and otherwise have only corrected minor errors. In doing this, the legitimate desires and some concrete suggestions from reviewers are ignored; they could only be incorporated as part of a completely revised new edition. For his initiative in undertaking this translation and for his perseverance in the project, we thank Jim Eisenbraun personally. Thanks are also due to Nancy Rahn (Berne); she has actively and quickly been of great help in proofreading the English translation.

The title of the English edition corrects the idea that theologies are not something that should be considered only as the purview of the Bible and that, on the other hand, ancient Near Eastern cultures only had to do with religions. In many of the chapters in this book, we have called out examples of Egyptian and other theologies. At the same time, we fully understand that biblical theology and the practice of the religion by the general population are not always identical.

What we wish for is that this translation and us as authors may encounter open, curious readers—a colorful combination.

Fribourg and Berne, April 2015

---

2. Lukas Vischer, "Kalenderblätter? Zu Othmar Keel und Silvia Schroer, *Schöpfung: Biblische Theologien im Kontext altorientalischer Religionen*," *Evangelische Theologie* 64 (2004) 294–400.

Introduction:
The Primacy of Exodus Theology
over Creation Theology?

Ever since Gerhard von Rad's famous essay "The Theological Problem of the Old Testament Doctrine of Creation" (1936; English, 1966),[1] the thesis that the First Testament's belief in Yhwh was primarily a belief in election and salvation has been repeated countless times. What was considered specific to Israelite revelation was a historical event, the Exodus. This credo of dialectical theology has been refuted in the course of events since the 1960s by Old Testament scholarship but tenaciously hangs on as an idealized construct. Even in recent theological publications, creation theology has been subordinated, neglected, minimized, or in any case usually not treated as a starting-point or basis for theological thought.[2]

Generally, a great gulf exists between the "propositions" of theology and the religious requirements and experiences of wider, more-or-less Christian groups of people. For many, just a few decades ago, praying the Rosary or the Stations of the Cross might have been at the heart of their Christian piety. Today, by contrast, the literature racks of churches and the devotional calendars or books, especially from evangelical but also from mainstream Protestant and Catholic publishers, are overflowing with nature pictures: leaves, trees or forests, flowers, lawns and meadows, sea and beach, brooks, lakes, sunrises, sunsets, all kinds of animals, and faces of men, women, and children from all over the world. Whether these pleasant pictures—which are not specifically Christian in any way—are combined with appropriate Bible verses or not obviously does not make the slightest bit of difference. The pictures themselves signify comfort and refreshment in every possible circumstance; they encourage the assurance of security in the breadth of creation, from the supportive powers of nature. This development ought to be a wakeup call or a red flag for theologians, both men and women. For the faith of modern man, creation faith is obviously more basic than salvation history. And this has probably often been the case

---

1. For the relation between creation and salvation history, see the interesting and suggestive article by Rolf Rendtorff (1991).
2. For Gerhard von Rad (1962: esp. 121–28), Deut 26:5ff. was the original credo of Israel. Walther Zimmerli began his *Foundation of Old Testament Theology* (1972) with Exod 20:2f. (likewise Deissler 1972). Dorothee Sölle in *To Love and To Work* (1985: 17) developed virtually her entire creation theology out of belief in the primacy of salvation history. Even in 1991, H. D. Preuß makes Yhwh's historical acts of election the programmatic center of his entire *Theology of the Old Testament*. For Preuß, creation in the Old Testament belief structure and hence in Old Testament theology explicitly has no theological weight of its own (1991: 271). Rainer Albertz (1992: 70) also still speaks of the Exodus as the decisive "impulse that set the religious history of Israel in motion." Otto Kaiser, to be sure, pays close attention in his *Theology of the Old Testament* to the creation traditions, with detailed and nuanced expositions, but only after dealing with all other aspects of faith in Yhwh. He prefaces the creation chapters with a statement in the form of a proposition that Old Testament discourse on the creation of the world and man is "not the expression of a belief, but a self-evident logical presupposition that Israel shared with its predecessors and contemporaries" (1998: 210). With this ingenious but, with respect to the ancient Near East, entirely artificial distinction betweeen "belief" and "logical presupposition," the theological meaning of creation is once more *a priori* denied. Also, Erhard S. Gerstenberger's otherwise conceptually innovative publication (2001: esp. 192ff.) on *Theology in the Old Testament* heads, as far as creation theology is concerned, right back into the old ruts.

throughout the history of Christianity, because, significantly, only the major Christian feasts with "natural substrates"—Christmas (birth, winter solstice) and Easter (awakening of nature)—have withstood the waves of secularization. What is alarming is not that all faiths, including Christianity, refer to creation, but rather that romantic nature pictures do not directly promote concern for nature but usually function as empty promises and spiritual hiding-places. It is not uncommon to find that the same people who have a poster of an unspoiled mountain meadow in full flower over their bed are the same ones who attempt with a noisesome machine to destroy every so-called weed and bit of crabgrass in their yard in order to achieve a sterile lawn, and have two cars in the garage.

The traditional theory, that the experience of the escape from Egypt was foundational and original and that belief in God, creator of heaven and earth, only secondary has meanwhile been massively shaken by exegetical and (reli-gion-)historical research. The priority of memory of the Exodus is hardly used at all any more as a basis for dating biblical texts, and in recent Palestinian ar-chaeology and the religious history of Palestine/Israel, the picture of the origin of Israel has greatly changed in the past few years. The village population that began to settle in the highlands after the collapse of Egyptian dominion at the start of the Early Iron age, around 1200 B.C., were not, according to current un-derstanding, immigrants from foreign lands but for the most part Canaanites by descent. At the time of Egyptian domination, their ancestors had lived in the land as nomads. The small Exodus groups, which previously had emigrated to Egypt, who under extraordinary circumstances managed to flee to Palestine, had given an enormous impulse to the nascent Yhwh religion, but the worship of this fierce, warlike God did not yet constitute a full-blown religion. Its founda-tions were much more strongly marked by the worship, long rooted in the land and in Canaanite culture, of gods who were responsible for the prosperity of the land, people, animals, and plants—in short, precisely for creation.

The Israelites did not adapt some poor imitation of belief in a foreign, say Ugaritic, creator to Yhwh. Instead, over a long period, processes involving merger, adaptation, and selection took place, and these led to the coming into existence of Yhwh monotheism.[3] The dynamic of some developments that can be found in the Bible demonstrably usually leads from references to creation and existential questions to historical ones. The creation festivals of Canaan were secondarily historicized; the prayers of Yhwh-believers, for example, were secondarily linked with events in the Davidic history.[4]

The primacy of the Exodus and liberation tradition can thus no longer be maintained on the basis of its historical foundations, either.

Here is where our book begins, by taking seriously the creation traditions of the First Testament as foundational witnesses to belief in the Yhwh religion, all the while attempting to look at and organize aspects that are somewhat new, at the same time also confronting current questions, continually inquiring into what is incipient and provocative for today's Christians. We acknowledge clos-est spiritual affinity to the positions of the Dutch Catholic feminist theologian Catharina J. M. Halkes (1990), in whose small book *To Renew the Face of the Earth* we were delighted to encounter some familiar thoughts while working on ours. While Halkes turns to biblical passages only among others, in this book we are attempting a radical rethinking in the direction of a fundamental review of bib-lical creation traditions. Against the background of developments in theology

---

3. Keel and Uehlinger 2001. A summary sketch of recent history of religions research is found in Schroer 1996.
4. Psalms 3, 34, 51f., 54–57, 59f., 60, 63. See the excursus to chap. III.7 below, pp. 64ff..

during the twentieth century (chap. 1), when Catholic exegesis and theology was of very limited significance for decades,[5] our contribution is unmistakably an attempt to counterpose an alternative to the position of Protestant "orthodoxy" that is still predominant in German-language Old Testament exegesis, an alternative with its roots in liberal and Catholic theology with its broader understanding of revelation, as well as in engagement with liberation theology and feminist theology; and not least, this enterprise possibly can be formulated somewhat less guardedly in countries such as the Netherlands or Switzerland than in Germany.[6]

---

5. But see the recent Catholic publications of Clifford and Collins (1992) and Löning and Zenger (1997). If in what follows no Catholic exegetes are mentioned for long stretches, this is not to say that there were none at all but that they played no decisive or even leading role in the major developments. See the overview of research in R. G. Kratz and H. Spieckermann, "Schöpfer/Schöpfung, II: Altes Testament," *TRE* 30 (1999): 258–83.

6. It is striking that Switzerland continues to provide energy for unexpected theological developments and that exegetical "peculiarities" can arise there (K. Barth, L. Ragaz, V. Maag, etc.). One, but certainly not the only, condition for this possibility probably is the peripheral position of Switzerland in terms of significance, not merely geography, with respect to the dominant heartland of theology, Germany.

I. The Status of Creation Traditions in Several Twentieth-Century Currents of Christian Theology

1. In the History of Religions School and the Liberal Theology of the Turn of the Century

For more than two thousand years, Jews and Christians considered the Bible a work written by prophets to whom God had directly revealed everything they wrote down. In this revelation, the Jews sought instructions for living, and the Christians searched the Old Testament (as the Hebrew Bible has been called since the second half of the second century A.D.) for prophecies about Christ on which to found their faith. This supernatural (preternatural) understanding of the Bible was dominant into the seventeenth or eighteenth century. After the first seventeenth-century forerunners (Hugo Grotius, Baruch Spinoza, Richard Simon), the era of critical investigation of the Bible began with the Enlightenment. Contradictions and textual strata were discovered in the Pentateuch, and attempts were made to place the Psalms, whose Davidic authorship was now coming into doubt, in chronological order. An encounter with the ancient Near East could not yet occur, since nothing at all was known about it beyond what was found in the Bible and in the notices of a few Greek and Roman writers. Johann Gottfried Herder (1744–1803) considered the Old Testament the oldest records of the human race and the creation story the natural first view of the universe. It was Julius Wellhausen (1844–1918) who declared that knowledge of the Old Testament and a few pre-Islamic traditions about ancient Arabia fully sufficed for the understanding of ancient Israel.[1] Georg Friedrich Grotefend's initial successes in the decipherment of the Persian column of a little trilingual cuneiform inscription from Persepolis, all the way back in 1802, had no effect on the principles of the exegetes. Only much later did they recognize the implications of nineteenth-century archaeological discoveries for their discipline: the rediscovery of the Egyptian and Mesopotamian civilizations abruptly changed the Bible from the oldest book of humanity to a relatively late testimony of ancient Near Eastern spiritual life.

1.1. The Rediscovery of the Ancient Near East

The scholars whom Napoleon brought along on his Egyptian campaign (1797–1801) published the first detailed description of Egyptian antiquities. Their discoveries and the preparation of the related material (including the Rosetta Stone) made possible Jean-François Champollion's 1822 decipherment of the ancient Egyptian hieroglyphic script. In 1843, the Turin native Paul Emile Botta, who worked under French auspices, began to expose the reliefs in the palace of the Assyrian king Sargon II at Khorsabad (27 years before Schliemann's excava-

---

1. After the Council of Trent, Catholic theology was largely uninterested in the historical investigation of Scripture and concerned itself primarily with philosophy, principally the neo-scholasticism that arose in the nineteenth century.

tions at Troy). Two years later, the Englishman Austen Henry Layard followed with successful excavations at Nimrud and Nineveh. In 1852, Hormuzd Rassam found Assurbanipal's library of some twenty thousand cuneiform tablets. A few years later (1857), Edward Hincks (whose laurel has generally been awarded to H. C. Rawlinson; Daniels 1994, 1995) and other savants definitively completed the decipherment of cuneiform. In 1872, Rawlinson's successor, George Smith, after the discovery of cuneiform tablets with portions of a Babylonian Flood story, presented a lecture on the Babylonian epic of the creation of the world and its relationship to the Old Testament narratives of creation. Four years later, his book *The Chaldaean Account of Genesis* appeared in London, with translations of the Babylonian epic of the creation of the world and the Babylonian Flood narrative juxtaposed synoptically with the comparable biblical passages.[2] From Egypt too came more and more news of amazing discoveries. In 1887, the correspondence of the revolutionary pharaoh Amenophis IV (Akhenaton) with princes in Palestine was discovered in his archive at Amarna in central Egypt. In 1890, William Matthew Flinders Petrie, who had previously dug in Egypt, initiated scientific excavation at Tell el-Hesi, which Petrie believed was Lachish, about twenty kilometers northeast of Gaza. Thus, in the big picture of the rediscovery of the ancient Near East, tiny Palestine also received increasing attention from archaeologists, Assyriologists, and Egyptologists.

1.2. The Theological Consequences

Only in 1890 did German theologians associated with the young Hermann Gunkel (b. 1862), among them Hugo Gressmann and Wilhelm Bousset, begin to reflect systematically on the consequences of the new archaeological discoveries for the understanding of the Bible. The *history of religions* school welcomed the rediscovery of the ancient civilizations.[3] It represented a liberal theology,[4] strongly influenced by the historical sciences and ethnology, directed against Lutheran orthodoxy and its particularistic positivism toward revelation, and it stressed the connection between Israel's traditions and humanity's in general. One of its favorite topics was creation traditions, much of which Israel shared with neighboring cultures.[5]

Gunkel's *Creation and Chaos in the Primeval Era and the Eschaton* appeared in 1895. Here he shows that creation was understood in Babylonia as a conquest in a war with chaos (the dragon), that this concept also appears in the Old Testament (Psalms 74, 89) and exerted influence even into the Revelation of St. John (Revelation 12). The careful reconstruction of the progress of a Babylonian myth into biblical Scripture was received with the utmost interest by the world of German scholarship: some hailed the book as a Copernican revolution; others condemned the approach and methods of the young scholars from the ground up, including the aforementioned leading exegete, Julius Wellhausen (b. 1844), who was firmly convinced of the theological irrelevance of the antecedents of biblical content and considered the investigation of the biblical writers' material a task not for exegetes but for antiquarians at best (Klatt 1969: 71). In his indignant

---

2. Along the same lines, see Lambert 1965 and Keel and Küchler 1983.
3. See J. Hempel, "Religionsgeschichtliche Schule," *RGG* 5 (3d ed., 1961): 992–94; on Gunkel's theology, see Klatt 1969.
4. See H. Graß, "Theologischer und kirchlicher Liberalismus," *RGG* 4 (3d ed., 1960): 351–55.
5. See Gunkel 1997 and such typical titles as Karl Marti's *The Religion of the Old Testament among the Religions of the Near East* (*Die Religion des Alten Testaments unter den Religionen des Vorderen Orients*; 1906). For the history of this period of research and the history of religions school, see Klatt 1969, Kraus 1982: 295–367, Lehmann 1994, Lüdemann 1996.

reply to the criticism, Gunkel charged that the entire older generation of exegetes was interested only in the individual personalities of the biblical writers, with no concern whatever for the history of the peoples and their religions that constituted the background of the text. Theologically, in the process, he freed himself from the preternatural interpretation of revelation and the romantic idea that the individual genius is the main medium of divine revelation. Instead, he enthusiastically stressed that all of human history encompasses revelation and therefore called for an appropriate piety in the face of the evidence of the ancient Near Eastern religions. Gunkel enlisted the old theological declaration "The seed of divine revelation was not sown only on Jewish ground," which already appears in similar form in the church fathers Origen and Eusebius,[6] to honor the historical forerunners of his own tradition. In his opinion, only through profound understanding of them could the understanding and evaluation of the details of biblical tradition grow, as he had made clear by example in *Creation and Chaos*. He did not consider it a leveling of the properties of Israelite religion but rather a demonstration of its special qualities, which previously others had merely asserted. Gunkel was convinced that the Old Testament had collected and illuminated the wisdom bestowed by the ancient Near East.

Not everyone interested in connections between the ancient Near East and the Bible was so cautious and argued with as much discrimination as Gunkel. On January 13, 1902, thirty years after George Smith's sensational discoveries, the Assyriologist Friedrich Delitzsch delivered a lecture in Berlin before the German Oriental Society and in the presence of the Emperor—that is, to the ears of the general public—entitled "Bible and Babel" (see Johanning 1988, Lehmann 1994), in which he attempted to derive the entire Pauline doctrine of redemption from a single Babylonian cylinder seal. For Assyriologists and Old Testament scholars, this was nothing new, but what was new was the widespread publicity. Representatives of the churches, particularly, reacted with indignation and anger.[7] Delitzsch had burned his bridges behind him and in further lectures in the heated debate trapped himself with the assertion that all of biblical revelation was a "great deception." The so-called Pan-Babylonianists, principally Hugo Winckler and Peter Jensen, undertook a veritable orgy of deriving the entire Old and New Testaments from Babylonia. Gunkel reacted to this extremism with great good humor and irony (Klatt 1969: 102), but this cannot conceal the fact that over the long term the interests of the history of religions school were severely compromised by the extreme distortion.

For legitimate research into the relations between the ancient Near East and the Old Testament, more important than the noisy quarrel were the scholarly publications of those years, such as Alfred Jeremias's great work, *The Old Testament in Light of the Ancient Near East* (1905), Hugo Gressmann's anthologies of ancient Near Eastern texts and pictures relating to the Old Testament (1909), and the study published in 1924 by Adolf Erman, "An Egyptian Source of the Proverbs of Solomon," in which he shows that Prov 22:17–24:34 depends on the Egyptian book of wisdom of Amenemope.

In the 1920s and 1930s, when Nazism was in political ascendance, the position of the history of religions school became ever more difficult in the German-speaking world. Nevertheless, history of religions work continued in Scandinavia during the War. A student of Gunkel's, Sigmund Mowinckel, in several articles going back to the 1920s commenced a concentration on the ritual

6. The first inklings of this idea are already found in Paul's sermon on the Areopagus (Acts 17:22–31).
7. As late as 1912, Hermann Klüger's book, *Friedrich Delitzsch, the Apostle of the New Babylonian Religion: A Warning Cry to the German People*, appeared in Leipzig.

history of ancient Near Eastern and Old Testament religion. While this school was decried by ancient Near Eastern and Old Testament scholars alike as a last bastion of Pan-Babylonianism, excavations at Ugarit (beginning in 1929) were already promoting renewed interest in the concrete cultural context of ancient Israel, resulting in even a sort of Pan-Ugariticism (Mitchell J. Dahood). For the first time, the Ugaritic myths supplied a more-complete self-presentation of a religion that had been acknowledged in the Bible: the Canaanite religion and its gods Baal, El, Asherah, Astarte, and so on (see Haag 1962).

Theology since the late nineteenth century has also been challenged by revolutionary discoveries in biology and anthropology and a new natural philosophy, cosmology, and behavioral science. Charles Darwin (1809–1882), Ernst Haeckel (1834–1919), and others laid the foundations of the theory of evolution, which represented a serious challenge to the hitherto unquestioned reading of the reports of creation as reports of actual events, but many interpreted evolution as primarily calling faith into question. The churches rejected these provocative theories unconditionally; governing boards forbade the teaching of evolution in school curriculums. A positive reception of evolutionary theory was met first in liberal theological circles. But their famous representative, Adolf von Harnack, at the same time was defending a Marcionite critique of the canonicity of the First Testament in general, so no moderation of the positions resulted. The topic was literally put on ice by both Catholic and Protestant theology until the 1980s, with the result that the protracted conflict has not been resolved to this day and remains political poison.[8]

2. In the Dialectical Theology of the 1930s

Against the rabid nationalism that gained the upper hand with World War I, liberal theology had nothing to offer that could match the irrational, archaic thought of this period. It was, at least in part, sucked into the Zeitgeist.[9] The enlightened spirit of liberal theology was formulated by some of its representatives, either openly (Adolf von Harnack) or implicitly (Rudolf Bultmann), at the expense of Judaism.[10] In any case, most liberal theologians, including Old Testament scholars (Albrecht Alt, Otto Eißfeldt, Gustav Hölscher, Wilhelm Rudolph), were not prepared for the political insanity. They endeavored to pursue their academic research unperturbed. Others were completely blind to the dangers of a "natural theology,"[11] whose "ethnic" variety was linked with Nazi "blood

---

8. A small selection of the immense literature may be mentioned: Daecke 1981, Westermann 1984, J. Hübner 1987, Gräb 1995, Mortensen 1995, Welker 1995, Esterbauer 1996, Schmitz-Moorman 1997. Further bibliography in S. Daecke, "Darwinismus, II: Religionsphilosophisch," RGG 2 (4th ed., 1999): 585f.; J. Hübner, "Darwinismus, III: Systematisch-theologisch," RGG 2 (4th ed., 1999): 586; P. Hefner, "Darwinismus, IV: Ethisch," RGG 2 (4th ed., 1999): 586f. On the relation between science and theology, see J. Hübner, "Evolution, III: Evolution und Schöpfungsglaube," RGG 2 (4th ed., 1999): 1753f.

In the U.S. and Israel, especially in the early 1980s, battles raged between "evolutionists" and (biblical) "creationists." Today the fundamentalist opponents of teaching evolution in the U.S. call themselves "creation scientists." They use the Internet to spread their ideas and plead in court, under the banner of freedom of religion, that the biblical creationism du jour be taught in schools (see Webb 1994) [at this writing, the current term is "intelligent design" –trans.]. Then, as now, the question of the origin of the universe is an effective index of unresolved problems between theology and evolution regarding scientific theory, because coarser and coarser biblicistic and creationistic discourse regarding the creator God is placed before the public in order to contrast cosmologies.

9. For Old Testament scholarship between 1933 and 1945, see especially Crüsemann 1989 and C. Weber 2000.

10. On anti-Judaism in Harnack and Bultmann see von der Osten-Sacken 1978.

11. The concept is problematic and incorporates a variety of positions. In the twentieth century, Protestant theology no longer had a "natural" theology in the narrower sense, comparable to the theologia naturalis of Catholic tradition. See W. Sparn, "Natürliche Theologie," TRE 24 (1994): 85–98.

and soil" myths, or to the dangers of the central teaching of neo-Lutheranism that the state is the "order of creation" (Ebach 1989, esp. 104f.). The Old Testament scholar Artur Weiser, who considered himself both a confirmed Nazi and a Christian, in fact defended the revealed character of the First Testament and assented to Israelite belief in election (on nationalistic grounds!) but rejected the "legalistic religion." "Legalistic religion" was—and not just for Weiser—the label for one of the lines, the Jewish line, that developed out of ancient Israel, while the second line was supposedly the one that ran toward Christ. The Old Testament scholar's task was to cast aside the Jewish forms of expression and thought from the claims of revelation in the First Testament. The renowned Old Testament scholar and (beginning in 1927) editor of the *Zeitschrift für die alttestamentliche Wissenschaft* [*Journal for the Academic Study of the Old Testament*], Johannes Hempel (1891–1964), an interested member of the "German Christians," firmly maintained the significance of the First Testament for Christian theology, but reacted to the "people's ideology" of the Nazis by calling attention to the special place held by popular and election thought in the Old Testament and from it deduced that the "people" is an entity created and blessed by God (C. Weber 2000). The partition between Judaism and the, in effect, Christian occupation of the First Testament remained fundamental in Old Testament studies for the duration of the Nazi period.

It was only the dialectical theology of Karl Barth, Friedrich Gogarten, and others,[12] whose thought was becoming accepted in the 1930s, that managed to oppose on the theological level the unholy developments of the time. Dialectical theology contrasted the particularism of election with the religious universalism of the turn of the century; the psychologized religions understood from below it contrasted with the entirely different revelation bursting from above, the *kerygma* addressed to the believer. The unique and particular in Israel's tradition was stressed, just as in the political and social spheres internationalism was stressed over the popular and national, and the horizontalism of democracy was contrasted with the verticality of a leadership—a Führerdom—decided by fate. In this critical distancing from the idea of rulership, however, a then unrecognized advance in the direction of the thought of the enemy lay hidden. The word of *the* "Führer" was contrasted with the word of the true "lord," *the* "history" with the history of Israel, *the* "Heil" with the saving power of the God of Israel. The works of the new generation of great Old Testament scholars, such as Gerhard von Rad, Hans Walter Wolff, and Martin Noth, are contributions to this new theological conception. Von Rad fought the isolation and prioritization of creation theology that might have led to the sacralization of certain elements of nature (and of the state). Wolff devoted himself intensively to the word of God and of the prophets in the First Testament, Noth to the law and covenant of God with Israel. Creation and wisdom as components of human knowledge of God were pushed to the background,[13] creation traditions subsumed under covenant theology and soteriological concepts. To some extent, they theologically blocked off the areas that might have been able to partake of Nazi ideology (Rendtorff 1991), without, to be sure, realizing that talk of the "people," or of salvation (*Heil*), salvation history, election, and leadership (*Führung*) of a people

---

12. See W. Pannenberg, "Dialektische Theologie," *RGG* 2 (3d ed., 1958): 168–74; D. Korsch, "Dialektische Theologie," *RGG* 2 (4th ed., 1999): 809–15.

13. The biblical wisdom writings, especially Job and Qohelet, continued to be read, but with very specific questions in mind. Thus, for Barth's theology Job was an important datum point under the aspect "witnesses to the truth," which he went into in great detail in the central chapter on the doctrine of atonement of his *Church Dogmatics* (IV/3).

was and is a most fragile subject when undertaken by inhuman ideologies.[14] Well into the 1950s, given the historical catastrophe, stress on the singularity, the irreversibility, even the arbitrariness (election) of the biblical God, whose unreasonable demands humanity can endure only by grace, remained an acceptable answer.

At this point, we may also call attention to the accomplishments of the Swiss biblical theologian Leonhard Ragaz (1868–1945). Karl Barth and Leonhard Ragaz remained in close contact and exerted strong mutual influence, but Ragaz distinguished himself from Barth by the expressly political content of his theology and founded the religious-social movement in Switzerland. Ragaz, a lifelong prophetic antimilitarist and peace activist,[15] in his last year, shortly before the end of the Second World War, prepared a comprehensive interpretation of the Bible (posthumously published in 1947), the first part of which deals with the Primary History. It also fell to him to counter the atrocities of his time, to formulate the Other, the True, the Universal on the basis of the biblical tradition. He did this not because he was limiting himself to Exodus and election theology, but because in the context of the horror of Nazi dominion and the Second World War he planned a creation theology that was pointedly critical of dominion: The creature must not set himself in the place of the creator.[16] Despite the fact that his starting point was rooted in dialectical theology, Ragaz adhered to some basic ideas of liberal theology: for instance, the thought that among heathen peoples major or minor kernels of truth were regularly to be found, in the "religion" of the peoples could be found the primeval revelation of God (1947: 112–19).[17] He directed the epithet "heathendom" against Christianity, intending to criticize its idols. Ragaz also—like his Catholic contemporary Teilhard de Chardin—based an idiosyncratic theological theory of evolution on his creation theology. Creation, and the creature man as well, was for him in continual development—that is, evolution—which in man aspires ever more to perfection. Creation should be understood not as a single act but as a perpetual process proceeding from God and to God. This holds also for man, who never *is*, but always first must *become* (1947, esp. 93–97).

3. In the Ecumenical Theology of the Post-War Period

The influence of dialectical theology on German-speaking Old Testament scholars was powerful and remains so today, albeit no longer monolithically.[18] Dialectical theology was dominant especially in the generation of exegetes following World War II. In their works, the "Primary History" became an early history of Israel extended backward (von Rad 1962, Kraus 1982: 393–434). In explicating

---

14. For the concept of "people" (*Volk*) in Old Testament scholarship during Nazism, see C. Weber 2000. It would be equally worthwhile to compare the biblical notion of "shalom" with the Nazi discourse on "Heil."

15. For his significance, see Lindt 1956; Mattmüller 1957, 1968; Böhm 1988.

16. In Ragaz's theological plan, Israel's creation theology was fundamentally different from that of the heathen peoples. Its distinctive characteristic was for him—though in the interim we have learned that it was not unique at all—that ethically it was consistently directed toward greater justice. Free creation by the living God is the original and basic form of miracle (1947: 29).

17. Ancient Near Eastern materials should not be used, said Ragaz, to devalue biblical presentations, because the pillars of the ancient traditions were incorporated into the new structures (1947: 34). He names hardly any names, but in the context of the Bible–Babel debate he must have been aiming at the "Pan-Babylonianists" (see chap. I.1 above, pp. 4f.).

18. As late as 1970 (393–417), H. D. Preuß, trapped in this exegetical tradition, could write that the Old Testament evidences for wisdom-endowed attitude were "passages that lead on to the proper biblical kerygma."

biblical creation texts, the anti-mythic was stressed above everything else, and in mythical creation statements (e.g., in Psalms 74 and 89), a typically Israelite historicizing of myth was immediately assumed, while the equally common and important process of mythologizing of history was completely overlooked.

The catastrophe of World War II, however, had brought the Nazi movement provisionally to an end. Everywhere, borders opened; the formation of the U.N. and international trade commissions, not to mention burgeoning mass tourism, brought to the foreground encounters with other cultures and religions and questions that concerned all humanity. On December 24, 1968, upon emerging from radio blackout behind the moon, the American astronauts Frank Borman, William Anders, and Jim Lovell read the first ten verses of Genesis. The continual internationalization of politics during the 1960s and 1970s provided an opportunity to consider the universally human, the timeless or less time-bound concerns of the Bible.[19] In the 1950s and early 1960s, Protestant theology cautiously began to reopen itself to a strongly universalistic way of thinking. While for Gerhard von Rad Genesis 1–2 still represented a sort of preface to the history of Israel, the creation texts now began to be understood ever more strongly as statements about fundamental orderings, not as protology. Thus, Claus Westermann in his commentary on Genesis (1966: 89–95; English 1994) stressed that the Primeval History was not just a prologue to the history of Israel but that universal human traditions were given expression in it.[20] The Swiss Old Testament scholar Victor Maag, a liberal theologian and history of religions adherent who survived the era of dialectical theology practically unscathed, already in the 1950s interpreted Genesis 2 entirely from the perspective that the texts were concerned not with history but with what is timelessly valid (Maag 1954, 1955).

Hand in hand with the rediscovery of the creation stories as discourses on the basic organization of life goes the reawakening of the Sleeping Beauty of wisdom literature from more than thirty years' slumber. One of Victor Maag's students, Hans Heinrich Schmid (1966), returned the significance of international wisdom traditions for the First Testament to the foreground of German-language exegesis with great success,[21] after this shift had been accomplished in other countries some years earlier.[22] The connection between creation traditions and wisdom traditions is causal, because the orderings laid down in creation are the same as those traced out by the wise in order to give instruction for successful life.[23] Their proximity also is apparent in the fact that in both of them gods who are specific to regions or peoples retreat in favor of a founder god and in that both are international. Creation theology and wisdom theology share a certain direct accessibility.[24] From the example of Gerhard von Rad's theology,

---

19. The depth psychology interpretation of the Bible, for example, stressed this universal, just as generally at that time interest in political ideology gave way to interest in psychological categories.

20. See his student Rainer Albertz's work, *World Creation and Human Creation* (1974).

21. His book, *Justice as World Order: Background and History of the Old Testament Concept of Justice* (1968), was frankly revolutionary. Dialectical theology had understood *ṣedeq* and *ṣedaqah* as relational concepts, especially on the basis of Gen 15:6; Rom 4:3, 9, 22; and Gal 3:6. Schmid showed that in some places in the First Testament this concept is to be understood more appropriately in the sense of the ancient Near Eastern, objectivizing world-order notion and of Egyptian *maʿat*. Cf. also Schmid 1974. Schmid's work, strongly oriented to the history of ideas, is criticized by Halbe 1979.

22. See the mostly English articles in the Festschrift for H. H. Rowley, which appeared in the prestigious series "Supplements to Vetus Testamentum" under the title *Wisdom in Israel and in the Ancient Near East* (Noth and Thomas 1955).

23. In Egyptian mythology, Maat, the goddess of the world order, is associated especially with the world-sustaining sun-god Amun-Re, and in biblical passages, *ḥokmah* is associated with the God of Israel (cf. chap. X.2 below, pp. 177ff.).

24. This is why we can intuitively understand a New Kingdom Egyptian hymn to the sun or Psalm 104 and why Christian festivals that are closely connected with natural cycles enjoy wider popularity than those that are specifically Christian. Creation theology and wisdom theology unite religions and survive changes in them.

the cowardly solutions of dialectical theology's doctrines can be recited. If von Rad initially denied the existence of Israelite belief in creation (1936; English, 1966), he nuanced his position gradually (1957: esp. 149ff.; English, 1962) and later devoted himself increasingly to biblical wisdom theology (von Rad 1970; English, 1972), in which connection he noteworthily spoke of the "self-evidence of creation" (see Rendtorff 1991, esp. 102f.). The conviction of Israel's wise that creation by God can be questioned and that knowledge of the primeval order is available to all caused von Rad increasingly to doubt some of the premises of the theology of his time and its doctrine of the total hiddenness of God (von Rad 1971: 153f.).

Catholic exegesis, which had been paralyzed by the anti-modernist movement, after World War II began to recover, partly because Pius XII permitted exegetes to interpret the Bible within the framework of their cultural contexts with the encyclical "Divine afflante spiritu," published in 1943. For the first time, Genesis 1–2 could be read as teaching about creation rather than as a report of historical events (so Renckens 1957), without fear of sanctions from the church bureaucracy. The Second Vatican Council also decreed theological openness, which resulted, for instance, under pressure from North American bishops, in the acceptance of the doctrine of religious freedom. On the other hand, there was no reconciliation of the Catholic church with the thought of the paleontologist, philosopher, and theologian Pierre Teilhard de Chardin (1881–1951). This Jesuit was reprimanded several times by prohibiting him from speaking and publishing, and it was only after his death that his writings could finally be published; even then, the Holy See in 1962 declared them unclear and erroneous. His brilliant attempt, in collaboration with universalistic thinkers familiar with various sciences and regions of the world to meld philosophical anthropology and biblical salvation history with the scientific theory of evolution aroused too many suspicions.

4. In the Contextual Theologies of the 1980s and 1990s

It was typical for theology after World War II, when it was once again open more to the environment than it was to humanity and hence to traditions of creation and wisdom, to deal primarily with the history of ideas.[25] Conversely, the theology of the 1980s and 1990s is marked especially by downsizing and the retreat of idealistic proposals. Universal triumphalism yielded to disillusion and the need to alter existing conditions rather than discuss universal systems. Political and feminist theologies, liberation theologies, and others of this sort are characterized by their concrete concerns, their sensitivity to the power-political, social, and most recently biological presuppositions of theological proposals. Creation theology is marked by a greater awareness of issues of power, but especially with regard to its relationship to ecology and the urgent need for a new definition of the relationship of Christianity to other religions.

An example of the significance of these developments is that anthroposophy (founded by Rudolf Steiner at the end of the nineteenth century), which for decades had been under massive bombardment from the theologians (*inter alia*, on the grounds of gnosticism and pantheism),[26] at the same time displayed an uncommon broadening. Anthroposophy as a doctrine never gained general

---

25. See the notes on Old Testament exegesis in the first three quarters of the twentieth century in Keel ed. 1980: 12–30.
26. See the detailed presentation of the successive stages of the debate in Geisen 1992.

currency, but its principles for biologically appropriate agriculture and its na-
ture-sensitive connection with all things having to do with everyday life set
standards of behavior that were more appropriate to creation, for Christians as
well. In view of ever more critical ecological problems, old controversies became
meaningless; the proof of the pudding is in the eating.

4.1. Liberation Theology

Liberation theology's connection with creation traditions in the 1980s was
at first stuck firmly in the ruts of dialectical theology. In the initial phases of
Latin American liberation theology, Exodus and the Prophets were the only
portions of the Old Testament consulted; wisdom and creation played a very
limited role.[27] If creation is mentioned, it involves a challenge, as already was
the case for Leonhard Ragaz, to formulate a creation theology that is critical of
dominion. Dorothee Sölle's greatest concern, in the context of rigid American
creationism, is the potential misuse of creation theology (1985: 22–25, 1990:
61–74). "All fundamentalist theologies turn the orders of creation into an essential component of belief in creation and absolutize them" (1990: 65f.). Sexism,
homophobia, Apartheid, and slavery were and still are passed off as "consistent
with creation" and so legitimized. Because Sölle, in the tradition of dialectical
theology, considers liberation to be the primary *kerygma* of the Bible, she brings
out the liberating, even egalitarian, impulses of Genesis 1–2. Creation is an act
of liberation and a part of, not a prologue to, salvation history and redemption
(1990: 71f.). Sölle's creation theology remains soteriological. Pedro Trigo (1991)
also subordinates creation theology to historical discourse and the concern for
liberation, which he connects biblically to Deutero-Isaiah. Its central object is a
new creation of humanity and the world in the global context of injustice.

Interestingly, feminist theology of the 1990s is marked by a retreat from "Exodus" as the model for women's liberation. In her book *Again We Stand at Sinai*
(1990, esp. 96–107), the Jewish feminist Judith Plaskow formulates a far-reaching
skepticism regarding Israel's consciousness of election that is bound up with
biblical liberation traditions, a consciousness that inexorably leads to discrimination, exclusion, and the erection of hierarchies.[28] In more recent feminist
proposals, the Exodus still plays its proper role, but no longer as a paradigm of
the exodus of women from patriarchal institutions. It symbolizes rescue and the
finding of identity through delimitation, but the search is for symbols that make
association possible, transcending international, interreligious, and intercultural
borders. The Exodus is not appropriate for this. A further noteworthy tendency
is a conspicuous increase of Catholic voices on the topic of creation theology
(Matthew Fox, Catharina J. M. Halkes, Rosemary Radford Ruether, etc.), a sign
that in the Catholic tradition, at least, the potential exists for solving problems
in the history of theology.

4.2. Ecology and Theology

In the background of the disillusionment that the creation theologies of the
last two decades document stand the signs of ecological crisis that have been

---

27. Under titles such as *Wisdom and Liberation* (Scannone 1992) mostly lurks the liberation theology
demand that one heed the people, its wisdom, and its piety, but not a real encounter with (biblical)
wisdom theology.

28. On the part of Christian theology, the plea for a farewell to consciousness of election grows ever
louder (see, most recently, Jörns 2001).

impossible to ignore since the 1970s. The Club of Rome announced the "Limits to Growth" (Meadows et al. 1972).[29] In 1967 the American historian Lynn White Jr. was the first to rebuke Christianity for historical complicity in the exploitation of nature. At that time, the euphoria of progress still ruled, and theologians were certainly proud of the fact that Christianity had done its part by demythologizing and dedeifying the world. This boomeranged. White's theories found champions in the German-speaking world in Carl Amery (1972) and Eugen Drewermann (1981). For Amery, Gen 1:28 was the executive summary for "anthropocentrism" and a real contribution to the destruction of the earth. Drewermann stressed that Hebrew thought and the biblical Scriptures themselves had radically ripped man out of nature, the few texts that said otherwise being not Israelite but Egyptian or Canaanite. In the following years, exegetes and theologians, without entirely denying the accusations, concerned themselves with refining the analysis.

One of the first to stake out a detailed position against Amery's charges that the biblical doctrine of creation, with its dedeifying and objectivization of the world, had prepared the way for modern exploitation of natural resources was Jürgen Moltmann (1985). His point was that the Bible's anthropocentric conception of the world was in fact more than three thousand [sic!] years old, whereas scientific-technical civilization had arisen no more than four hundred years ago. The Enlightenment, the progress of science and technology, and a philosophy that made man the measure of all things had, according to Moltmann, far more influence than the anthropocentrism of Genesis 1.

A sign of the social and religious changes of the 1980s was the European Ecumenical Assembly "Peace with Justice" held in Basel in 1989, where for the first time since the Middle Ages the churches of Europe gathered under the themes "Justice, Peace, and Preservation of Creation." Special attention was paid to the manifold threats to the environment that had concerned concilial proceedings in the churches for years before and after this event:

> We consider it to be a scandal and a crime that irreversible damage continues to be inflicted on creation. We are becoming aware that there is a need for a new partnership between human beings and the rest of nature. . . . We will work for an international environmental order.[30]

The creation-theological statements of the final document of the conference concentrated on an interpretation, fundamentally critical of dominion, of faith in God as the proprietor of *all* creation. With this claim, broad circles of Christianity took the first step out of the shadow of the anthropocentrism of Genesis 1–2. The obvious need for a theological paradigm shift encouraged the widest possible comprehension of Old Testament creation traditions.[31]

4.3. Ecofeminism

Since the 1990s, the confrontation of theology with ecological questions has been led by feminist theologians.[32] As early as 1974, the Frenchwoman Françoise

---

29. See also Forrester 1972 and, for what follows, Rappel 1996: 11–21.
30. From §74 of the final document, quoted from Felber and Pfister 1989: 80. English text from the website http://oikoumene.net/eng.home/eng.regional/eng.reg.basel/eng.reg.basel.7/index.html. For the biblical foundation of the themes coming from Basel, see especially Duchrow and Liedke 1989.
31. For the cycle of problems of ecology and theology in the present see Hilpert 1987 (literature review) and Keel 1987; see also the comprehensive collections Altner 1989 and Hallmann 1994, as well as the more recent project "The Earth Bible" (Habel 2000).
32. Note the journal *Ecotheology* (formerly *Theology in Green*) edited in England by M. Grey and the Latin American *Revista Latinoamericana de Ecofeminismo, Espiritualidad y Teología*; additional bibliography

d'Eubonne coined the word "ecofeminism," which was then popularized primarily by the Indian scientist Vandana Shiva.[33] It is no accident that women in particular took up the discussion. In the dominant patriarchal symbol system, there is a distinctive connection between nature and femininity, and there are demonstrably complex associations between the destruction of nature and the oppression of women.[34] If women stand up for the protection of creation, they are naturally continuing to operate, on the one hand, under the terms of the patriarchal system. For example, they diligently and carefully separate their household recyclables, while the conglomerates continue to produce hazardous waste on a grand scale. On the other hand, something along the lines of a subversive alliance of the oppressed (woman and nature) seems to be taking shape.

Catharina J. M. Halkes (1990) begins with the connection in the history of ideas between the oppression of nature and of women, specifically relating the investigations of Carolyne Merchant (1980) to contemporary shifts in thinking. Tendencies toward the domination of nature and the feminine are expressed in the work of Francis Bacon (1561–1626), one of the founding fathers of modern science, especially empiricism; he was Solicitor General in the English court at the precise time when laws against witches in England were strengthened. The demonic in nature and the demonic in women combine in the idea of witches; both nature and woman are tortured into surrendering their utmost secrets. In writings from Bacon's time, Teacher Nature becomes submissive nature, offering herself up to the male researcher, although in Bacon's perspective, still within the I–Thou relationship. Belief in a divine world-soul disappears from the structure of philosophical systems. The world is understood as a mechanically functioning whole, with only its origin owing to a divine impulse. Almost contemporary with empiricism, in the footsteps of René Descartes (1596–1650), in France the current of rationalism arose. Rationalism methodically commenced with the thinking *I* in order to establish a sure foundation for knowledge, and in the process transformed the man–nature relationship into a subject–object relationship.[35] Halkes's sketch of philosophical revolutions unfortunately stops with Descartes, even though Immanuel Kant (1724–1804) developed a concept of reason that is particularly apposite for feminist inquiry, a concept to which the construction "the other" belongs, including (feminine) nature, the human body, desires, emotions, and so on (Böhme and Böhme 1985).

Halkes adds to feminist culture criticism her design for a renewed creation theology, which is similar in outline to that presented by us in this book but which—because it is not specifically a contribution to biblical studies—neither concentrates on the biblical sources nor makes their reexamination and reappraisal the starting point of her considerations. As a Catholic and feminist

---

in Halkes 1990: 131–52, Green and Grey 1994: 110–13; see also the special number "Öko-feminismus" of the journal *Schlangenbrut* 14 no. 52 (1996) with bibliography by K. Heidemanns and N. Hollmann (33f.). The encounter of feminist theologians with the biblical texts is disappointingly conventional. Genesis 1–3 exclusively occupies the center, with Psalm 104 and God's speeches in Job mentioned only occasionally.

33. Mies and Shiva 1995; see the articles by Chung Hyun Kyung, A. Gnanadason, A. Primavesi, and R. Radford Ruether in Hallmann 1984.

34. The word patriarchy (also kyriarchy) is to be understood, according to E. Schüssler Fiorenza (summary in 1994: 12–18) and others in the sense of a complex pyramid of dominion, as already found in the writings of Aristotle: some groups of men dominate other groups of men, women, children, strangers or "others," and creation. For the confrontation of the androcentric dualism of Western thought by feminist philosophers, see Hubbard 1989, 1990; Orland and Scheich 1995; Schiebinger 1995.

35. Simone Rappel (1996) has fundamentally redrawn these developments by concentrating on the work ethic in Christian tradition in connection with creation and the image of God. How responsible Descartes really was for the development of a technocratic understanding of nature is in any case controversial (Perler 1998, esp. 258f. contra Hösle 1991: 54ff.).

theologian, she develops her inquiry on dialectically stamped theology, the so-teriological reception of creation, and the overstressing of the transcendence of God, at the same time showing ways out of the crisis with her thoughts on the sacrality or sacramentality of creation, on the theology of blessing and Sabbath, and so on.

Rosemary Radford Ruether reveals herself to be very much biblically founded in *Gaia & God* (1992). The author, whose biography suggests connections with Judaism, Christianity, and other religions, situates herself expressly in the Christian/Western tradition and hence also in the biblical tradition. The earth is an ecosystem into which we humans are irrevocably interwoven. But we are marked by traditions that have defined nature as non-human (often sub-human) and non-divine. Ruether sees an escape from doom in a biblically based theology of covenant and in a sacramental tradition that can perceive signs of divine salvation in created reality. She goes back to the church father Irenaeus (second century A.D.), who related christ's act of redemption to all creation, not just to humanity, and to Teilhard de Chardin, who incorporated the findings of evolutionary theory into his cosmic Christology. For Ruether, the strength—not the weakness—of Christianity is its syncretistic past (1992: 230; cf. Schroer 1996).

Some years ago already (1991: 354f.), Ina Praetorius declared that a characteristic of ecofeminist theology is a tendency toward pantheism (or more precisely, panentheism, the doctrine that all is inspired by God) that grew out of the endeavor to subdue the androcentric dualisms of nature–history, nature–culture, nature–human, God–world, creator–creature. This tendency has meanwhile grown stronger, especially outside the Western world, because in these other contexts the confrontation with the creation traditions of other religions is alive for Christian women. In the small volume edited by Bärbel Fünfsinn and Christa Zinn, *The Sigh of Creation*, several Latin American women, including Christian theologians, explicitly advocate a panentheism that recognizes divinity not as a person above the world but in everything (1998: 14, 20). Theologians such as Ivana Gebara speak in this context of a new universal covenant (Fünfsinn and Zinn 1998: 36f.) of survival in sisterhood. Most of the contributions to this volume concern conceptions of God and creation in the indigenous cultures of Latin America. What appears problematic to us is not the panentheism and the questioning of the Christian claim to unconditionality, but that the conversation with the biblical tradition is simply broken off. The ominous separation and neglect of creation theology, which is a late successor to dialectical theology, portends the danger of a break with the Jewish and Christian tradition, because it appears impossible to unify the tradition's doctrine of creation with the pressing needs of the present. This development is also problematic to the extent that it implies a truly romantic understanding of nature and compares other religious traditions (Hinduism or the indigenous cultures of Latin America) utterly uncritically as just as good as the Christian religion. In this case, the approaches especially of Matthew Fox, Catharina J. M. Halkes, and Rosemary Radford Ruether seem more mature; they combine the desire for a renewed encounter with creation theologically with the sacramentality of the created, and so, always in dialogue with other religious traditions, develop a panentheism that bears a Christian stamp.

II. Contemporary Challenges for a Christian Creation Theology

1. The Contemporary Situation

Some thirty years after the report of the Club of Rome, the destruction of the environment continues practically unabated despite the fact that we have global conferences, the World Wildlife Fund, Greenpeace, and growing ecological consciousness.[1] Globalization, increasing mobility, and a higher standard of living in Western Europe, the U.S., Japan, and elsewhere have resulted in an utterly irresponsible wasting of resources. There is virtually no hope for a future reversal of these developments. Shortly before the turn of the millennium, scientists such as the Austrian Franz M. Wuketits (1998) spoke of "Man, the natural catastrophe" and proclaimed, if not the end of the world, then at least a deep-seated evolutionary pessimism regarding humanity, which at one time proudly considered himself the "crown of creation." In fact, the insight that humanity is, evolutionarily speaking, a parasite—that is, a species that multiplies uncontrollably at the expense of other species—can scarcely be dismissed. Nonetheless, the reference to "Man, the natural catastrophe" is debatable. To declare the human species bankrupt benefits no one, because in this case no liquidation of assets is possible. This self-certified, scientifically embellished, and childish report card cripples any motivation for action; in the best case, it serves to suppress guilt feelings and, in the worst case, in a cynical way it leads to further exploitation of the earth; in any case, it robs us of responsibility. Instead, the question must be how we shall act responsibly on behalf of the generations that will follow us.

Moreover, in the last few years a virulent phemomenon, "ethnonazism," as it has been labeled by Urs Altermatt (1996), has appeared. After the demise of Nazism at the end of World War II, such cancers were wrongly thought to have been eliminated. In view of recent examples of "ethnic cleansing" and nationalistic schisms (Rwanda, former Yugoslavia, etc.), creation traditions should have reminded us that allegiance to creation and to humanity is more fundamental than ethnic, national, or religious allegiance. Creation possesses greater (because it is primary and fundamental) dignity than achievement, namely, "redemption."

In view of these developments, the need for a responsible Christian theology of creation remains undiminished. The historical sketch of the discipline in the previous chapter furnished a few relevant details. Mostly conditioned by the history of Europe in the first half of the last century, reservations regarding creation theology grew ever greater. Salvation history, liberation, and Exodus appeared to offer a degree of immunity from the clutches of Nazism and for decades after were at the foreground of exegetical interest. That even these traditions were not immune from harmful political misuse was not appreciated.

---

1. Rosemary Radford Ruether (1992, esp. 88–111), using documentation from the U.N.-cofounded World Watch Institute, describes the worldwide crisis under five headings: population and poverty; feeding the world's human population; energy, climate, and pollution; extinction; and militarism and war.

Like the Spanish Conquistadors centuries earlier, for example, the Boers justified their land-taking and Apartheid on the basis of passages in Joshua and Deuteronomy.[2] The religious conviction that salvation comes from a specific people chosen by God was shamelessly recoined by the Nazis into the credo that "German nature" would promote the renewal of the world. To this day, however, in some Christian circles—and perhaps especially among theologians—fear of the sacralization of nature seems far greater than fear of the theological promotion of status-quo politics and belief in progress. But why should it be more dangerous to sing, in concert with Chief Seattle, "Every part of this earth is sacred to my people"[3] than "Praise to Yʜᴡʜ, the Almighty, the King of Creation"?

2. Jewish Signposts toward a New Theology of Creation

The doctrine of creation has received hardly any attention in recent Jewish theology.[4] The field has largely been left to secular science. Franz Rosenzweig (1886–1929), however, provided the first modern Jewish impetus for a renewed creation theology with his *Star of Redemption* (1921), at exactly the time when dialectical theology, and along with it creation-forgetting Christian theology, was becoming consolidated (Staubli 2001). For Rosenzweig, creation is not a question of physics (that is, secular science) or of philosophy; nor is it the object of revealed belief. Rather, creation is the basis for the discovery of faith. Creation doctrine deals with a higher truth than the truth of science; it is a metascience. It deals not with what is but with what should be. Rosenzweig relates revelation and creation to each other in an extremely unusual way that is diametrically opposed to the spirit of his time and far distant from the theological developments of the twentieth century. In his view, revelation serves the renewal of creation; it restores the natural. As regards its entire content, revelation is already foreseen in creation; it is the "fulfillment of the promise made in creation" (§97). The recognition of creation is made possible by revelation in the narrower sense, but creation is itself already revelation, namely, revelation of the creative power of God. Here Rosenzweig's theology proves to be a wisdom theology in the tradition especially of the book of Job, even though it appears only occasionally in his exposition. Despite all the injustice and suffering that befall him, Job remains entirely confident that his "redeemer" (*go'el*) lives (19:25). The one who reveals himself to him at the end is the creator God. Creation itself reveals this creator, but in order to recognize this fact, Job in his affliction requires a direct encounter with God, who shows the believing complainant the overpowering greatness of creation, until he recognizes it and no longer needs to resort to citations of what is incomprehensible and miserable about the created order in order to slander the divine plan for the world, the wonder of wonders.

From the circle of Rosenzweig's friends emerged something that remains virtually unknown in our times: a circle of editors who collaborated on the periodical *The Creature*, of which, however, only three volumes appeared, between 1926 and 1930. With this programmatic title, Martin Buber (Jewish), Joseph Wittig

---

2. For the Conquistadors, see Delgado 1991: 20–36; for the role of Deuteronomy in the history of South Africa, see Deist 1994.

3. The famous address of the chief to the president of the United States in 1855 has of course been overlaid with European-American romanticism and is not historically authentic (Gerber 1988, esp. 225ff.).

4. See N. M. Samuelson and G. Stemberger, "Schöpfer/Schöpfung, IV: Judentum," *TRE* 30 (1999): 292–96.

(Catholic), and Victor von Weizsäcker (Protestant) together defied the unholy spirit of the times:

> What binds us three editors together is an affirmation of the bond of the created world, the world as creature. Faith in the source that is common to our three communities of study and service is materially present in the certainty of its inherent createdness and in the expanding life that grows from it, along with all created things. This periodical will deal with the world—all beings, all things, all phenomena of this present world—in such a way that its createdness is recognizable. It will not promote any particular kind of theology, but rather, in spiritual humility, cosmology. If it remains ever mindful of creation, every creature to which it turns must be worthy of consideration. If it trusts in the doer, it must trust the deed. Trust also in the growing race, the century rising from secrecy.[5]

3. The Direction for a Theology of Creation in the Twenty-first Century

And so we stand at a point in the history of theology where we should be able to draw lessons from its twentieth-century past and also leap over its shadows. Catharina J. M. Halkes (1990, esp. 92–112) has made noteworthy comments regarding the course theology needs to adopt in the matter of creation. A responsible Christian creation theology must on the one hand not abandon the Jewish credo that no secular factor be absolutized. Nothing created can claim to be like God and be worshiped like God. There is thus no question of resacralizing or divinizing creation in a narrow sense, but the baby—in this case, the numinous character of creation—must not be thrown out with the bathwater. The time has come to give back to creation its soul, its dignity, to liberate it from its humiliation in which it is deemed an entirely godless opposite to the creator, as purely the product of a God whose sovereignty and transcendence are overly stressed and as the object of human science and exploitation.

The Bible suggests that the created world be viewed as a work of art, the work of the hands, even the fingers, of God (Ps 8:4). The sacramental nature of creation is a key idea stemming from the Catholic tradition that can be sufficiently nuanced to label the new perspective. All creation can transparently become divine reality, can become a sign and realization of the presence of God in this world. The "sacrament" makes it possible for us to experience God's holiness in creation but at the same time signals his inaccessibility. "Do not destroy it, for there is blessing in it," says Isa 65:8 of the cluster of grapes. In the biblical understanding of blessing, there is also respect for the numinous, the sacramental in nature (M. Fox 1983). Appealing to mystical traditions, it is even possible to understand creation as the body of God.

Nature must no longer be imagined and experienced in terms of ownership and property. It is rather the dwelling-place of all living things, and at the same time, according to Christian understanding, it is inhabited by God in three persons. Jürgen Moltmann (1985, esp. 166ff., 191) has already emphasized the significance of a trinitarian approach for creation theology. The Christian doctrine of the Trinity implies that God is also in loving (not hierarchical) relationship, obligation, and community with creation, that the "kingdom of God" also signifies hope for the complete indwelling of the triune God in the world (cf. Halkes 1990: 107). Many theological possibilities that have the potential to further a

---

5. Final section of the foreword to the periodical *Die Kreatur*, signed by the three editors. Our attention was drawn to this important—for its time—document by Peter Galli (Baden-Baden).

nuanced devotion with respect to all creation have not yet been worked out practically, though they are contained in the notion of "holiness."

Our book is more than anything an attempt to indicate the Old Testament foundations for these new approaches, as we show that ancient Israel, despite belief in a creator God, did not abandon the numinous character of creation. With respect to contemporary challenges, it is not a matter of reducing theology to creation theology but of placing theology on the sturdier pillars of creation theology.[6]

4. What Theologians Can Do

1. In the world of A.D. 2000, nature and culture can no longer be separated from each other. Virgin, wild nature—all those calendars and travelogues notwithstanding—scarcely exists any more, and so the romanticizing of nature no longer helps with ecological problems and even serves to deafen observers to the ever-mounting problems. The preservation of nature does not mean a naïve "back to the wilderness," the protection of creation does not mean "back to God's original plan," but both mean humanity's compassion and cooperation in the service of God's *Gesamtkunstwerk*, his all-encompassing work of art, "the world." "Maker-mentality" is generally not needed for the preservation of nature, but rather a cessation of "permissiveness." On the one hand, political means must be used to prevent the clearing of the rainforests, to stop the poisoning of the environment, to protect species from extinction or to reintroduce them, to create national parks; but, on the other hand, ecological niches, little pieces of wilderness, must be allowed to return, by our—for once—doing nothing, not interfering, not steering. Creation is not a machine, not some mechanical device functioning in man's interest but a work of art that derives its meaning independent of purpose; it is unconditionally worth preserving. Theologians in alliance with the appropriate conservation organizations can promote this basic concept in community activities, in schools, adult education, and universities.

2. To provide a new status among the various disciplines of theology for creation and wisdom theology and to incorporate them into theology to the fullest extent is one of the most important tasks of the new century. There also needs to be a deepening continuation of the dialogue between theology and science, which already involves the most recent developments in genetics, neurology, and astronomy.

3. Because the worldwide ecological catastrophe is an expression and consequence of the same corruption and exploitative dominion that oppresses women and children, people of color, and the "other" of every kind, a new creation theology cannot come into being without the formulation of a new, less androcentric anthropology that takes human life seriously as corporeal and frail as well seeing it as included in and dependent on its environment.[7] The biblical tradition appears to us to offer sagacious and realistic concepts for the relationship between humanity and the environment, so long as one does not focus narrowly on Genesis 1–3. It challenges us on the one hand to speak of

---

6. Jürgen Ebach (1989: 105) argues against the isolation of creation theology on the basis that neither justice nor solidarity with the weak nor love of neighbor can be derived from nature and its laws. But here he does not distinguish sufficiently between nature and creation, since, biblically seen, having been created by God can be connected throughout with the idea of equality (of rich and poor) or solidarity (of man and animal). "Law of nature" and "law of creation" are not identical (see the excursus to chap. VI 3 below).

7. Schroer and Staubli 2001, esp. 1–40.

creation in the face of (cosmic, historical, individual) suffering and death but on the other to come to God with wondering praise. The consecration of creation and the consecration of God belong together; to both are due an attitude of respect and thankfulness.

4. The exploitative hold on the natural resources of our living world goes hand in hand with a disregard for the Sabbath commandment that is regularly gaining more ground. In Jewish tradition, Sabbath is part of the order of creation. Because God paused to rest after six days of work, in Israel, on the seventh day, any sort of work and production is to cease as well. The interruption of the activity of planning, separating, gathering, regulating, blessing, making, and delegating holds for all living things that are included in productive activities, including domestic and working animals. The ability to rest gives human creative power its value—work without pause is drudgery, is "slavery in Egypt." The protection of the work-free and business-free Christian Sunday must, given this background, become an urgent goal of the Christian community who are committed to creation and ecology. We dare not unlearn the "release" of creation, the contemplative pause in our relation to the world.

5. Some grounds for optimism are found in current legal discussions. For a few years, the possibility that "nature," which in constitutional law has the status of a thing (res in Roman law), might be elevated in status to a subject having legal rights has been seriously entertained.[8] After Europe-wide scandals regarding intensive livestock farming and its consequences, more and more groups, including church groups, took stands for the rights of animals.[9] First attempts to grant nature a value of its own in the law, not just to protect it when people feel like it, have already been incorporated into the Constitution of the Swiss Federation. Even if nature is not able to make its own interests known, it would still be possible to appoint lawyers for the legal entity "nature" and so combat and punish any sort of long-term destruction of the environment much more effectively than was previously possible under the law. It is certainly the case that this new sort of legal proposal is dependent on a formal anthropocentrism, insofar as man must be considered the only subject of morality.[10] Yet, this development would be a decisive break with material anthropocentrism: man would no longer be the measure of all things. At base, this is a shift of models. The relationship between man and nature has always been a question of power, and until not so long ago the victory of man over nature had not yet a priori been decided; and today and in the future, it probably still is not decided, because the setbacks that nature has thrown in the way of human encroachments are becoming more evident all the time. But if the model of conquest is retained, all that can happen in the future is that the victor—in his own interest—stops short of destroying his entire plunder or brings himself to the realization that

---

8. Saladin 1992, Teutsch 1995, Rappel 1996: 369–401, Praetorius 2000 (with many references to the ethical discussion).

9. The German animal welfare organization "Animals' Angels" and—throughout the German-speaking area—the "Aktion Kirche und Tiere" (AKUT) association, which since 1988 has been gathering signatures throughout Europe for the "Glauberg Confession" of Christian disregard for animals (included in *AKUTe Nachrichten: Mitteilungen der Aktion Kirche und Tiere* 1 [2001] [AKUTe news: Contributions of "Action Church and Animals"]), reflect Christian motivations (compare Deut 25:4 with 1 Cor 9:9).

10. Simone Rappel (1996) argues against the general abandonment of anthropocentrism. She rightly points to the necessary distinction between "formal" and "material" anthropocentrism (see also Metz 1962) and pleads in the final analysis for a sort of paternalism, for a good dominion of man over creation. On the whole, her arguments are quite apologetic and not very courageous. She does raise the question of what value humanity will have after the abandonment of anthropocentricism, if, in principle humanity has no higher interests than that of other life. Sigurd Daecke (1989) seeks to overcome the opposition between anthropocentrism and cosmocentrism through the fact that both nature and man receive their value only through being created by God, so that neither has an intrinsic value of its own.

his own survival is dependent on the survival of nature. A completely different model would be that of nature as "world cultural property" or "God's *Gesamtkunstwerk*." The fact that someone owns a Picasso does not give them license to destroy it. Similarly, nature has an unconditional right to further existence, independent of man. In the history of law, another emancipation and its documentation have application here: slaves and women were long considered by the law as things; their gaining legal status was hardly imaginable at one time. All theologians, not only ethicists, are challenged to get involved in this debate, being careful to consider the biblical traditions, because the wisdom-oriented creation texts present non-anthropocentric models. It is high time that we escape from the undertow of Genesis 1.

III. Traces of a Numinous Approach to the Environment in the Hebrew Bible

Art thou, fair world, no more?
Return, thou virgin-bloom, on Nature's face;
Ah, only on the Minstrel's magic shore,
Can we the footstep of sweet Fable trace!
The meadows mourn for the old hallowing life;
Vainly we search the earth of gods bereft;
And where the image with such warmth was rife,
A shade alone is left!

Cold, from the North, has gone
Over the flowers the blast that kill'd their May;
And, to enrich the worship of the ONE,
a universe of gods must pass away!
Mourning, I search on yonder starry steeps,
But thee no more, Selene, there I see!
And through the woods I call, and o'er the deeps,
No voice replies to me!

In this excerpt from his famous poem "The Gods of Greece" ("Die Götter Griechenlands," ca. 1790; trans. Edward Bulwer Lytton, 1852), Friedrich Schiller bemoans the fact that biblical monotheism has obliterated magic from the world. Carl Amery's "Great Pan is dead" (1972: 213) sounds a similarly elegiac tone. In the second half of the twentieth century, the allegation has been made from many sides[1] that biblical teaching about Creation, with its dedeifying and thorough objectivization of the world, has paved the way for contemporary exploitation of its natural resources. This is not entirely false, but, as Jürgen Moltmann (1985: 40f.) has noted, rather one-sided, because Enlightenment philosophy and the natural sciences surely have been more influential than the anthropocentrism of Genesis 1. After all, Genesis had been read for more than two thousand years before the advent of the Industrial Revolution. Moreover, there is more to the Bible than an anthropocentric worldview (on which more later). Furthermore, talk of a creator god does not all by itself rob the world of the numinosity that we experience and expect from it, as we shall now explain.

Latin *nuere* denotes the (divine) will, indicated by nodding of the head, or the majesty, especially of the Roman emperor, that governs one's free movement. "Numinosity" is understood as the mysterious emanation belonging to one endowed with divine power; it refers to superhuman strength of unparalleled greatness. Numinous emanation is answered on the human side by the emotion of *pietas*, of dependency, of grateful love and of respect, all of which stand in the way of the quick grab, of clear-cutting the forest, of harvesting the field down to its last kernel and its very edge. A sense of holistic concern was already gladly affirmed, with lucid explanations, in biblical times. Thus, in Ps 104:16, the special quality of the YHWH-trees of Lebanon is attributed to God having personally planted the mighty conifers. Contact with the numinous was difficult and was

---

1. White 1970, Amery 1972, Drewermann 1981; cf. chap. I.4 above (pp. 11ff..).

eased by means of strict rules or taboos. For example, the fruit of a tree was not to be consumed during its first four years (Lev 19:23–25).

In terms of the history of religions, the numinous interpretation of the world that can be glimpsed in biblical texts can be traced back to belief in the activity of specific, often still identifiable, deities in the ancient Near Eastern pantheon. Thunder and rain manifest Baal; flocks come under the blessing of Astarte; even shortly before the Exile, in the Jerusalem Temple itself the Sun-god was worshiped. The divine names—although not with great success prior to the Exile—are pushed into the background in favor of a monotheistic symbol-system, but belief in the numinosity of Creation has obviously not been shaken to its foundations. The most diverse texts in the Bible include formulations of the idea that YHWH is present in the cosmos and in his creatures. Heaven and earth are filled with God (Jer 23:24), his glory (*kabod*; Isa 6:3), his kindness (*ḥesed*; Ps 33:5), his spirit (Wis 1:7). Rarely, however, is numinosity explicitly reduced to its core, a divine power of YHWH. More often, it is presupposed as a sort of giving of religious experience, without explicit reference to YHWH. The metaphors of acting, reasoning, speaking and spoken-to attributed to the cosmos, heaven, earth, mountains, etc. are rooted in the numinosity inherent in them from the beginning. Biblical texts are often extremely reticent in suggesting this background. Conversely, of course, inherited conceptions of a God of Heaven are emphasized: for example, that YHWH created the heavens (e.g., Ps 96:5, 102:26, 104:2), that they belong to him (Ps 115:16), that God dwells or is enthroned in heaven (Ps 103:19, 115:3). Despite this clear objectivization, Heaven appears quite often as a personal, acting agent,[2] and occasionally a passage still transparently refers to a divine Heaven, as in Hos 2:23f. and Isa 45:8 (cf. comprehensively Houtman 1993).

The transmission of these traces of the numinous has been placed under lock and key—sometimes drastically—in the Septuagint, the ancient translation of the Bible into Greek. In its translation (that is, interpretation) of the Hebrew text, major mythological terms such as *tehom*, as well as designations for God such as "Rock" or "Shaddai," or divine manifestations such as Wisdom, are drastically trimmed or made to disappear by various means, so that a monotheism in which Creation and Creator are no longer separate is propagated.[3]

Excursus:
On the History of Human Interaction with Nature

It would be wrong to romanticize the past with respect to human interaction with nature. The man–nature relationship must have been ambivalent from the very beginning. Anyone who gathered plants or even hunted wild animals knew themselves to be in a relationship of dependency and responsibility with Earth the Mother of Plants, the goddess of flocks, or the "lord of the animals." Respect for the divine donors continued to be expressed in ancient Near Eastern art of the first millennium B.C. (cf. figs. 27–29, 40–41, 60–61 below). During the Neolithic Revolution, around 10,000 B.C., humanity gradually shifted from purely consuming to partially producing its means of subsistence. With animal husbandry and farming, humans began in some respects to be creators themselves. Their surroundings henceforth were divided into one segment that was managed by people and one part that was inaccessible to

---

2. As witness, e.g., in Deut 4:26, Ps 50:4, cf. Jer 2:12, 4:28; rejoicing and praising God in Ps 19:2, 50:6, Isa 44:23, etc.; cf. the excursus to chap. 6 §2.1 below.

3. Cf. Fritsch 1943; Gard 1952; Orlinsky 1959–61; G. Bertram, "Septuaginta-Frömmigkeit," *RGG* 5 (3d ed., 1961): 1707–9; Küchler 1992: 131f.

1 Cylinder seal from Mesopotamia (3300–2900 B.C.). A nude male uses a spear to defend a calving cow from a rampant lion. The composition symbolizes the development of fundamental conceptions of "culture" and "nature." The owner or shepherd battles heroically on behalf of his herd against the wild animal. "Culture" must be defended against wilderness. (Keel 1992: 27 with fig. 12)
2 Early Sumerian cylinder seal (3300–2900 B.C.). A prince in a net skirt and another worshiper bring a slaughtered predatory cat, its feet cut off, and an oversized string of pearls to the temple of the goddess, which is represented by its façade. Behind them can be seen two juxtaposed sheep walking between stalks of grain. The goddess is presented not just with the achievements of culture but also with their defeated enemy. (Frankfort 1939: 19 fig. 2)

them, the latter commonly experienced as hostile. As early as the third millennium B.C., the development of a concept of culture opposed to "nature" as wilderness can be identified in Mesopotamian iconography. "Culture" is represented by the feat of domestication and owning of herd animals, "nature" by the threat of a savage, dangerous world in the shape of wild animals that attack the herds—that is, the **Figs. 1–2** "culture." This age-old polarization functions in the face of all rational argument to the present day, as, for example, in the resistance to reintroducing certain wild animals such as the wolf and the bear into Italy and Switzerland. The subjugation and killing of living things is unflinchingly legitimated by the necessity of protecting culture, although as a result the basic premises have been stood on their head, with the protecting and protected protagonists changing places.[4]

This glance into the development of thinking of this kind in an advanced ancient Near Eastern civilization should prevent us from romanticizing. Respect for the

---

4. Already in antiquity, the end justified the means. As early as the third millennium B.C., killing lions and game animals was sometimes depicted apart from its original purpose of protecting the useful herds; it became a manly deed of heroes and rulers. It increased prestige.

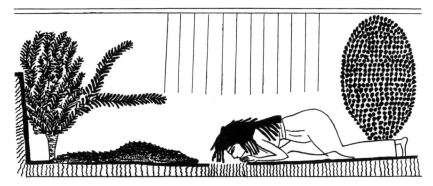

3 Book of the Dead papyrus of the Heruben from the 21st Dynasty (1085–950 B.C.). The dead man prostrates himself before a crocodile, which is a manifestation of the god Sobek. (Drawing by Inés Haselbach after Piankoff and Rambova 1957: no. 1)

4 (Top, right) Scarab from Palestine/Israel (12th–11th century B.C.). A man with a harpoon lifts up a crocodile by the snout. (Keel 1978 fig. 84a)

5 (Left) Late Egyptian bronze (6th–1st century B.C.). A priest kneels, bearing a platter of offerings on his head, facing a monumental representation of a seated goddess with a lion's head. (Keel 1977a: 36, fig. 19)

6 (Bottom, right) Scarab from Egypt (1300–1200 B.C.). The striding pharaoh, with the Blue Crown and wearing a short kilt, aims an arrow in his drawn bow at a lion, which appears to be sitting on its hind legs. Branches in the background may signify agriculture. Behind the lion is the hieroglyph *nfr* 'beautiful', and behind the pharaoh is the sign *wsr* 'strong'. (Keel 1997c: pl. 10D)

numinous was not an absolute value, but ever a value in competition with others, such as nourishment, luxury, or prestige. The tension of the relationship also be-

Figs. 3–6 comes clear from the fact that the same animals, such as the crocodile and lion, on the one hand represent powerful deities (Sobek, Sekhmet, etc.) and on the other can be mercilessly hunted. The value of ivory in ancient times already resulted in the extinction of the African elephant across much of Egypt. The Syrian elephant was also already extinct in the ninth/eighth century B.C.

Indeed, the prophet Amos (3:15, 6:4), an astute social critic, portrays ivory in a rather bad light, but the extinction of the elephant was not his concern. On the other hand, biblical voices do address the deforestation of the coniferous forests of the Lebanon. Every empire of the ancient Near East participated in this ecologically disas-

Fig. 7 trous plundering, with the result that cedar-wood was already scarce by 1100 B.C.[5] Their monumental entries in the roll-call of history can still be seen today in the rocks at Nahr el-Kelb, not far from Beirut. The coveted wood of the conifers was hauled and shipped great distances with unimaginable effort, requiring the conscription of countless draft animals (cf. Isa 37:24). Both the annals and the reliefs of Sargon II

Fig. 8 (721–705 B.C.) portray how gigantic these expeditions were. Only a few pathetic cedar groves remain in Lebanon today.

Israel, too, played a part—fairly small, to be sure—in the deforestation of the Leb-anon.[6] According to 1 Kgs 5:16–25, 27f., 7:2, etc., wood for building the Temple in Jerusalem came from the Lebanon, which, on account of its proud forests, appeared to the people of ancient Israel to be the garden of God.[7] Cedar wood radiated not only scent but also prestige, which is why people in times of deprivation were re-luctant to do without it (cf. Hag 1:4, Ezra 3:7). In any event, it was so expensive that only the upper classes—at the expense of the working peasants—could obtain it. Prophetic criticism of its use is therefore primarily social criticism (Isa 9:8f., Jer 22:13–15). The memory preserved in Ps 104:16 of the numinous character of the great trees of Lebanon did not preserve them from a tragic fate. But the prophets of Israel felt such trespasses to be sacrilegious. Thus, in Isaiah 14, the derision over the death of the Great King—originally Sargon II, and then in later reinterpretation the king of Babylon—is heightened when the trees of the Lebanon, which have now gained permanent respite from the tyrant, speak:

> "Now that you are laid to rest,
> there will be none to cut us down." (Isa 14:8)

Sennacherib (704–681 B.C.), too, is mocked by the population of Judah after his departure from Jerusalem, because he had proudly boasted of the sacrilege he had committted in the forest of Lebanon (2 Kgs 19:22f.).

The prophet Habakkuk, who was active during the time of the Babylonian expan-sion at the beginning of the sixth century B.C. and had an eye for the intertwining of ecology, colonialism, and power, pilloried the outrage committed in the forest of Lebanon and the cruelty inflicted on animals, probably draft animals:

> For the violence done to Lebanon shall cover you,
> and the destruction of the beasts shall terrify you;
> Because of men's blood shed, and violence done to the land,
> to the city and to all who dwell in it. (Hab 2:17)

Fig. 9 In order to inflict long-term damage on conquered cities, the soldiers of the Assyr-ian army would systematically cut down fruit trees. Deut 20:19, conversely, forbids

---

5. Cf. Brown 1969, Meiggs 1982, Elayi 1988, Bleibtreu 1989.
6. See Keel 1993b, esp. 58–71.
7. For the tradition of God's garden on the Lebanon heights, see 2 Kgs 19:23ff., Ezek 31:9, 16ff. (Stolz 1972), and the Lebanon metaphors in the Song of Songs (4:8, 11; 5:15; Keel 1986a: 145, 156, 194).

7 Part of a relief of Pharaoh Sethos I (1290–1279 B.C.) from the outer wall of the temple at Karnak. Canaanites fell trees from the Lebanon for Egyptian construction works. The accompanying inscription describes the Canaanites in the picture as "the great chieftains of the Lebanon." The artist who drew the image knew the felled trees only as beams, which he turned back into trees simply by adding leaves. (Keel 1993b: 59 fig. 5)
8 Part of a relief from the Khorsabad palace of the Assyrian king Sargon II (721–705 B.C.), depicting a scene from his Lebanon campaign. Phoenician seamen are busy transporting beams and pillars. (Keel 1997a: 74 fig. 84)

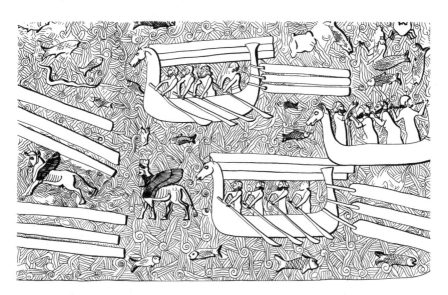

"making war" on trees. But even in peaceful times, stands of trees could be uprooted in order to create farmland (Josh 17:14–18), and it was permissible to hunt animals.

Sensitivity to the divine in every creature, in all of nature, was thus even in ancient times not taken for granted. Many Old Testament commandments regarding the

9 Part of a relief from the SW palace of the Assyrian king Sennacherib (704–681 B.C.) in Nineveh. After conquering a city, soldiers cut down its date-palms. (Drawing by Inés Haselbach after Paterson 1915: pl. 94)

protection, for instance, of animals show that despite awareness of their numinosity it was necessary to concretely define the boundaries of human access and—in the name of the god—to establish rules. Forbidden access thus turns into "sacrilege." The performance of sacrifices was especially important for the regulation of the contact-point in the relationship between humankind and God. Through the sacrifice, the divinity is recognized as the giver of produce and cattle, and the person through the voluntary (return) donation of part of the gift expresses his gratitude and in the exchange also receives exemption from punishment and the right to use what has been given. The consumption of meat in ancient Israel thus remained extensively bound up in ritual slaughter (cf. Leviticus 17). In ancient Greece too, and up until the dawn of the Common Era, it was usually sacrificed meat that people ate communally.

1. Numinous Aspects of the Sea and Rivers

Again and again in the Bible, the sovereignty of Yʜwʜ over the sea is highlighted. But at least as many passages unmistakably demonstrate that it is precisely the raging, roaring sea, that retained very powerful traces of the divine, that could strike fear and awe into the hears of the people of ancient Israel (Ps 89:10, Prov 29:11) and even, later, the moved Christian community (Luke 21:25) into reverential awe and retained very powerful traces of the divine. Texts that mention the roar of the sea are laden with myth, and the fear-inspiring din of enemy peoples is often compared to it:

> Ah! the roaring of many peoples
>   that roar like the roar of the seas!
> The surging of nations
>   that surge like the surging of mighty waves!
> But God shall rebuke them, and they shall flee far away . . .
>   (Isa 17:12f., cf. Jer 51:55)

The floods that lie under the earth and supply the sea and the heavenly ocean can serve as a source of blessing (Gen 49:25, Deut 33:13). More commonly, however, the forbidding power of chaos is embodied in the form of monsters to whom mythic names such as Leviathan, Rahab, Tehom, and Tannin are applied.[8] Even the usual Hebrew word for 'sea', *yam*, is not devoid of mythic content; in the Ugaritic myths, 'sea' designates a divine adversary of Baal. Again,

---

8. For details, see chap. V.3 below, pp. 97ff. For the roaring of the sea, cf. Ps 65:8, 93:3; Isa 17:12; Jer 6:23, 50:42. Cf. M. Görg, "Drache," *NBL* 1 (1990): 444–46.

10 Greek hydria (early 4th century B.C.). The god Poseidon rides a wingless hippocampus (seahorse). His left hand holds a long trident, his right reaches out to a young man, who addresses him (perhaps Pelops before his race for Hippodameia). In Greece, too, the sea and its lord took on increasingly negative connotations. Poseidon existed on the edge of the civilized world; myths and religious developments also attest to his marginalization within the pantheon. (Drawing by Inés Haselbach after LIMC VII,2 366 Poseidon 158)
11 Cylinder seal of the Akkad period from Ur (2350–2150 B.C.). The god of fresh water, Ea/Enki, is enthroned in a chamber in the deep. His insignia are the streams of water, accompanied by fish, issuing from his shoulders. An attendant kneeling to the right grasps the gatepost of the underwater residence. The gate divides the deep and its fresh water from chaos, which is represented here as a winged lion being forcibly restrained. The small god with flaccid, dangling arms is an evil (night) god, who surrenders. The sun-god Shamash enters between the wings of the lion-dragon; he can be recognized by the rays on his shoulders and the "saw" in his hand. Another light- or sun-god, perhaps Marduk, appears in the same triumphal pose as Shamash and ascends the mountain with the Gate of Heaven and salutes the enthroned Ea. The combined powers of the three gods may have been thought to provide the seal-bearer with reliable protection against danger. (Keel 1997a: 48, fig. 43)

Job 38:8 says of the sea that it burst forth from the womb—that is, the conception intended in Gen 1:10 and Ps 95:5, that God "made" it just like the other works of creation, could manifestly not be sustained in post-exilic times. The

12 Cylinder seal from a grave in Jericho (18th century B.C.). In Old Babylonian and Classical Syrian cylinder seal glyptic, a nude hero, usually with six tresses and streams of water, plays a role alongside the storm-god. In the second millennium B.C., in Anatolia and Syria he takes on the role of god of springs and rivers. It cannot be coincidence that two seals with this image have been found at Jericho, of all places, which had a powerful spring.
The seal shows a prince before a goddess in a layered garment. To the left is the nude hero with streams of water. The water flows from his shoulders directly into two small jars at his feet. To the right, below, is a sphinx treading on a rebellious serpent. In the context of the spring god at the left, the motif is probably to be interpreted as representing the damming of the dangerous floods of chaos. (Porada 1983: 774 fig. 354)

sea retains its personal-divine properties, even though it is not considered (as in **Fig. 10** Greece) a positive entity.

The God of Israel sets the sea's boundaries and holds it in check (Ps 33:6–9, etc.); less often, he divides it, on an ancient model, like the dragon of chaos (Ps 74:13; cf. figs. 20, 112 below). Yʜwʜ commands Yam, dominates him, so that he flees, etc. In Ps 104:26, he toys with Leviathan, but it is doubtful whether this grand view of things can really be sustained. Even in Daniel (7:3) and Revelation (13:1), very serious opponents of Yʜwʜ emerge from the sea, and the early Christian community longed for a new world without a sea (Rev 21:1).

Wells and rivers are much less laden with numinosity than the sea in biblical stories. On the other hand, among Israel's neighbors, as well as in Greece and especially in Roman times, wells and rivers play a significant role.[9] In Akkad **Fig. 11** Period cylinder seals (ca. 2300 B.C.), Ea/Enki appears as lord of the groundwater. In Jericho, with its important spring, the representational art provides evidence **Fig. 12** that a divine hero was venerated as Lord of the Water. When the Kishon Brook comes to the aid of the Israelites against Siscra alongside their allies the stars (Judg 5:21), or the Jordan alters its course in light of the miracle of the Exodus (Ps 114:3), a hint of the divine, independent existence of watercourses shines forth. The oldest strand of the story of Jacob's fight at the Jabbok (Gen 32:22–32) concerns the struggle between the archetypal forefather and a river demon that lurks in the shadows to prevent crossing the ford but loses its strength at daybreak.[10] The healing power of the waters of the Jordan in the story of the ailing Syrian Naaman (2 Kgs 5:10, 14) is also an indication that rivers possessed "supernatural" powers.

---

9. F. Graf, "River gods," *BNP* 6 (2009).
10. The remarkable name "Spring of him who cries out at Lehi" in Judg 15:19 might recall a spring-demon, suggests M. Görg, "Quelle," *NBL* 3 (1998): 227f.

13 Relief from Assur, found in a fountain in the temple of Asshur (1800–1500 B.C.). This 136-cm-high relief showing a combination of spring gods and mountain or plant gods can be considered a ritual image on account of its size, the quality of its workmanship, and the frontal representation of the gods (making it a devotional image). The bearded mountain god, recognizable by the scale pattern on skirt and cap, simultaneously embodies vegetation, fertility, and life. From his hips spring two stems with clusters of fruit. He holds two more in his hands, happily being nibbled by mountain goats. He is flanked by two spring goddesses with jars gushing water in their hands. Trees and water serve to characterize the mountain as a realm of life. (Black and Green 1992: 80, fig. 63)

14 Kassite cylinder seal (14th century B.C.). Between forested mountaintops, the lord of the mountains and waters rises majestically. He has dominion over the streams of water that he holds in his hands. They flow directly from the heavenly jars (rain) into the water jars of the earth (springs, rivers). (Matthews 1990: no. 130)

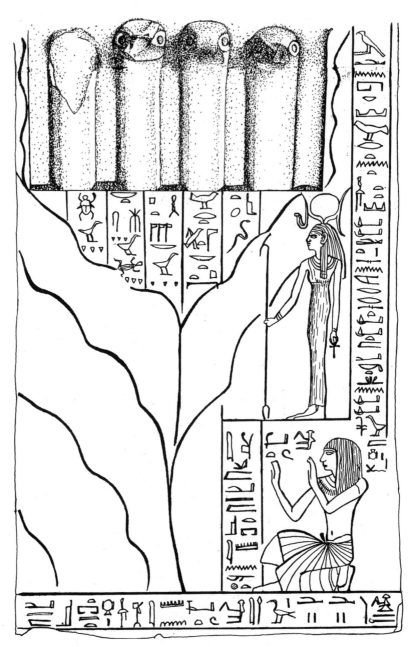

15 Stela from Deir el-Medina (13th century B.C.). In the New Kingdom, the mountain peak above the necropolis of Thebes was called the "Western" or "Great" mountaintop; in the eyes of the people, it had the appearance of a goddess and was especially identified with the serpent-shaped goddess Meretseger. (Drawing by Inés Haselbach after Tosi and Roccati 1972: no. 50059)

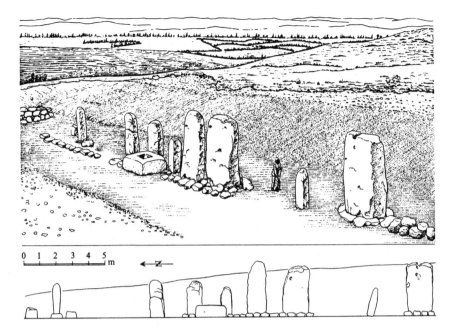

16 Stela sanctuary at Gezer (ca. 1600 B.C.). Sacred stones without images, alongside or in place of statues and sculptures, could express the presence of divine power. The famous ten monoliths of the open-air sanctuary at Gezer could have represented both gods and goddesses. (Galling 1977: 207, fig. 49)

2. Numinous Aspects of Mountains, Rocks, and Stones

High mountains are the preferred seats of gods—such as, for example, Baal-zephon (Exod 14:2, 9; Num 33:7)—but the mountain can also represent the deity itself. The "eternal" or "primeval" mountains bestow blessings (Gen 49:26, Deut 33:15), probably referring concretely to mountain springs. Mountains offer security to those who live on them (Jdt 7:10). Those who pray lift up their expectant eyes to them and in them find reassurance that YHWH is their help (Ps 121:1f.). That the God of Israel is a God of Mountains was also known to Israel's neighbors (cf. 1 Kgs 20:23, 28). Important events of Israelite revelation history take place at the foot and on the peak of "God's mountain." The mountain is thus much more than the seat of God and the locus of encounters with YHWH. At the very least, it is so powerfully incorporated into the theophany that it can kill (Exod 19:12). This may be why overturning the mountains at their foundations in Job 28:9 is considered a deed of insufficient *pietas*.[11] In this connection, the worship of the "mountain peak" (*t3 dhnt*) above the Necropolis at Thebes (modern *el-Qurn*) is worthy of mention. Among the common people, it enjoyed the status of a goddess and was identified with Hathor or Meretseger.[12] In the thanksgiving prayer on the stela of Nefer-Abet (13th century B.C.),[13] its great and fearsome power is praised:

Figs. 13–14

Fig. 15

> Take care before the mountain peak,
> For a lion is in the mountain peak!

---

11. R. Zimmermann 1994: 88f.; and for more on Job 28, see chap. III.3 below, p. 40.
12. Cf. E. Otto, "Bergspitze," *LÄ* 1 (1975): 709f.
13. Translation by J. Assmann, *TUAT* II 876f.

17 Stela with vulva from Tel Kittan south of the Sea of Galilee (1750–1650 B.C.). A row of ten small *maṣṣebôt* made of boulders was found in front of a building, perhaps a temple, on Tel Kittan. Two somewhat larger stones were placed in front of this row. One of the stelas in the main row is a very crudely executed nude female figure with prominent vulva. The discovery shows that *maṣṣebôt* in Israel were not exclusively associated with male gods, as was long assumed. (Keel and Uehlinger 1998: 36, fig. 26b)

It strikes with the blow of a furious lion,
it is a burden on whoever trespasses there.

The fearsome appearance of YHWH from the mountains is a theme in Ps 76:5, but the meaning of "mountains of prey" [NRSV footnote] (*meharrérê-ṭarep*) is unclear. When the Bible speaks of mountains, it usually stresses YHWH's supreme power, but mountains possess a certain intrinsic power of their own.[14] Thus, in Mic 6:1 mountains and hills are summoned as cosmic witnesses of YHWH's lawsuit with Israel.

Rocks, too, are not perceived merely as ordinary masses of stone. The designation or name "rock" (*ṣûr* or *selaʿ*) for YHWH is especially favored in the prayer language of the Psalms, as well as in other texts. In Deut 32:18 (cf. 32:4, 31), Israel is accused of forgetting "the Rock that begot you." Originally, then, divinity lived in the rock. In order to preclude any misunderstanding, the Septuagint, the ancient Greek translation of the Bible, frequently translates the Hebrew word for "rock" simply with "God" or with abstract terms.[15]

Fig. 16   Large standing stones, whether undressed or engraved with image or inscription, served various purposes,[16] but always the stone also bore numinous power. The *maṣṣebôt* that belonged to even the smallest, simplest sanctuary were regarded as sacred stones that, among other objects, were anointed (Gen 28:18; cf. the sacred legend of Bethel). *Maṣṣebôt* clearly could be associated with both male

Fig. 17   and female powers. The worship of stones that bore no image in ancient times—contrary to modern interpretation—was not considered to be in antithesis to the worship of representational images of gods, but was seen as an alternative, parallel form of veneration.[17] The worship of stones was especially widespread in Transjordan (among the Nabataeans).[18] In Jeremiah 2, the leadership of the House of Israel is accused of worshiping wood and stone, and in this case the connotations of wood are male and of stone female:

14. Ps 89:13, 90:2, 97:4f., 104:32, 121:1f. The sense is: YHWH created the mountains, the mountains tremble before him, etc. For what follows, cf. Keel 1997a: 20, 113–20, 179–83.
15. Thus, the "rock" of Ps 18:3 is rendered "steadfastness" (Gk. *stereoma*) in the Septuagint (17:3).
16. Boundary, treaty, grave, memorial, victory, or votive stones (Schroer 1987a: 357–75).
17. For discussion, see Mettinger 1995, van den Toorn ed. 1997, Lewis 1998.
18. For iconless worship among the Nabataeans, see, e.g., Mettinger 1995: 57–68.

18 Cylinder seal from Shadad near Kermansha in Iran (ca. 2500 B.C.). In the center of the impression is an earth-goddess whose upper body rises from the earth and who, like a tree, gives off branch-like growths on which the animals (to the left in the picture) feed (cf. Gen 1:11f., 24). On the right may be the same goddess, in her fully human form. (Keel 1996: fig. 493)

> They who say to a piece of wood, "You are my father,"
> and to a stone, "You gave me birth." (Jer 2:27)

The target of the criticism here appears to be ancestor worship with images of ancestors carved in wood and stone; elsewhere, these are called "teraphim."[19] Prophetic criticism increasingly was directed against any sort of "stone cult," and Deuteronomistic criticism was addressed above all against the sacred stones and trees of the open-air sanctuaries (*bamôt*).[20]

3. Numinous Aspects of Farmland and the Depths of the Earth

In ancient times, both earth in the sense of fertile farmland (Gk. *ge/Gaia*; Hebr. *'adamah*) and also the depths of the earth, the underworld (Gk. *chthon/chthonios*; Hebr. *'ereṣ, še'ol*, etc.), were treated respectfully, as quasi-divine forces. In Greek mythology, Gaia (perhaps Indo-European 'childbearer') is the personification of the earth as the basic principle of all existence.

Traces of an Earth considered to be divine, which by itself is generative and is not regarded as the result of divine creation, are found in Gen 1:11a, 12a, 24a "Let the earth bring forth . . . / the earth brought forth every kind of plant / all kinds of living creatures" (cf. Ps 90:3, 5; Isa 34:1). In the Sumerian *Prologue to the Disputation between Wood and Reed*,[21] the bearing of plants is still clearly the result of insemination of the earth by An, the god of heaven:

> An, the illustrious heaven, inseminated the wide earth [. . .]
> the earth stepped in to joyfully bear the plants of life.

Furthermore, earth-goddesses who sprout plants appear in the iconography of the Near East from the third millennium B.C. onward. A cylinder seal from Mari shows the supreme god, El, enthroned on a mountain between the streams of the primeval flood, flanked by vegetation deities. A spear-carrying god indicates that the balance of powers was not achieved without a battle. The cooperation

Fig. 18

Fig. 19

---

19. S. Schroer, "Terafim," *NBL* 3 (2001): 816f. Cf. Hos 4:12 for consulting wood.
20. Cf. Jer 3:9, Ezek 20:32, Hab 2:19, and for criticism of the *maṣṣebôt*, 1 Kgs 14:23; 2 Kgs 17:10, 18:4, 23:14, etc.
21. Translation by W. H. P. Römer, *TUAT* III 357–60.

19 Cylinder seal of the Akkad period from Mari (2360–2180 B.C.). A bearded god with a royal scepter (Anu, Ea, or El) is enthroned on a ridge between the two wellsprings of the primeval flood. Half-tree, half-human vegetation goddesses, who emerge from the flood, display their reverence to the father of the gods. A war-like god (at the left) uses his spear to hold the upsurging water of chaos in check for the benefit of the plants. (Keel 1997a: 47, fig. 42)

20 Classical Syrian cylinder seal (1850–1700 B.C.). A warlike god with a horned crown strides across two mountaintops. His left hand brandishes a weapon, his right thrusts a spear into the maw of a partially standing up serpent. His partner, the nude goddess, stands on the same level, on a platform. She protectively raises a hand over the stylized world tree in the middle. The tree clearly embodies the ordered world, whose existence is guaranteed on the one hand by the protection of the goddess and on the other by the storm-god, who successfully battles chaos in the form of the menacing serpent (Rahab, Leviathan). The serpent symbolizes the menacing floods, which the storm-god brings under control. (Keel 1997a: 51, fig. 46)

of the chaos-battling Syrian storm-god with his partner, the earth-and-plant goddess, as it is represented in the first half of the second millennium B.C., has the goal of preserving the (stylized) cosmic tree. This world tree symbolizes the thriving of vegetation, the nourishment and life of animals and humanity.

Figs. 20–21

Much more common in Palestine/Israel than in Syria is the earth-goddess type who appears as Lady of the Plants from the Middle Bronze Age onward (1750–1550 B.C.). This erotic, attractive goddess (Schroer 1989) appears between trees, holds branches in her hands, or wears vegetation as headgear. She emerges in the form of a woman as if from the ground, whereas the later Egyptian tree-goddesses with the tree crown have a mixed appearance. Her womb is associated with the powers of vegetation. Even when the goddess is no

Figs. 22–23

21 Classical Syrian cylinder seal (1750–1550 B.C.). Two goats or ibexes rear up on a highly stylized world tree, flanking it. The tree symbolizes nourishment and life for land animals (caprids), birds of heaven (above), and aquatic animals (two fish below). Its cosmic significance is also accented by the astral symbols above it. On both sides, worshipers approach. To the right, a storm-god with his plant-scepter strides into the composition. While in fig. 20 the goddess in human form stands opposite her partner, here the icon of the world tree and its animals symbolizes the presence of the goddess and her blessing-filled furtherance of the plant and animal worlds. (Keel 1998: 126, fig. 13)

longer fully depicted, from her pudenda or navel grow branches that portend life. In the course of the history of Israelite religion, the responsibilities of the earth-and-vegetation goddess early on passed over to YHWH, who now appears to have sole control of the productive powers of the earth (Hos 2:8). Traces of a unification of the God of Heaven with the Goddess of Earth are found, however, in verses in which YHWH is explicitly mentioned as a great power bringing about fertility, as in Hos 2:23 and in the metaphors of Isa 45:8.

Figs. 24–25

The commandment to allow farmland to lie fallow periodically was originally motivated by respect for the numinous nature of the earth, and then later it increasingly took on social explanations. Thus, in the Holiness Code (Lev 25:1–7), fields and vineyards are to be worked and harvested only six consecutive years. Whatever grows in the seventh year is *nazir*, dedicated to the spirits of fertility (Elliger 1966: 257, 350); only the animals may eat of it.[22] In the formula "sabbath for YHWH," the spirits of fertility are replaced by YHWH. According to the Book of the Covenant (Exod 23:10–12), the fallow year is commanded for the benefit of the poor of the land and the cattle, because the entire yield of the fields, olive trees, and vineyards is theirs while the land lies fallow. Similar instructions— with or without social foundations—exist for the vintage and grain harvest. There are multi-year moratoria on reaping firstfruits, and fields and vineyards may not be harvested down to the last stalk or grape.[23]

---

22. Anything that grows wild from such a field or vineyard may be consumed, but not the secondary growth from the previous year.

23. Lev 19:9–10:23–25, 23:22; Deut 24:19–22 (the latter has an especially strong social component). G. Fohrer (1989: 440–42) finds a reminiscence of the respect for the divine protectors of the earth in Job's great oath of purification:

If my land has cried out against me
till its very furrows complained;I
If I have eaten its produce without payment
and grieved the hearts (*nephesh*) of its tenants;
Then let the thistles grow instead of wheat
and noxious weeds instead of barley! (Job 31:38–40)

But whether the field is here presented as a living being, whose future is directly strengthened or weakened by the vitality of its (divine) masters, the field spirits, remains questionable, because many semantic markers in these verses point to a social transgression (such as nonpayment of rent). Fohrer's

22–23 Scarabs from Gezer (1650–1550 B.C.) (Schroer 1989: 97, no. 6) and from Aphek (1650–1550 B.C.) (Schroer 1989: 97, no. 9). Both stamp seals show a nude goddess, her head in profile. The first holds in each hand a long branch or tall tree. The branches appear to stand directly on the goddess's feet. Conspicuous in this image are the navel, the necklace, the hip-girdle, and the two branches sprouting from the pudenda. The scarab from Aphek shows a goddess standing between branches with her arms at her sides, the pubic region in the shape of a leaf. The combination of pubic triangle and branch(es) is already attested in pictorial representations from the third millennium B.C.

24–25 Decorative pendants from Ugarit (14th/13th century B.C.) (Keel 1986a: 165, fig. 96) and from Tell el-Ajjul south of Gaza (1550–1480 B.C.) (Keel 1986a: 165, fig. 97a). The electrum pendant in fig. 24 shows the head of a goddess with Hathor's hairstyle and a necklace. The breasts are only suggested, while the pudenda are very prominent. From them grows (cf. fig. 22) a tree stylized as a branch. In the gold pendant (fig. 25), the little twig grows not from the pudenda but from the navel (for the interchangeability of pudenda and navel, cf. also Song 7:3). The direct gaze of the highly stylized representation of the goddess (an icon), with a beautiful shoulder-length hairdo and lissome neck, gives the piece the character of a devotional portrait.

Figs. 26–27 The earth is occasionally represented as a womb from which humanity is born and to which it returns.[24] Job reacts to the blows of fate with these words:

> Naked I came forth from my mother's womb,
> and naked shall I go back again. (Job 1:21)

---

suggestion gains strength from the fact that in the Old Testament tradition the outcry against great injustice always comes directly from the offended entity, so in this case the earth itself must have experienced violence. Furthermore, a (later) social interpretation of a no-longer-understood earlier commandment would correspond with the aforementioned tendency of providing social rationales for commandments that were originally taboo-based.

24. See Ps 139:15, Sir 40:1, and possibly Job 17:14.

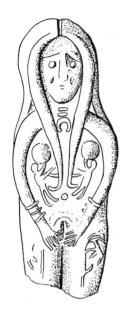

26 Figurine from Revadim (1250 B.C.). Parts of small goddess figurines, all pressed from the same mold, have been found in three different sites in Palestine/Israel. The most complete figurine, from Revadim, is shown here. The nude goddess is portrayed frontally, with long, straight hair, a crescent moon or Ω-pendant on her neck, and bracelets. Her hands open her vulva. Two infants nurse at the goddess's breasts. On each upper thigh, alongside the vulva, is a palmetto tree with a high-climbing caprid (cf. fig. 21). Once again, the tree is very close to the goddess's pudenda. At the same time, the motif of goats feeding on the tree is associated with the nourishing aspects of the divine mother. (Keel and Uehlinger 1998: 75, fig. 82)

The "back again" makes sense only if it refers not to the physical womb but to the mythic womb of Mother Earth.[25] Those who pray the Psalms know that their life began in the dark deeps of the earth:

> nor was my frame unknown to you
> When I was made in secret,
> when I was fashioned in the depths of the earth.
> (Ps 139:15c)

Jesus ben Sira (40:1) describes the time between leaving one's mother's womb and returning "to the mother of all the living" as one's arduous lifespan. And Isa 26:19 expresses the hope that the dead may be born a second time from the earth, like the birth of children from the womb.[26] The burial of the dead beneath sacred trees, still occasionally practiced in early Israel, must belong to the same realm of thought.[27]

The divine properties of the earth and the earthly realm remained in memory, but the depths of the earth appear straightaway to have been bound up with taboo and avoidance. True parallels to the Egyptian god of the underworld, Osiris, or the Greek chthonic gods (Hades, Demeter), or chthonic appearances by gods (Hermes, Zeus) did not exist in Palestine/Israel. YHWH is not a chthonic god but a heavenly deity whose realm is mountains, heights, and the heavens rather than the underworld, which was associated with darkness and death. Sheol is explicitly described as a place where the praise of God no longer resounds (Ps 6:6, 88:11–13; Isa 38:18). The underworld does not belong to the majestic realm of the God of the living. The ancient name Sheol, used without the definite article, certainly seems to be highly mythic. The usual Northwest Semitic word for the realm of the dead is *'ereṣ* 'land' or 'earth' (Tromp 1969). When in Num 16:30–33

---

25. Less mythically, Gen 3:19b and Ps 90:3 speak of returning to the dust of the earth. The expressions in Job 17:14 are both gruesome and grotesque: "I say to the pit, 'You are my father,' and to the worm[s], 'My mother,' or 'My sister.'"
26. Cf. Job 3:3–19, etc.
27. According to Gen 35:8, Deborah was buried under a mighty tree near Bethel (cf. Judg 4:5); 1 Sam 31:13 has the bones of Saul and his sons under a mighty tree in Jabesh.

the cultivated land, or the earth, devours the guilty, so that they enter Sheol alive (cf. Gen 4:11, Ps 106:17), the mythological coalesces with the numinosity of the earth.

Other themes also reflect a mood of resentment against contact with the depths of the earth. Job 28 contains a vehement critique of mining, which people are very good at and practice with much ambition and pride. But rooting around in the earth or the mountains to extract ore is criticized by the wise of Israel as sacrilege and trespass on the sovereignty of the Creator (Zimmermann 1994: esp. 88f.):

> The earth, though out of it comes forth bread,
> is in fiery upheaval underneath. (Job 28:5)

Obviously, it was considered particularly repugnant to intrude into the depths of the very earth that nurtured humanity. Although the darkness of caves offered the most secure refuge (Judg 6:2; 1 Sam 13:6, 24:4; 1 Kgs 18:4, 13; 1 Macc 2:31, 36), the psalms never speak of God metaphorically as a saving cave. While in Egypt the inner sanctum of a temple can be considered the "cave" of the god and many gods lived in rock temples, Elijah had to emerge from the cave and stand on the mountain in the presence of Yhwh in order to experience God (1 Kgs 19:11, 13). In the Psalms, heights, crags, mountain fastnesses, luminescence, and resplendence are all living metaphors with which Yhwh is praised as a refuge. Only with the rise of the Christian community do fundamental changes begin. Under the influence of mystery cults, central religious symbols shifted to the underworld. Caves came to be preferred sacred places for believers, even when this shift resulted in overt contradictions of the biblical tradition. Thus, for example, in the early church, the place where Jesus celebrated the Passover with his disciples was thought to be not in the city but in a cave on the Mount of Olives.[28]

4. Numinous Aspects of the Plant World

Throughout the Bronze Age (ca. 3000–1200 B.C.), especially in Palestine, a close connection can be discerned between portrayals of a nude goddess and vegetation (trees, branches).[29] Over time, branches were growing from the pudenda or navel of the anthropomorphic goddess (cf. figs. 22–25 above), then she was flanked by branches, and eventually, in some contexts, the cultivated sacred tree (*ašerah*) or "green tree" was interchangeable with the anthropomorphic goddess.[30]

Figs. 27–29

Hebrew *'elah* means 'mighty tree' but also 'goddess'. In the iconography of Palestine/Israel, from the middle of the second millennium B.C. onward, the tree or the icon of animals on the tree came to be a substitute for the goddess. Jacob used sprigs of green wood to promote the fertility of his flocks (Gen 30:37–41). Underlying this magical rite must have been the branch-goddess's function of protecting the flocks (cf. figs. 36–41, 60–61 below).[31]

Figs. 30–32

In the older traditions, Yhwh could appear in a tree or bush (Exod 3:1–5, Deut 33:16). Yhwh and his messengers frequently appear under specific large trees, as he did to Abraham and Sarah (Gen 18:1, 8; cf. Gen. 13:18) and Gideon (Judg

---

28. Kopp 1959, esp. 456f.
29. Schroer 1987b, 1989; Keel 1998: 20–57; Winter 1987: 434–41.
30. Cf. Keel and Uehlinger 2001: 31, figs. 10–12c; 33, figs. 14a–16; 63, figs. 49, 52–53; etc.
31. The Hebrew word *maqel* designates the riding crop and the traveler's staff but in Hos 4:12 plays an obscure role in connection with a tree cult and oracles about which we know very little.

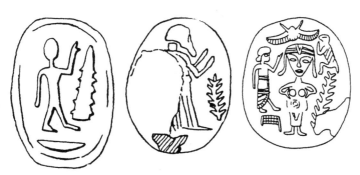

27–29 Scarab from Tell el-Farah South (945–713 B.C.) (Keel 1998: 146, fig. 84); scaraboids from Samaria (930–730 B.C.) (Keel 1998: 146, fig. 85) and from Lachish (8th/7th century B.C.) (Keel 1998: 146, fig. 86). All three seal-amulets show a more-or-less stylized worshiper, who stands with hands upraised in greeting or adjuration before a sacred tree. The one on the left shows a cut-down sacred tree (in biblical usage, an *ašerah*), the middle one a young sapling. In the third scaraboid, which could be of Phoenician origin, the goddess (*Ašerah*) appears in her anthropomorphic form in the middle of the scene as well as in the symbol of the tree, on which, furthermore, an ape sits. The sacred tree, as the biblical polemic against *Ašerah/Ašerim* suggests, cannot be separated from the presence of the earth-and-vegetation goddess that are experienced in it.

6:11). Bread and water, Elijah's portion (1 Kgs 19:5), recall the gifts of Egyptian tree goddesses (Keel 1992: 61–138). Sacred trees serve as oracle trees (Gen 12:6; cf. Judg 9:37). They are typical of sanctuaries (Josh 24:26) and are thought to have been planted by venerable figures, such as Abraham (Gen 21:33). Charismatic leaders dispense justice under mighty trees (Judg 4:5; 1 Sam 14:2, 22:6). The illustrious dead are buried beneath them (Gen 35:8, 1 Sam 31:13).[32]

In Hosea—trumping the tree cult that was widespread in the land—we still find a tree metaphor:[33]

> Ephraim! What more has he to do with idols?
>   I have humbled him, but I will prosper him,
> "I am like a verdant cypress tree"—
>   Because of me you bear fruit! (Hos 14:9)

Literary metaphors of this kind were no longer possible in later times. Tree worship was hit much harder by the Deuteronomistic reform than was the cult of the New Moon (chap. 3.7).[34] Rituals under the sacred trees of the goddess are systematically condemned in the prophetic books, beginning with Hosea (4:12f.):

> You shall be ashamed of the terebinths which you prized,
>   and blush for the groves which you chose. (Isa 1:29)

> When I had brought [your fathers] to the land I had sworn to give them, and they saw all its high hills and leafy trees, there they offered their sacrifices, there they sent up appeasing odors, and there they poured out their libations. (Ezek 20:28)

Deuteronomy forbids the planting of *Ašerim* (Deut 16:21f.), the most commonly leafless cult trees that originally, as is suggested by extrabiblical inscriptions from Palestine/Israel of the 9th/8th century B.C., had a place in the YHWH cult.

---

32. Keel 1989b: 70–75; cf. overall also Elan 1979: 89–101; Jaroš 1982: 119–50.
33. See most recently Wacker 1996: 297ff.
34. For the following, see Schroer 1987b; Keel 1998: 54–57.

30 Cylinder seal from Megiddo (14th century B.C.). The nude goddess appears beside a tree flanked by caprids. A stag flanked by a lion and a bull forms her counterpart, so that the bull and lion simultaneously flank the goddess as "Lady of the Animals." A male figure with arms raised in worship and a cherub [lionlike figure] sitting on its hind legs also flank the tree, with which the goddess is closely connected. (Keel and Uehlinger 1998: 55, fig. 52)

31 Painted vessel from Lachish (14th/13th century B.C.). Imitating the style of the ancient combination of the erotic and vegetation-enhancing aspects of the goddess (cf. figs. 22–23), in the Late Bronze Age the stylized tree against which goats rear up is conveniently altered, by very obvious overdotting, into the pubic triangle of the goddess. (Schroer 1987a: 7, fig. 14)

32 Painting on a vessel from Megiddo (14th/13th century B.C.). Wild goats and birds are grouped around a stylized tree. The agility of the animals is emphasized by the technique of the drawing. The pictorial composition as a whole represents the life-supporting and life-enhancing divine power manifested in the sacred tree (cf. fig. 21). (Amiran 1969: 162, no. 166)

The *Ašerim*, because of their transparent connection with the goddess, were later radically eradicated (2 Kgs 23:6f.). Only wisdom still appears in the form of trees and shrubs, in Sir 24:12–19. According to Ps 52:10 and 92:13f., trees still stood in the forecourt of the Jerusalem temple, but, according to Hecataeus of Abdera,[35] they were cut down in the fourth century B.C. in order to avoid the impression that sacred trees were being worshiped. The seven-branched candelabrum and the *lulab*[36] may represent survivals of the sacred tree and tree rites.

Restrictions on the use of fields, which at least partially were given secondary social interpretations,[37] are a further indication of the numinous conception of the plant world. The fruits of a tree were not to be consumed during its first four years (Lev 19:23–25). In the case of war, cutting down a city's useful trees during a siege as raw material for siegeworks is expressly forbidden in Deuteronomy (cf. fig. 8 for the opposite perspective):

> When you are at war with a city and have to lay siege to it for a long time to capture it, you shall not destroy its trees by putting an ax to them. You may eat their fruit, but you must not cut down the trees. After all, are the trees of the field men, that they should be included in your siege? However, those trees which you know are not fruit trees you may destroy, cutting them down to build siegeworks with which to reduce the city that is resisting you. (Deut 20:19f.)

War is not to be made against trees, the explanation goes, but behind the rationalization (sparing a source of food) might also lurk *pietas*.

Judaism celebrates New Year for Trees (*Tu bi'Shevat*) on the 15th of Shevat (Daum 1994: 21–49). This date marks the calculation of the three-year harvest delay for the fruit of saplings, but in addition, the day became more and more a festival of trees and nature, a time in modern Israel when trees are planted and new fruit is eaten.

Excursus:
The Goddess, the King, and the Cosmic Tree

The motif of the (sacred) tree in ancient Near Eastern art enables us to trace interesting developments in the history of culture.[38] The tree, especially the palm, because it casts physical shadows and provides nourishment and indicates the presence of water, is a primary symbol of protective and nourishing divine powers and the fullness of life that has its source in them. In the iconography of the ancient Near East, ever since the third millennium B.C., the tree represents, substitutes for, or accompanies various goddesses, but in Egypt a tradition of tree goddesses does not appear until the fifteenth century B.C. As late as the 7th/6th century B.C., stylized trees or the motif of goats standing against the sacred tree still transparently refer to the goddess, just as in Hebrew the designation "Asherah" for a green or felled tree never quite lost its connection with the goddess of the same name. The composition of Late Bronze Age cylinder seals (15th–13th centuries B.C.) proves the equation tree = goddess (cf. fig. 30 above). Similarly, the stylized tree, also from the third millennium onward, plainly appears as a symbol of the ordered world, even without explicit reference to the goddess. Beginning in the second millennium, these sacred trees are surrounded by wild animals, birds, or hybrid creatures, or flanked by worshipers.

Fig. 33

---

35. Quoted by Josephus, *Ag. Ap.* 1.199.
36. Cf. Lev 23:40, Ps 118:27.
37. Exod 23:10–12; Lev 19:9f., 23:22, 25:1–7; Deut 24:19–22. Cf. chap. III.3 above, pp. 35ff..
38. For the following, cf. S. Schroer, "Lebensbaum," *NBL* 2 (1994): 602f.; Winter 1986a, 1986b; Keel 1992: 61–138; most recently, Jeremias and Hartenstein 1999.

33 Cylinder seal of the Mitanni period (15th/14th century B.C.). The stylized cosmic tree is flanked by pairs of stags, winged sphinxes, and wild goats. This image of a good, well-ordered creation is enhanced by the group of figures to the right. Two assistants come to help a nude winged goddess support a winged disk, probably a symbol of heaven. The central, world-supporting powers are thus, along with tree and goddess, probably imagined as female. (Keel 1978: 120, fig. 66)

The first millennium B.C. introduces a significant alteration in tree symbolism. In Assyrian art, the stylized tree becomes a metaphor for the kingdom or the king that guarantees the world order. In precisely the same way, Ezek 31:2–9 describes the Egyptian king as an august world tree in the garden of paradise, towering over all; under his protection birds nest, animals bear their young, and people dwell (cf. Dan 4:7–9, 17–19). It is no longer tree and goddess that appear interchangeably in com-

Fig. 34 positions, but tree and king.

The cosmic tree is often represented as something that is in danger and therefore under protection. Whereas on the older Middle Bronze Age cylinder seals (fig. 20 above) the storm-god and his female partner still undertake the task of protection together—the god actively battling chaos, the goddess supportively blessing—beginning in the Late Bronze Age, the protection of the world tree is increasingly taken over by male heroic figures such as the "lord of the animals." These heroes conquer the dangerous world of chaos, represented by wild animals, whom they pull away from the sacred tree, the symbol of the inhabited world. Later on, in the tradition of the "lord of the animals," the Assyrian or Persian Great King—rather like YHWH in God's first speech in Job 38:39–39:30—takes over the role of protector of the cos-

Fig. 35 mic order. The protagonist to be protected—the ordered world as represented by the tree—points to its protector and increases his renown and worship-worthiness, whereas originally the tree pointed to the divine powers to which it and all living things owed their existence and which manifested themselves in the tree. The subtle iconographic changes in the tree motif between the third millennium and first millennium B.C. are an indication that, long before Genesis 1, there were developments that resulted in a desacralization of creation and an impetus toward the patriarchal *dominium terrae.*

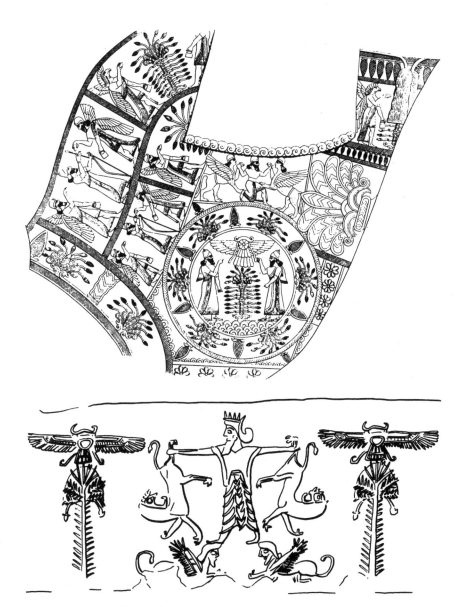

34 Breastpiece of a garment depicted on a relief of Assurnasirpal II (883–859 B.C.) at Nineveh. Winged genii alternately flank the Assyrian king and a stylized sacred tree. The power upholding the cosmos is thus represented primarily by the king and his rule, and they can be represented by the world tree. It is no longer the goddess who guarantees the liveability of the world by ordering nature, but human exercise of rulership. (Layard 1849: pl. 6)

35 Cylinder seal from the Persian period (5th/4th century B.C.). The Persian Great King, in the dynamic role of "lord of the animals," subduing lions and standing on winged sphinxes, takes over the protection of the ordered world, which is represented by a stylized palm under a symbol of heaven. (Keel 1978: 121, fig. 69)

5. Numinous Aspects of the Animal World

Throughout the ancient Near East, deities appear in the form of animals or, alternatively, animals represent divine powers.[39] Palestine/Israel was no different. Old Testament texts disapprovingly record recurring incidents of bull and serpent worship in Israel (Exodus 32 and 1 Kgs 12:28; Num 21:4–9 and 2 Kgs 18:4), not just here and there in remote places, but at the central ritual sites.[40] Archaeological discoveries bear out these records to a great extent. Obviously, though, the worship of images of animals became more and more problematic for certain circles—though for a long time not for all, as Ezek 8:10–12 makes abundantly clear. In Deut 4:17f., they are strictly prohibited.

But many animals nevertheless remain close to the divine sphere in the religion of Yhwh. Depictions of bulls and lions played an important part in the furnishings of the Temple in Jerusalem. The walls were decorated with carvings of winged sphinxes (cherubs), palms, and flower motifs. The bronze sea rested on a sculpture of twelve oxen (1 Kgs 7:25); lions, oxen, and winged sphinxes decorated the panels of the wheeled stands (1 Kgs 7:29); winged sphinxes formed the throne in the Holy of Holies (1 Kgs 6:23–27). The prophet Isaiah saw winged seraphs (spitting cobras) above the majesty of Yhwh in the temple (Isa 6:1–7). The comparison of Yhwh with a lion (Hos 5:14), a bull, or a vulture[41] protecting his brood (Exod 19:4, Deut 32:11) was not viewed negatively. Even in the New Testament, the Holy Spirit, the Pneuma, is visible in the form of a dove (Mark 1:10 and parallels), and Christ appears in the early Christian community as a programmatic symbol, the "Lamb."[42]

Some animals, such as the hairy billy goat (cf. Keel 2003: esp. 216–28), are connected with demonic spirits.[43] In Job, the world of wild animals—though all are creations of Yhwh—also stands for the threatening powers of chaos (Job 38:39–39:30). The hippopotamus and crocodile likewise plainly appear as mythological embodiments of chaos and evil (Job 40–41).

The world of real animals remains numinous to a great extent: in the Deuteronomistic expression šegar ʾalapeka weʿašterot ṣoʾneka 'the increase of your cattle and the issue of your flocks' (Deut 7:13),[44] the names of a North Syrian deity, Shagar, and a Canaanite fertility deity, Astarte, peep through. The divine protective patronesses of the flocks, who were responsible for the health and fertility of the animals and the thriving of their young, were only gradually replaced by Yhwh as protector of the flocks.[45] Gazelles and hinds, which are sworn by in Song 2:7, 3:5, are the love goddess's symbols (Keel 1986a: 89–94).

A sort of divine motherliness is recognized in the relationship between mother animals and their young, which is why they are not separated immediately after birth:

Figs. 36–37

Figs. 38–41

---

39. For the theme of animals, see especially Keel, Küchler, and Uehlinger 1984: 100–181; Keel 1985a, 1993; Janowski, Neumann-Gorsolke, and Gleßmer 1993; Riede 1993, 1997, 2000; Reinke 1995; Schmidt et al. 1996; Precht 1997; Schmitz-Kahmen 1997; Münch and Walz 1998; Janowski and Riede 1999; Keel and Staubli 2001. Cf. also P. Riede, "Tiere," NBL 3 (2001): 849–58.

40. Cf. Keel 1993a. On the numerous representations of animals in pictorial form in the First Testament, see Schroer 1987a: 69–135.

41. An ostracon from Samaria dated to the first half of the eighth century B.C. attests the name 'glyw 'a bull is Yhwh' (Lemaire 1977: 53). Cf. also the bull and wild animal metaphors in Num 23:22, Deut 33:17. Concerning the vulture (Heb. nešer), a highly respected bird in the ancient Near East, and the biblical metaphors, which are normally incorrectly translated by 'eagle', see Schroer 1998.

42. John 1:29, Acts 8:32, 1 Pet 1:19, Rev 5:1–13, etc.

43. Lev 17:7; 2 Chr 11:15; Isa 13:21, 34:14.

44. Similarly in Deut 28:4, 18, 51; cf. Delcor 1974, Görg 1993.

45. Gen 30:37–43 tells the tale of a remarkable piece of analogic magic used by Jacob to increase the fertility of his flocks (cf. chap. 3.4). Jacob's use of branches could possibly point to a goddess of flocks.

36 Classical Syrian cylinder seal (1750–1550 B.C.). In front of an enthroned prince in a layered garment stands the Syrian goddess, lifting her skirt in an invitation to love. The erotic goddess is accompanied by a recumbent griffin and a suckling goat or ibex (behind her) and an ape. The animals symbolize various aspects of her nature. (Keel 1980: 101, fig. 66)

37 Classical Syrian cylinder seal (ca. 1750 B.C.). A nude goddess propositions a warlike prince or (deified) king, who holds a club. Goddess and prince look in the same direction. Her intent is unmistakeable: she draws her robe back, appearing to touch him with one hand in an attempt to attract his attention, perhaps also offering him fruit. In the detailed secondary scene, which is divided by a braided band into two registers, below are a pair of copulating deer, a suckling caprid, and a pair of copulating fattail sheep; above, a crouching lion striking a caprid, and two sphinxes. The lower scene represents the life-bestowing aspect of the goddess, the upper her dangerous, frightening side. (Keel-Leu and Teissier 2004: no. 333)

> When an ox or a lamb or a goat is born, it shall remain with its mother for seven days; only from the eighth day onward will it be acceptable to be offered as an oblation to Y{\scriptsize HWH}. You shall not slaughter an ox or a sheep on the same day with its young. (Lev 22:27f.; cf. Exod 22:28b–29)

It was sacrilegious to cook a kid in the milk of its own mother (Keel ed. 1980). The corresponding prohibition in Exod 23:19b, 34:26, and Deut 14:21, originally a taboo out of respect for the mother–child relationship, had major cultural consequences, because the original meaning was misunderstood and the commandment became the foundation of the separation of dairy and meat cuisines in Judaism.

Out of pious respect for the fertility of animals, Deuteronomy forbids taking a mother bird together with her eggs or chicks:

> If, while walking alone, you chance upon a bird's nest with young birds or eggs in it, in any tree or on the ground, and the mother bird is sitting on them, you shall not take away the mother bird along with her brood; you shall let her go, although

38 Middle Assyrian cylinder seal from Assur (1400–1250 B.C.). A suckling fattail sheep in front of a small tree. The star above the ewe is the 'god' determinative DINGIR, which marks the entire group as a genuine divine portrait. (Keel 1980: 115, fig. 87; cf. Keel and Schroer 2010: fig. 208)

39 Neo-Assyrian cylinder seal (9th/8th century B.C.). A bull mounts a nursing cow. Above the cow's head is a crescent moon, above her back the eight-pointed star of Ishtar, and above the bull the Pleiades. A small tree is indicated in front of the cow. The man standing in front of the animal, who appears to grasp a horn with one hand and feed her with the other, is indisputably recognizable from comparable seals of the period as a worshiper. The fertility of the animals, represented by the mounting of the cow and the already born calf, is the embodiment of divine power and therefore worthy of worship. (Keel 1980: 123, fig. 103)

40 Conical stamp seal from Taanach (1200–1000 B.C.). In Early Iron Age Palestine/Israel, the favorite icon of divine motherhood, whose care causes life to grow and prosper, is the suckling caprid (goat, wild goat, or ibex). On this seal amulet, the mother is accompanied by a scorpion, which expresses the characteristic of sexuality. (Keel 1980: 115, fig. 90)

41 Ivory plaque from Fort Shalmaneser at Nimrud (8th century B.C.). Wherever expensive cattle could be kept and elegant ivory carvings could be afforded, as in Phoenicia and from time to time in the Northern Kingdom of Israel, instead of the suckling goat, the motif "cow and calf" appears as a representation of the divine power protecting the herds. (Keel 1980: 135, fig. 118)

you may take her brood away. It is thus that you shall have prosperity and a long life. (Deut 22:6f.)

The prohibition of castration (Lev 22:24) similarly prevents interference with the reproductive capabilities of animals. Thus, there were in the biblical world no steers (neutered males).

Other legal regulations show that, on the one hand, domestic animals were accorded rights, and these rights were protected; on the other hand, for animals, just as for people, these rights carried responsibilities, even if those responsibilities were limited (Exod 21:28–36). The third chapter of Jonah reports that, at the order of the king, both man and beast in the city were required to fast and summoned to repentance. Cattle and donkeys have a right to rest on the sabbath (Deut 5:14, cf. Exod 23:12). Thirsty cattle must be led to water even on the sabbath. Both the neighbor's donkey and cattle must be offered help in case of an accident (Exod 23:4, Deut 22:4). A dangerous ox, in the case of an incident that the owner could not predict and thus cannot himself be charged with negligence, can be sentenced to death (Exod 21:28–31). The commandment not to muzzle an ox during threshing (Deut 25:4) likewise testifies to great respect for the cattle. By New Testament times, Paul could no longer imagine that the Torah confirmed the protection of animals in God's name, because in 1 Cor 9:9 (cf. 1 Tim 5:18) he interprets this prohibition allegorically. Living and dead cattle played a special role in rituals, for example, in expiating an unexplained death (Deut 21:1–9; cf. also Numbers 19) or in consummating contracts. Passing between the parts of a slaughtered calf was the highest possible commitment one could make to fulfilling a covenant. If a contract was breached, the one who had performed the ritual would receive the same fate as the animal (Gen 15:19ff., Jer 34:18ff.).

Excursus:
The Secret Wisdom of Animals

Traces of the numinous nature of cattle are also found in the tale of the return of the Israelites' war totem to Israel (1 Sam 6:7–12). After the Ark was captured by the Philistines, it brought nothing but misery to Philistia, and the local priests and prophets resorted to a very specific oracular query. Two nursing cows were hitched to a cart bearing the Ark. Even though their calves were taken from the cows and kept in their stalls, the mother-animals drew the wagon directly to Beth Shemesh, as if they were responding to a different divine voice. This "contrary-to-nature" behavior (cf. fig. 41 above) was interpreted as the oracle's response that it was YHWH, the god of Israel, who had caused the misery.

The donkey, too, even though it held no religious/cultic significance in Israel, was credited with having a sensitivity to the numinous. Balaam's clairvoyant ass (Num 22:22–35), unlike her master, was able to sense the signals of divine power directly (Schroer 1994b). She saw YHWH's angel standing in the road and sidestepped him. Upon being beaten, the beast began to speak as in a fairy tale in order to explain its behavior.

Animals served as lessons for people (Riede 1997), who observed them in wonder:

Four things are among the smallest on the earth,
  and yet are exceedingly wise:
Ants—a species not strong,
  yet they store up their food in the summer;

Rock-badgers—a species not mighty,
　yet they make their home in the crags;
Locusts—they have no king,
　yet they migrate all in array;
Lizards—you can catch them with your hands,
　yet they find their way into kings' palaces. (Prov 30:24–28)

In their mysteriously guided behavior—the arrival of the vulture at carrion (Prov 30:19), the directing of the stork (Jer 8:7), the ability of the cock and ibis to predict rain and flood (Job 38:36; Keel 1981)—people not blinded by the explanations of natural science discerned divine wisdom that surpassed human comprehension. In Greece, even early on, human nature was experienced as non-animal nature, and the essence of humanity was defined by opposition to the animal; humanity in ancient Israel, however, was clearly viewed as related to animals, which were both feared and admired and with which they shared both origin and deadly fate.[46] The sense of connection was not limited to corporeal existence. Animals were credited with wisdom and, as the following passage shows, even knowledge of God:

But now ask the beasts to teach you,
　and the birds of the air to tell you;
Or the reptiles on earth to instruct you,
　and the fish of the sea to inform you.
Which of all these does not know
　that the hand of God has done this?
In his hand is the soul of every living thing,
　and the life breath of all mankind. (Job 12:7–10)

Observation of animals offered people the possibility of becoming wise, of coming closer to the divine order (of nature) and thus to God himself:

Go to the ant, O sluggard,
　study her ways and learn wisdom;
For though she has no chief,
　no commander or ruler,
She procures her food in the summer,
　stores up her provisions in the harvest. (Prov 6:6–8)

Unlike people, animals respect the order of things that has been put in place by God to support life. They do not forget that God nourishes them (Job 38:41; Ps 104:21, 147:9; Joel 1:20) and that they belong to him (Ps 50:10f.). And that is why they praise their creator (Ps 148:10, Isa 43:20).

6. Numinous Aspects of the Storm and Other Forces of Nature

The frequent rains and thunderstorms of the winter months are always interpreted in the Levant as manifestations of divine power, especially of the storm-god.[47] Akkad-period cylinder seals (ca. 2200 B.C.) show the storm-god and his female partner in concerted action. In the second millennium, the storm-god assumes the active role alone, while in Palestine/Israel his partner takes on the role of earth-and-vegetation goddess more completely (cf. figs. 20–23 above). The affiliation of the storm-god with his symbol, the bull, predominates.

Fig. 42
Fig. 43

Figs.
44–46

46. For this and for Daniel 7, see Keel 2000.
47. For climate, see Keel, Küchler, and Uehlinger 1984: 38–53.

42 Cylinder seal of the Akkad Period (2350–2150 B.C.). At the end of the third millennium B.C., the watering and fertility of the land was represented as the result of active cooperation between a rain goddess and a storm-god. The nude goddess with streams of rain in her hands stands in front of her partner, who bears a horned crown and a scepter. The two deities are carried or accompanied by winged lion-dragons spewing fire or water. Another lion-dragon can be seen at the right alongside the tempest or storm-god. At the far right, a hero tries his strength against a rampant lion. (Keel-Leu and Teissier 2004: no. 79)
43 Two-sided engraved plaque from Palestine/Israel (1700–1550 B.C.). One side of the seal amulet shows the storm-god with a blossom in his left hand, which indicates his responsibility for the thriving of vegetation. He wears a tall cap and a loincloth and is surrounded by apotropaic uraeus serpents and an Egyptian 'life' sign. The uplifted arm is a gesture of triumph, which expressing the already victorious of the storm-god's battle against heat and drought. On the reverse, two dancers and a worshiper, who with his triumphal gesture and a branch in his hand imitates the god's pose, celebrate the arrival of the storm-god, who is manifested in the spring rains. (Keel 1989c: 266, fig. 73)

In the second half of the second millennium, a merger of the Canaanite Baal type with the warlike Egyptian Seth appears (cf. figs. 116–118 below). This Baal-Seth figure constitutes the background to the biblical conflict between Baal and YHWH. As early as the ninth century B.C., prophetic circles, discernible in the biblical text in the person of Elijah, attempt to create a distinctive image of YHWH to contrast with Baal. Hosea, too (2:4–7), is essentially concerned with informing an agriculturally oriented population that YHWH—not Baal—is the bestower of the natural gifts of the land (Keel 1998: 50–53). The competitive relationship arose because YHWH as storm-god and rain-bringer was treading, in terms of the history of religion, on Baal's territory. This complex process is documented in

44 Relief from the temple of the storm-god in Aleppo (10th/9th century B.C.). The Syrian storm-god mounts a wagon drawn by a powerful bull with mighty horns. Both the pose of the god, who appears to be springing lightly into the wagon, holding the reins loosely but skillfully with one hand and with the other his scepter, and the galloping motion of the animal communicate potency and dynamism. (Drawing by Hildi Keel-Leu after Kohlmeyer 2000: pl. 17 top)

45 Neo-Assyrian cylinder seal (7th century B.C.). In fig. 44, the storm-god appears as a dynamic, active, young hero, but the later seal impression here shows him quiet and dignified, standing on his symbol, a bull, which lies quietly. The bearded, older-than-typical god holds lightning bolts in each hand. This clearly is the portrait of a god, because the bull is lying on a pedestal. A praying man stands in front of what appears to be a shrine or dais that holds the portrait of the god. To the right appears a scorpion-man bearing a sky god in a winged disk, alongside the god Marduk's spade and the god Nabu's stylus, as well as a ten-pointed star. (Keel-Leu and Teissier 2004: no. 234)

many biblical passages. The well-known Psalm 29,[48] a true YHWH theophany in the storm (cf. Job 37:1–6), theologically no longer needs to be seen as pasting a new label, the name of YHWH, onto an old tradition. In a very sophisticated way, Psalm 65 transfers a Canaanite hymn that honors the rain-giver (Baal) to YHWH and reworks it in the context of Israelite belief in the God on Zion who

---

48. Cf. Loretz 1988, with a bibliography of some two hundred items, including fifty special studies and two monographs on Psalm 29—which has enjoyed excessive attention to biblical studies.

46 Neo-Assyrian cylinder seal (9th/8th century B.C.). The lower register of the seal impression contains a plowing scene with two bearded men. One man directs the plow with the bull, and the man following him clearly is an assistant. The upper register shows the storm-god on a pedestal, with three ears of grain in his hand. He is received by a goddess, probably Ishtar, with a timbrel. The soaring dove can hardly belong to the plowing scene, but to the upper register, where it flies as love's messenger from the goddess to her partner. A servant leads and feeds the storm-god's bull. Strewn about the background are astral symbols (Pleiades, crescent moon, eight-pointed star). The theme of both registers is agricultural fertility. Plowing and sowing are the human contribution to raising plants, but only the blessing of the appropriate gods (Ishtar, storm-god, possibly also the favorable influence of the stars), especially the spring rains, guarantees a rich harvest. (Keel-Leu and Teissier 2004: no. 220)

47 Cylinder seal from the Akkad Period (2350–2150 B.C.). Ea/Enki, the god of wisdom, who rules the realm of groundwater and the deeps, can be represented as a judge. In this scene, he is recognizable by the streams that flow from his shoulders, which are marked by the two fish as fresh-flowing water. Two subordinate gods bring to the throne a bird-man, the destructive hurricane bird Zu, to be condemned. Serving as plaintiff is a god recognizable from the plow on his shoulders as a vegetation god. This is thus a trial that is vitally important for the prosperity of the land. (Keel 1997a: 207, fig. 285)

48 Old Babylonian cylinder seal from the environs of Borsippa in Iraq (ca. 1800 B.C.). A storm-god is shown quite small on this seal; he has a bundle of lightning bolts and a bent staff in his hands and he stands on a vomiting lion-dragon. Associated with him is a nude worshiper, farther to the right. The pictorial composition is dominated, however, by four winged beings with blowing hair; they may embody the four points of the compass. One anthropomorphic storm demon spreads his wings; an armed demon with bird's talons holds his wings together behind him; opposite him, in a greeting pose, is another creature with braidlike patterns on the lower body; and behind him an anthropomorphic storm demon with outspread wings bends over. Numerous additional symbols are scattered throughout the background of the seal. (Drawing by Julia Müller-Clemm after Collon 1987: no. 867)

is also the Creator god.[49] Heaven, too, makes an appearance as rain-giver (Judg 5:4; Ps 68:9; Hos 2:23f.). Although the Old Testament texts unfailingly stress that heaven is a work of Yhwh's and his dwelling-place, the idea of a "sacred marriage" between the god of heaven who emits a shower of semen and the earth-goddess thus fertilized seems not to have been fully forgotten, as the picturesque figure of speech—heaven streaming down and earth opening wide her lap—in Isa 45:8 also attest.

Figs.
47–48
Not only in thunder and rain, but also in the storm, in the rain-heavy black clouds, in fear-inspiring flaming lightning, and in the pounding of hail is Yhwh experienced.[50] In prophetic speech, they are described as instruments of Yhwh's punishment[51] and in Psalms and wisdom writing as subordinate messengers of Yhwh,[52] although the subordination of these natural phenomena was not without controversy among all segments of the population. When in the Synoptic tradition Jesus quiets the storm on the sea (Mark 4:35–41 and parallels), he reveals himself as someone with divine power over the elements, but even here the storm is represented as a divine opponent (Mark 4:39). What must be fundamentally realized is that natural elements accompanying theophanies are not to be understood in the sense of straightforward attributes or vehicles of divinity; instead, they have a certain share in the godlike nature of the power that is revealed. Elijah appears to consider Yhwh's manifestation not only *in*, but *as* the storm (1 Kgs 19:11ff.). The *ruaḥ* of Yhwh, the superstorm, has not only a dangerous and destructive but also a creative effect. According to Gen 1:2, this *ruaḥ* is the way in which the divine is present in the not-yet-ordered world before creation. It is recognizable in Ezekiel's famous vision of the revivification of

49. Schroer 1990 and "Regen II," *NBL* 3 (1998): 303ff.
50. Ps 18:10–15, 97:2–4, 135:7.
51. Isa 30:30, Jer 23:19, Ezek 13:11ff.
52. Job 37:6, 12:15, 38:35; Ps 104:4.

49 Assyrian bronze statuette with a bail on its head (7th century B.C.). In Mesopotamia, the hot desert wind was linked to the winged demon Pazuzu, the lord of all evil spirits of the air. The Pazuzu figure in the illustration could be hung on a cord and probably served as an apotropaic amulet, because the portrait of a demon could ward off that demon or a different one. On the back of the statuette is the inscription "I am Pazuzu, son of Ḫanpa, king of the evil spirits of the air, who fiercely issues from the mountains and enters raging, I am he." (Keel 1997a: 82, fig. 93)

the dry bones of the people of Israel (Ezekiel 37) as the divine power that made human life possible in the first place.

YHWH led the Israelites out of Egypt in the form of a pillar of cloud (Exod 13:21, 14:19f.). The rainbow also remained numinous in Israel; in Gen 9:12–16 (P) it took on a rational interpretation as the "sign of the covenant" of YHWH with Noah. In Ezek 1:28, Sir 43:11f., and then Rev 4:3 the "bow" (Heb. *qešet*) is a sign of divine majesty.

An important role in Palestinian/Israelite meteorology is assigned to the dew, which in the summer months replaces the declining rains as a source of water for many plants and is interpreted as the blessing of heaven, the gift of YHWH.[53] In Hosea, God himself says in a promise of salvation:

> I will be like the dew for Israel:
> he shall blossom like the lily. (Hos 14:6)

The saying on the "dew of life" in the Apocalypse of Isaiah draws on the regenerative power of the dew, which even awakens the dead to life:

> But your dead shall live, their corpses shall rise;
> awake and sing, you who lie in the dust.
> For your dew is a dew of light,
> and the land of shades gives birth. (Isa 26:19; cf. also Ps 110:3)

The destructive strength of hot desert winds (Ps 6:3; 102:4f., 12), which in Mesopotamia were feared as demons, were commonly recognized in Israel as acts of judgment from YHWH.[54] The *mashit*, the 'destroyer', which in the oldest Passover tradition (Exod 12:23) threatened the tents of the nomads, must lie behind the demonic personified might of the desert wind that compels the sheep- and goat-herding nomads to abandon the steppe (Keel 1997a). Death-bringing aridity and drought, embodied at Ugarit as Baal's adversary, the god Mot (Ugar. *mt* 'death'), nonetheless, like the impenetrable darkness, retained the *tremendum* of the holy.

Fig. 49

---

53. Gen 27:28, Deut 33:28, Hag 1:10, Zech 8:12.
54. Ps 11:6, 18:11, 83:16; Hos 13:15; Sir 39:28.

The same holds for natural forces such as earthquake and fire, which represent the traditional components of Israelite Yhwh theophanies.[55]

7. Numinous Aspects of the Skies

The heavenly bodies[56] in the day and night skies put the practice of exclusive Yhwh worship to an ongoing, rigorous test until post-Exilic times, especially because they were all always visible and their worship was not bound up with cult images and cultic structures (cf. Deut 4:19, 17:3).[57] Thus, religious ideas between the ninth and seventh centuries b.c., as demonstrated by iconographic evidence from Palestine/Israel, succumbed to the undertow of successive waves of solarizing, astralizing, and lunarizing that swept the entire ancient Near East.[58] In the metaphors of the Song of Songs, fascination with the divine astral world is preserved when the man says of his beloved:

> Who is this that comes forth like the dawn,
> as beautiful as the moon, as resplendent as the sun,
> as awe-inspiring as bannered troops? (Song 6:10)

The Priestly version of Creation (Gen 1:14–17) attempts to represent everything, including the sun and moon, as Yhwh's creations, as mere lights in the firmament that function purely as signs.[59] The account uses expressions that are obvious circumlocutions, avoiding the usual Hebrew words for sun (šemeš) and moon (yareaḥ), because they just as well could mean 'sun god' and 'moon god'. The amount of apologetic conjuration is a clear index of the virulence of astral worship at this time.

7.1. Sun Worship

Palestinian place-names such as Beth Shemesh and Jericho are proof of very ancient native sun and moon cults in the land. The sun, and perhaps also its companions, dusk and dawn, must have been worshiped at the pre-Davidic temple in Jerusalem, as the quotation from the Book of Jashar ("Book of Songs") in Josh 10:11 shows, where sun and moon are charged not to intervene on behalf of Jerusalem against Yhwh.[60] Under Solomon, legitimated by a decree from the sun-god himself, Yhwh received a permanent lease on this temple, as did the king. The Greek (LXX) text of Solomon's Temple dedication address (3 Kgdms 8:53) can be literally translated as follows:

> *Then Solomon said* about the house when he had completed its construction:
> The sun in heaven let *the Lord* know.
> *He said he intends to enthrone in the dark.*
> *Build my house, a noble house for you,*
> *in order* therein forever *to be enthroned anew.*
> Behold, it is not written in the Book of Songs.

---

55. Exod 3:1–5, 19:18; 1 Kgs 19:11f.; Ps 18:8f. Cf. R. Kratz, "Erdbeben," *NBL* 1 (1990): 558f.; W. Zwickel, "Feuer," *NBL* 1 (1990): 669ff.; M. Görg, "Finsternis," *NBL* 1 (1990): 673f.
56. For the following, see especially Keel 1998: 60–120.
57. For worship of constellations in Israel, see Schroer 1987a: 257–300.
58. Keel and Uehlinger 2001: 322–429.
59. Cf. also Ps 8:4, 104:19, 136:9.
60. For details on the sun cult, see Keel 1994b, Keel and Uehlinger 1994. That the Jebusite population ascribed special importance to the sun cult is shown also by the names of their city's kings, Adonizedek (Josh 10:1) and Melchizedek (Ps 110:4): both are connected with a deity that dispenses righteousness.

50 Cylinder seal of the Akkad period (2350–2150 B.C.). With a powerful leap, the sun god Shamash breaks through between the mountain peaks. He is identified by the flames that shoot out of his shoulders and by his symbol, a saw. The mountains are mythologized by the two gateposts adorned with lions. Three divine helpers guard the gate. Two of them swing open the Gate of the East for Shamash. (Keel 1997a: 23, fig. 9)

51 Cylinder seal of the Akkad period found in Jerusalem (2350–2150 B.C.). This imported cylinder seal was found in a tomb in Jerusalem (8th–6th century B.C.); the valuable burial object was already antique. In the center of the composition, the sun god Shamash is represented once again, though in this case enthroned as sovereign between the opened gates of heaven, a pose typical for Shamash as judge. (Drawing by Hildi Keel-Leu after "Welt und Umwelt der Bibel" no. 16 (2000): 12 [top])

Only the italicized portions of the verse are also included in the Hebrew text of 1 Kgs 8:12f. But there must have been an older Hebrew version underlying the Greek translation. Its wording can be reconstructed by back-translation. The crucial verses must have read as follows:

> The sun announced from heaven:
> YHWH will dwell in the dark.
> Build my house, a noble house for you,
> in order (therein forever) to be enthroned anew.

The dedicatory address probably intended a cohabitation of the most high sun god and the warlike YHWH on the model of the Egyptian coexistence of the

52 Cylinder seal of the Akkad period (2350–2150 B.C.). Shamash, who drove out the darkness every morning, was at the same time the god of law who brought light into the darkness of chaotic evil. As the god of judgment, he here sits on a throne formed of mountains. A man identified by the rays on his shoulder as the sun god's helper, with the assistance of another man brings a lion-headed demon before the court. (Keel 1997a: 208, fig. 286)

53 Cylinder seal of the Akkad period (2350–2150 B.C.). The sun god is enthroned at the right on a pedestal. In his hand he holds his symbol, the saw. A priest approaches from the left with the scale of justice in his hand, which he presents to the god on a small altar. Behind him stands a worshiper carrying a kid that will be presented as an offering. What the small figure behind the worshiper is doing cannot be made out. (Drawing by Hildi Keel-Leu after Eisen 1940: no. 42)

sun-god Re and Seth, who in the prow of the sun's bark pursued active battle against Apophis (cf. fig. 116 below).[61]

Near Eastern and Egyptian sun traditions have left behind equal traces of their influence in Palestine/Israel.[62] In the Near East, the image of the sun god was triumphal. Like a hero (cf. Ps 19:6), he breaks through the mountain peaks in the morning and runs his course; at the same time, he is represented as enthroned sovereign and judge, and every morning he establishes his lordship anew.[63] References to the sun cult are also found in the narrative of the destruc-

Fig. 50

Figs. 51–53

---

61. On the sun tradition of the Jerusalem temple and the Temple dedicatory address, see in detail Keel 2002.
62. On the aftermath of the solar theology of Akhenaten, see further chap. VI.2.1 below, pp. 127ff.
63. In Psalms, the judgment of YHWH appears as an important form of his advocacy of law and justice (Ps 35:1–3, 23f.; 54:3, 7; 74:13f., 22).

54–56 Two-sided engraved seal amulet from Judah (ca. 750 B.C.) (Keel and Uehliger 2001: 299, fig. 263b); Scarab from Judah (ca. 730 B.C.) (Keel 1977a: 96 fig. 67); and seal impression on clay from Lachish (ca. 700 B.C.). In the last third of the eighth century B.C., Judahite state solar symbolism came to the forefront of graphic art as propaganda. The double-sided engraved seal of *šbnyw*, a minister of King Uzziah (773–735 B.C.), shows on one face two winged sun disks (fig. 54). The scarab in fig. 55, which belonged to a certain *'šn'*, minister of King Ahaz (742–726 B.C.), shows a sun disk with a huge *Atef* crown guarded by uraeuses. In the time of Hezekiah (725–697 B.C.), winged sun disks became predominant, sometimes drawn only in outline; they appear on the many *lmlk* stamp seal impressions used by the royal administration to mark storage jars from Judah (fig. 56; Galling 1977: 305 fig. 78.29).

tion of Sodom and Gomorrah, at sunrise, in Gen 19:23f. (Keel 1979). The two messengers who were supposed to investigate whether the people of Sodom were behaving justly were, in the original version of the tale, sent by the sun god. The only one who was able to stand before them was urged to leave the city as quickly as possible at the break of dawn. The rising sun god hurled fire and brimstone on the city to destroy it utterly. This tradition is taken up by Isaiah (1:9f.) in connection with the central concept of justice, *ṣedeq*. Shamash, the god whose light drove out the darkness and, with it, the evil powers, in the Near East served as guardian of law and justice. This role was obviously transferred to YHWH without much difficulty.[64] In the east-oriented sun temple in Jerusalem, YHWH was seated invisibly on the cherub throne, originally perhaps only as a sojourner legitimated by the real lord of the temple. Increasingly, though, YHWH became solarized (Stähli 1985). According to Ps 84:12, he bore the title "Sun and Shield." Praise of the law of solarized YHWH is also sung in Psalm 19.

Kings were regarded as champions and heirs of the "sun of justice" (2 Sam 23:3f., Psalm 72), as were the god-fearing devotees of YHWH (Mal 3:20),[65] for whom the sun or dawn of justice (Ps 110:3, Isa 58:8) is always the source of renewed life, youthful vitality, and salvation (Schroer 1998). This solar regeneration symbolism is Egyptian in origin. Judahite kings of the eighth century B.C., especially Hezekiah (725–693 B.C.), disseminated the winged sun disk or the winged scarab beetle, representing the waxing morning sun, as the official symbols of their reign: it has been found on thousands of seal impressions. In the course of his reform, King Josiah made sure that the horse and chariot of the sun god, dedicatory gifts given by the kings of Judah, were banished from the Jerusalem Temple (2 Kgs 23:11; Schroer 1987a: 282–300). The effects of the reform do not seem to have lasted very long because, at the beginning of the Exile, Ezekiel (8:16), to his horror, in precisely this sacred location observed a group of dignitaries, perhaps including even priests, quite openly performing a ritual adoration of the sun.

Figs. 54–56

Figs. 57–59

---

64. Cf. the secondary use of Genesis 19 in Amos 4:11 (a god) and Ezek 16:50 (YHWH).
65. Cf. also Matt 13:43.

57–59 Seal impressions (left, middle) of Hezekiah (725–697 B.C.) (Cross 1999: 43; Galling 1977: 305 fig. 78.28) and scaraboid (right) from Judah (8th century B.C.). Alongside the winged sun disks, scarabs with two or four wings adorn the royal administration's seals from the reign of Hezekiah onward. In Egyptian solar symbolism, the scarab represents the rising sun (Egyp. *ḫpr* means 'become, arise, appear'). Just as the real dung beetle deftly rolls a ball of dung across the floor, so the mythical scarab pushes the ball of the sun across the horizon. The seal impression (bulla) in fig. 57 bears the inscription 'for Hezekiah (son) of Ahaz, King of Judah'. Fig. 58 is an administrative seal from the time of Hezekiah. The scaraboid (fig. 59), which according to the inscription belonged to an Israelite named Saul, in the middle register shows two kneeling worshipers praying in front of a four-winged scarab. (Drawing by Ulrike Zurkinden after Avigad and Sass 1997: no. 1175)

The prolonged territorial conflict (solarized Yʜwʜ vs. sun god) did not hinder the perpetuation of the sun's numinosity. Dawn and twilight, familiar from the Ugaritic texts as the gods Shaḥar and Shalim (KTU 1.23), never became entirely profane phenomena. In the earliest version of the story, the river demon with whom Jacob wrestled at Jabbok fled at the light of dawn (Gen 32:24, 26). At daybreak, the men who were raping the Levite's concubine stopped (Judg 19:25). And again, in Job 38:12–13, the dawn itself, albeit at Yʜwʜ's behest, shakes the wicked off the ends of the earth.[66] This tradition makes it clear that Israel ascribed divine assistance to the morning light (Janowski 1989).

7.2. Moon Worship

Deut 33:14 preserves the tradition, disguised as a possibly ancient tribal blessing, that the moon brought (successful) harvests. This may refer to the sequence of harvests throughout the year but also may be a covert reference to the fertilizing powers of the moon. In Joseph's blessing in Gen 49:25f., the power of the stars to bless is replaced by the blessing that comes from fullness of breasts and womb.

Figs.
60–61

The sequence of phases of the moon that governed the division of time was of great importance, and bound up with it was the cult of the moon (Theuer 2000), which is also very well documented iconographically for Palestine/Israel. In the pre-Exilic period, we hear of New Moon ceremonies, which took place both within the family (1 Sam 20:5, 18, 24, 27, 34) and publicly (Hos 2:13, Isa 1:13f.).[67] What is certain is that, during the New Moon festival, no work was

---

66. In Ps 101:8, it is the king who assumes this task.
67. Whether the Hebrew word *ḥodeš* designates the entire lunar cycle of invisibility and reappearance, the interlunium, corresponding to the Babylonian *bubbulum*, as suggested by K. van der Toorn (1997), is worth investigating, but is not provable in most biblical references. In 1 Samuel 9–10 and 20,

60–61 Stamp seal impression from Palestine/Israel (7th century B.C.). (Drawing by Hildi Keel-Leu after an original photo in the Department of Biblical Studies, Freiburg, Switzerland); and stamp seal impression from Palestine/Israel (7th century B.C.). Special influence over the fertility of animals was ascribed to the stars. In the course of the trend toward increasing astralization in the seventh century B.C., the old icon of the suckling female was often associated with the star of Ishtar or a crescent moon. (Bickel et al. 2007: 47, fig. 1; cf. Keel 1997a: 578–79 Akko No. 136)

62–64 Cylinder seal from Mount Nebo in Transjordan (8th/7th century B.C.) (Keel and Uehlinger 1998: 299, fig. 300); stamp seal from Tawilan, in the environs of Petra (end of the 8th century B.C.) (Keel 1977a: 288, fig. 209); and button seal of unknown provenance (8th/7th century B.C.) (Keel 1977a: 295, fig. 220). Mediated by the Arameans, the cult of the moon god at Harran was also a great favorite in Palestine/Israel. The crescent moon adorned with two tassels and mounted on a staff is worshiped like an anthropomorphic image of a god. Musicians with double-flute and lyre play in front of the pedestal supporting the divine symbol, and a stylized tree is beside it (fig. 62). A Palestinian specialty is the representation of the moon symbol between two cypress-like trees, which underscore the adoration appropriate to the divine symbol and perhaps are meant to represent the gate of heaven in which the moon appears (fig. 63). A pair of worshipers sometimes appears in place of the flanking trees (fig. 64).

done (Amos 8:5). Holy men were sought out on such days (2 Kgs 4:23), possibly to consult oracles.[68] The cult of the night stars experienced a period of strong growth because of the Assyrian-Aramaic occupation of Palestine in the seventh century B.C. The cult of the moon god of Harran (Keel 1994a) became very popular, especially in the west (2 Kgs 21:3ff.). The Josianic reform was supposed to have abolished this cult (2 Kgs 23:5).[69] The Deuteromonistic school based the eradication of the

van der Toorn has found clues that, as in Babylonia, family sacrifices in honor of ancestors were offered in Israel during the interlunium.

68. Promulgation of oracles at the new moon is presupposed by Isa 47:13, especially with regard to Babylonia. Arad ostracon 7 also appears to contain a reference to the observance of New Moon day (Loewenstamm 1992). Cf. R. North, "*ḥdš*," *ThWAT* 2. 759–80, and R. E. Clements, "*yrḥ*," *ThWAT* 3: 939–47.

69. On Zeph 1:5, Uehlinger 1996: 75–78; on the Josanic reform, cf. Uehlinger 1995b: 77–81.

65–67 Scaraboid (top, left) from Shechem (8th century B.C.) (Keel and Uehlinger 1998: 303, fig. 304); scaraboid (top, middle) from Transjordan (7th century B.C.) (Keel and Uehlinger 1998: 308, fig. 306c); and inscribed stamp seal (top, right) (6th century B.C.) (Keel 1998: 167 fig. 81). Sometimes, instead of the lunar standard, the moon god appears in human form, enthroned between the two cypresses (fig. 65). In Palestinian images of the 7th century, he can be enthroned as a favor-granting lord of heaven gliding across the sky in his (crescent-moon) boat, seated between two incense stands (fig. 66). The astral-symbol and human forms can obviously be combined without further complication, as shown in the case of priests worshiping the god in the crescent moon (fig. 67).

68 Relief plaque (right) from Tell Aḥmar (Til Barsip) in Syria (8th century B.C.). One side of the plaque (not shown) depicts a four-winged genius; the other (shown here), a god standing on the battlements of a city gate. Dressed in Assyrian garb, he is recognizable as the moon god by his high cylindrical (polos-like) crown with a horn in front and a crescent moon on top. Additional crescent moons adorn the staff in his hand (a scepter?) and the scabbard on his back. The god on the city wall is flanked by a pair of oversized crescent moon standards with tassels. He is probably intended to represent the moon god of Harran, because he appears as a warlike, armed type, perhaps in his function as vanquisher of darkness. (Seidl 2000: 94 fig. 4)

69 Neo-Assyrian cylinder seal (bottom left) (8th/7th century B.C.). A moon god of the same type as in fig. 68 appears on this cylinder seal, bristling with weapons, accompanied by a goddess, probably Ishtar, who appears similarly armed in a sort of garland of stars. A worshiper approaches the two divine images, which are raised on pedestals, in greeting. In front of him are the symbols of Marduk and Nabu, with the moon god Sin's crescent moon above. (Keel-Leu and Teissier 2004, no. 237)

moon cult on the fact that sun, moon, and stars had all been assigned to other peoples to worship, but not to Israel, which had a different experience of God (Deut 4:19). Job 31:26ff. takes up the matter of the seductive power of the great stars, but rejects it.

Figs. 62–64 Moon worship nonetheless survived into post-Exilic times, when the moon god could be represented either by his symbol, the crescent moon, or in human form. An indirect and unique testimony to the influence of the moon cult on Judahite religion of the 7th/6th century B.C. is represented by the central vision in the Zechariah cycle (Zech 4:1–6, 10f., 13f.; Keel 1997a: 274–327). The prophet sees not the traditional enthroned, anthropomorphic God (Isaiah 6, Ezekiel 1) but a lampstand between two trees. Ancient Near Eastern forerunners have long been assumed for this combination. The most persuasive archetype is the crescent moon mounted on a staff between two trees, which was very popular in the seventh century B.C.

Figs. 65–69

Even in Trito-Isaiah (Isa 66:23), the adoration of Yhwh at New Moon and Sabbath is a picture of the longed-for time of salvation. Psalm 81, very probably a post-Exilic composition, is very important for understanding numinous aspects of the astral world. Ps 81:4 contains an invitation to sound the shofar on New Moon day, and the Full Moon day (cf. Prov 7:20) is called "our feast (day)." This interpretation is obviously not self-evident, but no fewer than three terms (*ḥoq*, *mišpat*, and *ʿēdût*) follow the imperative, marking the obligatory nature of this practice ever since the time of the Exodus. This emphasis contrasts with the fact that the sounding of horns (*ḥaṣoṣerôt*, not the *šopar*) is cited elsewhere only in Num 10:10. The New Moon festival is otherwise never mentioned in the old lists of festivals.[70] Not once do the Priestly writings refer to this festival in their systematic presentation of the Jewish festivals in Leviticus 23. Whether the festival that in the Priestly festival calendar (Lev 23:23ff.) is announced on the "festival day with trumpet blasts"—that is, on first day of the seventh month, the month in which the festival of Booths is celebrated on the Full Moon (Lev 23:33–44)—is identical with the festival mentioned in Ps 81:4, which is not fixed to a specific day in the year, appears to us questionable (contra Körting 1999, esp. 154–62). The earliest attestation of this festival in a legal context is Ezek 46:1, 6f. (cf. 45:17). The only other citation is in the late addition to P in Num 28:11–14. Here the festival is accompanied by the same substantial sacrifices as, for example, the festival of unleavened bread (two young bulls, a ram, seven young rams, a billy goat). Martin Noth (1966: 192) was surprised only by the significant amount of sacrifices for this festival. Commentators at the beginning of the twentieth century were less hesitant in their interpretations. They thought that the New Moon festival was very deeply anchored in popular piety and therefore was taken into account by later lawgivers willy-nilly.[71]

Instead of rejoicing that the First Testament retained traces of great respect and numinous perception of "nature," biblical scholars attempt to minimize, to devalue the festival, or ignore it completely. In contrast to nearly all of the important Jewish festivals, no attempt is made to historicize the New Moon festival. It is exactly this that accounts for its uniqueness and its allure: it is a pure creation festival. It is also interesting that in the cultures neighboring Israel, connections between the cycle of the moon and women's monthly cycle were seen.[72] This provides a possibly positive evaluation of menstruation, which in the biblical tradition was primarily problematized as "defilement."

Hos 5:7 appears to know the tradition, found in North Syria as well, of a warlike New Moon (cf. figs. 68–69 above).[73] This concept was unknown to the later

---

70. Exod 23:14–17, 34:18–23; Deut 16:1–17. Post-Exilic texts mention the New Moon festival several times (2 Chr 8:13, 31:3; Ezra 3:5).

71. H. Holzinger (1903: 42) remarks: "That the provision for festivals in Leviticus 23 ignores the New Moon [. . .] an original 'Baal day' proper, is characteristic of P: the restoration theology beginning with Ezekiel (cf. 46:1, 3, 6f.) assimilated everything and incorporated it into the system, regardless of any traces of older traditions that might remain or if its origins made it questionable."

"Possibly as a popular festival it was associated with heathen practices, and, therefore, intentionally ignored by the early lawgivers (JE, D). It may have regained its place in this later law partly on account of the importance of the new moon in fixing the calendar and the due succession of festivals, and partly in accordance with the tendency to preserve but transform customs that had a great hold on the people" (Gray 1903: 410, quoted from Budd 1984: 316).

72. V. Haas and D. Prechel, "Mondgott. A. II. Bei den Hethitern," *RlA* 8 (1995): 370f.

73. Keel 1994a, esp. 142f., 183f. A warlike moon god may also be symbolized on the eighth-century B.C. stele found recently (1997) in the outer gate area of Bethsaida (et-Tell). The stele depicts a frontal

scribal exegetes, so they emended *ḥodeš* into *haḥasîl* 'the locust'[74] or *meḥaddeš* 'conqueror'[75] or some other word written more or less similarly with a more or less similar meaning. Wilhelm Rudolph translates: "nun wird ein (einziger) Monat sie verschlingen samt ihren Grundstücken." But the word that is crucial for this understanding, "einzig," appears nowhere in the Hebrew. The passage is correct without having to provide any insertions into the text: "Now the new moon shall devour them along with their fields." The new moon, which they had worshiped so enthusiastically (Hos 2:13), has became their enemy (cf. 7:2). That the moon could be dangerous under certain circumstances is shown by Ps 121:6 as well.

Excursus:
Israel's Historicized Creation Festival
and the Temple as Guarantor of Fertility

The three main festivals in Israel, which are listed in the early festival calendars of Exod 23:14–17 and Exod 34:18, 22f., originally were harvest thanksgiving festivals that were celebrated at local or regional sanctuaries: the festival of Unleavened Bread in the grain-harvest month at the time of the barley harvest, the festival of Weeks at the time of the wheat harvest, and the festival of Ingathering around the end of the year (our late autumn), when grapes and olives ripen. All of these festivals are anchored in the Canaanite tradition of the land. The storm-god and his consort had received the gratitude of the people for rain and the prosperity of the growing plants since the Middle Bronze Age (cf. figs. 22, 23, 43 above). Naturally, the "day of rejoicing" (cf. Ps 126:6) originally could not have had a fixed date, but in Israelite times a quite early attempt was made to integrate it into the rhythm of the Sabbaths (Exod 23:10–12). The festival of Unleavened Bread in Exod 23:15 was at first loosely associated in date with the Exodus event ("for it was then that you came out of Egypt"). In the course of the Deuteronomistic reform, it was integrated into the festival of Pesach, which was growing in significance (Deut 16:1–8). Similarly, the festival of Pesach (Exodus 12f.) was originally an apotropaic ritual against the death-bringing "Destroyer" (Heb. *mašḥit*), the demon of heat and drought who came at the beginning of summer (Keel 1997), reflecting its source as the festival of nomadic peoples whose life is shaped by storm and season. Generally speaking, it has a more familial character than the three harvest festivals. According to the later Israelite interpretation, it is intended to commemorate deliverance from the slaying of the firstborn in Egypt, with the demonic Destroyer assigned a new role as YHWH's helper (Exod 12:23).

On the whole, the historicizing of Creation festivals succeeded more in the breach than in the observance. Thus, the command to observe the Festival of Weeks "for YHWH" (meaning: not for Baal!) in memory of the slavery experienced in Egypt (Deut 16:9–12) succeeded[76]—assuming that the intrinsic connection is not recognized. Lev 23:33–44 commands the Israelite sons and daughters to celebrate the Ingathering with fruit and branches, and this festival in the later calendar would be called the Festival of Booths (*sukkot*), because they had dwelt in booths during their escape from Egypt (v. 43). This amalgamation with the Exodus also is artificial and hardly convinc-

---

view of a highly schematic but undoubtedly armed figure with a bull's head. For details on the find, parallels to it, and its interpretation, see Bernett and Keel 1998.
74. Wolff 1974, on the basis of the Greek translation.
75. Jeremias 1983: 73; cf. also Rudolph 1966: 116ff.
76. The mood of revelry at the festival was emphatically decreed pointblank. Cf. the four cups of wine at the Jewish seder.

ing. The *sukkot* are temporary shelters—harvest booths, in fact—that were put up on the spot during harvest and subsequently garnered a place in festival observances.

Less unambiguous than the case of the old harvest festivals is the historicizing undergone by the Sabbath day, an observance that defined Israel's identity.[77] In Akkadian, *sabbatum/sapattum* designates the festival that was celebrated on the 15th day of the lunar month with sacrifices—thus, a Full Moon festival. In pre-Exilic times, and later as well (Ezek 46:3; cf. Isa 56:4), the Sabbath in Israel must also have been a joyful, widely celebrated Full Moon festival, celebrated just as the Canaanite population of the land had in earlier times (cf. the anti-Canaanite label "days of the Baals" in Hos 2:15), and as had the Phoenicians, Israel's northern neighbors.[78] This festival is often mentioned alongside the New Moon festival (2 Kgs 4:23, Isa 1:13, Amos 8:5, Hos 2:13). It was observed even during the labor-intensive harvest period (2 Kgs 4:18ff.; cf. Exod 34:21b), and it provided the model for the length of the festivals of Pesach and Booths. Under Babylonian rule, Israelite priests reformed the festival calendar. It appears that only in this late context do the priests introduce the Sabbath as a day of rest that cycled at an interval of seven days (Heb. *šabat* 'to stop, rest'), perhaps as an idea borrowed from the Assyrians and Babylonians, who believed in astrology and considered every seventh day to be work-free, "inauspicious days"—the 7th, 14th, 19th, 21st, and 28th of every month. Neh 13:15–22, a regulation regarding enforcement of the Sabbath, shows that as late as the fifth century B.C., the rural Jewish population, busy with agricultural production, was not entirely pleased with the prescribed interruption of work (cf. already Amos 8:5f.). The weekly-recurring Sabbath day was from the start obviously very much in need of legitimation. The two versions of the Decalogue that have been trasmitted interestingly provide two different explanations of the emphatic demand for observance of cessation of work, which now occupies the foreground instead of the old Full Moon days. Deut 5:15 provides social and historical reasons for the observance of a Sabbath "for Yʜwʜ." Everyone who works, whether sons or daughters, slaves or slavegirls, domesticated animals or sojourning foreigners (migrant/guest workers?),[79] has a right to a day of rest. It was because Israel itself had experienced slavery and been freed from bondage in Egypt that freedom from the burden of labor should be perpetuated. This explanation for the Sabbath command principally rests on the need for a recreational pause after six days of work, not, in the narrower sense, on the prescribed calendrical rhythm of seven.[80] Exod 20:11, on the other hand, grounds the Sabbath in creation theology, which refers back to the Priestly account of creation in Genesis 1 and its conclusion in Gen 2:3 and anchors the regular cycle of six workdays and a day of rest in God's work of creation itself. In keeping the Sabbath, Israel is imitating God the Creator, who established the sequence of day and night and blessed and hallowed the seventh day, after the creation of the world was completed. The Israelites were continually reminded of the mystery that the blessed and hallowed pause in work was inherent in the creation and thus somewhat "natural," as was true also of the episode of the manna, which on the seventh day did not fall from heaven and therefore could not be gathered (Exod 16:26). The question regarding whether one of the two versions of the Decalogue is older, and if so, which, has not yet been settled by Pentateuchal

---

77. Cf. A. Lemaire, "Sabbat," *NBL* 3 (1998): 388–91; B. Lang, "Sabbatgebot," *NBL* 3 (1998): 391–94; Dohmen 2000.

78. In Ps 81:4, Prov 7:20, the festival has the Phoenician name *keseʾ/keseh*.

79. Whether Israelite women were addressed implicitly by the commandment, or why they are not explicitly named, is an unsolved question (summary by B. Lang, "Sabbatgebot," *NBL* 3 (1998): 392). It is also possible to imagine that an interpretive loophole was deliberately left, because strict observance of rest from work without some basis for exceptions is scarcely feasible in an agricultural household; quite possibly, free Israelite women were intentionally not subject to this law.

80. Exod 23:12, 34:21, too, obviously does not involve a calendar, but one free day per six of hard work.

70 Relief from the palace of Assurbanipal in Nineveh (668–626 B.C.). The relief shows a temple site raised on a mountain. The immediate surroundings of the temple are indicated by trees and water. The water is brought in by means of an aqueduct. On the temple mountain it divides into several streams (cf. Gen 2:10–14). Beside or in the sanctuary, which is approached by a *via sacra*, is a stela with an image of a worshiping Assyrian king. (Keel 1997a: fig. 202)

studies. The suggestion that old taboo commandments, such as the requirement that fields be allowed to lie fallow, may underlie the trend toward historicizing the creation festivals and the subsequent attribution of social foundations for them finds some support in the fact that in Deut 5:15 an attempt is made to historicize (albeit loosely) a festal day that already exists—and in this case, the content is persuasive; thus, a secondary interpretation exists. Exod 20:11, on the other hand, must have arisen from the primary need of the Priestly circle to refashion the original Full Moon festival into a weekly "festival for YHWH," the God who stands sovereign over the world, and at the same time to create, using the rhythm of seven (cf. also the Sabbath year), a characterisitic of Israelite identity not dependent on land and Temple.

The (nearly) consistent, though not entirely trouble-free, amalgamation of Creation and History was, in view of the stability of the tradition, obviously a very successful union. Like the Jewish tradition, the Christian tradition also set its great festivals, Easter and Christmas, on top of the double layers of Creation and History. In these two festivals, the memory of the broad sweep of historical events, the birth and death/resurrection of the Nazarene, was celebrated. Beneath all this, however, lies a layer of "nature"—the course of the sun and the awakening of spring, birth and death as the basic facts of human existence, light symbolism (candles), signs of fertility (green tree, bunnies, eggs)—all of which originate in heathen festival traditions. These natural substrates have also ensured the survival of the festivals in the widely secularized Western societies.

It is not only the festival calendar that points to the ongoing close connection between agriculture and cult in Palestine/Israel. Every sanctuary—in Israel, the Temple in Jerusalem above all—as the abode of divinity on earth, as worship center and symbol, was the guarantor of fertility and prosperity in the land.

In ancient Near Eastern cults, the temple as the dwelling-place of divinity on earth also is a sort of link between heaven and earth.[81] The siting of sanctuaries, the configuration of their interiors, and their immediate environs had cosmological features.[82] "House of the foundation of heaven and earth," or something similar, is the name given to the great temple complexes of Mesopotamia. The Temple Mount, even when it is as small as Zion, possesses the value of a primeval hill—the first hill—that emerged from chaos and led the order of creation, for here chaos was first repulsed. The temple precinct is a little paradise on earth because of the nearness of divinity, a primeval garden, often with a temple spring or at least a symbolic representation of the connection with the cosmic primeval water. The temple is the place of origin of the cosmos, where mythic primeval time is recalled. In the Jerusalem Temple, YHWH is gladly worshiped as "Creator of heaven and earth" (cf. Ps 24:1ff., 134:1–3).

Fig. 70

At the same time, the Temple is the visible symbol of the world order created by the divinity and thus a confirmation of the existence of this order. The so-called basic Priestly writing sees the presence of YHWH in his sanctuary as the continuation of the divine act of Creation.[83] Blessings go out from the Temple to the entire land and especially to pilgrims: the water of the Temple spring[84] fertilizes the entire land; rain (Ps 84:7), thriving of animals and plants (Ps 65:10–14), and the blessing of children (Psalm 128) come from the sanctuary. Even after the Exile, the circles of the prophets Haggai (Hag 1:2–11, 2:15–19) and Zechariah (Zech 8:9–12) were certain that the Temple building and Temple worship were essential for the fertility and welfare of the land. However, fulfillment of the laws of worship and sacrifice were prerequisite for the functioning of this complex. Whoever participates in worship must approach with clean hands (Ps 24:5). The bringing of sacrifices by an individual or the community serves, among other things, to expiate sin and guilt (Ps 65:3f.); in a way, the sanctuary symbolizes the purification system of the land. In this sense, it contributes to the constant maintenance of the ecology and economy of creation (Joel 1–2). The prophets of Israel continually warned that Temple worship without genuine fear of God and readiness for righteous living before YHWH achieved nothing and earned no blessing (Amos 4, Isa 1:10–17). The connection between the cult on Zion, where YHWH is worshiped as creator of heaven and earth, and the prosperity of the land is wonderfully evident in Psalm 65, with which an ancient Canaanite hymn for rain has been interwoven (Schroer 1990). God on Zion makes atonement and forgiveness possible; his Temple provides blessing for his followers (65:1–5). YHWH has revealed himself powerfully as Creator God and in history (65:6–9). Above all, however, he made the earth fruitful through his rain (65:10–15).

The interior furnishings of the Jerusalem Temple also bore witness to the abundance of life due to the proximity of divinity. In Egyptian and Canaanite tradition, cult basins (the "bronze sea," cauldron carts) and plant and animal symbolism (lotus, pomegranate, palmettos, bull images, etc.) point to the cosmological, creation-maintaining function of the sanctuary.[85] Branches, grape leaves, and so on are

---

81. For the following, cf. Keel 1997a: esp. 111ff., and Keel 1996: 338ff., and Janowski 1993b.
82. Thus the points of the compass play an important role, as do geographical references of temple and landscape (cf. for Greece Schroer 2002).
83. The complex relations between the Priestly creation and Sinai narratives cannot be unraveled here. Cf. Janowski 1993b: 223–46; Frevel 2000, esp. 384f.
84. Ps 36:9f., 46:5, 65:10; Ezek 47:1–12.
85. Cf. Schroer 1987a: 46–66, 75f., 82–84, 121–33; Keel 1997a: 111–51; Keel and Uehlinger 2001: 189–96.

71 Roman denarius (54 B.C.). The obverse of the coin (not illustrated) depicts a woman's head with a crenelated crown; the reverse shows a kneeling, bearded man holding out a palm branch in front of a standing camel. The man is labeled "Bacchius Judaeus." Historically, this must be Aristobolus II, the last Hasmonaean king under whom the Judean kingdom was besieged by Pompey in 63 B.C. This coin would be evidence that some representatives of the Greco-Roman world sought to understand the Jewish religion as a Bacchus religion. (Keel and Staub 2000: 117 fig. 2 right)

72–74 (top) Silver shekel from the First Jewish War (A.D. 66–70) (Galling 1977: 233, fig. 56 no. 6); (middle) silver coin (Madden 1881: 236 fig 10); and (bottom) tetradrachma from the Second Jewish War (A.D. 134/135) (Reicke and Rost 1964: 1253f. no. 10). The obverse of the coin in fig. 72 shows a chalice (of salvation), the reverse three pomegranate flowers. The inscription reads 'Israelite shekel, year 2—Jerusalem, the Holy'. In fig. 73 (middle) a cluster of grapes, representing fertility, is on the obverse, and on the reverse, a lyre, representing Temple worship. The inscription reads 'Simon' (bar Kochba) and 'for the freedom of Jerusalem'. The obverse of fig. 74 (bottom) shows the front of the Temple and the ark for the Torah scrolls inside, with a star above. The reverse depicts the *lulav* (traditional vestal bouquet of branches of the 4 species) and a citrus fruit. The inscription reads 'Jerusalem, year 2 of the freedom of Israel'.

indispensible elements of worship and processions.[86] On the testimony of Flavius Josephus (*J.W.* 5.4 §210, *Ant.* 15.11.3 §395), Tacitus (*Hist.* 5.5), and the Mishnah tractate *Middot* (3.8c), there still was a monumental gold grapevine with clusters of

---

86. Cf. Ezek 8:17 and again at the Entry into Jerusalem in Mark 11:8 and parallels.

grapes as tall as a man over the entrance to the holy place of the Herodian Temple. The Dionysiac element was obviously not as foreign to the Jerusalem cult as 2 Macc 6:4, 7 would have it. When the Romans came to Jerusalem for the first time under Pompey, they considered the indigenous religion obviously Dionysiac, because an oscure coin (54 B.C.) of the Rex-Aretas type shows, next to the camel, a kneeling Jewish prince—perhaps Aristobolus II—with a festive bouquet and the inscription *Bacchius Judaeus*, 'Jewish follower of Bacchus'. Jewish coins of the First and Second Roman Wars regularly depict a ritual object or the façade of the Temple on one side, and a symbol of blessing, such as a pomegranate or cluster of grapes, on the other.

Fig. 71

Figs. 72–74

IV. Creation and Blessing

As shown in the previous chapter, traces of the numinosity of creation survive at every turn. "Numinosity," as we have already said, is a modern concept, borrowed from ancient Rome. The Hebrew word-group with a semantic field closest to this phenomenon—though not fully equivalent—are all derived from the root *barak* 'to bless, grant saving power'. We "Occidentals," with our extremely logocentric religion, are all too quick to associate blessing and benediction with the spoken word[1] and are especially interested in what exactly takes place in a benediction—how the blessing enters into something. The people of ancient Israel, and probably other peoples of the ancient Near East, quite reasonably began with the fact that blessing (*berakah*)—or, to put it even more simply, 'good' (Heb. *tob*)—is present in and can be experienced in much that is created: for example, in a pool that promises refreshment, which in Hebrew is precisely *berekah*. Trito-Isaiah records an adage:

> As the juice is found in the grapes,
>   men say, "Do not destroy them,
>   for there is a blessing in them." (Isa 65:8)

Folk wisdom warns us not to destroy unnecessarily something that inherently possesses fertility, growth, and maturity. In the Old Testament understanding, blessing is present wherever life prospers to the fullest extent; it is through blessing that life and prosperity advance. Rain that falls in its season and causes the seed to sprout is an embodiment of blessing (Gen 27:27; Ps 84:7, 85:13; Isa 45:8; Ezek 34:26; Joel 2:14); and so are the verdant tree, the good harvest (Ps 65:10–14, 67:7f.; Jer 31:12), the lavish table and warm clothing (Ps 132:15, Hag 1:6), the land that may be inhabited in peace, spared by war (Lev 26:6), the pregnant (Luke 1:42), the multiplication of offspring (Ps 37:26), the woman's full breasts (Gen 49:25; cf. also Luke 11:27), health (Deut 7:15), long life (Job 21:7), sound sleep (cf. Ps 127:2), increasing flocks (Deut 7:13 etc.), the nursing animal with her young, a neighbor's friendly greeting, and the day of rest from hard work (Gen 2:3, Exod 20:11).

In the art of Palestine/Israel and the ancient Near East, many of these blessings have been incorporated into icons that can be interpreted simultaneously as amulets, votive gifts, prayer offerings, or thank-offerings.

Archaeologists have excavated hundreds of little "pillar" figurines of the eighth/seventh century B.C. in dwellings and graves in the area of ancient Judah, and these discoveries are no doubt a healthy shock for the entire guild of biblical scholars, who have been forced to recognize the nature of the primary religious preoccupation of the people of the time. This preoccupation is clearly expressed pictorially and by example in the blessing icons depicted as presenting their full breasts. Biblical passages can be correlated with the little breast-presenting figurines, such as, for example, when the Teacher of Wisdom describes the woman as source of blessing for an Israelite household (Prov 5:18) or when Jacob calls down blessing on his sons Judah (Gen 49:11f.) and Joseph:

Figs. 75–76

---

1. Cf. the Greek *eulogein* and the Latin *benedicere*. In the early church, a *eulogia* was not simply the words of blessing but also the actual blessing-gift, donation, or even bread that was shared with believers as a substitute for communion.

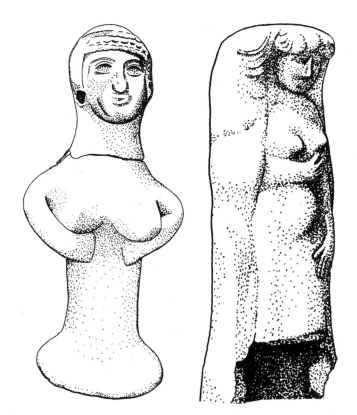

75 Pillar figurine from Judah (8th/7th century B.C.). The archaeologically best attested blessing icon from the Iron IIB–C period in Judah is the so-called pillar figurine. It portrays a woman with highly stylized lower body presenting her full breasts. In the Bible, too, breasts plainly symbolize nourishment and the fullness of life. These little figures have been found in many houses, and they were also interred with the dead as a final blessing for the darkness of the grave. (Drawing by Hildi Keel-Leu after Keel and Schroer 2010: 188, no. 161, with photo on p. 4)

76 Terracotta figurine from northern Israel or Phoenicia (6th/5th century B.C.). Depictions of pregnant women are later and less common. The figurines symbolize nourishing fullness and divine blessing in a manner that significantly transcends the actual role of nursing mother; the little figurines of pregnant women must have expressed the particularly urgent desire in contemporary society for children and the hope for rapid conception, sound pregnancy, and healthy birth. (Drawing by Inés Haselbach after Keel and Schroer 2010: 220f., no. 208)

> [because of] The God of your father, who helps you,
>   God Almighty (*Shaddai*), who blesses you,
> With the blessings of the heavens above,
>   the blessings of the abyss that crouches below,
> The blessings of breasts and womb,
>   the blessings of fresh grain and blossoms,
> The blessings of the everlasting mountains,
>   the delights of the eternal hills. (Gen 45:25f.; cf. Deut 33:13–16)[2]

---

2. The etymology of the divine name "(El) Shaddai" is not entirely clear, but the meaning 'god of the wilderness' and a connection with the "lord of the animals" is most likely (Knauf 1999).

77 Cylinder seal from Cyprus (ca. 1500 B.C.). The seal impression depicts intercourse. The man and woman lie on a luxurious bed, under which a scorpion lurks. The scorpion, the wild goat lying down, and the fish above must symbolize the aura of the protective goddess responsible for the perpetuation of life. That the coitus of this couple—perhaps a prince and his consort or a priestess—was a sacred act is suggested by the presence of a worshiper in a tasseled skirt who approaches the bed from the right and blesses the couple. The fertility of husband and wife is explicitly blessed in Genesis 1. (Winter 1987: fig. 366)

78 Grave stela of Sobek-aa from Moalla (2100 B.C.). The owner of the grave is shown as a father lying on his bed, playing with his children—an unusual scene. The caption reads 'enjoy yourself'. The interpretation of this scene as a depiction of coitus is in our opinion not correct; instead, the scene portrays joy in the blessing of children. (Drawing by Inés Haselbach after Wildung 1984b: fig. 18)

Every promise and covenant, purity statute, law and ordinance, wisdom admonition, as well as prophetic utterance, the entire religious enterprise, and kingship—all ultimately serve to maintain and promote blessing. For an Israelite, hoped-for blessing and its results were not spiritual but consisted of very concrete gifts. Job sadly recalls (Job 29) the times when he was still under God's protection, himself blessed and also a blessing for others. But not only does he despair over the loss of God's blessing and experience of an unjust curse on his life, he is also appalled that the blessings deserved by the just are often granted to the godless:

Why do the wicked survive,
grow old, became mighty in power?

Their progeny is secure in their sight;
  they see before them their kinsfolk and their offspring.
Their homes are safe and without fear,
  nor is the scourge of God upon them.
Their bulls gender without fail;
  their cows calve and do not miscarry.
These folk have infants numerous as lambs,
  and their children dance.
They sing to the timbrel and harp,
  and make merry to the sound of the flute.
They live out their days in prosperity,
  and tranquilly go down to the nether world. (Job 21:7–13)

The withholding of blessing created fears that were just as concrete: drought, barrenness, illness, and war infesting the land.

For the biblical writers, the fount and origin of all blessing is for the most part YHWH, though sometimes it is the place of his earthly dwelling, the Temple.[3] The Priestly account of creation embeds God's original blessing on man and the creatures of the air and the water[4] as well as the Sabbath directly in the creation of the world and in the assignment of fertility to all living things (Gen 1:22, 28, 2:3). Yet, this primeval blessing required constant renewal (cf. already Gen 5:2, 9:1) on the part of God and effort on the part of humanity. The deity can also turn away its friendly gaze, which signifies blessing (Num 6:22–27, Ps 67:2); blessing can turn to curse and curse can turn to blessing (Deut 23:5, 1 Kgs 8:31–43, Mal 2:2). The Flood is a powerful—but never spoken out loud—curse from God upon humankind (Gen 8:21). Only through renewed blessing can the power of this primeval curse be broken. In Deuteronomy, the Israelites are faced with the fundamental choice between blessing and curse (Deut 11:26, 28; 30:1, 19; cf. also Leviticus 26). This is what Deuteronomy promises to those who uphold YHWH's law:

Figs. 77–78

> As your reward for heeding these decrees and observing them carefully, YHWH, your God, will keep with you the merciful covenant which he promised on oath to your fathers. He will love and bless and multiply you; he will bless the fruit of your womb and the produce of your soil, your grain and wine and oil, the issue of your herds and the young of your flocks, in the land which he swore to your fathers he would give you. You will be blessed above all peoples; no man or woman among you shall be childless nor shall your livestock be barren. YHWH will remove all sickness from you; he will not afflict you with any of the malignant diseases that you know from Egypt but will leave them with all your enemies. (Deut 7:12–15)

Very similarly, Hesiod of Boeotia (ca. 700 B.C.) lays out the alternatives of law and blessing versus lawlessness and curse for the entire polis.[5] Finally, the whole relationship between Israel and its God is organized around the preservation of this sort of concrete, divine blessing.

The central figures of the history of the primeval ancestors,[6] the king (Ps 21:7, 72:17f.), and every righteous person (ṣadiq; Psalm 37, Prov 28:20, etc.) all served as mediators of blessing. The power of blessing proceeds from them or from

---

3. Cf. the Excursus to chap. III.7 (pp. 64–69).
4. That the land creatures are not blessed and fertility is not assigned to them is not chance. They are man's rivals in settling the land (for *dominium terrae* see chap. VI.2.3.2 below, pp. 144ff.).
5. *Works* 224–72. The parallels in the concretizing of the fertility blessing vs. curse in Hesiod and Deuteronomy are astonishingly close and deserve further investigation. In Hesiod, generally, the gods are directly involved in carrying out reward and punishment for human actions. In biblical belief, blessing and curse can also be engaged without direct divine intervention (cause-and-effect connection; cf. Koch 1955). For the metamorphosis of the theme into the stuff of tragedy, compare the opening of Sophocles' *Oedipus Rex*, where sterility that has gripped city and land sets the tragic events in motion.
6. Gen 12:2f., 18:18, 22:18, 27:29, 28:14, 48:20.

79–80 Relief in the temple of Edfu (237–57 B.C.) (Keel 1997a: 286, fig. 389); and Relief in the Chons temple of Karnak from the time of Ptolemy II (246–221 B.C.). (Keel 1997a: 287, fig. 389a). The two temple reliefs dating to the Ptolemaic period show the pharaoh in his priestly capacity performing fertility rituals. In the first case, the king cuts sheaves of grain in front of Min, the god of fertility; in the other, holding a serpent staff, he brings before the god four various-hued calves for threshing. This rite, too, according to the accompanying text, is intended to increase the harvest. In the ancient Near East, direct influence is attributed to the royal performance of fertility rituals, including the "sacred marriage," whereas the Bible connects the fertility-promoting powers of the king to his ethical behavior.

their name. Inasmuch as the king creates law in the land, he himself becomes like rain (Ps 72:6), sun, and thus fertility and blessing on the land, as David affirms in his last words:

> He that rules over men in justice,
>   that rules in the fear of God,
> Is like the morning light at sunrise
> on a cloudless morning,
>   making the greensward sparkle after rain. (2 Sam 23:3f.)

According to Psalm 72, King Solomon personified law and along with it divine blessing of the highest sort, thus creating fertility upon earth. The prosperity of city and land (72:16) depends on the king, who is blessed, blesses, and hence becomes blessing.[7]

Figs. 79–80

The Bible understands humanity to be fully empowered in many respects with regard to blessings and curses. Humanity acknowledges and reinforces the good by its power to bless—thus, everything beneficial that humanity experiences, whether in things or in other human beings, in the final analysis comes from God.

People cooperate with God's blessing, but they are also in a position to diminish life through their curse. Yet it is impossible for them to bless or curse contrary to the curse or blessing of God.[8] Furthermore—in Judaism, to this day—people also bless God as the source of all good gifts and the creator of all life (Psalm 103).

In the Bible, receiving blessing and granting blessing are most closely bound up with creation and the God who is revealed in it and its good gifts. Amnesia regarding creation in twentieth-century theology, with its extreme concentration on soteriology,[9] has led almost inevitably to the exclusion of blessing from theology, community, and everyday life. Karl Barth connected blessing quite directly to the acts themselves. Indeed, confessional differences regarding blessing theology are striking. Only in 1998 did two comprehensive monographs on the theme of blessing appear, simultaneously and independently, authored by Protestant theologians (Frettlöh 1998, Greiner 1998). Both authors are sensitive to the obvious need for blessing of the church's foundation, and they investigate the causes of silence regarding blessing in their Protestant tradition and recognize a connection with the decline of creation theology. Both formulate approaches to a new theology of receiving blessing and granting blessing and in the process wrestle tirelessly with the results of the old theology, such as, for instance, the general suspicion of magic in the context of receiving blessing and the word-fixation that often accompanies granting blessing, and, last but not least; finally, they grapple with the idea, so difficult for dialectic theology, that the divine can be revealed in creation. Even though Catholic biblical studies has long sailed in the wake of Protestant exegesis and, similarly, did not investigate the topic of blessing in great detail, Catholic theology found this notion much less problematic, because it does not find the notion of Creation's sacramentality to be alien. Thus, the Dominican Matthew Fox, in a series of

---

7. Cf. Ulysses' song of blessing (Hom. *Od.* 19.107–14), according to which the king's righteousness is directly responsible for the prosperity of grain, fruits, flocks of sheep, and fish (see Auffahrt 1991: 524–29). For Psalm 72, see now Arneth 2000.

8. Cf. Num 22:12, 23:8, 20–23; 1 Sam 14; 2 Sam 16; Prov 26:2.

9. There have been scarcely any exegetical publications on this topic, other than a small book by Claus Westermann (1992) and a dissertation by Gerhard Wehmeier (1970). Westermann, significantly, attempted to separate the blessing of God from his saving acts. Exegetical research has taken even less interest in curse than in blessing (Schottroff 1969; cf. Wyss 1984). For the impact of the Assyrian *adê* on Deuteronomy 28 see Steymans 1995, and for the punishing storm-god or Adad curse, Grätz 1998, esp. 7–131.

publications since the 1980s (in German translation 1991, 1993)—and considerably more impartially than Frettlöh and Greiner—has been able to devise a comprehensive theology of blessing and creation and combine it with a cosmic Christology (Fox 1998). Fox's theology, which is strongly marked by mysticism, is primarily a spiritual way and a spiritual wisdom and is built on the sacramentality and divinity of creation. The rediscovery of the great primeval blessing of creation becomes the key to a renewed connection with earth's natural resources and the basis of a far-reaching alteration in lifestyle for humanity, which owes its existence to the generative powers of creation. That major topics of theology remain underexposed in Fox's theology, and considerable counterpoint is shunted aside, is a legitimate criticism.[10] But this should not distract us from the fact that Fox has grasped a central challenge to twentieth-century theology very precisely and has taken it on in an impressively constructive fashion. In any case, the rehabilitation of creation theology, if it is biblically based, will go hand in hand with the rehabilitation of blessing and wisdom traditions.

---

10. Rosemary Radford Ruether (1994: 252–54) and Dorothea Greiner (1998: 250–65) distance themselves from Fox for similar reasons. Both complain of a certain superficiality, imprecision, and simplification with regard to theological traditions.

V. Ideas of the Origin of the World

The classification of creation traditions is not unproblematic.[1] There are various basic ways of organizing the variety of Near Eastern approaches:

a. Classifying texts and images by origin (Egyptian, Mesopotamian, Israelite)
b. Classifying texts by agent
c. Classifying texts by technique of creation
d. Classifying texts by object or goal of the origin or creation

Anthologies of Old Testament and ancient Near Eastern creation texts are usually organized by *origin*.[2] This classification takes into account the conceptual autonomy of each culture (Landsberger 1926 = English trans. 1976), but it is ill-suited for presenting the (usually later) biblical creation traditions against their ancient Near Eastern background.

Somewhat better is a classification by *agent*. When we begin with the fact that earth- and mother-gods played a predominant role in Sumer, the sun-god in Egypt, and storm-gods in Canaan, we are still too close to the inadequate principle of classification by origin. Of course, we could sort the various gods by type, but it soon becomes clear that various types can belong to various contexts or even to texts from the same culture. The Egyptian sun-god's résumé does not correspond to that of the Mesopotamian sun-god and judge Shamash. And even within Egyptian sources, the sun-god can appear in various roles: sometimes as a member of a pantheon in a polytheistic system, sometimes as the only god, monotheistically. The Egyptian god Ptah of Memphis was originally a craftsman-god, creating the uraeus on the potter's wheel, but in the *Monument of the Memphite Theology* he appears as the primeval god, who creates entirely by thought and word but not by deed.[3]

Still better is a classification of creation texts by the *technique* of creation.[4] Jean Piaget, the father of child psychology, in his groundbreaking work *La représentation du monde chez l'enfant* (1926 = English trans. 1929) distinguishes artificial and biological ways of thinking. He traces this conceptualization back

---

1. See G. Ahn, "Schöpfer/Schöpfung I. Religionsgeschichtlich," *TRE* 30 (1999): 250–58, esp. 250ff.
2. Eliade et al. (1959, 1964) offer Egyptian, Sumerian, Akkadian, Hurrian, Hittite, Canaanite, and Jewish [sic] creation texts; Brandon 1963 contains texts from Egypt, Mesopotamia, Israel, Greece, and Iran; Blacker and Loewe (1975) survey a total of nine culture areas (Egypt, Sumer, Babylon, Israel, China, India, Islam, Scandinavia, Greece); O'Brien and Major 1982 is limited to Mesopotamia, Israel, and Greece; Clifford (1994) includes Sumerian, Akkadian, Egyptian, Canaanite, and biblical texts; the extensive anthology "Texte aus der Umwelt des Alten Testament" organizes the material by origin (*TUAT* III/3 Sumerian, III/4 Akkadian and Hittite, III/5 Egyptian), as do R. G. Kratz and H. Spieckermann, "Schöpfer/Schöpfung II. Altes Testament," *TRE* 30 (1999): 258–83.
3. With regard to the Bible, a division between myths and legends oriented to a single god and those that are explicitly polytheistic is conceivable, but one would be advised to foreground only the differences between Israel and the ancient Near East, not their similarities. Both early (e.g., the *Lugal* myth) and late (e.g., the *Monument of the Memphite Theology*) creation legends that are introspective, other than those of Israel, which concentrate on the acts of a god, are less interested in the gods than in their works. Although in Egypt several gods (Re, Ptah, Khnum, Neith) could play the role of creator-god, the idea was also maintained that all life originated in a single primeval god not precisely identical with the creator-god. See J. Assmann, "Schöpfergott," *LÄ* 5 (1984): 676f.
4. Ancient Near Eastern and Egyptian examples of creation by procreation and birth are discussed in Keel 1997a: 26–29, 201f., and figs. 25–32; by crafts, 204f.; by magic, 205f.; by battle, 47–55, figs. 42–52; see also Keel 2001a.

---

to Aristotle, who according to Piaget described the world both as the work of a transcendent *artifex* (nature or the divine mover) and also as a living being (1929: 253ff.). Children are for Piaget in general "artificialists," because on the basis of their everyday observations they see all things as the result of (divine) manufacture. Nonetheless, in order to explain the origin of the sun and moon, they speak directly of birth (1929: 263ff.). In addition to these two methods (God "made" or "gave birth to" the moon), children also claim the numinous idea that tricks or magic were used,[5] which in ancient creation texts corresponds to the terminology of power words, miracle, or magic. In addition to the techniques of creation already mentioned, in the ancient Near East, creation through battle plays an important role. The frequent blending of methods, such as the combination of artificial and biological elements in Sumerian and Akkadian myths of the creation of humanity, and the forming of the world egg on the potter's wheel in Egyptian mythology, makes classification by technique problematic, but as an aid to understanding ancient ideas of creation it is most helpful. The most important methods of creation are therefore briefly presented here in both word and image. Fundamentally, however, it must be kept clearly in mind just how speculative these ideas of creation are. The thought, pictorial representations, and language of people of that time were generally symbolic— that is, neither entirely concrete nor purely abstract. A cow that bears a calf or the sky-woman who bears the sphere of the sun are not expressions of naive, childlike fantasies regarding the origin of the world but philosophical developments of thought that were able to form and formulate more abstract notions (the coming into being of the world) from concrete experiences (cattle, birth, etc.). This kind of representation is not simple realism but reflects an interest in the powers that operate and appear in the concrete world. Empiricism and reflective thinking, technology and speculation, science and myth are not polar opposites but are interwoven facets of the same realities.[6]

Excursus:
Ancient Near Eastern Images of the World
and the So-called "Ancient Near Eastern Image of the World"

People in the ancient Near East did not conceive of the earth as a disk floating on water with the firmament inverted over it like a bell jar, with the stars hanging from it. They knew from observation and experience with handicrafts that the lifting capacity of water is limited and that gigantic vaults generate gigantic problems in terms of their ability to carry dead weight. The textbook images that keep being reprinted of the "ancient Near Eastern world picture" are based on typical modern misunderstandings that fail to take into account the religious components of ancient Near Eastern conceptions and representations.[7] All ancient Near Eastern world images imply the involvement of divine powers that, especially at the beginning, make possible the cohesion and functioning of the parts of the cosmos—that is, they grapple with the transcendental. Job, too, in God's first speech is questioned about his knowledge of the divine power underlying everything, in

---

5. Cf. Fetz and Oser 1985 and Reich 1987.
6. See Assmann, Burkert, and Stolz 1982 and K. Hübner 1985.
7. For ancient Near Eastern images of the world, see especially Keel 1986b, 2001a; most recently in detail Janowski and Ego 2001; on representations of heaven in detail, Houtman 1993. B. Lang, "Weltbild," NBL 3 (2001): 1098–1105, with his very schematic sketch of the principal spheres of a vertical cosmography (fig. 27), has once again left out the most important characteristic of an ancient Near Eastern image of the world, namely, the participation of divine powers.

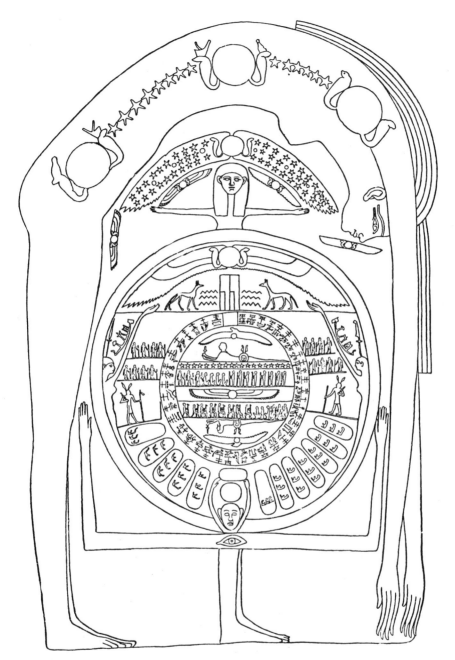

81 Relief from a coffin lid of the 30th Dynasty or the Ptolemaic period, from the necropolis of Saqqara (4th–3rd century B.C.). Discussed in the text. (Keel 1997a: 38, fig. 33)

connection with the entirety of the world (Job 38:5–38). Who, if not (one) God, could have established the pillars of the earth, fixed the boundaries of the sea, or determined the arrangement of the universe?

Ancient Near Eastern images are conceptual, not photographic. They combine aspects of (empirical) experience of the world and worldly outlook, sometimes in

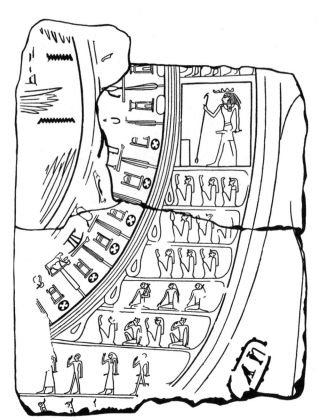

82 Limestone block dating from the end of the Old Kingdom (1500–1200 B.C.) or slightly later. This fragment proves that the much later image in fig. 81 is connected with an ancient tradition. Preserved especially is a part of the representation of alien lands, which are seen complete in fig. 81. (Keel 1997a: 40, fig. 34)

a (to our mind) grotesquely mixed-up way, as when, for example, the legitimacy and divinity of an Egyptian crown prince is proclaimed by showing him suckling at the breast of a goddess who, except for her breast and arms, appears entirely in the form of a tree.

Figs. 81–82

One of the most complex Egyptian representations of the world is shown in figure 81. Nut, the sky goddess, bends protectively over the world disk. Her naked body, which is also the course of the stars, bears the tent of stars and the sun-disk at its rise, zenith, and setting. The sun is flanked by a pair of cobra guards, which personify the sun's fiery breath. The sky is represented a second time, below the female body. The winged—that is, protective—sun-disk in front of the goddess's pudenda represents the newborn rising sun, while the sun setting in the west is about to be swallowed by the goddess's mouth.

The circular world-disk in the middle is surrounded by an empty outer ring, representing the ocean, which in turn merges into the sky-ocean. Emerging from the inside of this ring, shown as women, are the goddesses of the east on the left and the west on the right. The goddesses of the east guide the sun's bark from the ocean of night to the ocean of day, and the goddesses of the west do the reverse. At the zenith, once again a winged sun-disk appears.

The next ring represents the alien lands. They are identified by the lords of the eastern desert, Sopdu (left), and the western desert, Ha (right). Above them, the sign for chieftain appears sixteen times, and in the lower half of the ring, in twelve ovals, appears the sign of the seated man, which designates the entirety of subjugated alien peoples.

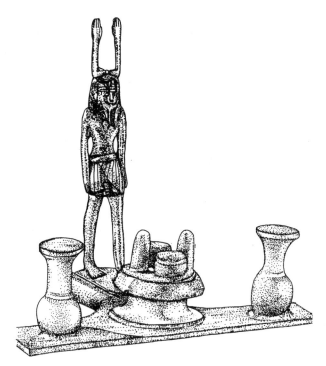

83 Bronze figure from Egypt (6th–1st century B.C.). In Egypt, the Ka is a life-giving power bestowed on humanity by the gods at birth. It can also stand for nourishment. On this offering plate, the Ka appears in human form, surmounted by the hieroglyph of the Ka (the up-raised arms), alongside offering vessels and gifts on a table. (Drawing by Inés Haselbach after Schoske and Wildung 1992: 99 no. 67)

An upper segment of the second ring is marked off separately. Two jackals, representing the waterless wastelands, flank the gate of the kingdom of the dead, which is inscribed with the hieroglyphic signs for water (here, water wasteland)[8] and (funeral) stela. The non-Egyptian world—the margins of the earth—in Egyptian thought is close to the world of the dead; the world at its core simply is Egypt.

The third ring is filled with the forty-one standards of the Egyptian nomes: it encloses a central circle that can be identified by the figures in it as the world of the dead (Duat) and is shown by the ribbon of stars that appears in it to be night. The winged sun-disk, shown three times, traverses this world of the dead every night.

The entire world disk is held up by the hieroglyph for "Ka," which is provided with feet and an eye. It is this divine lifting ability that every morning brings the sun **Fig. 83** and humanity into life. Above the feet of the Ka is a figure represented only by its head and arms, possibly Nut again, this time embodying the primeval ocean.

The most complex surviving Mesopotamian image of the world can be seen on a twelfth-century B.C. Late Kassite *kudurru* (boundary stone). Like the Egyptian im- **Fig. 84** age, it shows the world in several parts, which here are arranged quite practically in storeys. The largest section of the boundary stone takes on the appearance of a mighty fortress whose foundations are encircled by a horned serpent. A second serpent encloses the peak of the entirety, which is formed from a bull of heaven (not visible here). The two serpents symbolize the upper and lower oceans. The register

---

8. Waterless and water wastelands are two variations of the description of the pre-world. In the biblical creation tales, Gen 2:5 begins with a waterless wasteland and Gen 1:2 with a water wasteland.

84 Late Kassite *kudurru* (boundary stone) from Susa (ca. 1180 B.C.). The multi-part picture of the world distinguishes an upper heavenly sphere, an earthly realm, and the underworld. Discussed in the text. (Keel 1997a: 46, fig. 41)

below the serpent of heaven displays the symbols of the gods that can be recognized in the constellations (Seidl 1989). The fortress most probably represents the city of the underworld, with its awe-inspiring gates (cf. Ps 9:14, 107:18). Its towers constitute the pillars or foundations of the earth (Ps 18:8, 75:4, 82:5). The earthly realm, the register below the symbols of the gods, shows a procession. On earth, the worship of the gods, which involves plants and animals, is carried out.

Comparable Greek images of the world have not been preserved in representational art. But that they existed and that in structure and content they were clearly influenced by the Near East is suggested by Homer's detailed description of the shield made by the smith and craftsman Hephaestus for Achilles (*Iliad* 18.468–608). The earthly domains are represented in detail in several scenes on this shield. The description in the Iliad begins, however, with the cosmic framework and the firmament:

> In it was earth's green globe, the sea and heaven,
> Th' unwearied Sun; the Moon, exactly round,
> And all the stars with which the sky is crown'd,
> The Pleiades, the Hyads, and the force
> Of great Orion; and the Bear, whose course
> Turns her about his sphere observing him
> Surnamed the Chariot, and doth never swim
> Upon the unmeasured Ocean's marble face. (*Iliad* 18.483–89, trans. George Chapman)

The ocean stream is finally mentioned as the last image on the shield. Apparently, it winds around the other images:

– 82 –

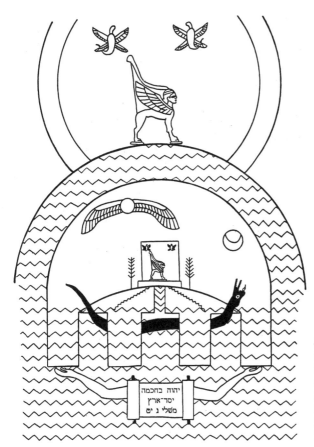

85 Reconstruction of the Israelite image of the world on the basis of biblical passages and iconographic elements from Palestine/Israel and its surroundings. (Keel 1985b: 161, fig. 14)

About this living shield's circumference,
He wrought the ocean's curled violence,
Arming his work as with a crystal wall. (*Iliad* 18.607f.)

No iconographically complete image of the world, like those just described for Egypt and Mesopotamia, has survived from Palestine/Israel. Nonetheless, in numerous miniature objects and in small details of other objects and from biblical passages, a corresponding picture—one of many possibilities—can be sketched. The heavenly **Fig. 85** sphere above the sky ocean (Hebr. *mabbul*; Ps 29:10, 104:13, 148:4) is marked by the presence of YHWH, who is enthroned on cherubs, surrounded by winged seraphs (cobras), and worshiped without an image. Corresponding to the heavenly presence is the earthly presence of God in the Jerusalem Temple. Here, YHWH dams up the waters of chaos that crash against the earth and transforms them into life-giving streams (cf. Ps 104:5ff.).[9] Stylized trees characterize the Temple as a realm of intensive life. The horned serpent, which is imported from fig. 84 and represents Leviathan, recalls that this cosmos is always in danger from the waters of chaos. The wonderful power and wisdom of YHWH, represented here by the outstretched arms and the torah scroll with the quotation from Proverbs 3, prevents the sinking of the inhabited earth into the deep waters of chaos and guarantees the elevation of cosmos-constructing

---

9. For the cosmological significance of the temple, see Keel 1997a: esp. 113–20, 171–76; on the connection between Temple and Creation in the Priestly conception of holiness, cf. Janowski 1993a.

86 Cylinder seal of the late Uruk period from Khafajah in Iraq (ca. 3000 B.C.). In the up-per register of the impression is a procession of cattle; in the lower register, cattle gather around a hut in the center of the image. On the roof of the hut rise three staff-and-ring symbols of the goddess Nintu(r), the "Lady of Birth." From either side of the hut itself emerges a calf, each with its own feeding trough. The message of the composition must be that *Nintur*, the Lady or Goddess of Birth, brings forth livestock, especially cattle. The pictographic writing on the hut has the reading *tut/tur* 'birth'. (Black and Green 1992: 155)

differentiation through creation. "YHWH by wisdom founded the earth, established the heavens by understanding" (Prov 3:19a). The motif of the arms is imported from fig. 81. The "eternal arms" that support the earth from below are also mentioned in Deut 33:27 [NRSV footnote].

1. Creation as Conception and Birth or Growing and Becoming

The experience that new plant and animal life originates through conception and birth was carried over to explanations of the origin of parts of the world throughout the ancient Near East and in Greece as well,[10] and in Egypt, it was applied to the entire world. What happened in the past and in primeval times is associated in Egyptian texts and images from the earliest periods with episodes of masturbation, self-insemination, and birth. The coming into existence of all beings from One or the primeval god stood in creative tension with sexuality, which was experienced as a principle inherent in the world and was retrojected along complex paths of thought and systems back to its beginnings (Troy 1997). The biblical creation texts, except for some hints in Prov 8:22–31, do not expli-cate aspects of gender with respect to the God who creates. In Genesis 1–3, the theme of sexuality is in the foreground as a purely human concern. Indeed, the statement that male and female are created in God's image (Gen 1:26f.) subtly implies that the creating divinity contains within itself the polarity of the sexes. The abstractness of this theological thought, however, puts it at a significant distance from most ancient Near Eastern ideas of creation.

In the Sumerian *Prologue to the Disputation between Wood and Reed*, An, the sky god, inseminates the earth, which thereupon bears plants.[11] Traces of this idea of creative bearing by the earth survive in Gen 1:11f., 24, where the earth causes vegetation to sprout (see chap. III.3, pp. 35ff.), and in Hos 2:23f., where

10. Hesiod's *Theogony* tells of the coming into being of the not-yet-sexualized divine powers, then—after Eros appears—of their sexual union (Bonnafé 1996).
11. Translation by W. H. P. Römer, *TUAT* III 357–60.

87 Old Babylonian terracotta relief from Tell Asmar (ca. 1800 B.C.). The relief plaque shows a goddess striding to the left, in a tiered or layered garment and with a head covering that resembles the entrance to a shrine or temple. She holds a nursing child to her right breast, which is not covered by the garment. Her raised right hand holds an unidentified object. From each shoulder protrudes the head of a man or child. This goddess may be compared with goddesses known from texts, such as Ninhursanga or Nintu(r), since she is flanked by two large Ω-shaped signs and two emaciated childlike figures sitting at her feet. These might represent fetuses, miscarriages, or premature births. Their wandering spirits were greatly feared in ancient Mesopotamia. The Ω-signs above them may be intended to restrict their baleful activities. (Winter 1987: fig. 390)

88 Scarab from Tell el-Far'ah North (ca. 1700 B.C.). In Anatolia–North Syria and Palestine, very small faience stamp seals have been found, having their undersides worked in raised relief, not the usual incised relief. An important motif in this group is the Ω-sign. It probably is a highly simplified representation of a woman's uterus, a symbol simultaneously of the birth and mother goddesses. That the seals are commonly found in graves, two of them children's graves, suggests that the motif was intended to provide the dead with a fragment of the security of the mother's womb on their final journey. In the Bible, the word 'womb' (Hebr. *reḥem*), so important both for anthropology and the divine image, is the equivalent of this symbol. (Keel 1989b: 47, fig. 16)

heaven goes in to the earth so that it can bear fruit.[12] The Sumerian goddesses Ninhursanga and Nintu(r) served as divine bearers of humans and flocks. That **Fig. 86** mother goddesses were originally responsible for the prosperity of flocks was still understood by the Israelites. Litters are brought into relation with Shagar, flocks with Astarte (Deut 7:13; 28:4, 18, 51). In Middle Bronze Age Palestine/ Israel (1750–1550 B.C.), people, especially the infants, were reassured by Ω-signs

---

12. Compare the notion of the cosmic conception of "justice" with the union of heaven and earth in Isa 45:8.

89 Classical Syrian cylinder seal (1850–1750 B.C.). The nude goddess on her consort's symbolic animal, the bull, often appears on Classical Syrian cylinder seals. The warlike storm-god, to whom she turns, strides across the mountains. The goddess unveils herself before him, thus inviting him to the "sacred marriage." Two processions of worshipers in the subsidiary scene stress the sacral character of the encounter between god and goddess. (Winter 1987: fig. 270 = Keel and Schroer 2010: 112f., fig. 66, and Keel-Leu and Teissier 2004: no. 344)

Figs. on amulets, symbols of the divine womb, which implied the protection given
87–88 by the lady of all life.

If the life of those who pray the Psalms is fashioned deep in the womb of the earth (Ps 139:15), the return of human life to the womb of the earth (Job 1:21) presupposes that it also comes from there; according to Isa 26:19, the earth gives birth again to the shades (of the dead), and behind these images stands belief in the (re)generative powers of the "body of earth":

> For it was you who formed my inward parts,
>   you knit me together in my mother's womb.
> I praise you, for I am fearfully and wonderfully made.
>   Wonderful are your works;
> that I know very well.
>   My frame was not hidden from you,
> when I was being made in secret,
>   intricately woven in the depths of the earth.
> Your eyes beheld my unformed substance. (Ps 139:13–16; cf. 33:15, 94:9; Isa 44:24)

Psalm 139 contains the archaic idea of coming into being in the depths of the womb or the earth (which is identified with the womb), alongside the idea of an actively artistic God who forms the child in the womb. It is not the God of Israel himself who gives birth to humanity, but he is somehow involved in their coming into being in the womb and in the birth process. The idea that a male god watches and accompanies the mysterious process of birth is also transmitted in the *Childbirth Incantation* from the Akkad period (ca. 2300 B.C.). As in Psalm
Text 6 139, in this much older text, the event that takes place in the womb has already been fused with an origin in the depths of the earth. In the Akkadian birth incantation, the depths are clearly described as the watery depths of a distant ocean, while the psalm is silent about the character of the depths of the earth. But since pregnancy and birth always go together with amniotic fluid, the psalm could also be describing aqueous depths. Water is also connected by people in ancient Egypt with pregnancy. In Egyptian hymns to the creator god, the work of the god in the womb and after birth is praised:

90 Scarab, probably from Jericho (1700–1550 B.C.). A woman, by bending forward, invites a (dancing?) man to enter her. The meaning of this very tersely presented motif in stamp seals can be confirmed from Syrian cylinder seals that show variants of this scene with additional context. (Keel 1995: 221, fig. 483; cf. Keel 1996a: 13, fig. 16)

Who makes seed grow in women,
Who creates people from sperm;
Who feeds the son in his mother's womb,
Who soothes him to still his tears.
Nurse in the womb,
Giver of breath,
To nourish all that he made.
When he comes from the womb to breathe,
On the day of his birth,
You open wide his mouth,
You supply his needs. (370b, trans. Miriam Lichtheim)[13]

YHWH, like a midwife, also delivers the newborn from the womb and places it at the mother's breast (Ps 22:10, 71:6). As God initiates the creation of individual people in general, it is also he who protects or abandons children and opens or closes the woman's womb.[14] In apocalyptic and in the New Testament (John 16:20–22, Rom 8:19–23), hope for a new creation is illustrated with images of birth, with the cries and pains of labor.[15]

Many facets of life related to transcendence, genealogies, life-giving fertilization, and even politics (Zimmermann and Zimmermann 1999) were connected with the idea of a "sacred marriage," the sexual union of god and goddess. Examples of this union include the rain coming from the storm-god or sky-god and impregnating the earth-goddess (cf. fig. 112 below), and a god might unite **Fig. 89** with a human partner, such as the prince of a city or a priestess. Although it remains far from clear whether and how this idea of a union between the divine and the human world, which is frequently portrayed in iconography,[16] was ritually enacted (perhaps as analogic magic); it is nonetheless evident that the fertility of the land in a comprehensive sense was expected to follow (Keel 1996a). The coitus that reflects this ideology is depicted on Classical Syrian seals, and stamp seals of the same period from Palestine/Israel also depict the sex act. Crit- **Fig. 90** ical analysis of Gen 6:1–4 needs to take into account the ancient mythological topos of "sacred marriage" between the sons of God and the daughters of men (Zimmermann and Zimmermann 1999). In 6:3, the unique quality arising from this union between a nature endowed with divine *ruaḥ* and one that is merely mortal flesh is quantitatively constrained by YHWH himself through limiting the

---

13. From the *Great Amarna Hymn* (Assmann 1999: no. 92.59–67 = text 10).
14. Cf. Gen 18; 25:21; 29:31; 30:1f.; Ps 113:9.
15. Sutter Rehmann 1995. Cf. also John 3:3–7, the conversation between Nicodemus and Jesus about the possibility of being born again without returning to the mother's womb. In Christian iconography after the fourteenth century, the return to the mother's womb again became a peculiar, strongly myth-laden icon in the image of the Pietà, of Mary holding her dead son to her womb.
16. In detail, Winter 1987: 252–368. For the question of cultic prostitution, see Wacker, "Prostitution," *NBL* 3 (1997): 201–3; for "sacred marriage," comprehensively, see also Zimmermann 2001: 56–87.

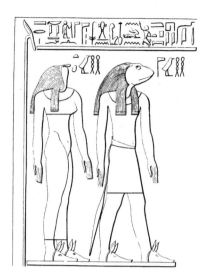

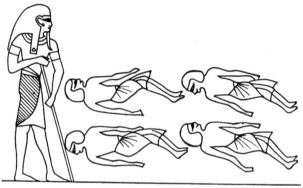

91 Relief of Ptolemy VIII from the Opet temple in Karnak (145–116 B.C.). The world before the world is occasionally represented by four pairs of primeval gods, the Ogdoad of Hermopolis: Nun and Naunet (primeval water), Kek and Keket (darkness), Heh and Hehet (eternity), Amun and Amaunet (secrecy). In some visualizations, these primeval gods, here Hehu and Hehet, wear jackal-head slippers. The jackal heads may refer to Upuat, "opener of the way," but they might, in contrast to the frog heads that evoke water, represent the dry wastelands that were part of the world before creation. (Keel 1997a: 334, fig. 481)

92 Relief from the tomb of Sethos I in the Valley of the Kings (beginning of the 13th century B.C.). The Egyptians conceived of the primeval water quite radically as a timeless-and-spaceless condition. Spacelessness is represented in the New Kingdom Book of Gates by the four exhausted cardinal directions, drifting, over which the sun god Atum keeps watch as primeval creator-god. The god Atum guards "these tired ones," four figures lying down completely stretched out, which symbolize the cardinal directions that are eventually lifted up and functioning in the world. (Keel 1997a: 334, fig. 480a)

lifespan. The proximity of God and humanity is blocked by the mortality of mankind. Although the Hebrew text is not unambiguous, the memory of a *hieros gamos* might also be preserved[17] in the words of Eve after the birth of her first son:

---

17. E. Lipiński, "*qnh*," *ThWAT* VII (1993): 63–71, esp. 67; Zimmermann and Zimmermann 1999: 352 n. 115.

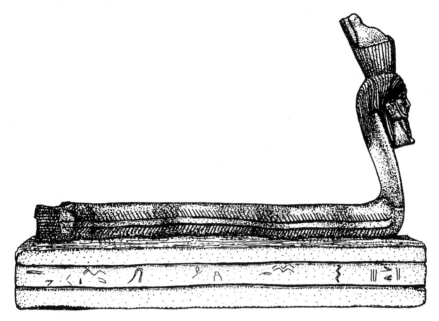

93 Egyptian bronze (6th–1st century B.C.). The god Atum appears in the form of an eel. The eel embodies the swampy, misty primeval place from which all life arises. (Drawing by Inés Haselbach after Keel and Staubli 2001: 92f., no. 95)

I have produced a man with the help of Yhwh. (Gen 4:1)

That fertility rituals that included sexual unions were known in Israel is made clear by the polemic raised by the prophet Hosea (Hos 4:13f.) and later prophetic tradition against the dirty deed and is also reflected in the delight shown in special, large trees (tree goddesses).[18] Whether sexual contact was understood as the consummation of a "sacred marriage," however, remains unclear.

The Egyptians have left a number of images of the pre-world, including both water and waterless wastelands in which there are no compass points and hence no orientation or order. The creator-god Atum is sometimes represented as an eel, which represents the as-yet-unformed, dank, primeval material that nonetheless contains the entire potential of the world.[19] Time generates itself: the Ouroboros, a serpent swallowing its own tail, causes Atum as a youthful sun to proceed from itself. But the creator-god also emerges from death as the primeval god. The origination of everything from the One is represented by the image of the masturbating Atum. **Figs. 91–95**

In Egyptian art, the origin of the habitable world is evoked by the cohabitation of the sky-goddess (Nut) with the earth-god (Geb). Earth and sky are divided by the air-god Shu or some other power, but this would not be possible without a secret magical power, the divine Heka (Egypt. *ḥk3*). In many of these representations, the sphere of the sun follows its course, swallowed by the sky-goddess in the evening and reborn from her womb in the morning. The sky can be represented as a cow as well as by a woman.[20] **Fig. 96** **Fig. 97**

---

18. Schroer 1987b.
19. Cf. Mysliwiec 1978: 131–38 and pls. 35–42.
20. On the Egyptian myth of the cow of heaven, see in detail Hornung 1997. The birth of the sun is also a subject of 19th–21st Dynasty scarabs from Palestine/Israel, which are influenced by the miniatures in Egyptian Books of the Dead (cf. Keel and Schroer 1998).

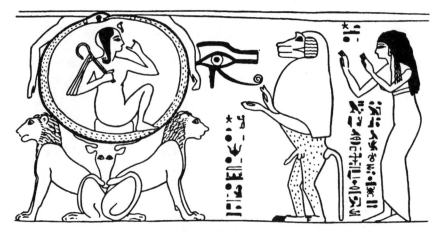

94 Book of the Dead papyrus of Heruben (ca. 1000 B.C.). A baboon and the deceased worship the youthful sun-god who is emerging from the Ouroboros (the serpent swallowing its tail), which is supported by the "Great Flood" cow between the lions of the horizon and which is being received by the arms of the sky goddess Nut. (Keel 1997a: 44, fig. 39)

95 Book of the Dead papyrus of Chentawi (ca. 950 B.C.; illustration spans both pages). (1) Between the lions of the horizon, Atum appears as an Ouroboros (serpent or dragon eating its own tail) surrounding the sun, which is represented by the Osiris fetish. (2) Atum as the youthful sun (scarab) emerges from the winged serpent, which is identified by the caption as "Death, the great god, who made gods and men." (3) Atum is a preliminary stage of sky and earth, and as such, already identified by the caption as the earth-god (Geb), takes his phallus into his mouth. Atum's masturbation is a common metaphor for the origin of everything from One. (4) The appearance of the actually existing world is then specified by the cosmic powers Nut and Geb, sky and earth. (Niwiński 1989: 200 fig. 74)

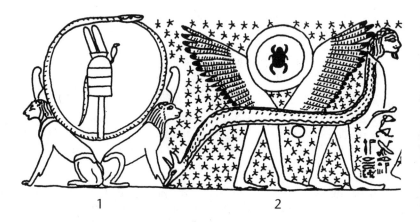

1   2

Less spectacular, but central to Egyptian ideas of creation, are the contributions of plant images, particularly the lotus. Marsh plants, whose flowers close in the evening and reopen in the morning on the surface of the water, from the New Kingdom on were an omnipresent symbol of vitality and regeneration. Like many similar natural events, such as the emergence of fry from the mouth of the tilapia perch, which incubates its young in the mouth—therefore giving

96 Scene on a sarcophagus of the 21st Dynasty (1085–950 B.C.). The star-spangled body of the sky goddess Nut is spread like a tent-roof over the earth-god Geb, who lies worn out on the floor after his union with the sky-goddess. Beside him coils the frightful Apophis serpent, which here probably represents the realm of the underworld. The god Shu controls the air and habitable region opened up by the separation of earth and sky. He bears the plane of the sky and the bark of the sun on his upraised arms. The noose on his head is a sign of his divine magical powers by which the structure of earth and sky is miraculously maintained. In the Psalms, this miracle is attributed to Yʜwʜ's inscrutability (Ps 8:2, 19:2, 89:6, 97:6). Two divine falcons with flails and 'life' signs flank Shu. Two winged uraei watch over the pictured cosmos and the powers that sustain it. (Niwiński 1988: pl. 17A no. 317)

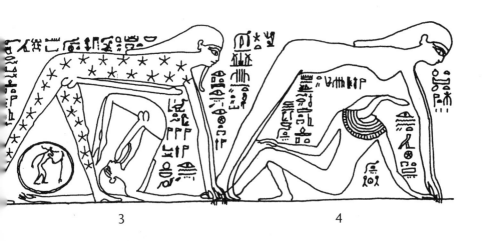

3   4

the impression of sudden appearance of life from the (primeval) depths—and the appearance of the lotus blossom would have been associated with sunrise and especially also with birth.[21] The dead are reborn from the lotus blossom, **Fig. 98**

21. For Egyptian lotus symbolism, see Morenz and Schubert 1954; Schlögl 1977; Weidner 1985; Ryhiner 1986; E. Brunner-Traut, "Lotos," *LÄ* 3 (1980): 1091–96; for biblical lotus symbolism, see the summary by S. Schroer, "Lotus," *NBL* 2 (1994): 670.

97 Ceiling painting in the tomb of Ramses VI in the Valley of the Kings (1141–1135 B.C.). A ceiling painting with scenes from the "Book of Days" represents sunrise and the sun's daily course beneath the starry body of Nut. The sun's sphere is born of the sky goddess, who is shown—in Egyptian art a rarity—frontally, kneeling, attended by two (divine) midwives. Above, the winged scarab pushes the sun disk over the imaginary horizon; below, the god Shu, standing in the sun's bark, elevates it with his arms. Beneath, the sun's two barks—one for day, one for night—are shown on a smaller scale. (Rambova 1954: 383–88 with fig. 130)

98 Vignette from the Papyrus of Paqrer accompanying the Book of the Dead saying 81A (12th/11th century B.C.). A giant lotus blossom with the head of the deceased grows from a pond. The saying reads, "Spell: Take on the form of a lotus blossom." (Keel 1984: 156, fig. 62c)

and, later, out of the "sun child" known from the art of Palestine/Israel. In the Book of the Dead, the sun-calf is important as a representation of the rising young sun. Traces of Egyptian sun-calf symbolism can be found in the book of Malachi (Schroer 1998), where those true to YHWH are told: *Figs. 99–101* *Fig. 102*

> But for you who fear my name, there will arise
> the sun of justice with its healing rays;
> And you will gambol like calves out of the stall
> and tread down the wicked. (Mal 3:20)

In Egypt, from the Middle Kingdom on, the (world-)egg also served as a symbol of new life: the egg is laid by the "great cackler," out of which a primeval god hatches; in addition, it was generally accepted that Khnum or Ptah had fashioned the egg on the potter's wheel.[22] Even in modern advertising, the egg has continued to retain its basic generative significance. *Figs. 103–104*

Biological notions of creation are found remarkably seldom in the Bible, with no references to the flow of semen, emanation, or emergence from the egg.[23] In only a few places is Israel's God said to have begotten or borne.[24] Divine begetting of the king is borrowed from Egyptian royal mythology in Ps 2:7, but the people of Israel (Isa 45:10f.) can also be understood as begotten by God. In Num 11:12, YHWH's motherhood of Israel is indirectly invoked, in the context of contesting the suggestion that Moses bore Israel and had to suffer for it. In Deut 32:18b, the people are reproached for forgetting "the God who gave you birth" (cf. Jer 2:27b).

Texts occasionally indicate original divine procreation or birth. Personified Wisdom in the book of Proverbs, for example, is legitimized by the fact that she was already born prior to all of the other works of creation:[25]

22. Cf. R. A. Caminos, "Ei," *LÄ* 1 (1975): 1185–88.
23. Cf. J. Assmann, "Schöpfung," *LÄ* 5 (1984): 677–90, esp. 679f.
24. On the whole, the First Testament carefully avoids sexual imagery in speaking of the God of Israel. Only the metaphor of YHWH as bridegroom of the faithless or faithful Israel is not felt to be repugnant, an image in which the legal aspects predominate, usually explicitly including sexual promiscuity on the woman's part (Hosea 1–3; cf. Jeremiah 2–3, Ezek 16:23, etc.).
25. Cf. Keel 1974a, esp. 13–21. Cf. details on personified Wisdom in Proverbs in chap. X.2 below.

99 Phoenician ivory from Samaria (9th century B.C.). Sitting in the lotus blossom is the sun child with the typical gesture of fingers pointing to the mouth. The motif symbolizes the coming into existence of the rising young sun and the ideas of regeneration connected with it. (Keel 1984: 154, fig. 58)

100 Egyptian bronze situla (end of the 7th century B.C.). The young sun-god, here depicted as a standing child, emerges from the lotus blossom, which is flanked by two winged goddesses. (Drawing by Hildi Keel-Leu after Page Gasser 2001: 139–42, fig. 35)

101 Double-sided engraved seal from Judah (8th–7th century B.C.). The young sun-god can be seen on the lotus blossom on this seal, which belonged to a man with the typically Judahite name ʿAsyo son of Yokim. The first name means 'Yʜᴡʜ made', the second 'Yʜᴡʜ caused to rise'. (Keel 1986a: 81, fig. 34)

102 Painting from the tomb of Irinefer in Deir el-Medina (Thebes West, 1190–1075 B.C.). In Irinefer's tomb, the deceased stands worshiping the sun-calf, who emerges from between two sycamores. This scene also belongs with the Book of the Dead vignettes and illustrates Book of the Dead spell 109: "[1] I know that eastern gate of the sky . . . [7] I know those two sycamores from turquoise, [8] between which Re emerges . . .[19] I know the eastern powers: [20] Harachte it is, the sun calf it is, the morning star it is." (Keel 1997a: 301, fig. 233)

When there were no depths I was brought forth,
   when there were no foundations or springs of water;
Before the mountains were settled into place,
   before the hills, I was brought forth. (Prov 8:24f.)

103 Part of a Roman-period relief from Philae. The pharaoh offers a sacrifice before the ram-headed Khnum, who shapes the world egg on the potter's wheel. In the 18th Dynasty (1540–1292 B.C.), it was the body of the future king that he formed on the potter's wheel. The old motif is used here to give priority to an artisanal model (potter) over the biological (egg) model of creation. (Keel 2001: 53, fig. 9a)

104 Part of a Roman-period relief from Philae. The pharaoh offers a sacrifice before Ptah, the craftsman-god of Memphis, who shapes the world egg on the potter's wheel. (Keel 2001: 53, fig. 9b)

The image of the sea that brings forth from the womb (Job 38:8) and of the reliable presence of God "before the mountains were begotten" (Ps 90:2) suggests that, although it is not stated explicitly, in Prov 8:24f. the coming to birth of the primeval floods and the shapes of the hills is intended. In a sarcastic question playing on *ḥokmah* as creation's firstborn (Job 15:7), Eliphaz rebukes his friend Job with the fact that, as a human being, he scarcely has the status of creation's firstborn and, hence, divine wisdom. The texts that have been mentioned offer no precise information on who might have borne the floods, the mountains, or wisdom. The book of Job must be alluding to—disguised in the form of a rhetorical question—the traditional understanding that rain, dew, ice, and frost arise through procreation and birth (Job 38:28f.).

According to Ps 110:3, the dew is born from "the womb of the morning." Behind this image, at least originally, stands a divine greatness, because the cognates of the Hebrew word *šaḥar* ('morning') at Ugarit, Emar, and elsewhere are used to name a god.

Despite the reticence of the Priestly writings concerning the model of "creation as birth," they approach the origins of heaven and earth—that is, the entire world—as *tôledôt* ('generations' or 'conceptions').

2. Creation as Handicraft

Conception or birth (biology) and craftsmanlike (artisanal) creation are not mutually exclusive. The best-known form of an artificially created object is pottery. Thus, the Egyptian god Khnum, in the myth of the birth of the god-king (15th/14th centuries B.C.), throws on the wheel the body and the *ka* of the royal

105 Part of a Roman-period relief from the birth-house at Dendera. Even in the Roman period, the god Khnum is shown, working at the pottery wheel, shaping the royal child whom the queen conceived by the god Amun, as the enthroned goddess Hathor extends an Ankh sign to him in order to turn him into a living being. (Drawing by Inés Haselbach after Daumas 1959: pl. X)

Fig. 105 child who will be born.[26] Both Khnum and Ptah, as already mentioned, are depicted as the potters of a world egg. In the Bible as well, artisanal terminology is found in the immediate context of biological terms. Those who pray the Psalms praise YHWH as the one who created and formed them in the womb:

> Truly you have formed my inmost being;
> you knit me in my mother's womb. (Ps 139:13; cf. 33:15, 94:9, Isa 44:24)

The view best attested in the Bible is that creation and its individual acts are shaped by a *deus faber*. God is a *yoṣer*,[27] a potter or sculptor. This image of God is understood beyond metaphor, since the act of creation is sometimes described very concretely as the shaping of clay:

> Your hands have formed me and fashioned me;
> will you then turn and destroy me?
> Oh, remember that you fashioned me from clay!
> Will you then bring me down to dust again?
> Did you not pour me out as milk,
> and thicken me like cheese?
> With skin and flesh you clothed me,
> with bones and sinews knit me together,
> Grace and favor you granted me,
> and your providence has preserved my spirit.
> (Job 10:8–12, 33:6; cf. Ps 119:73, Isa 64:8)

But the verb *yaṣar* should not always be taken this literally. The root has as its object the formation of mountains (Amos 4:13), earth and dry land (Isa 45:18, Jer 33:2), animals (Amos 7:1, Gen 2:19) and Leviathan (Ps 104:26), humans (Gen 2:7f.) and all their parts (Ps 33:15, 94:9), the entire world (Jer 10:16 = 51:19), as well as light (Isa 45:7), the seasons (Ps 74:17), and specific historical events, but not the sea. In ancient Near Eastern creation stories, the material for the creation of humans is usually earth, mud, clay, and possibly blood.[28] The material is shaped and modeled. In addition to the manufacture of ordinary pots, *yaṣar* also refers to shaping and molding an image or manufacturing sculptures from mud, clay, and other materials.[29]

---

26. The myth is older but is attested from the time of Hatshepsut and Amenophis III. See the translation by H. Sternberg el-Hotabi, *TUAT* III 991–1005.
27. Cf. W. H. Schmidt, "*yṣr*," *THAT* I 761–65; Schroer 1987a: esp. 320f.
28. Cf. chap. VI.1 below (pp. 108ff.).
29. Cf. Uehlinger 1988, 1998.

When the creator-god is clearly portrayed as a craftsman, this does not exclude technical prowess. Rather, the picture of the potter and his pots serves—often explicitly—to stress the competence of God in contrast to humanity and the frailty, fragility, and impotence of human existence (Isa 29:16, 45:9–12; Jer 18:1–10). Alongside *yaṣar*, other craftsmanlike activities of the *deus faber* are presented, all of which accentuate his absolute sovereignty over what has been created. He lays the foundations for the earth (Ps 24:2, 89:12, 102:26, 104:5), spreads out the sky like a tent or fastens it (Ps 104:2, Prov 8:27), hammers out the breadth of the earth (Ps 136:6), plants vegetation (Ps 104:16), and weaves cloth (Ps 139:15). Overall, God reliably supports his creation, the heavens, the earth, and humanity, establishes (*kun*), makes (*'asah*) everything; everything is his work (Ps 104:31; 145:9, 17), the work of his hands (Ps 19:2, 102:26) or his fingers (Ps 8:4).

The notion that divine wisdom or wisdom sent by the gods reaches fruition in technical mastery and craftsmanlike perfection is a familiar commonplace throughout the ancient Near East. The real builders and architects of temples and cities are often gods, and the execution is taken over by kings (cf. also Exod 25:9, 40; 1 Chr 28:19).[30] Without the divine master-builder, human building is in vain:

Unless Yʜᴡʜ build the house,
    they labor in vain who build it. (Ps 127:1)

According to the general ancient Near Eastern understanding, although it is supplanted in biblical sources by a rationalistic polemic against idols, cult images also arise as a result of divine decisions and by means of divinely inspired craftsmen endowed with special wisdom,[31] including all the skills necessary for erecting a sanctuary (Exodus 35–40, 1 Kings 7).

3. Creation as Battle

The inhabited world does not always come into being peacefully by natural or artificial means. Sometimes, in ancient Near Eastern thinking, creation comes about through a battle between primeval powers or after a series of gory battles among various gods (theomachy). In *Enuma elish* (tablet IV, esp. 59–146), which was perhaps reworked from Old Babylonian material around 1250 ʙ.ᴄ., Marduk dismembers Tiamat, the monstrous briny deep, in order to use part of her corpse to fashion the cosmos.[32] The chaos-battle is also the theme of Hesiod's *Theogony* (ca. 700 ʙ.ᴄ.), which presents the development of the world from its origin through its completion under Zeus as a succession of battles of the generations of gods (Fuchs 1993: 43–49). The best-known echo of the ancient Near Eastern idea of chaos-battles in Greek thought probably appears in Heraclitus (fragm. 53), who gets the militaristic *logos* of the world directly in his sights with his statement "War is the father of all, the king of all" (Keel 2001a; cf. chap. 11).

But creation, in the ancient Near Eastern mind, is neither completed by nor secured with the initial act of creation. Instead, every creature, from the moment of its inception, finds itself in ever-present danger of being annihilated by

---

30. This is also true for other culture-creating acts, such as the opening of irrigation canals by the pharaoh in the Old Kingdom (Staub 1985).
31. Berlejung 1998, Lorton 1999, Walker and Dick 1999.
32. Eliade et al. 1964: 141f.; cf. the translation by W. G. Lambert, *TUAT* III 565–602, esp. 585–87.

106 Seal impression from Tell Asmar (2500–2400 B.C.). In the lowest register of the impression, a hero triumphantly holds up two of the heads of a seven-headed serpent. From the left approaches a dog or lion with a branch-like tail. Another snake rears up in the top register between the claws of two pairs of scorpions. Pairs of scorpions, perhaps in copulating posture, can also be seen in the narrow central frieze and below left. (Frankfort 1955: pl. 47 no. 497)

107 Cylinder seal from Tell Asmar (ca. 2300 B.C.). A god with a spear grasps a seven-headed monster from the front. Three heads already hang limp; a fourth has been pierced. Flames shoot from the back of the monstrosity. A second, very similar god grasps it from behind. Both of the worshipers looking to the right should be understood as being at the left of the scene. (Keel 2001b: 16, fig. 52)

108 (Opposite, top) Greek vase painting (590 B.C.). Heracles and Iolaus slay the many-headed Hydra. (Keel 2001b: 17, fig. 6)

109 (Opposite, bottom) Monumental relief from the Ninurta temple at Nimrud in Iraq (870 B.C.). The god Ninurta, shown as the storm-god possessing the wings of the storm and two lightning bolts, drives the lion-dragon out of the temple precincts. (Frankfort 1969: 88 fig. 38)

Figs. 106–114 the powers of chaos. From the third millennium on, heroic figures or gods take on serpent- and dragon-like monsters[33] or demons of darkness (cf. Job 38:12f.), in order to prevent creation from falling back into chaos (Keel 2001b). These "lords of the animals" hold the world of wild, dangerous animals in check (cf. figs. 146–166 below).[34]

---

33. For battle as one understanding of creation, see Keel 1986a; Fuchs 1993, esp. 11–64; for battle with dragons, Uehlinger 1991, 1995; McBeath 1999; Keel 2001b; for battle with dragons in ancient Greece, Sauer-Gaertner 2001; further references in chap. VI.3, pp. 147ff.
34. Cf. Job 38:39–39:30 with Keel 1978.

110 Neo-Assyrian cylinder seal (ca. 700 B.C.). Ninurta drives off the lion-dragon with bow and arrow. A supplicant worships the god with the typical Assyrian oath-gesture of the pointing finger. (Keel-Leu and Teissier 2004: no. 226)

111 Neo-Assyrian cylinder seal (8th century B.C.). Ninurta stands on a scorpion-tailed lion-dragon, using his bow to drive away a bird-tailed lion-dragon (cf. fig. 109) into the mountains. The name of the worshiper at the right reads "Yappahaddu" in Aramaic, a person who by profession is a dream interpreter. (Sass and Uehlinger 1993: 81 fig. 8)

112 Classical Syrian cylinder seal (18th/17th century B.C.). The Syrian goddess disrobes in front of the storm-god. He treads on a semi-erect serpent, piercing its head with a tree-shaped weapon, swinging a club or scepter in his upraised other hand. The protagonist who is protected by the battle with chaos may be represented by the caprid between the goddess and god (cf. figs. 20–21). The kneeling worshiper at the far right underlines the sacral nature of the event. (Drawing by Hildi Keel-Leu after Gorelick and Williams-Forte 1983: pl. 1 no. 3)

113 Seal impression from Nuzi in northern Iraq (15th/14th century B.C.). The storm-god, holding two lightning bolts, stands on a Mesopotamian lion-dragon. His helper kills the horned serpent. At the left are two rearing goats and another quadruped. (Keel 2001b: 20, fig. 29)

114 Neo-Assyrian cylinder seal (9th/8th century B.C.). The storm-god, shown running, wields his cluster of lightning bolts over the serpent-dragon. (Keel-Leu and Teissier 2004: no. 179)

115 Book of the Dead papyrus of Amunnacht from the 19th Dynasty (1292–1190 B.C.). The deceased holds the Apophis serpent down with a spear. This vignette accompanies Book of the Dead spell 15B, a hymn to the dawn sun-god. Prerequisite for the sun's successful rising is the neutralization of the deadly Apophis. (Keel 1992: fig. 230b)

The Egyptian sun-god, with the support of his energetic military subordinates, night after night had to overcome the dangers of the dark night and the frightful Apophis. In this Egyptian tradition, the menacing antagonist appears not just as a danger, but as evil. One of the sun-god's assistants is the god Seth, who in the art of Palestine/Israel ca. 1200 B.C. merged with the Canaanite storm-god who battles the chaos-serpent. The Israelite god YHWH assumes the mantle of Baal-Seth, still imagined as a storm-god, but with a greater emphasis on the battle against evil. Israel did not take over another Egyptian tradition, of

**Figs.
115–118**

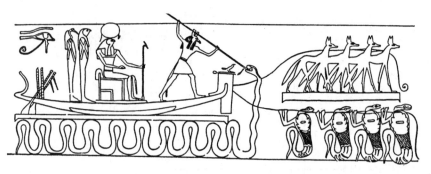

116 21st Dynasty papyrus (1075–945 B.C.). Seth, the god of the storm and foreign lands, is shown dragging the head of a weird animal whose precise zoological identification cannot be determined. As the assistant to the sun-god, who must endure the dangers of the night in his bark drawn by jackals and guardian serpents, Seth battles the dangerous Apophis. Seth was especially popular in the 19th Dynasty (1292–1190 B.C.). (Keel 1992: 248, fig. 229)

117 19th Dynasty scarab (1292–1190 B.C.). The god Seth strikes down a serpent whose head appears to have several horns. At the god's head is the inscription 'beloved of the sun-god'. (Keel 2001b: 24, fig. 53)

118 Egyptian scarab (13th/12th century B.C.). Not Seth, but the Near Eastern storm-god Baal, with the typical tall hat with ribbon, attacks the rearing chaos serpent. The god is shown with wings, which give him greater strength. From his forehead protrudes the head of the Seth animal. Thus, the storm-god is merged with warlike Seth. The warrior who takes on threatening drought and the subduer of the ocean floods simply turns into a warrior against enemy evil. (Keel 1992: 228, fig. 225)

120 Wall painting from the tomb of Ramses VI (1145–1137 B.C.) in the Valley of the Kings in Thebes West. This representation in the tradition of a magical victory over the Apophis serpent stands alongside many others. Here, too, Isis stands conjuring in the bow of the sun's bark. A god, possibly Seth, pilots. Two gods hold the head and tail of the Apophis still, while a third one carefully cuts it in half. (Keel 1992: 249, fig. 231a)

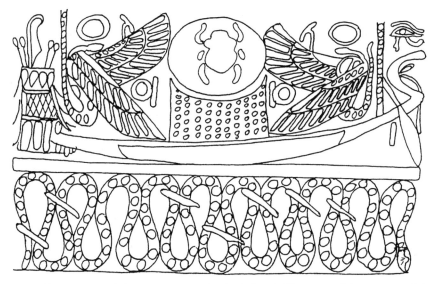

121 Coffin painting of the 21st Dynasty (1075–945 B.C.). The magical destruction of the Apophis was a favorite idea alongside the destruction-by-battle version around the turn of the first millennium, after Seth fell into ever more disrepute. The dangers of the journey of the sun-god, who appears as a scarab in the bark, are overcome by magical knives stuck into the body of the Apophis. (Keel 2001b: 26, fig. 62)

119 (opposite, bottom) Wall painting in the tomb of Thutmosis III in the Valley of the Kings in Thebes West (1479–1426 B.C.). In the middle of the sun's bark, protected by a serpent, stands the ram-headed sun-god. His journey, which is necessary for the preservation of the cosmos, after reaching its deepest point at midnight, is threatened at the beginning of its rising by the Apophis serpent, on its sandy beach. The serpent is confronted by the magical Isis (identified by a caption, not shown here) in the bow of the sun's bark. Behind her stands the "oldest magician," who according to Erik Hornung is identified with the god Seth. The scorpion-goddess Selket has thrown a noose around the neck of Apophis, and the next figure has tossed one around its tail. Knots and nooses are a means of magic as much as they are tools of a restraint of power. The figure with the noose around the tail is called "the one over his knives." The name reveals that this figure is responsible for the six knives stuck into the Apophis's body. They also appear to have been impaled there by magic rather than by a physical confrontation. The four figures to the right of the Apophis have significant names: "Binding Together, Cutting, Punishing, Destroying." (Keel 1992: 249, fig. 231)

– 103 –

122 Relief from the Ramesseum in Thebes West, from the time of Ramses II (1301–1234 B.C.). Like a god, the pharaoh in his war chariot breaks into the crowd of enemies. Men, horses, and chariots tumble over each other in panic. The jumble of enemy soldiers succumbs to the ordered royal power; the "rage of the people," the assault of the chaotic enemy powers, is successfully fended off. (Keel 1997a: 298, fig. 405)

Figs.
119–121
the overpowering of Apophis through divine magic leading to his being butchered with knives.

The notion that the inhabited world was constructed first through battle, especially between the creator-god and the all-threatening water of chaos (e.g., Job

38:8–11), was also current in Israel, as well as the idea that battle was necessary in order to prevent this world from falling back into chaos. A cosmos-preserving battle is already the theme of the well-known Ugaritic myths, in which Baal with the help of Anat fights against Yam and Mot for his divine kingdom and thus for the preservation of the earth. Creation is locked in a permanent battle, and a positive outcome that preserves life can, in the biblical view, be guaranteed only by YHWH. Thus, the God of Israel very often appears in the role of a warrior against chaos (Job 40–41; Ps 74:12–18, 89:10ff.), one who overpowers the cosmic threat in various forms (darkness, wilderness, enemies, but above all, water)[35] and one who in the process reveals himself as Creator (Kapelrud 1979, Stolz 1992). Yhwh battles against Leviathan, the "coiler," who in Isa 27:1 is compared with the accursed serpent. He battles against Rahab, the "oppressor" or "turbulent one"; against Tehom, the "primeval flood"; and against Tannin, the dragonlike "Monster."[36] When enemy peoples attack, these great deeds are recalled, so that victory can be snatched from the jaws of chaos. How similar the ideas of craftsman-based and warrior-based creation are is shown, for example, by Ps 74:13–17, where the memory of God's victorious battle against the heads of Leviathan is followed directly by praise for the foundation of creation by the establishing of times and boundaries. Historical events, too, are readily clothed in the mythic sense of a cosmic battle with chaos. The popular opposition of history and myth is by no means operative in the ancient Near East (cf. Assmann 1996); instead, they play off one another.[37] The entire ancient Near East understood the commission of the royal ruler, the legitimate son of the god: his task was to ward off enemies, whether through battle against external aggression or through intervention against agitators within, as a contribution to the preservation of the cosmos.

Fig. 122

4. Creation as Magic, Command, and Decree

The sovereignty of the creator-god over what was created is further emphasized when this god does not need to act either by craft or by battle but can bring about everything through his powerful and wise word alone: it brings order.[38] The divine word as a potent cosmic force that creates and destroys is also known in Mesopotamia and Egypt at various times.[39] It first became a key concept in creation theology in the Egyptian *Monument of the Memphite Theology* (cf. chap. VI.2.2 below, pp. 135ff.). God's word creates saving ordinances that bring order to the community, on whose account the heavens were created. God orders the things that are created to obey like a disciplined army:

> For upright is the word of Yhwh,
> and all his works are trustworthy.
> He loves justice and right;
> of the kindness of Yhwh the earth is full.
> By the word of Yhwh the heavens were made;
> by the breath of his mouth all their host.
> . . .
> Let all the earth fear Yhwh;
> let all who dwell in the world revere him.
> For he spoke and it was made;
> he commanded, and it stood forth. (Ps 33:4–6, 8f.)

When Yhwh orders the dawn or the sea (Job 38:11f.; cf. Sir 39:17) or hurls lightning (Job 38:25), all of these forces obey unquestioningly. Once again there

---

35. See Wakeman 1973, Day 1985, Kloos 1986. More detail in chap. VI.3 below, pp. 147ff.

36. Leviathan in Ps 74:14, 104:26; Isa 27:1. Rahab in Job 9:13, 26:12; Ps 87:4, 89:11; Isa 51:9; cf. Ps 74:13, 149:7; Prov 8:29; Isa 27:1. Tehom (akin to the goddess of the briny deep, Tiamat, in the Babylonian *Enuma elish*) in Gen 1:2, 8:2; Job 38:16; Ps 33:7, 42:8, 77:18, 107:26; Prov 8:24, 27f. Tannin in Gen 1:21; Exod 7:9 (serpent); Job 7:12; Ps 148:7; Isa 21:1, 51:9; Ezek 29:3 (crocodile). For the meaning of the various terms, see the precise analysis in Wakeman 1973, esp. 56–82.

37. The Exodus, for example, is mythologized as a battle with chaos (Ps 77:15–21; Isa 43:16, 51:9). On the results of myth, see Assmann, Burkert, and Stolz 1982.

38. Genesis 1; Ps 147:15, 18, 148:5; Sir 39:17, 42:15, 43:5, 10, 13f., 26; Wis 9:1. In ancient Israel, a reality-creating power inhabits the word, especially the divine word, independent of ideas of creation.

39. See J. Bergman, "*dbr* 1. Ägypten," *ThWAT* II 92–98; H. Lutzmann, "*dbr* 2. Mesopotamien," *ThWAT* II 98–101. For the creating word in Memphite and Jewish theology, see Koch 1965, esp. 271–75.

appears a mingling of modes of creation, for Yhwh the warrior against chaos can also display his power through a spoken prohibition (Job 38:12) or at least through his scolding, rebuke, or fear-raising cry.[40] Although creation by means of the word is rarely viewed statically in the Bible, because of the commanding position of Genesis 1 at the beginning of the Pentateuch, it has taken on an (overly) exalted significance in the interpretive tradition.

Excursus:
Naming as an Act of Creation-Appropriation

In the Priestly account of Creation, the narrative of how God divided the light and darkness, the heavens and dry land, is followed by the note that God named the works thus created and divided (Gen 1:5, 8, 10). Those who prayed the Psalms (Ps 147:4) deduced that God knew every star by name. Naming, however, is very rarely practiced by God (Isa 49:1). Everywhere else in the entire Old Testament tradition, it is exclusively a task delegated to people, even when God frequently exercises influence over the choice of name. The responsibility to name is also an expression of mastery. In Genesis 2, Yhwh restrains himself from any influence and leaves the naming of the animals to the earthling alone:

> Whatever the man (’adam) called each of them would be its name. (Gen 2:19)

In the naming of children, animals, places, etc., humanity carries out its cooperative part in God's work of creation. The name does not express the nature of the named thing itself but the significance of encountering it and its appearance. When people name something that has been created, they recognize it by their encounter with it and in the process endow it with an excess of life over and above existence "in and for itself." Only through this act of recognition, which is a "post-creation" act, does a child become a person[41] and a fellow human being becomes a woman partner (Gen 2:23, 3:20), an animal a fellow creature, a place a historically significant location.[42] On names hang curses or blessings—but always a meaning, an important one—around which stories gather. Name changes correspond to existential crises and new life-beginnings (Gen 17:15, cf. 32:29, 41:45); they can also serve as arbitrary demonstrations of power by the strong over the weak (2 Kgs 24:17). Men seek honor and greatness and try to make a name for themselves through imposing monuments (Gen 11:4). The disappearance of a name by the death of a person was that person's greatest sorrow in ancient Israel:

> My enemies say the worst of me:
> 'When will he die and his name perish?' (Ps 41:6)

This background helps to explain why the disclosure of God's name is so important for Israel. The revelation of the name makes Yhwh's real power accessible, almost in the sense of bringing it into "existence." Especially in deuteronomistic theology, the Name of God takes on its own divine importance, becoming worthy of worship as such, just as in Egypt pharaoh's names (in cartouches) or god's names, such as Amun's, were worshiped, and there is much evidence for this in seals from Palestine/ Israel (Keel and Uehlinger 2001: esp. 124–28).

---

40. For "rebuking" (g‘r) the powers of chaos, see Klopfenstein 1997.
41. In ancient Greece and Rome, a newborn must be lifted up from the earth in the *pater familias* rite in order to become a person.
42. Most naming of children in the First Testament is done by women. Of the 45 namings, 26 are by women, 14 by men, and 5 by delegation or command of God (see Winter 1987: 22–25). Naming by the mother is more common in the older texts, while in the later texts the fathers do more (compare J's version in Gen 4:25, where Eve names Seth, with P's in Gen 5:3, where Adam does).

VI. The World as Manifestation of Divine Activity

Although traces of a numinous valuation of the environment are found in the First Testament, traces that take on entirely new and specific significance in view of the modern ecological crisis, as a rule its world appears less as a bearer of numinous properties than as an object dominated by a sovereign or as a counterpart to divine activity.[1] YHWH is the most high god and "creator of heaven and earth" (*qoneh šamayim waʾareṣ*).[2]

When classifying creation texts, a *distinction between goal and object of the origin or creation* seems helpful. Therefore, we proceed from what was more accessible to human experience than were the agents or methods of production, both of which must always remain speculative; that is, we proceed from the end product, such as humanity, the entirety of what has been created, the supply of water, etc. It will be seen that specific types of gods and methods of origin are associated with particular parts or aspects of the world that has come into being or has been created and that particular cultures prefer one or the other of the traditions so defined.

1. Humanity at the Heart: Anthropocentric Creation Texts

In one group of creation narratives from the ancient Near East, including Gen 2:4b–25, humankind is the central object, while the rest of the world, to the extent that it is even taken into account, is defined entirely by its relationship to humanity. The oldest Near Eastern texts that attempt to answer the question of why humankind is on earth are the Sumerian and Akkadian texts from Mesopotamia.[3]

In the Sumerian myth of *Enki and Ninmah* (ca. 2150–2000 B.C.),[4] and much more dramatically in the Akkadian *Atra-hasis* (ca. 1750 B.C.),[5] the reason for the creation of man is a conflict among the gods and goddesses. The higher deities compel the lower to perform difficult and exhausting labor, such as digging canals. In order to reserve the divine world for the cosmos-endangering conflict,

Fig.
123

---

1. O. Kaiser's chapters (1998: 210–318), which are rich in material and provided with much bibliography, are a useful supplement to what follows.

2. Gen 14:19, 22; this is also the interpretation of the sequence of letters *qnʾrṣ* 'creator of the earth' on an early 7th-century B.C. ostracon from Jerusalem (Avigad 1972: 195f. and pl. 42β). Hebr. *qanah* can denote a creation in both the generative and the artificial-craftsmanlike senses, but in any case it emphasizes the sublime ascendancy of God over the creation (for *qanah*, see Keel 1974a: 15–21). This is also expressed in the creation term *baraʾ* favored by P and Deutero-Isaiah, which aims to express an absolutely incomparable and free creation or re-creation in the realm of nature and history (see W. H. Schmidt, "*brʾ*," THAT I 336–39; J. Bergman, "*brʾ*," ThWAT I 769–77).

3. See the collections of texts in Gressmann 1926, Pritchard 1969, and TUAT III/3–4; as well as Maag 1954, Lambert and Millard 1969, Pettinato 1971, van Dijk 1973, Jacobsen 1976, von Soden 1979, and Bottéro and Kramer 1989.

4. Pettinato 1971: 18, 22–23; Kikawada 1983; Sauren 1993; translation by W. H. P. Römer, TUAT III 386–401. These texts are preserved in Middle Assyrian copies but go back to a Babylonian origin (16th century B.C.) or perhaps even to Sumerian tradition.

5. Lambert and Millard 1969: 57–61, von Soden 1979, Tropper 1987, translation by W. von Soden, TUAT III 612–45.

123 Akkad-period cylinder seal (2350–2150 B.C.). In Mesopotamia, the gods are considered the founders and actual builders of the temples. The seal shows Marduk, on the left, killing an opponent, who represents the power of chaos. The god in the middle raises his arms in horror, triumph, or mourning. At the right, six subordinate gods (the Annunaki) are busy with the temple-building that follows the victory over chaos. At the lower left, a divinity with a hoe prepares the mud. Another, above him, packs mud into a wooden brick-form. A third carries the bricks in a basket up a ladder onto the building being erected. A fourth waits above, ready to take the load from him. A fifth throws materials up to a sixth figure. The seal was grooved much later, probably so that a Bedouin woman could wear it on a cord as a necklace. (Keel 1997a: 175, fig. 240)

in *Enki and Ninmah* Nammu, the primeval water—here still viewed positively—gets the idea of creating man. She persuades Enki, who together with Nammu, **Text 1** Ninmah, and other mother-goddesses creates man. The procedure of creation remains somewhat unclear. The involvement of the mother-goddesses suggests a biological element; the clay that is referred to implies an artificial element; and the *sig-en* or *sig-sar* (according to Pettinato, 'model'), perhaps a formal element. Herbert Sauren's more recent translation (1993), on the other hand, insinuates a thoroughly biological creation procedure. **Text 2**

In *Atra-hasis*, the initiative comes from Enki, who persuades the Belet-ili, the 'Lady of the Gods'. Here, too, the procedure of creation is not terribly clear. **Text 3** One of the cuneiform texts from Assur, which probably come from the 16th century B.C. but go back to older traditions (KAR 4), requires the blood of a **Text 4** craftsman-god, and *Atra-hasis* requires the flesh and blood of a god in order to equip man for his intended role. In the version included in *Enuma elish* (written down ca. 1250 B.C.), it is Marduk alone, the chief god of Babylon, who conceives and carries out the plan. **Text 5**

It goes without saying that this view of the origin of humanity was very convenient for temples and their functionaries. It was so widely accepted in Mesopotamian society that the king himself was represented as the prototypical **Figs.** man in this role. By involving the birth of a child, Enki and the mother goddess **124–125** could be reminded that a safe birth and a healthy child lay in their own personal interest, as in the Akkad-period *Childbirth Incantation* (2300 B.C.). **Text 6**

It is interesting that in the Sumero-Akkadian traditions discussed thus far, the origin of humanity as man and woman, male and female, is hardly mentioned. **Text 2** In *Enki and Ninmah*, after the birth of the man from Nammu, the birth of the woman and her destiny as child-bearer was taken up. In the Epic of *Gilgamesh* (ca. 1200 B.C.), the first two tablets of the twelve-tablet version tell how Enkidu, created from clay by a mother-goddess, through an encounter with a prostitute **Text 7** changed from a wild man living among the animals into a civilized man. There

124 Part of a relief plaque from Tello (ca. 2500 B.C.). That the king appears as its master-builder highlights the significance of the temple in this period. The dedicatory plaque from Tello (not fully shown here) presents a religious festival in the context of the court and the royal family in connection with constructing a temple. King Urnanshe, who according to the inscription built temples for several gods, presents himself as master-builder. On his head, he carries a basket of building materials. (Keel 1997a: 269, fig. 361)

125 Central motif on a stone stela of Assurbanipal from Babylon (668–627 B.C.). King Assurbanipal is still portraying himself in the role of a humble hod-carrier for his lord, the god Marduk. Throughout the ancient Near East, unless subordinate gods undertake this role, it is a primary task of the king as representative of the god to build a house for him. The First Testament portrays Solomon as the great founder of the Jerusalem Temple (1 Kgs 5:17ff.). Later generations took care to explain why King David had not already built a temple for YHWH, which is why Ps 132:1–5 presents David, in accordance with the image of an ancient Near Eastern ruler but contrary to all historical criteria, as master-builder of a temple. (Keel 1997a: 269, fig. 362)

are obvious parallels to Genesis 2–3: the male human, formed of clay, first lives with the animals, and then through an encounter with a woman is estranged from the society of animals and introduced to civilization. But the woman, in contrast to the biblical creation narrative, is merely a small part of an episode that turns Enkidu into a "man" and makes his comradeship with Gilgamesh possible. The differences are more significant than the parallels (Bailey 1970).

The basic question of these texts, Why is humanity on earth?, is answered as follows: humanity unburdens or replaces the gods in order to prevent the outbreak of class warfare in heaven or at least to relieve the gods' boredom. Labor, in these texts, is always described as forced. These creation stories are properly by their nature theocentric. Humanity sees itself in utterly irrevocable dependency on and subordination to divinity. Humans are not created of their own will. Reflexes of this view are found in the biblical Psalms, where those who pray remind Yhwh that, when dead, they are of no further use to him, because in Sheol the praise of God is silenced (Ps 88:12–14, 115:17, etc.). The creation of humankind, at first the task of mother-goddesses, in time becomes a theo-political concern, and the powerful gods seize the role of creator for themselves. Thus, the birth process and related matters recede entirely into the background. In Sumerian texts, the creation process is mixed in form (formation, emerging), and then in the Akkadian texts formation clearly comes to the fore (pinching off clay; cf. much later, Job 33:6). On the other hand, the gods bestow on humanity a part of themselves, of their nature, in that they slaughter one of their own. Being in the gods' image is the necessary correlative to the purpose of humankind, since the latter must be capable of being addressed by the gods. Nonetheless, the creation of a sort of duplicate is a means of self-deprivation and self-abandonment on the part of the divine world. By creating, the gods renounce their uniqueness.

In *Enuma elish*, which probably goes back to Old Babylonian traditions (back to the 18th century B.C.), the idea that the creation of humanity involved some admixture of evil first appears, and something similar is found in the *Babylonian Theodicy*:

	Enki and Ninmah (ca. 2000 B.C.) Text 2	Atra-hasis (18th century B.C.) Text 3	KAR 4 (before 16th century B.C.) Text 4	Enuma elish (ca. 1250 B.C.) Text 5
Justification	Difficult labor of the gods. The lower gods complain (less dramatically).	Outcry among the gods (dramatic uprising of the *Igigi*); relates to heavy labor, yoke).	Boredom of the gods. Only afterward does it emerge that the creatures are to work for temples, guarantee worship, and rule over animals.	Babylon/Esagila should be built for the relief of the gods.
Initiator	Nammu, the primeval water, the mother of Enki (here positive) assumes the initiative.	Enki suggests that Belet-ili cause humankind to be made for relief.	Enlil asks: What shall we do now? The great gods (An, Utu, Enki, etc.) answer.	Marduk, as victor, has the initiative; Ea only advises.
Creation/Process	Enki creates, with the assistance of Nammu-Ninmah and others; abstract process (with a sort of model plus formation).	Belet-ili, Mami create humankind with Enki.	They slaughter Lam-ga-gods in the temple of Nippur. Aruru appoints the rule of germination from blood or seed.	Ea creates on the instruction of Marduk; no mention of birth or goddess.
Elements	*sigensigšar*, clay, water.	Flesh/blood of a god and spittle of the great gods.	Blood of the lamga-gods (craftsman gods?), earth.	Blood of a rebel god.

Narru, king of the gods, who created mankind,
And majestic Zulummar, who dug out their clay,
And mistress Mami, the queen who fashioned them,
Gave perverse speech to the human race.
With lies, and not truth, they endowed them forever.[6]

In *Atra-hasis* and the Epic of *Gilgamesh*, the emphasis is on human mortality, which was bestowed at creation. Giovanni Pettinato interprets the passage in **Text 3** *Atra-hasis* (I 214–17) as follows:

Let the spirit of the dead reside (in man) on the basis of (the presence of)
    the god's flesh.
Let it proclaim (to him, the) living (= so long as he lives) its sign (of death),
So that this be not forgotten let the spirit of the dead be present (in him).[7]

The *eṭemmu* 'spirit of the dead' is the shadowy mode of existence after death, the spirit of the deceased, which dwells in the underworld like a demon but can escape from it. Mortality is thus already bestowed on the creature at birth. The Epic of *Gilgamesh* reads:[8]

O Gilgamesh, where are you wandering?
The life that you seek you never will find:
    when the gods created mankind,
    death they dispensed to mankind,
    life they kept for themselves. (trans. A. George 1999: 124)

Genesis 2–3 contradicts both accounts. The created human beings, in the eyes of the biblical writer, were not marked for good or evil from the beginning but were subjected to a divine plan. Sin and mortality belong only to the corrupted order of creation after the Fall. Good and evil are neither created nor desired by God (cf. still Sir 15:11–21) but irrupt as powers of the ever-lurking pre-world chaos, wherever no ordered world (cosmos) confronts them (cf. Gen 4:7).

The situation of humanity in Egypt is entirely different from what it is in Mesopotamia. In Egypt, the king, as the son of the gods, is pledged to serve the gods. But this is a normal son's duty and has nothing to do directly with the role of humankind and the maintenance of cosmic peace. In the *Instruction for King Meri-ka-Re*,[9] the sun-god's sorrow for humanity is commemorated in the con- **Text 8** text of a theodicy. The love of this creator-god for his creatures is portrayed as completely selfless. Everything has been created for humankind, including the temple, so that the god may be near them as well as functioning as the magical guard against sickness. In a few motifs, such as the idea that humans are the image of god, as well as in its strongly anthropocentric overview, the text can be fully regarded as a forerunner of the anthropology of Genesis 1.[10]

In Egypt, as in Greek origin narratives (Bonnafé 1996), myths of the creation of humanity have a very limited place. Much more important is the cosmogony, which to a great extent is a theogony.[11] When we recall that the original interest of such narratives was the preservation of humankind, the security of their birth

---

6. Lambert 1960: 88f. lines 276–80.
7. An emendation of the translation by Lambert and Millard (text 3). Cf. the very similar translation and interpretation by Tropper (1987).
8. Meissner-Millard tablet from the 18th century B.C. (iii 1–5); translation after K. Hecker, *TUAT* III 665f.
9. The *Instruction for King Meri-ka-Re* comes from the early second millennium B.C., but the passage under consideration is probably an addition from the 14th/13th centuries B.C. (Bickel 1994: 214–23 no. 198).
10. E. Otto 1971, Ockinga 1984, Lorton 1993.
11. J. Assmann, "Schöpfung," *LÄ* 5: 677–90. In Egypt, the myths of the creation of the *world* serve more directly for the glorification of individual gods than for the sustenance of the world, although sustaining the world was always a central theme.

and of their existence overall, this might mean that humans in ancient Egypt felt less threatened in their existence. The creation of humanity by God is a prime reason for rejoicing.

1.1. The Creation Story in Genesis 2:4b–25

In ancient Israel, the coming into being of an individual person was regarded both as having a mysterious origin and growth in the depths of the earth (cf. chap. V.1, pp. 84ff.) or the womb (Ps 139:15) and also as the work of a *deus faber* who forms the baby in the womb (Ps 139:13). In the mythical narrative in Gen 2:4b–25,[12] in contrast, the miracle of the first creation of humankind is presented as purely artificial and surprisingly soberly, as the work of a single God who takes earth, forms the earthling, and vivifies him. The creation narrative in Genesis 2 reveals many correspondences to Sumerian and Akkadian traditions but differs from them in several aspects, especially in two points. (1) The creation of humankind does not take place purely for the use of the creator-god but is the gift of God. God creates the human, provides for his nurturing and overall well-being, especially seeing to it that he be not alone, and even, when he banishes him from the Garden of Paradise, does not leave him unclothed. And the burden of labor (at first not difficult), unlike the rest of Near Eastern tradition, falls only on humankind, not the gods. (2) The creation of man in two kinds, male and female, is a central theme. In this point, the biblical account of the creation of humankind differs from the Egyptian traditions as well.[13]

Claus Westermann rejects the comparison of Genesis 1 with Genesis 2, as it has commonly been posited since the time of Hermann Gunkel. For Westermann, Genesis 2 is purely an account of the creation of humankind. But his arguments are unpersuasive.[14] Humanity does undeniably stand at the center of Genesis 2, but the creation of humanity is surrounded by a miniature creation of the world.

The tradition of the creation of man in Genesis 2–3 now stands in close connection with the story of God's garden, the violation of the commandment, and the banishment from the garden:

2:5	"While as yet"—the earth was wasteland.
6	God causes water to stream from the earth (an oasis, where it seldom rains).
7	God forms the earthling from dust.
8	*Garden in Eden*
9a	God makes trees grow from the farmland as food.
9b	*Tree of life, etc.*
10–14	*Geography of Paradise*
15*	God gives the garden (*Eden**) to man for cultivation.
16–17	*Prohibition*
18–20	Plan for a counterpart so that *'adam* may not be alone. Creation of animals as a first unsatisfactory attempt.

---

12. Especially important German commentaries on Genesis 2–3 are Gunkel 1901 (translated, 1997), von Rad 1949 (translated, 1961), Westermann 1966 (translated, 1994); see also Steck 1970 (= 1982); Keel and Küchler 1983, esp. 80–84, 92–97; Dohmen 1988.

13. In the *Story of Two Brothers*, to be sure, Re-Harakhti bids the creator-god Khnum "O, fashion a wife for Bata, that he may not live alone!" (Brunner-Traut 1990: 66).

14. C. Westermann asserts that the motif of nurturing is a typical component of ancient narratives of the creation of humankind, but his principal piece of evidence, the Amun hymn (Assmann 1999: no. 87E), is neither ancient, nor a myth, nor a narrative of the creation of humankind. The classic Sumerian and Akkadian creation of humankind texts are concerned only that humans nurture the gods, not vice versa.

21–23　Creation of woman as successful masterpiece.
’*adam* recognizes their solidarity.
24–25　Utilization, etiology (marriage as the Sitz im Leben)

From a critical point of view, approximately only two independent texts need to be reconstructed, while from a tradition-historical point of view, there are clearly two elements. One concerns the creation of man and his most important interests and relationships—namely, work, animals, and the opposite sex. In creation from dust or clay and in referring to work—that is, orchard duties[15]—the text connects with ancient Near Eastern traditions. The other element has to do with a sojourn in God's garden (Eden) and the subsequent banishment from it (cf. Ezek 28:11–19, 31:9).[16]

The narrative of the creation of man, in which the word 'farmland' (’*adamah*) plays a key role, comprises approximately 2:4b–7, 9a, part of v. 15,[17] and vv. 18–23. The narrative begins, as do so many ancient Near Eastern creation narratives, with the description of conditions "not yet . . ." and paints these conditions as yearning for the post-paradisical world. The great Akkadian epic *Enuma elish* begins:

> When skies above were not yet named,
> Nor earth below pronounced by name,
> Apsu, the first one, their begetter
> And maker Tiamat, who bore them all,
> Had mixed their waters together,
> But had not formed pastures nor discovered reed-beds;
> When yet no gods were manifest,
> Nor names pronounced, nor destinies decreed,
> Then gods were born within them. (I 1–9).[18] [trans. S. Dalley 1989: 233]

But in the Old Egyptian Pyramid Texts as well, the description of the pre-world is also couched in "before . . ." sentences:

> N.N. was born in Nun
> Before there was sky,
> Before there was earth,
> before there were mountains [i.e., the two mountain chains that border the Nile valley and were viewed as supports of the sky],
> Before there was strife,
> Before fear came about through the Horus Eye.
> (Pyr 486 § 1040 [trans. Lichtheim 1973: 47])[19]

In Genesis 2, the world before creation is described not as a water wasteland, as in Genesis 1, but as a dry wasteland, in which not even the poorest desert shrubs grew,[20] let alone the vegetation that would serve man as food (Ps 104:14; cf. Gen 1:11, 29). "Bringing rain" is an act of creation (Job 38:25f.). Precisely this had not "yet" happened. And also missing was ’*adam*, the earthling, who as his name implies is from the earth and cultivates the earth (2:5; cf. 3:23). Creation

---

15. For God as orchard-keeper, see also Ps 104:16; for the connection of Genesis 2–3 with the tradition of ancient Near Eastern royal gardens, see Jericke 2001.

16. According to E. Otto (1996), the story was constructed quite late and inserted into its present place in order to make the transition from Creation (Genesis 1) to the Flood (Genesis 6–9) comprehensible. But P has a transition of its own (Gen 6:11f.: "mighty deed"), and this explanation has nothing to do with Genesis 2–3.

17. The feminine object suffix on 'cultivate' and 'care for' probably refers originally to the 'farmland' with the trees in v. 9 and not to the (grammatically masculine) 'garden' of v. 15a.

18. Translation after W. G. Lambert, *TUAT* III 569; Bauks 1997a, 1997b; Löning and Zenger 1997: 20–40.

19. Translation after Bauks 1997a: 156f.

20. For *siyah*, cf. Gen 21:15, Job 30:4, 7.

in these verses is thus understood as a sort of cooperation between divine and human acts. The coming into being of the world is not wedded to romantic ideas of nature but originally was already represented as a culture-creating act. According to Gen 2:9, Yhwh caused trees to grow from the farmland, but to cultivate this farmland no man yet existed. The first irrigation took the form of a mysterious flood (cf. fig. 70 above).[21]

1.2. The Creation and Nurturing of the Earthling

Yhwh "pots" the man from the moist soil. The "potting" can but need not be taken literally (cf. chap. V.2, pp. 95ff.), since God also "pots" the eye (Ps 94:9) and even seasons (Ps 74:17). The word 'adam literally means 'red', 'reddish-brown'. He is made of loose clods of 'adamah, the red-brown soil, the iron-bearing *terra rossa*, into which he will also decompose. The term 'apar, usually translated 'dust', does not necessarily refer to dry, powdered earth. In Lev 14:42 it stands for moist clay or plaster used to plaster walls. Job also parallels 'dust' with the Hebrew word for 'clay' (ḥomær) in the context of the creation of man:

> Oh, remember that you fashioned me from clay!
> Will you then bring me down to dust again? (Job 10:9)

Every ancient Near Eastern tradition of the creation of man clearly distinguishes between the forming of the body and that body's vivification. Already in Egypt, two gods—one male, the potter, and one female, who holds the 'life' sign—take part in the creation of man (cf. fig. 105 above).[22] The connection between the body and the vivifying power is loose. When God takes back his breath of life or his spirit of life (*ruaḥ*), every living creature collapses into dead material:

> If you hide your face, they are dismayed;
> if you take away their breath, they perish
> and return to their dust.
> When you send forth your spirit, they are created,
> and you renew the face of the earth. (Ps 104:29f.; cf. Job 34:14f.)

The living thing that God created must be nurtured. The subsequent verses are devoted to this manifest, pressing need. God himself assumes the responsibility for his creation and organizes the necessary work. Just like an eastern potentate, he lays out a royal garden (cf. Jericke 2001). In 2:15, the garden (the keyword "Eden" probably did not originally belong to this narrative) is assigned to the earthling for cultivation, so he was meant to live as a vegetarian (cf. Gen 1:29f.). His task consisted of cultivating (cf. 2:5) and caring for this plot of earth.[23] Light work, in which income and expenditure are happily balanced, is anticipated for him. Cultivating, protecting, and guarding were considered the basic forms of human activity. Only after the expulsion from the garden did this labor become a burden, a daily struggle with the (accursed) stony ground. In fact, Palestine/Israel was a land that yielded sustenance only with perpetual backbreaking toil.

---

21. 'ed, found elsewhere only in Job 36:27, is probably a loanword from Akkadian *edû*, 'field-watering flood, springtime high water'.

22. In Amarna letter 143:10f. (from the Canaanite prince Amumira; 14th century b.c.), too, man is imagined as a combination of the breath of life and "dust."

23. 'Cultivate' and 'care for' are provided with feminine suffixes referring to 'adamah. Contrary to Detlef Jericke (2001: esp. 172), it must be stressed that in le'abedah ulešomerah the administrative aspect certainly does not take the foreground. In a primeval society that did not yet have division of labor, like that described in Genesis 2, protection and guarding (šamar can have both meanings) are both part of cultivating a garden. The earthling does not earn his livelihood through an administrative position, as might have been possible in some limited circles in ancient society but would only be possible to a greater degree in modern society.

1.2.1. The Encounter of Man and Animal

If food is the most urgent necessity of the new creation, an additional necessity comes in a close second: reliance on interactions with fellow creatures. In a first attempt to relieve the loneliness (on which more below) of the earthling, God creates the animals. The encounter with the various animals,[24] which focuses on their being assigned names by the earthling, shows that the environment, including the animals, belongs to humanity in the same way that labor does (Janowski, Neumann-Gorsolke, and Gleßmer 1993). But the animals turn out not to be an ultimately satisfactory relief for loneliness, because they cannot be man's equal counterpart. Nor are they seen, as in Genesis 1, as the object of human care and dominion(!) but instead as beings on the periphery of human society (Schmitz-Kahmen 1997).[25] The unsatisfactory outcome of the attempt to associate the animals with humans as equal counterparts, however, should not mislead us about how much they are in fact counterparts, how closely they are related to humanity. This relationship between human and animal is also fore-grounded in many other biblical passages. Little distinguishes humans from the animals. They share with animals the spirit of life (*ruah*) and the fate of death:

> For the lot of man and beast is one lot; the one dies as well as the other. Both have the same life-breath, and man has no advantage over the beast; but all is vanity. Both go to the same place; both were made from the dust, and to the dust they both return. Who knows if the life-breath of the children of men goes upward and the life-breath of beasts goes earthward? (Qoh 3:19–21; cf. Ps 49:13, 21)

In the Priestly creation story in Genesis 1, land animals and humans are created together on the sixth day of creation, and originally both are intended to be vegetarians (Gen 1:29f.). In the Flood, both man and animal are to be destroyed, they are saved together in the Ark (Gen 6:5–9:17), and the expected time of final salvation brings them to ultimate reconciliation and peace (Isa 11:4–9). At the end of the story of Jonah (4:11), YHWH justifies to the frustrated prophet his re-fusal to destroy Nineveh on the basis that the city contained not just people but also much cattle. According to the Bible, man and beast often find themselves in the same boat. Whether by Flood or by drought (Jer 14:5f.), they are equally afflicted, and the fate of one has repercussions for the other. That man and woman are formed in God's image, as programmatically formulated in Genesis 1 and Psalm 8, thus distinguishing them from the animals, is justified not by biology but purely on a theological basis as a deliberate act of God. The Israelites thus certainly considered themselves closer to the animals than we do. They also used some 40 animal names as personal names (Riede 1993), and only one animal name, "Dog," was an insult, and even this one was not originally so. Countless metaphors and comparisons show how people in ancient Israel were observant of animals and their behavior. A closer look at the nearness of this relationship and the common destiny of man and animal might have calmed somewhat the upheaval in theology that resulted from Darwin's theory of evo-lution. In our Western civilization, however, Greek anthropology has prevailed in this case: man is perceived as absolutely distinct from animals, a viewpoint that also underlies the book of Daniel (Daniel 7).[26]

---

24. The animals that are named are the cattle, the birds, and the wild animals, but not the aquatic animals, which an "earthling" would not encounter (at least at first) and which in Israel had no par-ticular cultural significance.

25. A proper person behaves toward the animals as toward the weakest in society (Exod 20:10; Deut 5:14, 25:4); note the similarity of Prov 12:10 to the prohibition of oppressing the alien (Exod 23:9).

26. Hesiod (*Works* 275–80) stresses that while fish, wild animals, and birds eat each other indiscrim-inately, Zeus gave man law and justice. For the interpretation of dominion over animals and the Son of Man, see Keel 2000.

1.2.2. God's Measure against Human Loneliness: The Creation of the Sexes

Genesis 2 is distinguished from the preserved creation narratives of Israel's neighbors by the overt topic of the relation between man and woman.[27] The entire second and longer part of the story presents the problem of the loneliness of the earthling. It begins with God's, not man's, determination that "It is not good for the man to be alone (*lebad*)" (see Seidel 1969). Thus, in this text, God does not demand that humans meet all their needs in God (for an opposing point of view, see 1 Cor 7:32–35). The insight drawn from life experience, that solitude is not good for man, is also found in the wisdom literature:

> Two are better than one: they get a good wage for their labor. If the one falls, the other will lift up his companion. Woe to the solitary man! For if he should fall, he has no one to lift him up. So also, if two sleep together, they keep each other warm. How can one alone keep warm? Where a lone man may be overcome, two together can resist. A three-ply cord is not easily broken. (Qoh 4:9–12; cf. Ps 25:16)

After the animals proved unsatisfactory in this respect, the woman was created as "help" (*'ēzer*) for the solitary earthling. "There was no one to help" elsewhere in the First Testament refers to a man abandoned by his friends; he is alone and sorrowing.[28] The view in the Psalms is that God can fill this gap (Ps 33:20, 70:6, 121:1f., etc.). And if a man has been abandoned by father and mother, help is to be found in Yнwн (Ps 27:9f.), and this help consists of God's closeness. The Hebrew word *'ēzer* is thus sometimes an attribute of God, though it does not denote in the least any associations of a subordinate, serving helper. The "help" for the solitary earthling is a genuine counterpart, born to the same station, as stressed by *kenægdo* 'opposite him' or 'corresponding to him' in v. 18.[29] When, later, the real dominion of the man over his partner observed in everyday life is discussed, such dominion is regarded as the result of disobedience of God and as a corruption of the original order of creation:

> Yet your urge shall be for your husband,
> and he shall be your master. (Gen 3:16)

Mastery is the man's answer to the woman's longing for pairing. Only in the joy of lovers can this sanction be lifted and that which was intended from the beginning be rewon (cf. Matt 19:8), so that the woman rejoices:

> I belong to my lover
> and for me he yearns. (Song 7:11)[30]

The sexual differentiation of the earthling—a piece of the *'adam* is built into a new variant of the human species—has the purpose of creating a remedy for loneliness. It is not a punishment, as in Aristophanes' myth in Plato's *Symposium* (189c–191) but an enhancement for the better. On the contrary, the creation of woman appears as the climax of the experimental activity of the god of creation.[31] While the motif that a creator-god at first fails at all sorts of experiments is widespread,[32] it is never realized elsewhere in terms of the creation of

---

27. On the significance of this text for all of Western anthropology and discussion of the place of women, see Schüngel-Straumann 1997.
28. 2 Kgs 14:26; Ps 72:12, 25:16, 107:12.
29. For *nægæd* see also Job 10:17 and Qoh 4:12. On equal station as a prerequisite for true partnership, see also Sir 13:15–23.
30. The word used in both of these quotations, *tešuqah*, occurs only three times in the Hebrew Bible. Its only other appearance is in Gen 4:7.
31. The god of the primeval history is educable, as is also clear from Gen 6:5f. and 8:21.
32. Such as the frustrated attempts in the Sumerian *Enki and Ninmah* (translation by W. H. P. Römer, *TUAT* III 386–401; cf. Kramer 1997: 71f.).

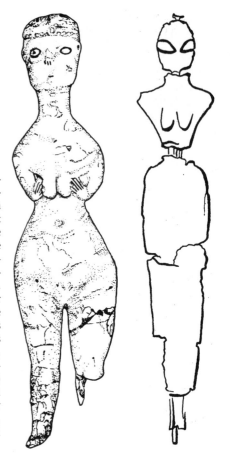

126–127 (right) Reconstructed clay sculpture from ʿEn Ghazal on the outskirts of Amman (8800–7000 B.C.). Several large human sculptures or busts have been found in a pit of the Neolithic settlement of ʿEn Ghazal. The size of the head is exaggerated. The eyes are accented with chalk inlays and a black substance; the mouth is only suggested. The female figure shown here presents her breasts. The materials used—clay or lime plaster over a reed or rush—stand for flesh and bone, the materials from which the Bible also believes man was created. On some of the sculptures traces of red and black color were preserved, though the significance is unknown. (Drawing by Inés Haselbach after Ibrahim 1988: 22) (far right) Prehistoric female figurine from Egypt (4000–3000 B.C.). This Egyptian clay figurine is also constructed on a reed support, which represents the human skeleton. (Keel 1975: 75)

a female variety of man. It is unique to the narrative dynamic of Genesis 2 that the woman is the masterpiece of the god of creation.

The woman receives from the earthling at first only the framework, but this is the foundation of the relationship between man and woman, similar to the way in which in the Sumero-Akkadian myth the relationship between humanity and divinity is expressed by a substance taken from the gods (blood or flesh) being needed for the creation of man. In Genesis 2, the animals are not created from a piece of ʾadam—the primary difference from the creation of the woman. The Hebrew word ṣelaʿ comes from the terminology of building, not of anatomy. Banah,[33] too, in biblical usage is connected with the concrete activity of building, hardly ever with creation. Interestingly, though, the meanings of the cognate Akkadian words are 'rib' and 'creative building', which provides evidence that Gen 2:21f. has a tradition-historical origin in the Mesopotamian milieu (Uehlinger 1988, 1998). Behind the basic idea that God built a piece of the earthling into a new being must be experience from the world of handicraft. The construction of an interior structure from reed or struts of clay or other materials is

---

33. Cf. Isa 9:9, Ezek 27:5, 2 Chr 11:5, etc. In the First Testament, the word is used only once (Amos 9:6) for the activity of creation!

128–129 (Right) Scaraboid from Megiddo (1700–1600 B.C.) (Keel and Uehlinger 1998: 48, fig. 43) and scarab from Palestine/Israel (1700–1600 B.C.). In the first half of the second millennium, depictions of couples were favored. The scaraboid from Megiddo shows a ruler in a rolled-hem garment and a woman with a long, thick braid in close embrace. In the background are a bud and an open flower. The scarab at the right shows a man in a loincloth and a nude woman, both holding a flower. Two persons holding a plant, which signifies blossoming and fertility, was a ceremony used to solemnize covenants. In Mal 2:14, marriage is conceived as a covenant (Hebr. *berit*). (Keel and Uehlinger 1998: 46, fig. 42)

130 (Left) Ivory tablet from Ugarit (1400–1350 B.C.). The ivory carving shows a highborn couple, perhaps a young prince of the city and his consort, in loving embrace. The woman's slightly rounded belly might indicate pregnancy. An erotic encounter such as this, however, represents not merely the coming into being of new life but also the creative-generative powers of love in general. (Keel 1997a: 285, fig. 387)

attested since the Neolithic.[34] Bones and flesh, which are likewise central in Gen 2:21–23, are represented by two different substances in handicraft. The newly created being, unlike the earthling in Gen 2:7, is not awakened to life through God's breath. It is living from the beginning—like the animals (Hebr. *ḥayyat* 'living being')! This could be a narrative shortcut (to avoid repetition), but surely this is not the case. In Gen 3:20, the woman is named mother of all living things (*ḥawwah*), so the fact that women themselves bring forth life might here find a reflex. The woman is from the beginning living and life-giving.

Figs. 126–127

---

34. See, for example, the Neolithic statue fragments from Jericho (Amiran 1962). The suggestion that the shaping of female statuettes in bone, such as the widespread bone amulets from 9th/8th century B.C. southern Palestine depicting a sexual, nude woman, underlies Gen 2:21 (so Uehlinger 1988, 1998) is less likely, since the bone is worked by carving.

The creation of the woman occurs during a deep sleep (*tardemah*), in a mysterious state of consciousness induced by God.[35] Job's friend Eliphaz describes such an experience as something like a nocturnal vision:

> In my thoughts during visions of the night,
> when deep sleep (*tardemah*) falls on men. (Job 4:13; cf. 33:15, Gen 15:12)

The deep sleep automatically teaches the earthling that the new creature is related to him, as the biblical text says, "Bone of my bones and flesh of my flesh."[36] The relationship is also particularly clear in the naming that follows the encounter. The man, *'iš*, and the woman, *'išah*, bear related, similar-sounding, even mirror-image names. This is why two people who fall in love call each other "brother" and "sister," titles by which lovers address each other already in Egyptian love poetry and then in the Song of Songs (4:9–12, 5:1f.).[37] The mutual attraction of man and woman, like the creation of man, is simultaneously a primeval occurrence and an event that is repeated perpetually. In the tale of the search for Isaac's bride, the miracle of this meeting is experienced as brought about by God (Gen 24:12, 40, 50). When Ruth finds Boaz, she finds *menuḥah*, shelter and rest (Ruth 1:9, 3:1). According to Deut 12:9 (cf. 1 Kgs 8:6), *menuḥah* is a promised ultimate blessing of salvation: even God seeks *menuḥah* (Ps 132:14, cf. also Sir 24:7ff.).[38] The attraction of man and woman works in miraculous, mysterious ways. The teachers of wisdom, too, treated the powers and intuitions operating between the sexes as a sort of natural miracle when they assert:

> Three things are too wonderful for me,
> yes, four I cannot understand:
> The way of an eagle in the air,
>   the way of a serpent upon a rock,
> The way of a ship on the high seas,
>   and the way of a man with a maiden. (Prov 30:18f.)

In this androcentric perspective, it is true that the mutuality of the event seems to be lost. In fact, the teachers of wisdom—unlike the lawgivers, who counted the wife among the possessions of a free Israelite (Deut 5:21)—hold to the position that it is a gift from God when a man finds a woman.[39] Nonetheless, this "gift from God," in the context of a patriarchal way of thinking, quickly came to be regarded as a sort of special prize and exalted possession of the husband.

According to Genesis 2, when the not yet sexually specified earthling *'adam* encounters the *'išah*, he becomes an *'iš*. Only in Gen 2:25, in typical patriarchal fashion, do "person" and "man" become directly identified. In this equivalence, on which the interpretation of the entire narrative hangs, lies an important starting point for the hierarchical sexual relationship later derived from Genesis 2.

While the story so far has been played out in primeval time, a shift into the present, the time of the narration, follows. The original human pair in fact had no parents. So the "this is why" in Gen 2:24 shows that the narrative is to

---

35. See Thomson 1955: esp. 423. This state is not simply 'lethargy' (so *HALAT* 4.1645) and still less a form of narcosis but a conscious state that is frequently induced by God (1 Sam 26:12, Isa 29:10, cf. Judg 4:21, Jonah 1:5f., Dan 8:18).

36. This relationship formula is also used in Gen 29:14; Judg 9:2f.; 2 Sam 5:1, 19:13.

37. Cf. as well Goethe's declaration of love "To Charlotte von Stein" (in a letter from April 14, 1776):

Tell me, what's our destiny preparing? Tell me, how we're bound in such a knot? From an old existence were we sharing? You're the wife, the sister I forgot? (trans. John Frederick Nims, in *Goethe's Collected Works, 1: Selected Poems*, ed. Christopher Middleton, p. 61 [© Boston: Suhrkamp/Insel, 1983, repr. Princeton University Press, 1994])

38. According to a very old Christian interpretation found in the Gospel of Thomas and in the book of Hebrews, God finds the shelter and rest he sought in Jesus (see Schroer 1986).

39. Cf. Prov 18:22, 19:14; also in Sir 26:3f., where, contrary to the common translation, the woman is not called a "possession" but a *meris agathē* (Hebr. *manah tobah*), that is, 'generous gift' or 'destiny'.

be understood as an etiology explaining why the sexes at the present time are powerfully attracted to each other. It is thus not primarily an etiology of marriage.[40] Marriage was usually arranged based on the needs of family politics and economics and probably cured "loneliness" only to a limited extent. Exceptions do occur, however, such as the tale told in Judg 14:1–5a of Samson's marrying a Philistine for love.[41]

In the patrilineal organization of Israelite society, it was not the man who left his parents, but the woman who left hers (Genesis 24, etc.). Therefore the *'azab* in the text indisputably means not 'leave' but 'neglect' or 'abandon'.[42] Parents would resent this neglect or abandonment by a son who has 'clung' (Hebr. *dabaq*; cf. Gen 34:3) to a wife but still lives in his parents' house—obviously more strongly than they would resent neglect by a daughter who had left her parental home (Bravmann 1977: 593ff.). This representation of things is obviously androcentric. That fathers in ancient Israel paid no, or very little, attention to their daughters cannot be ruled out (Seifert 1997). But the strength of the mother–daughter bond is hard to discern on the basis of the patriarchally influenced texts. The strongest prior bonds of kinship were, in any case, considerably loosened or broken by the new connection of man and wife. "One flesh" in v. 23 means a relationship that is as close as the closest blood relationship (cf. Gen 37:27, Lev 18:6, Isa 58:7).

With respect to v. 25, it should be noted that in the Hebrew Bible the word "naked" has practically no erotic connotations but primarily means 'unprotected' (Job 1:21, Qoh 5:14). Clothing expresses a person's status, and nakedness means that a person has no status. Thus, prisoners of war were generally led off naked (Isa 20:2, 4). Hebrew *'arom* thus corresponds more closely to our word "bare." The saying means that the lovers stand before each other bare and unguarded. Goodwill and trust, which allow one to stand bare-naked before one's partner or before God, disappear with the suspicion brought into being by original sin (cf. Gen 3:7). In this sense, 2:25 introduces Genesis 3.[43]

It is noteworthy that in Genesis 2 the creation of man and woman, the powerful attraction of the sexes, and the basis of lifetime companionship seem to be completely disconnected from the topic of begetting and raising children. Fertility is closely connected with the creation of the two sexes in the image of God only in Gen 1:27f. In Genesis 2, it is not explicitly in the picture—although subsequently, in Gen 3:16, the woman's pains in childbirth are obviously presupposed. In Genesis 2, the central impulse behind creating two varieties of humans proceeds from God's single thought that it is not good for the earthling to be alone. The prevention of loneliness is the real reason for the creation of the sexes. Today, this goal—prevention of loneliness—can also be the basis for establishing the value of same-sex partnerships, on the basis of the creation-theology explicated here.

---

40. However, the small book of Tobit (8:6f.) already saw an etiology for marriage in Genesis 2, probably because, on one hand, marriage is an ideal and in part in practice satisfied the sexual urge, and on the other hand, perhaps because marriage increasingly had become the only legal means for the expression of the sexual urge. The indicative of Genesis 2 is the basis of the tradition that underlies Jesus' prohibition of divorce (Mark 10:2–12 and parallels). Where the experience of the indicative—God joined together two persons—fades or disappears, the imperative—the prohibition of separation—can become nothing more than a shackle, sometimes even a vicious shackle.

41. There were occasions, such as festivals, and places where young people could meet, for which (among others) the love poems of the unmarried in the Song of Songs provide the best evidence.

42. In Neh 13:11, *'azab* concerns the abandonment of the House of God; in Prov 4:2 the forsaking of a father's instruction.

43. It would not be enough, however, to see 2:25 merely as a contrast to 3:7 (Westermann 1994: 250ff.). If it were, one would expect to see "were not *yet* ashamed." Etiologies begin with *not yet, when not yet.*

Until recently, representatives of the Catholic Church never grew tired of stressing that the only purpose of the sexual partnership was the creation of progeny. However, in any case, Genesis 2–3 does not share this perspective. Once again, the suspicion arises that a common androcentric viewpoint has led to shortsightedness. Giving birth and children were reckoned throughout the Orient—as is proved by extrabiblical images and texts, as well—as strictly women's matters. The topic of having a baby turns up, astonishingly, only after the Fall, since this is when the burden of difficult, life-threatening childbirth is imposed on the woman (3:16), corresponding to the man's toil at difficult field work (3:17b–18). Work and childbirth belong to the natural, standard way of life granted at creation, but hard labor and labor pains are the result of a distortion of the original order of creation. In ancient Israel, having children was not a voluntary matter, since without children there was no societal security. The distress of a childless woman was great, and not all men recalled, as did Jacob (Gen 30:1f.) or Elkanah (1 Sam 1:4–8), that the love between man and woman is prior to the children that result and that only God gives the gift of children.

Excursus:
Functions of Biblical Discourse on
the Creation of Humanity

In the First Testament, it is not only in Genesis 2 that God's creation of humanity plays a role. The origin of any individual at any time can be understood, by analogy to primeval times, as direct creation by God (e.g., Job 33:6, Ps 139:13–15). This amalgamation of the primeval creation of humanity with the present-day event of the birth of an individual baby is already found in the Old Akkadian *Childbirth Incantation* and in *Atra-hasis*.[44] As a way of promoting successful birth, creation is recalled. What the gods did then, they are to do now, so that the new creation will turn out to be a good servant.

Text 6

In the First Testament, the topic of the creation of humanity comes up for various reasons:

1. The mystery of the origin of humanity and the miraculous omnipotence and majesty of God are recalled:

> Just as you know not how the breath of life (*ruaḥ*)
>   fashions the human frame in the mother's womb,
> So you know not the work of God
>   which he is accomplishing in the universe. (Qoh 11:5)

Psalm 139 (cf. chap. V.1, pp. 84ff.) is especially emphatic: the text does not predicate God's total control[45] but the fact that God knows us better than we know ourselves and is closer to us than we are ourselves because he created us. We, as we come to know ourselves better, gradually get on the track of the mysterious workings of God:

> My frame was not hidden from you,
>   when I was being made in secret,
> intricately woven in the depths of the earth.
>   Your eyes beheld my unformed substance. (Ps 139:15f.; cf. 33:15; 94:9; Isa 44:24)

God's sovereignty as creator can be grasped in the context of birth but also when death is considered. Job, fearing death, recalls:

---

44. I 272–306; trans. W. von Soden, *TUAT* III 612–45, esp. 625f.
45. But for the reception history, see Moser 1976.

"Naked I came forth from my mother's womb,
   and naked shall I go back again.
Y нwн gave and Yнwн has taken away;
   blessed be the name of Yнwн!" (Job 1:21; cf. Qoh 5:14)

The deepest insight into the dependency of human life on God's sovereign creative will is always—and in many lands until this day—preserved by women. In birth, especially for women, life and death echo off each other. Never are the woman and the child so close to death as in birth; never are new life and the utmost fulfillment of life so near to each other.[46] It is not accidental that programmatic passages in both Testaments rejoicing in God's sovereignty are placed on the lips of someone like Hannah, who has already given birth, and of someone like Mary, expecting her first child (1 Sam 2:1–10, Luke 1:46–55). In the Song of Hannah, the formula expressing God's sovereignty, "Yнwн puts to death and gives life" (1 Sam 2:6), explicitly evokes God's power over life and death. Islam also holds strongly to the absolute authority of Allah, the creator, over creation. In the Near East in modern times, women celebrate the birth of their child with a song to the sovereign creator, a hymn of inversion (Granqvist 1950: 58):

He brings to life and He sends death.
   He makes rich and He makes poor.
He feeds and He withholds.
   All is from God! praise and thanks be to God!

2. Recollection of God's miraculous creation of humanity is a request-granting motif in the laments and a motif of confidence. There is a close relationship between creator and creation. Oppressed creatures rely on this close relationship to attempt to obtain vindication from the creator. The created motivate God to grief, experiencing pain and suffering for the humans he called to life by the act of creation:

Your hands have fashioned me and formed me;
   will you then turn and destroy me?
Oh, remember that you fashioned me from clay!
   Will you then bring me down to dust again? (Job 10:8f.)

Those who pray Psalm 22 express a great need for God's help and appeal to the creator's closeness to his creation that exists from birth on:

You have been my guide since I was first formed,
   my security at my mother's breast.
To you I was committed at birth,
   from my mother's womb you are my God. (Ps 22:10–12; cf. Isa 63:15f., 64:8)

The certainty that God will not leave his creatures in the lurch extends from the Exile to the future of the entire people of Israel. It is a matter of eschatological hope in a new creation when Ezek 37:5–10 transfers the image of the creation of humanity to the people as a whole. In 2 Maccabees, the recollection of humanity's creation even becomes the basis of an eschatological hope for new life after death for the righteous. Convinced of God's creative power, the heroic mother encourages her seven sons to martyrdom:

I do not know how you came into existence in my womb; it was not I who gave you the breath of life, nor was it I who set in order the elements of which each of you is composed. Therefore, since it is the Creator of the universe who shapes each man's

---

46. Precisely the same holds true for men's experience of war, for in war everything is at stake, including life itself, for which life was put in play. The formula of God's sovereignty can encompass women's experience of God in childbirth as well as the experience of rescue in war (Deut 32:39, Ps 18:28). This proximity is also expressed in the prophets' comparison of the pain of war to the pangs of childbirth (Jer 4:31, 6:24, 30:6, 49:22; Mic 4:9).

beginning, as he brings about the origin of everything, he, in his mercy, will give you back both breath and life, because you now disregard yourselves for the sake of the law. (2 Macc 7:22f.; cf. 7:11, 28)

3. In a class-based interpretation of interpersonal relationships,[47] the recollection that all people have a common origin provides an egalitarian impulse (Doll 1985: esp. 15–39). In the presence of the creator-God, rich and poor have equal standing. This fundamental insight—not merely being created in the image of God—is what anchors the biblical idea of human worth. This thought is something of a precursor of modern arguments from natural law. In the ancient Near Eastern and biblical view, people are "by nature" quite different from one another: they are "naturally" rich or poor (see the especially emphatic and detailed Sir 13:15–23); nonetheless, in several passages this "natural law" is contrasted with a "creation law." Although the prophets denounce the oppression of the poor in the name of God as scandalous, and the memory of oppression in Egypt is usually incorporated into the prologues of legal codes in order to justify commandments affecting social relations (but cf. Exod 20:11, which appeals to the creation of heaven and earth in seven days), wisdom texts as early as the period of the monarchy are careful to ground the prohibition of exploitation and oppression on the basis of creation theology:

> Rich and poor have a common bond:
> Yhwh is the maker of them all. (Prov 22:2; cf. 29:13)

> [God] who neither favors the person of princes,
> nor respects the rich more than the poor,
> For they are all the work of his hands. (Job 34:19; cf. 33:6)

These aphorisms must not be misunderstood as fatalistic assertions of the common existence of rich and poor, such as are also found throughout the wisdom of the ancient Near East. In the mouth of a highly responsible elder in the gate, for example, these sayings strengthen the weak and set boundaries for the rich:

> He who oppresses the poor blasphemes his Maker,
> but he who is kind to the needy glorifies him. (Prov 14:31)

The previously wealthy Job refutes an accusation that he had disregarded the rights of his slaves, who like him were created by God:

> Had I refused justice to my manservant
> or to my maid, when they had laid a claim against me,
> What then should I do when God rose up;
> what could I answer when he demanded an account?
> Did not he who made me in the womb make him?
> Did not the same One fashion us before our birth? (Job 31:13–15; cf. 33:6)

Behavior toward one's fellow humans is the measure of one's relationship with God in these texts. In other proverbs—which are still more basic but beyond legal prescription—it is one's internal attitude toward fellow humans that determines one's relationship with God:

> He who mocks the poor blasphemes his Maker;
> he who is glad at calamity will not go unpunished. (Prov 17:5)

---

47. The wisdom literature has no illusions regarding the distinction between rich and poor and its consequences: see Prov 10:15; 13:8; 14:20; 18:23; 19:4, 7.

2. The Origin and Sustenance of All That Is:
Cosmocentric Creation Texts

Just as love, sickness, death—and especially birth—are occasions for pondering what a person is, so also a sunrise, the experience of the warming spring sun, or the sun on the sea are appropriate for illuminating the world as a whole, its origin (cosmogony), and its miraculous sustenance. A collection of myths has survived from the Sumerian tradition in which the cosmos is presented both as a whole and in fine detail—the *Dilmun* myth (or *Enki, Ninsikila, and Ninhursaga*).[48] The cosmogony proper is founded on the creative preparation of fresh water by Enki. Life comes about in a theogony that encompasses several generations, proceeding from Enki's sexual union with the earth and birth goddess and his daughter, granddaughter, great-granddaughter, and so on (Alster 1978).

Much more numerous, beautiful examples of sustenance of the cosmos are found in the Egyptian hymns to the sun- and creator-god Amun-Re. These hymns must go back to ancient traditions. Although life in the Old Kingdom appears to have been largely secular, bits of evidence are found, for example, in the visual arts of the 5th Dynasty (2500–2350 B.C.), at the time of Sahure and Niuserre, that processes in nature, such as the propagation of animals, were related to acts of the gods, particularly the sun-god. Based on two of the three Egyptian seasons that are represented in the "world chamber" of the solar sanctuary of King Niuserre (2425 B.C.), which also depicts the Egyptian nomes, the world created by Re is divided into the the realms of air, water, field, and animals. Many of the wild animals, including gazelles and antelopes, which walk in long lines through the bush and forest, are in the process of giving birth to young. Near the reliefs there would have been a platform on which an obelisk **Fig. 131** was erected as the gnomon of a sundial. The reliefs are a portrait of and paean to the life-giving acts of the sun-god that pervade every sphere of life—he is the god to whom plants, animals, and humans owe their lives (Wildung 1984a). The creator-god's image underwent continuous transformation during the Middle and New Kingdoms (Bickel 1998). In the Middle Kingdom, creation is treated preeminently in connection with the fate of the deceased and by analogy to the origin of Atum in primeval time, whereas in the New Kingdom the dead came to be compared with the sun-god, who was reborn daily. This led to listing created works in praise of the creator-god. The origin of heaven and the cosmos, in contrast to the human and divine world, became increasingly important, as did the role of the creator-god as guarantor and perpetual sustainer, not merely as source, of all life. In the New Kingdom, wʿy 'the only one' in the sense of a "solitary" creator-god turned into wʿy 'the One'. From the 18th Dynasty on, the Egyptian creator-god was treated as king of the entire world, of gods and humans.

The Egyptian hymns to the sun and creation are not single compositions but belong to an extensive and varied tradition. In the New Kingdom (ca. 1550–1150 B.C.), the hymn to the sun assumed a central position.[49] Even before the fundamental reform of Akhenaton[50] (1353–1336 B.C.) and the rise of Thebes as the capital, the god of the Theban empire, Amun-Re, assumed a preeminent position. The texts that celebrate him are marked by the polarity between the **Fig. 132** distant One and the proximate details of creation, down to the worms and flies. **Text 9**

---

48. *ANET* 37–41; Eliade et al. 1964: 111–17; translation by W. H. P. Römer, *TUAT* III 363–86. The text comes from the Isin-Larsa period (20th century B.C.) but consists of nearly unaltered earlier myths (Attinger 1984).
49. Assmann 1983, 1999: 71–365.
50. Assmann reads Yati for Aton and so Akhenyati for Akhenaton.

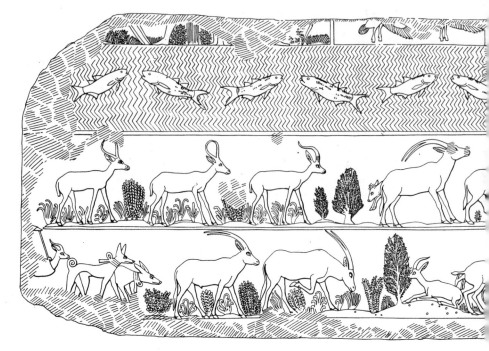

131 Parts of the originally painted relief from the "world chamber" of the solar sanctuary of Abu Gurâb near Abusir (ca. 2400 B.C.). Discussed in the text. (Edel and Wenig 1974: 22f. lines 250–52)

To the extent that humanity appears in this hymn at all, it is alongside the cattle between the fish in the river and the birds in the sky.[51] People join the chorus of every creature, from the gods to the mouse in its hole, singing the praises of the One who miraculously created everything, who lovingly cares for his creations by providing light, air, and nourishment and watches over all the peoples (Egyptians, Asiatics, Nubians, and Libyans) like a careful shepherd. The One creates the multiplicity of living things not out of need or to reach a goal but out of pure joy in life. The creation of the One is, as Jan Assmann (1998) stresses, a *creatio ex Deo*. But Akhenaton's Aton-monotheism goes on to recognize in creation not only the work of a personal god but in fact the manifestation of the One. Aton is the cosmological principle of all that is; all that is created is simultaneously a transformation of the one god.

Akhenaton's religious revolution sharpened the polarity between creator and creatures in that not only are other gods excluded *ad hoc* but their very existence is denied. In this religion—which scholars have called the "Amarna" religion after the location of Akhenaton's newly built residence—the political subtext of its theology is also clear. This late offshoot of a glorious dynasty stresses not only the oneness of its god but also the oneness of his mediatorship, "For there is none who knows thee, other than thy son."[52] The love of the king for his family became a symbol of divine love. In the course of his radicalizing reform

Fig. 133

---

51. In a coffin text (ca. 2000 B.C.), humanity already figures in the world ordered by Atum, inconspicuously placed among falcons, jackals, swine, hippopotami, crocodiles, and fish (Eliade et al. 1964: 95f.)—in fact, somewhere between birds and aquatic creatures. The birds in the sky and the fish in the river constitute a favored merism circumscribing the entire world. On the relation between Amun theology and the Bible, see Görg 1997.

52. For Akhenaton, see Schlögl 1986, 1993; for Akhenaton's religion, Hornung 1999.

and establishment of a religion, Akhenaton denied all other gods, abolished worship of them, and attempted to do away with their images. This reductive monotheism, limited to the worship of the empirical sun, had the characteristics of an Enlightenment philosophy, centuries before the pre-Socratics, rather than being an establishment of religion (Assmann 1993). Because this reductive monotheism ignored many of the familiar requirements of ancient Egyptian religion, such as concern for life in the next world and the presence of specialized gods in various places in different temples, the cult released by Akhenaton was abandoned soon after his death. The post-Amarna restoration, however, did not eliminate the image, so strongly inculcated, of a sun-god who gives life and prosperity with his rays, but rebuilt it so that the sun-by-night was identified with Osiris, the ruler of the kingdom of the dead, with the result that the realm of the night and the dead that Akhenaton had excluded became integrated into the theology of the sun.

Figs. 134–135

2.1. Psalm 104 and the Egyptian Hymns to the Sun

Ever since the Egyptian hymns to the sun were discovered, Psalm 104 has been increasingly connected to this tradition. In fact, on a purely stylistic level, this psalm exhibits a love of detail that is otherwise foreign to the poetry of the Hebrew psalms. It is disputed whether it is influenced by Egyptian hymns to the sun in general or specifically by the worship of Aton and whether literary dependency on the Great Amarna Hymn of Akhenaton should be posited. What seems certain, in any case, is that no Egyptian hymn is closer to the Aton hymn than the Hebrew psalm is. The text of the Aton hymn can be divided as follows:

Text 10

1–14   It begins with the invocation of the name of the sun-god and the introduction of Akhenaton, the praying king.

132 Early Ptolemaic bronze statuette (3rd century B.C.). Amon-Re, the father of the gods (originally fitted out with staff and scepter), wears a tall double crown of feathers with which a sun-disk is combined. (Drawing by Inés Haselbach after Page Gasser 2001: 101–4, no. 25)

133 Scene from the Book of Gates (ca. 1350 B.C.). The universality of lordship of the sky- and sun-god in New Kingdom Egypt is expressed in his shepherding the peoples. The falcon-headed god Horus, leaning on his staff like a shepherd, protects representatives of the four types of humans: Egyptians, Asiatics, Nubians, and Libyans. The caption begins: "Horus says to these cattle of Re, to those who are in the underworld, fertile land, and desert: transfiguration be to you, cattle of Re, which has arisen from the great one who presides over heaven. Breath be in your nostrils!" (Cf. text 8). (Keel 1996a: 343 fig. 494)

134 Part of a relief in the tomb chamber of Maketaton in Tell el-Amarna (1353–1336 B.C.). The relief, which was originally painted, portrays sun worship from a universalistic perpective, as it is in Akhenaton's famous hymn to the sun. The royal couple (not shown in the part reproduced here) occupies a prominent place in this worship, bringing the sacrifice for Aton. In this image, the rays of the sun rise over the eastern horizon and bestow life on all creation; many details of the worship take place in the temple, which is indicated by tall columns. A large part of the service is carried out by the king, not just a few priests. Beneath the sun-disk with uraeus and Ankh sign, the animal kingdom is represented by ostriches, caprids, and hares, which appear to join in singing the praise of the sun-god. With wide-open beaks and wings spread wide, the ostriches lead this little procession of worshipers, and below them in two rows are leaping caprids with their young. (Keel 1997a: 211, fig. 289)

Text 10

135 Scarab of the 19th/20th Dynasty from Beth Shean (1292–1150 B.C.). Palestine must have been under more than the political control of Egypt at the time of Akhenaton. The monotheistic worship of Aton introduced by Akhenaton probably left its traces behind in distant regions. This scarab from Beth Shean might depict an ostrich worshiping the rising sun. The sun-disk has only a small carving above the raised wings. (Drawing by Inés Haselbach after Rowe 1936: no. 782; cf. Keel 1995: fig. 196)

The song of praise itself follows, in small units on various topics.

15–26   First, Aton is praised as the source of life and in his general appearance. Although he is distant, his rays are mysteriously everywhere.

27–37   When he sets in the west, darkness grips the earth. Night is a cosmological danger, the gateway to death, the grave, and evil.

38–58   The rising sun god banishes the menacing darkness. Then humans awake to their daily work, with prayers of praise. Flora and fauna begin to stir and grow in the warmth of the sun's rays. On the water, the ships, and in the water, the fishes, come to life.

59–75   Praise of Aton as creator and wetnurse of every human baby in the womb follows. But he pays an equal amount of attention to providing for the breath of the chick in the egg and the appointed time for its hatching.

76–109   Aton is praised as creator of all things, visible and invisible. He created man and animals. His efficacy and his plans transcend the borders of Egypt. Peoples' languages and skin colors are as much his work as is the stipulation that Egypt is watered by the Nile and the other lands by the Nile of the sky, namely, the rain. Aton causes the plants to thrive by the creation of the seasons (cf. the Old Kingdom season reliefs and fig. 131).

110–41   Aton is distant in the sky but at the same time nearby: realized in all that is and its transformations but at the same time visible (as a disk) above the earth. When he sets, all life is extinguished, no eye created by Aton sees anything any longer.[53] But the entire mind of the king, who alone completely comprehends Aton, even then is still directed toward the god. The sun god leaves the prosperity of all that is to his corporeal son. The hymn closes with the king's titulature.

The similarity of Psalm 104 to this hymn goes beyond individual motifs. Its basic structure is marked by the sequence heaven, earth, and sea:

1b–4   describe *heaven* and God as the lord of heaven, and light, clouds, winds, lightning, etc., appear as his attributes

5–24   the *earth* (note the keyword ha-ʾareṣ in vv. 5, 9, 24)

25–26   the *sea* including Leviathan

The largest block, dealing with the topic "earth," can in turn be subdivided as follows:

5–18   describe the accommodation of the earth as habitation for living things. The water supply is critical; its arrangement is described in two parts:

    5–9   recall the formation of the earth and the banishment of the waters of chaos from it.

    10–18   Springs, brooks, and rain create a variety of living areas (ecological niches) for plants, animals, and people, among which the narrow valleys "among the mountains" (10–12), the "mountains" with rainfall agriculture (13–15), and the Lebanon, or, generally, the "high mountains," are named (16–18) (cf. figs. 13, 14, 19, 20).

19–23   extend the spatial organization of the living areas to the temporal dimension, especially night and day, which once again represent different "ecological niches."

24   in closing, celebrates the great number and wisdom of the works that fill the *earth*.

From them an arc is drawn to the countless living things hidden in the water (fishes), the ships on the water,[54] and Leviathan (24–26). All living things—in

---

53. This motif is very common in the Amarna hymns and elsewhere as well. The sun god creates sighted beings so that they can see him and the world (e.g., Assmann 1999: no. 90 lines 12–17, no. 94 lines 14–19). With the darkness of night, they fall into a blindness and an inability to act that has cosmic dimensions; they are no longer fit for life. To live, they need sunlight.

54. For the tradition-historical background to ships and Leviathan, see Uehlinger 1990.

27–30, especially those on dry land—are entrusted to the nurturing creator god. When he hides his face and takes away their breath of life (*ruaḥ*), they die; when he sends it forth (again), they come to life anew (28–30).

The psalm closes with the wish that God may enjoy his creation, that the praise may please him, and that sinners and godless might disappear from the earth (31–35).

Quite clearly, Psalm 104 treads in the footsteps of the Aton theology (most recently, Assmann 1998a: esp. 255–60). Yhwh nurtures flora and fauna and cares for all his creatures. He created the alternation between fearsome night and sunlit day, the visible and invisible. Day is designated as the living space for people, night as the kingdom of dangerous animals. A difference from the Great Amarna Hymn is that the night in Psalm 104 is not adjudged purely negatively, as the realm of death and the absence of god, but also positively, as the work of God and a living space in its own right.[55] In the Great Amarna Hymn, as in Psalm 104, the description of the night is followed by the awakening of people to go to work:

Awake they stand on their feet,
You have roused them;
Bodies cleansed, clothed,
Their arms adore your appearance.
The entire land sets out to work.[56]

In accord with the perspective shared throughout the entire ancient Near East, in Psalm 104 night precedes day. This viewpoint is diametrically opposite of the modern sense that day begins with morning and night is merely a pause between two days. Throughout the ancient Near East, night is the embodiment of chaos and danger. The ordered, lighted world only escapes chaos with the surprise of every new morning. The consciousness that night is prior to day, that the world collapses into chaos again and again, presupposes a powerful orientation toward beginnings, which rhythmically become futures.[57] In Genesis 1, too, it is as if the light is torn from the darkness, and the days of creation begin with the evening ("evening came, and morning followed"). This order, night before day, is observed throughout the Bible and has been retained in the religious life of Judaism and in the Christian church as well, to this day. The sabbath and the great religious festivals begin with the sundown (Vespers) of the previous evening.

Ships and aquatic creatures are expressly named as living things in both Ps 104:24–26 and the Amarna hymn (lines 53–58). A conclusive argument for the dependency of the psalm on the Egyptian Aton hymn is v. 29, which does not fit very well into the Israelite conceptual world. According to the text, living things that depend on God's spirit die and (the same things) come back to life as Yhwh withholds or bestows *ruaḥ*. A death in the narrow, literal sense cannot be meant. The rhythm of dying and resurrecting must instead be dependent on the Egyptian hymns to the sun. This verse only makes sense against the background of the ideology of the sun god, who bestows and withholds in congruence with the alternation of day and night; during the day, he fills everything with warmth

---

55. A tomb painting ca. 1200 b.c. (Keel 1997a: fig. 54) shows serpent, crocodile, and gazelle fleeing the sun god. These animals already for the most part have a mythological significance, so that this painting might reflect the cosmic battle of the sun god with the representatives of chaos, while in the Aton hymn sun, night, and nocturnal animals are understood much more empirically.

56. Assmann 1999: no. 92 lines 42–45; cf. text 10.

57. Hesiod also (*Theog.* 122–24) views the darkness not as negation but as the mother of daylight; the day proceeds from the night (Bonnafé 1996: esp. p. 18).

and life and by night he temporarily leaves behind a sort of stillness of death through his disappearance, as expressed in several songs of the Amarna period:

Every eye, they see through you,
nothing can bring them to an end if your majesty founders.
You are up early to rise in the morning,
your light, it opens the eyes of the cattle.
If you set in the western mountain,
then they sleep as if in death.[58]

In the Aton religion, the sun's rays themselves become the breath of life:

The breath of life to their noses;
By the sight of your rays.[59]
(trans. Lichtheim 1976: 92 [she parses it differently from Assmann])

In both the Egyptian and the Hebrew songs of praise, dangers posed to humankind or creation are indeed mentioned (darkness, lawbreakers, wild animals), but they are marginalized. Positive joy in life and security under the gaze of a solicitous god predominate, connected with the deep conviction that creation is due not to chance but to an all-encompassing wisdom:

How manifold are your works, YHWH!
In wisdom you have wrought them all—
the earth is full of your creatures. (Ps 104:24)

How many are your deeds,
Though hidden from sight,
O Sole God beside whom there is none!
You made the earth as you wished, you alone, . . .
How excellent are your ways, YHWH of eternity![60]

Alongside motifs from the hymns to the sun, Psalm 104 also contains motifs of strictly Canaanite origin, such as the battle against the sea (vv. 6–9). Here, too, there are some differences. The heavenly bodies (vv. 19–24) are the object, not the agent, of creation. It is YHWH, not Aton, who owns the role of creator god. The Egyptian idea that all that exists is a development and transformation of the One cannot be detected in Psalm 104. The psalm should thus be considered an offshoot of the Egyptian hymns to the sun, probably from the Amarna period, mediated through the Phoenician civilization,[61] and theologically received and modified in Israel.[62] The ideas in the Aton hymn appear to have had no afterlife in subsequent Egyptian tradition, so it appears that Psalm 104 represents especially noteworthy testimony to its exclusive reception outside Egypt.

Excursus:
The Works of Creation Praise Their Creator

In both Egyptian and Israelite tradition, all creatures join in the praise of the creator god. A text on the rejoicing of baboons has been found in several solar sanctuaries:

The baboons who proclaim Re,
(when) this great god will be born at the sixth(?) hour in the underworld.

---

58. Assmann 1999: no. 89 lines 25–30; cf. no. 91 lines 26f., no. 94 lines 12–16, no. 95 lines 11f.
59. From the *Short Amarna Hymn* (Assmann 1999: no. 91 line 56).
60. From the *Great Amarna Hymn* (Assmann 1999: no. 92 lines 76–79); cf. text 10, pp. 203ff.
61. Compare the Lebanese topography, which has sea, ravines, hills, and high mountains, and note the mention of the Lebanon in v. 16.
62. On this question, see Steck 1978b, 1978c: 63–69; Auffret 1981: 133–316; Uehlinger 1990; Keel 1991: 80–103; Krüger 1993; Köckert 2000.

136 Papyrus of Anhaï from the 20th Dynasty (1200–1085 B.C.). The falcon of the sky with the sun disk on its head sits on the sign for 'west'. From bottom to top, the following adore the sun god: the dead (two soul birds), the gods (Isis to the right and Nephtys to the left), the animals (four baboons), kings with ceremonial beards (right), ordinary Egyptians (left), and representatives of foreign lands. Also included in the creatures' united praise of the god—unlike in Israel—are the inhabitants of the world of the dead. (Keel 1997a: 60, fig. 63)

They appear after he has risen,
while they are on both sides of this god,
at his rise in the eastern lightland of the sky.
They dance for him, they leap for him,
they sing for him, they clap for him, they shriek(?) for him,
(when) this great god appears in the eyes of the "subjects" and the "heaven folk."
Then these hear the "jubilation" of Nubia.[63]

Fig. 136 The baboons greet the rising sun god with loud cries, the birds with beatings of their wings (cf. figs. 134–135). According to Job 38:7, the morning stars and sons of God shouted for joy at the creation of the world before it was enlivened.

In the psalms, the works of creation are frequently summoned to join in praising God along with those who are praying (cf. Isa 42:10f., 44:23). Is this "merely" imaginative discourse and metaphor? How could we know for sure? Behind the notion that the earth, the sky, the sea, a mountain, or a forest can burst into praise for the power that has created everything there exists in any case a deep wisdom, difficult for us rational people to grasp, and at least the insight, at the present time largely absent, that creatures have a proper dignity of their own, independent of humanity. In the First Testament, this dignity is granted to the works of creation specifically when it is presumed that they stand in their own individual relationship to God, one that finds expression in spontaneous praise of God:

The heavens declare the glory of God,
and the firmament proclaims his handiwork.
Day pours out the word to day,
and night to night imparts knowledge;
Not a word nor a discourse
whose voice is not heard;
Through all the earth their voice resounds,
and to the ends of the world, their message. (Ps 19:2–4)[64]

Let the heavens be glad and the earth rejoice;
let the sea and what fills it resound;
let the plains be joyful and all that is in them!
Then shall all the trees of the forest exult. (Ps 96:11f.)

Let the sea and what fills it resound,
the world and those who dwell in it;
Let the rivers clap their hands,
the mountains shout with them for joy
Before Yhwh . . . (Ps 98:7ff.; cf. Ps 24:1; 93:3f.)

The united praise of God by all creation is found in Psalm 148,[65] which inspired St. Francis of Assisi to compose his *Canticle of the Sun*. The structure of the Psalm—from the sea via meteorological phenomena to earth, plants, animals, and humans—looks like a hymnic transformation of Genesis 1:

Alleluia.
Praise Yah, praise Yhwh from the heavens,
praise him in the heights;

---

63. Translation after Assmann 1999: 92.
64. Ps 19:4 is ambiguous. The Hebrew text can also mean: "Although no physical sound is heard, yet the heavens have a language of their own that is understood throughout the world" [NAB footnote]. One hears and yet does not hear. This thought also underlies Wis 13:1–9 and Rom 1:19–23, where the question is raised of how it is possible that some people are unable to recognize God by drawing an analogy from his works of creation. For additional expressions of praise by heaven, see Ps 50:6, 97:6, 89:6, 148:4; Isa 44:23, 49:13.
65. Cf. Psalm 136: in the first nine verses, as in Genesis 1, the works of creation are praised, after which are added God's mighty deeds in history. The most elaborate hymnic enumeration of this sort is found in the "Song of the Three Men in the Fiery Furnace" in LXX Dan 3:57–90. See Helbling 2001.

Praise him, all you his angels,
  praise him, all you his hosts.
Praise him, sun and moon;
  praise him, all you shining stars.
Praise him, you highest heavens,
  and you waters above the heavens.
Let them praise the name of YHWH,
  for he commanded and they were created;
He established them forever and ever;
  he gave them a duty which shall not pass away.
Praise YHWH from the earth,
  you sea monsters and all depths;
Fire and hail, snow and mist,
  storm winds that fulfill his word;
You mountains and all you hills,
  you fruit trees and all you cedars;
You wild beasts and all tame animals,
  you creeping things and you winged fowl.
Let the kings of the earth and all peoples,
  the princes and all the judges of the earth,
Young men too, and maidens,
  old men and boys,
Praise the name of YHWH,
  for his name alone is exalted;
His majesty is above earth and heaven,
  and he has lifted up the horn of his people.
Be this his praise from all his faithful ones,
  from the children of Israel, the people close to him.
Alleluia. (Ps 148:1–14)

2.2. The Science of Lists and the Monument of the Memphite Theology

During the 19th Dynasty (1292–1190 B.C.), Memphis achieved importance over Thebes. Two texts are bound up with this city through the creator god Ptah, the principal god of Memphis, and they attest to spiritual concerns and topics that much later played an important role in the formulation of Genesis 1.

One tradition is *Listenwissenschaft* (the "science of lists"), a sort of inventorying of creation. The inventorying of individual aspects of the world and their designations, such as all plants or plant-names, is the oldest form taken by science.[66] Thutmoses III had detailed pictorial inventories of plants and animals brought back from his campaigns chiseled into reliefs (Beaux 1990), including the flora of Syria and Palestine as well. The *Onomasticon of Amenope* (ca. 11th century B.C.), the most extensive Egyptian product of this sort of spiritual pursuit, with 610 entries, ascribes all of creation to Ptah. The "Instruction" begins with the sentences: **Fig. 137**

Beginning of the teaching for clearing the mind,
for instruction of the ignorant and for learning all things that exist:
what Ptah created, what Thoth copied down,
heaven with its affairs, earth and what is in it,
what the mountains belch forth, what is watered by the flood,

---

66. See von Soden 1965; Schmid 1966: 88f., 95–99, 223–26; J. Osing, "Onomastika," *LÄ* 4 (1982): 572; A. Cavigneaux, "Lexikalische Listen" [in French], *RlA* 6 (1983): 609–41. Pleasure in the process of inventorying, in which the creative-adoptive power of naming (cf. Gen 2:19) comes into play, must also have been the impulse underlying the planning of zoos by Thutmoses III, Hatshepsut, and Ramses II, as well as Assyrian rulers such as Assurnasirpal II and Sennacherib.

137 Relief in the festival chamber of Thutmoses III at Karnak (1479–1426 B.C.). A part of the relief showing plants and animals that Thutmoses III brought back from his campaign in Syria–Palestine. Above, it is easy to recognize various kinds of iris; below are pomegranates and grapevines. The inscription at the left reads: "Regnal year 25 of Men-kheper-reᶜ (throne name of Thutmoses III), may he live forever. Plants that his majesty found in the mountains of Retenu (Syria–Palestine)." (Wreszinski 1923–38: II pl. 31)

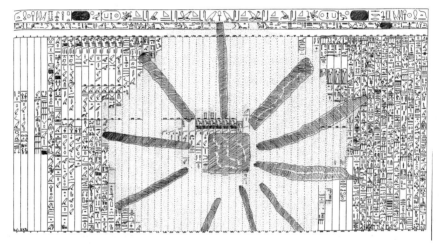

138 Basalt stone from the time of Shabaka (716–701 B.C.) bearing the *Monument of the Memphite Theology*. The hieroglyphic text is largely destroyed because of the stone's secondary reuse as a millstone. (Breasted 1901: pls. 1–2)

all things upon which Reᶜ has shone,
all that is grown on the back of earth. . . .[67]

There has been considerable discussion as to whether and how strongly biblical texts have been influenced by these and similar products of Egyptian *Listenwissenschaft*. But notwithstanding any misgivings, it is unlikely that passages such as Psalm 148, Job 38–39,[68] Dan 3:57–90 LXX ("Song of the Three Young Men in the Fiery Furnace"), and Sir 42:15–43:33 could have been composed without the influence of this sort of name-list. Whether 1 Kgs 5:9–14, where Solomon refers to plants, beasts, birds, reptiles, and fishes, refers to this sort of wisdom is hard to decide.[69] Solomon's wisdom is praised in this passage (also) as surpassing Egyptian wisdom. The text refers to knowledge of flora and fauna,

---

67. Gardiner 1947: 1: 2*.
68. So von Rad 1966: 131–43.
69. So Alt 1951: 139–44 = 1959: 90–99.

but above and beyond a simple inventory, it appears to have been cast in poetic form (1 Kgs 5:12). Such poetic-literary collection activity is historically credible, albeit attested only much later, namely, in the time of Hezekiah (725–693 B.C.), who, according to Prov 25:1, commissioned trained people to collect (and edit) proverbs.

In no way can the practice of organizing phenomena in a particular order—astronomical, meteorological, earth, plants, animals, humans—be regarded as derived from nature.[70] Orderings of this kind are not "natural" but culturally conditioned, stabilized in literary traditions, and thus "artificial," but by no means arbitrary.

The other important spiritual movement of that time is documented in the *Monument of the Memphite Theology*. The hieroglyphic text is on a basalt stone **Text 11** that is now preserved in the British Museum in London. It was inscribed, following an old papyrus, by King Shabaka (716–701 B.C.) and was later used as a millstone. It was probably composed during the 19th Dynasty (ca. 13th century **Fig. 138** B.C.).[71] In this highly theological composition, the principal god of Memphis, Ptah (-Tatenen), is celebrated as the primeval, creator god. The first portion announces that all gods who have anything to do with the creation of the world are in fact only the one Ptah. From Ptah, who as Ptah-Nun is father and as Ptah-Naunet is mother, originate the ennead of Heliopolis: from Atum (primeval god from the primeval water Nun), via Shu (sunlight and the airspace between sky and earth) and Tefnut (fire),[72] Geb (earth) and Nut (sky), to Osiris (vegetation), Isis (throne), Nephthys (lady in the house), and Seth (wasteland and foreign lands). The royal Horus proceeds from the coupling of Osiris and Isis.

The relation of the multiplicity of all living things to an original unity is based in what follows on an anthropological model,[73] which, to be sure, appears to modern people at first glance less obvious than the image of the sun and its rays. Seeing, hearing, breathing—that is, the senses—replace the "heart," seat of understanding and information. The tongue repeats what the "heart" thinks, and thus lends it existence. But this anthropology is—at second glace—not so foreign to us, because it proceeds from the fact that the "world" for a human being is first created through mental perception and its elaboration in a "control room"—which we know to be the brain. As in Genesis 1, this is a creation through thinking and speaking (Koch 1965). The diagram on p. 138 displays the creation of many from the one Ptah. The *Monument of the Memphite Theology* at the same time subordinates the ennead of Heliopolis to the god Ptah:

> Thus it is said of Ptah: "He who made all and created the gods."
> And he is Ta-tenen,[74] who gave birth to the gods,
> and from whom everything came forth,
> foods, provisions, divine offerings,
> all good things.
> Thus it is recognized and understood
> that he is the mightiest of the gods.
> Thus Ptah was satisfied after he had made all things and all divine words.[75]
> (trans. Lichtheim 1973: 55)

---

70. So the explanation by M. V. Fox (1986: 302–10).

71. For the dating to the Ramesside period, see Schlögl 1980: 110–17, Allen 1988: 43 (for the earlier discussion, see Junge 1974). Others date the *Monument of the Memphite Theology* not much earlier than the 8th century B.C. (Yoyotte 1996).

72. J. Assmann (1997a: 130) has, with good reason, thrown the received opinion of Tefnut as "moisture" into doubt.

73. The attempt of the *Bhagavadgita* (XI 15–19, 23f.) to describe the entire universe as the body of Vishnu is comparable.

74. *Tatenen* means 'the earth that rises up' (= primeval hill).

75. Cf. text 11 (pp. 206f.) and Junker 1940: 58 line 9 – 59 line 4 (no. 23). This does not exclude the

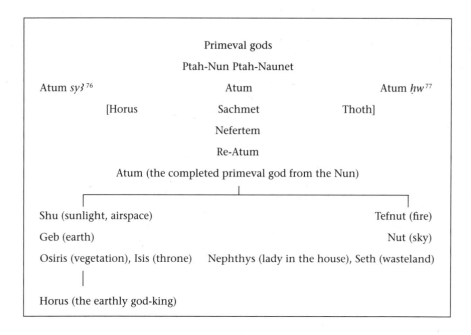

Primeval gods

Ptah-Nun Ptah-Naunet

Atum $sy\beta$ [76] Atum Atum hw [77]

[Horus Sachmet Thoth]

Nefertem

Re-Atum

Atum (the completed primeval god from the Nun)

Shu (sunlight, airspace) Tefnut (fire)

Geb (earth) Nut (sky)

Osiris (vegetation), Isis (throne) Nephthys (lady in the house), Seth (wasteland)

Horus (the earthly god-king)

The *Monument of the Memphite Theology* focuses considerable attention on theogony as part of cosmogony. But it also refers to the creation of all vital powers, the establishment of law, the creation of all crafts and occupations, the founding of cities and nomes, and the institution of worship of the gods through sacrifices, temples, and sacred images. Ptah's creative act is accomplished in primeval time, not in everyday time, and it is not understood to be cyclical.

2.3. The Creation Story in Genesis 1:1–2:4a

The best-known passage in the Bible that treats the entire richness of the cosmos and specifies that it is dependent on a single God is the Priestly creation story in Gen 1:1–2:4a. The centrality of this text is due not only to its positioning at the beginning of the First Testament and the introductory seven-day schema but probably also to the fact that it represents a little *summa* of biblical creation traditions. The author succeeded in gathering a variety of familiar traditions and motifs into a convincing, coherent system. Genesis 1 has endured an extremely complex reception history, which is discussed several times in this book. Even on Christmas Eve of 1968, when men first reached the moon, these verses were solemnly intoned by the Apollo 8 astronauts to the peoples of the world (cf. chap. 1.3). The results of the *dominium terrae*, the instruction to take dominion of the earth and its inhabitants, are today problematic. Also problematic, furthermore, is the fact that all life is said to come from a single God, whom at least the later interpreters understood as male.

But the significance of the tag line in Gen 2:4a should not be ignored: "These are the generations (*toledot*) of the heavens and the earth." It shows that, in con-

---

possibility that the text is an exposition of Heliopolitan cosmogony, as J. Assmann (1997a) suggests, but an exposition that promotes Ptah nonetheless.

76. Egyptian $sy\beta$, 'heart', represents knowledge, understanding, insight, and reason.

77. Egyptian hw means 'tongue', 'utterance', or 'command'.

ception and birth, P recognized the principle of life par excellence, from which all life comes and on which all life is based.

Time		Word	Effect/Act	Approval/Blessing/ Naming
1:1–2	pre-world	Superscription	Heaven and earth	
1:3–5 Living space Light	1st day	"Let there be light."	1. Separation of light and darkness	The light was good. Naming of day and night.
1:6–8 Living space Heaven	2nd day	"Let there be a dome."	2. Creation of the firmament	Naming of the sky.
1:9–13 Living space Land and plants	3rd day	"Let the water be gathered. . . ."	3. Origin of earth and sea	Naming of earth and sea; it was good.
		"Let the earth bring forth vegetation."	4. Growth of plants	It was good.
1:14–19 Chronometry	4th day	"Let there be lights."	5. Sun, moon, stars	It was good.
1:20–23 Living things	5th day	"Let the water teem."	6. Aquatic animals, birds	It was good. God blessed them.
1:24–2:1 Living things	6th day	"Let the earth bring forth."	7. Land animals	It was good.
		"Let us make man."	8. Humanity	God blessed them.
Allotment of living space and food				Result: Everything was good.
2:2–3 Rest	7th day		Cessation of all work by Sabbath rest	God blessed the seventh day and made it holy.
2:4a	Summary	Tag line	These are the *toledot* of heaven and earth	

The creation narrative begins with a *description of the pre-world* in 1:1–2 (for the following, cf. Bauks 1997a). The highly philosophical construct of a *creatio ex nihilo*, which appears in the historical record for the first time only in the second century A.D., arising in the early church, cannot be found in the Hebrew Bible. It developed from the ontological perspective that had its origins in the time of Aristotle and leads, in regard to understanding Genesis 1 and other passages, to error. Another verse frequently mentioned in this context, 2 Macc 7:28, is no support for a *creatio ex nihilo* of a Hellenistic character. It is a negative formulation: God did not make the heavens and the earth out of existing things (*hoti ouk ex onton epoiesen auta ho theos*). "Existing things," however, must here in good biblical tradition refer to 'created things' as opposed to a presumptive "pre-world." The Vulgate, to be sure, translates this formula in an ontological fashion: *quia ex nihilo fecit illa Deus* 'for out of nothing God created them'.[78]

Nor, according to Michaela Bauks, is the idea of preexisting primeval material correct. *Bara'* is a highly theological verb of creation, not a concept derived from craftsmanship.[79] Wherever it is used, it recognizes God's deed as unparalleled

---

78. For *creatio ex nihilo*, see Bauks 1997a: esp. pp. 15–30; for the history of research on 2 Macc 7:28 and Wis 11:17, Bauks 1997a: esp. pp. 20f. nn. 41f.

79. See W. H. Schmidt, *"br',"* THAT 1.336–39; J. Bergman, *"br',"* ThWAT 1.796–77. God creates (*bara'*) in the realm of nature and history. The use of the word focuses on the context of protological creation (the theology of history [Deutero-Isaiah]) and eschatological creation (Trito-Isaiah). Alongside the cosmological use of the word, there is also a soteriological use relating to Jacob, Israel, Jerusalem, and Zion. In pre-Exilic texts and Job, *bara'* does not occur.

creation. The agent is God, and there is never a mention of material from which God creates. Nor, then, in Genesis 1 can the intent of what follows be to mention materials.

Bauks proposes a translation of Gen 1:1–3 that recognizes the first verse as a sort of epigrammatic motto:

> In the beginning (it was), when God created the heavens and the earth (= the whole world). (Gen 1:1)

Syntactically, it is an anacoluthon, just like Gen 2:4a. Examination of the opening lines of Mesopotamian and Egyptian creation traditions shows that this is a traditional stylistic device. The meaning of bere'šit is not 'in the beginning' but 'at the time when. . .'. It is thus not a matter of a temporally ordered series of divine acts of creation; instead, the description of the pre-world logically precedes the report about creation. Gen 1:2 serves as a description of the contrast with the real creation narrative and is meant to emphasize God's sovereignty, in that the pre-world is depicted as void and negative, in the sense of presenting a comprehensive hostility to life.[80] A phase that is a frequent theme in ancient Near Eastern descriptions of the pre-world, the preexistence of a divine power that contains within itself all not-yet-differentiated creative potential, is skipped over in Genesis 1. The narrative begins with the "primeval state of affairs," in which the moment of transition to the origin of the world is already suggested and which contains one element of the world that is coming into being (water). The presence of flood and water in this primeval state of affairs indicates Egyptian influence, since the annual Nile inundation and reemergence of the land from the water was from time immemorial a cosmogonic experience for the people of Egypt.

When God created the universe, the habitable world did not yet exist; nor did light, nor dry land:

> In the beginning (it was), when God created the heavens and the earth.
> The earth was still Tohuwabohu, primeval darkness lay over primeval flood.
> God-powerful storm rattled over the waters. (Gen 1:1–2)

Parallels to the biblical portrait of the pre-world are found, for example, in pyramid and coffin texts with "not as yet" formulations, which describe the nonexistence of the habitable world, and in temple foundation inscriptions (Eridu). They are also found in texts in which properties of the pre-world are stated positively (as in the Monument of the Memphite Theology, with reference to the Ogdoad of Hermopolis) but which also note the lack of firmly structured order and distinction and express the need for differentiation and boundaries.

While the "pre-world" was and is hostile to life (darkness, water) despite the potential existing in it, the ordered series of acts by the creator god give rise to living space. Separation plays a large role in the process, as in the civilizations of Israel's neighbors (cf. fig. 96).[81] According to Genesis 1, the basic requirements of life are light, sky, dry land, plants, and the regulation of time (acts 1–5 in the table on Effect/Act). The living space that thus came about is prepared for animals and humans, which are now created (acts 6–8). The earth, including the animals, is entrusted to the humans for cultivation; a variety of vegetarian food is provided for both humans and animals (1:29f.). Genesis 1 is differentiated from the Monument of the Memphite Theology and other texts of Israel's neighbors by a surprisingly strong emphasis on time as a work of creation and

---

80. Ancient Near Eastern rulers similarly depicted the time before their accession to power as chaotic.
81. For the separation of heaven and earth in ancient creation myths, see already Staudacher 1946.

as the framework of creation. The rhythm of night and day originates in two acts, at the very beginning with the creation of light (1:4f.) and later on with the installation of the heavenly bodies to keep track of time (1:14–19). Timelessness (darkness) is a characteristic of the pre-world (1:2), while the establishment of the festivals, of the alternation of day and night, and of years is interpreted as an act of God and—with reference to the following verse—understood as the basis for the life of all creatures.

The Priestly creation account in Genesis 1 differs from most other biblical references to creation in its focus on the model of "creation by word or command" (cf. chap. V.4 above, pp. 106ff.). Klaus Koch (2000: esp. pp. 28–33) stresses that the word of God alone causes the act of creation and its result, so that the phrase "God made/created" that follows in several cases is not a secondary event but rather has the sense "and so (in this way) God made/created"; it contains the result of the preceding "God said." The previously preferred division of the Priestly creation report into an older report of a deed and a later report of a word has long since been shown by Odil Hannes Steck (1975) to be unnecessary. The alternation between speaking and doing or happening is instead to be understood as the distinction between plans/orders and execution or realization, a concept that is important to P in general[82] and is intended to emphasize that whatever happens is intentional and deliberate. This system, which recalls the *Monument of the Memphite Theology*, and the seven-day system are typical for P. The creation of the world is told as the initial event in perpetuity and as a divine model for history. The idea of a *creatio continua* (a 'perpetual creation'), unlike in the Jerusalem religious tradition, is nowhere to be found in Genesis 1. The world is presented as a kind of perfect machine, a well-regulated clockwork, an idea that especially in times of uncertainty would have had a calming and comforting effect.

Additionally, in its attempt to name every important area, the text must have been influenced by *Listenwissenschaft*. An indication of this genre is the phrase "according to its kind" appended to each category. A scientific and simultaneously demythologizing trait is betrayed when *yammim*, 'the sea', is called "basin of water" and when the sun and moon, forgoing their names *šemeš* and *yareaḥ*, 'sun (god)' and 'moon (god)', are prosaically defined as "lights."[83]

Genesis 1 has strong poetic traits as well. The lists of specific or "all phenomena," the onomastica, are easily transformed into hymns (Psalm 148, Daniel 3). This transformation has taken place in Genesis 1, because God is predicated as creator of all kinds. Even the introductory clause "In the beginning, when God created the heavens and the earth" is a variant transposed for the sake of narrative of a poetic predication—namely, the epithet *qoneʾ šamayim waʾareṣ* 'creator of heaven and earth'.[84] The many merisms (heaven and earth, light and darkness, day and night, aquatic animals and birds, etc.) and the refrain-like repetitions of "God saw that it was good"[85] are reminiscent of hymns. This latter sentence must not be misunderstood as a formula of divine approbation. When it is God—and not just anyone—who states that something is good, it is similar to a superlative (cf. Gen 10:9, Jonah 3:3).[86]

---

82. Compare Gen 6:13ff. with 6:22; 17:9f. with 21:4; Exod 12:28; but also Judg 6:36–40.
83. See chap. III.7 above, pp. 56ff.
84. Gen 14:19, 22; Ps 115:15, 121:2, 124:8, etc.
85. See Ps 8:2ff., 104:24, 136:1ff., 139:14.
86. M. Klopfenstein (1998) rightly stresses that God's vision does not examine, but elects in an acquiring way, as in Genesis 22, where God ultimately accepts a ram as substitute offering.

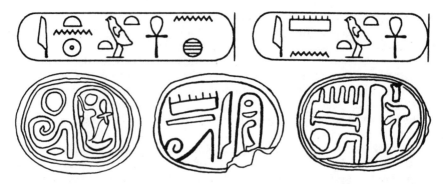

139–140 Cartouches with the royal names *Ytn twt ʿnh* (left) and *Ymn twt ʿnh* (right). Into his second regnal year, the son of Akhenaton, the twelfth ruler of the 18th Dynasty (1332–1323 B.C.), was called Tut-ankh-aton 'living likeness of Aton'; after giving up the residence in Amarna and the failure of the monotheistic revolution of Akhenaton, he was named Tut-ankh-amun 'living likeness of Amun'. The god's name is written first. (von Beckerath 1984: 232, nos. E1 and E3)

141–143 Scarabs from Tell el-Fara South (Drawing by Ulrike Zurkinden after Petrie 1930 pl. 12: 169) and from Tell el-Ajjul from the time of Amenophis III (1390–1353 B.C.) (Keel 1997a: 219 no. 344), and of the 19th Dynasty from Lachish (1292–1190 B.C.). On the scarab from Tell el-Farah South, the throne name of Amenophis III, *Nb-mꜣꜥt-rꜥ*, is accompanied in a cartouche by the epithet *tyt Rꜥ* 'likeness of Re'. On the example from Tell el-Ajjul, at the right, the throne name of Amenophis III is again engraved in a cartouche, next to it is his royal name, and at the far right the epithet *tyt Ymn* 'image of Amun'. On the scarab from Lachish appears, alongside the goddess Maat, the epithet *tyt Ymn Rꜥ* 'image of Amun-Re'. (Drawing by Ulrike Zurkinden after Tufnell et al. 1958: pl. 39–40 no. 372)

2.3.1. Man and Woman in the Image of God

The Christian shorthand "image of God" (Latin *imago Dei*) for the theological description of humanity originates in Gen 1:26f. Astonishingly, the Hebrew Bible does not take up Gen 1:26f. (cf. 5:2, 9:6); only Sir 17:3 makes reference to this verse (cf. also Letter of Jacobus 3:9). Being in the image of God was never central to the anthropology of the Talmudic and post-Talmudic Jewish tradition, but Christian theology can largely be regarded as a speculative imago-Dei theology, with a variety of strands of interpretation.[87] Old Testament scholarship has only occasionally ventured to escape from the pressure of dogmatic speculation.[88]

The idea fundamentally laid down in Gen 1:26f., that humans—and only humans, in contradistinction to the animals—are in the image of God must go back to Egyptian influence, where especially the ruler appears as the "image of god" (Ockinga 1984, Lorton 1993). The throne names and epithets of Egyptian kings perpetuate their "image of god-ness." Tutankhamun (*twt-ʿnh-Ymn*) means 'living likeness of Amun'. New Kingdom seal amulets (scarabs) have been found

Figs. 139–140

---

87. The Augustinian-Thomistic tradition developed the grace-full similarity of humanity to God, which enables mankind to relate to its creator within a covenant offered by God. The mystical tradition elaborated by Gregory of Nyssa, for instance, stresses the basis of the co-creative freedom of humanity, which inhabits the image of their character but also calls on similarity with God, thus providing a means of the indwelling of the Spirit of God. This tradition has been taken up in modern times, under the influence of Karl Marx, with respect to society, emphasizing human dominion over creation (Gen 1:28). According to this view, humans realize themselves as the image of God only when they succeed in setting aside alienated relations of production. Being in the image of God is offered to this day as a principal theological argument for the incontestable worth of humanity and basic human rights.

88. Humbert 1940; Stamm 1956, 1959; Groß 1993; Mathys 1998; Koch 2000; C. Dohmen, "Eben-bild," *NBL* 1 (1990): 453ff.

in Palestine/Israel as well; on them, the names of Thutmoses III and other pharaohs are provided with the annotation *tyt Rˁ*, *tyt Ymn*, or *tyt Ymn Rˁ* 'image of Amun/Re'.[89] But being in the image of God could also refer to human creatures in general. According to the *Instruction of Merikare*, which says of humanity that "They are his images, who came from his body" (*snnw.f pw prn m ḥˁw.f*), the relationship rests on the fact that humanity came from the body of the god.[90] The connection is clear, and it is clearly suggested in the Egyptian language.[91] The Egyptian numeral *snw* 'two' (Heb. *šanah*, *šenim*) is at the core of a broad semantic field to which, among others, the following concepts belong: *snwy* 'the two' (dual); *šnnw* 'second, companion, associate, colleague'; *šn* 'brother', *šnt* 'sister'; *šny* 'resemble, copy, imitate', *šnn* 'statue, image, icon', *šnnt* 'similarity'. "Similarity" is accordingly based on physical relationship and actually refers to a sort of "second edition" or "duplicate."

Additional background for "being in the likeness of God" in Gen 1:26f. is the belief, throughout the Orient, in the potent corporealization that an image represents. The statue or stela of an Egyptian, Assyrian, or Babylonian king, set up in a distant province of the empire, represents the king's power on the spot. The image of the god in the temple represents the presence of the god. The Hebrew word 'image' (*ṣelem*) points linguistically to the Mesopotamian cultural area. It can designate sculptures, statues, or reliefs, but primarily emphasizes their representative function.[92] The Akkadian word *ṣalmu* has a similar semantic spectrum. Like the Egyptian rulers, the Assyrian kings of the ninth to seventh centuries B.C. were often designated "image" (*ṣalmu*) of a god (Koch 2000: 19): it is clear that the notion of "being in the image of God" clearly developed from the conception of a representative image and was then probably abstracted. The word "likeness/form" (*demut*), which supplements *ṣelem* in 1:26f., designates the similar connection of the copy with the model. It alludes to the content of the image, the inner similarity in nature between human and God.[93]

It is often suggested, on the basis of the evidence that has been mentioned, that according to Gen 1:26 humanity is a sort of living image of God, in which divinity is active and which represents divinity on earth.[94] On the one hand, this can be considered a democratization of ancient Near Eastern thought patterns, since in Egypt and Southwest Asia it was preeminently kings who counted as representative images of divinity on earth. On the other hand, it is generally recognized that the writers of Genesis 1 understood the nuances of the highly complex theology of (religious) images of their environment (Berlejung 1998, Dick 1999). There is no question that the role of humanity within creation in Gen 1:28 and Ps 8:7 is presented as a dominion established and legitimated by God, and to this extent people (like kings) therefore represent God's power on earth. How closely this representative function in Gen 1:26f. was coupled with the idea of an actual image remains a question. Actual kingship, in any case, does not enter into the picture as a God-willed creation—quite differently from,

Figs. 141–143

Text 8

---

89. With reference to Genesis 1, it is noteworthy that on the stamp seals from Palestine/Israel Amun is represented approximately four times more frequently by his (secret) name than by an image (Keel 1995: §§582–85, Keel and Uehlinger 2001: 124–28.

90. Egyptian anthropology considers people "eye beings" that come from the eye of the creator, who as the sun god bestows on eyes, from the light of his eye, the ability to see. See J. Assmann, "Schöpfung," *LÄ* 5 (1984): 677–90, esp. 681.

91. Hannig 1995: 713ff., Hannig and Vomberg 1999: 349.

92. For this and what follows, see already Schroer 1987a: 322–32.

93. Both words are used in the Aramaic version of a bilingual statue inscription of the 9th century B.C. from Tell el-Fekheriye (Sikani, North Syria), while the Assyrian version has only *ṣalmu* (see Abou Assaf, Bordreuil, and Millard 1982: 64; Schroer and Staubli 2001: 3 with fig. 1). For a summary of the discussion, see Schroer 1987a: 322–32.

94. Most recently, Löning and Zenger 1997: 146f., Koch 2000: 13–24.

for example, the Persian texts from the time of Darius I, in which Ahuramazda is praised as creator of heaven and earth, of people and their welfare, and last but not least of the king and his rule:

> A great god is Ahuramazda, who created this earth, who created that heaven, who created man, who created fortune for man, who made Darius king.[95]

The biblical passages suggest that "being in the image of God" expresses a familiar relationship. In Ps 8:6, this relationship is not connected with the "image" but formulated as a comparison of the natures of "man" and "God"—with the plain result that the human species stands only a little lower than a divine being (*'elohim*). But the closest biblical parallel to Gen 1:26f. is in Gen 5:3. The similarity between Adam and Seth, father and son, is expressed in the same Hebrew words as in Gen 1:26, such that the son perpetuates the father after the latter's death. Representative dominion is not in view in Gen 5:3; association with an image of God is not implied. Thus, we can conclude for 1:26 that being in the image of God was related not only to notions of representation and dominion but especially expresses the highest possible relationship between God and man (cf. Ps 8:6, Sir 17:3). Humans are like God as children are like parents. This similarity explicitly holds for both sexes. Both the male and the female of the species emerge from a free creative will; they do not exist because of chance, misfortune, or as punishment.[96]

The Priestly understanding of "being in the image of God" connected not only with the far-reaching, albeit limited, authority of man. After the Flood, the earthling's similarity with God became the foundation of a taboo, from that point onward, on the shedding of human blood. Human life is sacrosanct. Whoever violates it—man or beast—is punished with death by God, the ultimate guarantor of the law:

> For your own lifeblood too, I will demand an accounting: from every animal I will demand it, and from man in regard to his fellow man I will demand an accounting for human life.

> If anyone sheds the blood of man,
>   by man shall his blood be shed;
> For in the image of God
>   has man been made. (Gen 9:5f.)

2.3.2. "Make the earth arable"

> God blessed them and told them: "Be fruitful and multiply; fill the earth and make it arable (*kibbešuha*). Have dominion (*uredu*) over the fish of the sea, the birds of the air, and all the living things that move on the earth." (Gen 1:28)

Fig. 144
The words used in Gen 1:28, *kibbeš* 'set the foot on' and *radah* 'tread, tread down, control', denote rulership, including the use of force if necessary (cf. fig. 1 above). Apologetic exegesis that attempts to exclude the aspect of force (Lohfink 1974; Koch 1983, 2000: 38–47) and foregrounds only the responsibility is not helpful in a careful examination of the reception history of this delegation

---

95. Old Persian inscription on a statue of Darius I (reigned 522–486 B.C.) found at Susa. Translation by U. Kaplony-Heckel, *TUAT* I 609–13, esp. 613.
96. The differentiation of the sexes ("male and female he created them"), which is emphasized and formulated in a completely programmatic manner, like the vegetarianism of the first human couple, could be an echo of Genesis 2.

144 Neo-Assyrian cylinder seal (750–700 B.C.). A hero with a scimitar rests his foot on a reclining calf and defends it against an attacking lion (cf. 1 Sam 17:34ff.). "To hold beneath the feet" or "tread" does not necessarily mean brutal, let alone arbitrary, subjection but can also imply the protection of the weak from the strong. (Keel 1997a: 59, fig. 60).

of authority.[97] Klaus Koch (2000: 38–47) has in detail teased out the entire semantic range of *kibbeš* and *radah* in the context of the related contemporary civilizations. The understanding of the intent of the pasage, with regard to both subduing the earth and dominion over the animals, is conditioned first and foremost by the necessity of creating and shaping living space for mankind once and for all. The land must be made arable and, in the process, living space for (wild) animals will—necessarily—be regulated. This implies neither a reckless despoliation of the earth nor an unlimited license to kill.

On the one hand, the context of the passage must be considered: humanity is in direct contact with the land animals, who are created, in fact, on the same, sixth, day of creation. The delegation of authority applies to aquatic animals, birds, and wild animals, but domesticated cattle (*behemah*) do not appear as an object of the exercise of power. The delegation of authority is followed in 1:29 by the regulation of food: God assigns to both man and (wild) animals as well as birds vegetarian food: fruits and seeds to the one, grasses and vegetables to the other. Dominion over the (wild) animals thus by no means includes a right to slaughter. Only to post-Flood man was meat given for food (Gen 9:3), and only then did all creatures begin to fear mankind (Gen 9:2; cf. Sir 17:1–4). Animal and human settle very close together in Genesis 1's order of creation.

On the other hand, the cultural context must receive primary consideration. Humans were in the minority, compared to animals; the animal world represented a real danger. Dominion and control, which created living space for humans, was more highly valued in this situation. Interestingly, God's instruction to be fruitful in Gen 1:22 extends only to the animals in the water and the air. No similar instruction to be fruitful is given to the land animals in 1:25, but in 1:28 it is given to the humans. On dry land, there is competition for living space between wild animals and humans. At any time, civilized land can revert to wilderness (Exod 23:29, Lev 26:22, Deut 7:22, 2 Kgs 17:25); the city, even Zion itself, can be transformed into ruins and wasteland,[98] and the wild animals **Fig. 145** swiftly will reclaim the territory from which they had been driven with so much

---

97. On the reception history of Gen 1:28, see Krolzik 1989. On dominion over the animals, see Uehlinger 1991b, Janowski 1993a, Rüterswörden 1993, Weippert 1998.

98. For Isa 13:19–22, 34:11–15; Jer 50:39f.; Mic 3:12; Zeph 2:12–15, see further chap. VII.2 below, pp. 156ff.

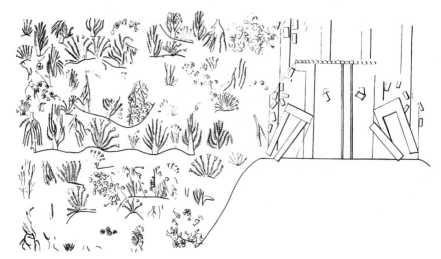

145 Limestone relief from the temple of Ramses II at Luxor (1301–1234 B.C.). The destruction of a city leads to "laying waste" in the literal sense. Weeds immediately take possession of the ruins. Where civilization was, chaos has entered. (Keel 1997a: 107, fig. 141)

effort. The state of civilization to which dominion over the animals belongs (Ps 8:7–9, Sir 17:4) can be understood to fit the situation in the sixth century B.C. In the minds of the exiles in Babylon, at least, wild animals had seized control of the Promised Land. According to a proverbial saying, these wild animals had turned it into a land that devours men (Ezek 36:3, 13f.).[99] P places this negative assessment in the mouth of the wicked scouts in the time of Moses (Num 13:32). This is the historical context in which mankind's task was described as to rule over the animals. Quite unmistakably, Psalm 8 also deduces from man's special place in God's created world that he should and shall have dominion over the animal world:

> What is man that you should be mindful of him;
>   or the son of man that you should care for him?
> You have made him little less than the angels,
>   and crowned him with glory and honor.
> You have given him rule over the works of your hands,
>   putting all things under his feet.
> All sheep and oxen,
>   yes, and the beasts of the field,
> The birds of the air, the fishes of the sea,
>   and whatever swims the paths of the seas. (Ps 8:5–9)

But that this dominion, according to Genesis 1, is not meant to be ruthless exploitation is already shown by the fact that primal man is conceived as vegetarian. After the Flood, when the use of living things is granted to humanity (Gen 9:3), even then the condition that animal's blood must never be consumed is stipulated (9:4). The alteration in power relations, moreover, is subtly equalized in that the animals that were affected by the Flood—namely, the birds and now explicitly the land animals—receive a new instruction to be fruitful.

---

99. Cf. the similar reference to thickets that consume men in 2 Sam 18:8 (on which, see Keel 1993b).

The seven-day system can also be understood in terms of the Exile situation. As long as Israel dwelt in its own land, the Sabbath—originally a Full Moon festival—was a foregone conclusion. In Babylon, the observance of a weekly day of rest "for YHWH" became foundational for the identity of the Exile community. Genesis 1 presents the Sabbath as part of the order of creation, not as something contingent and accidental. This order of creation was discovered by Israel when it depended on the direct action of God in the wilderness (the gift of quail and manna in Exodus 16P) and established that God does not work on the seventh day.[100] According to Gen 2:3, the life-enhancing blessing of God lay on the Sabbath—as on living beings. Moreover, God "hallows" (*wayeqaddeš*) the seventh day; that is, the Sabbath is removed from the profaneness of work days and everyday impurity through specific rituals and practices that mark it as a special time.

3. The Regulation of Bodies of Water: Hydrocosmological Creation Texts

The notion that creation came about through a struggle between divine powers (cf. chap. V.3, pp. 97ff.) and that its preservation required the damming up of life-threatening bodies of water was widespread in the ancient Near East. For this genre, too, the earliest attestation is in Sumerian literature, in the *Lugal* ('king') Myth. The text comes from Nippur, and though it was written down shortly be- **Text 12** fore 2000 B.C., it probably is considerably older. The hero of the myth is Ninurta, son of the storm-god and the lord of the earth, Enlil. Like his father, Ninurta is a warlike god but also a god of fertility. He made the earth habitable when he dammed up the destructive ice-cold water of the mountains, circled the land of Sumer with a great wall, and gathered the good water into the Tigris. The devastation that originally comes from the mountainous land is staged by a demon. This Asakku-demon embodies the mountain peoples who, among others, again and again invade the fruitful plain, wreaking devastation. This earliest literary form of the myth of the battle with chaos already has clear historical connotations (van Dijk 1983: 27).

What Genesis 1 is for the biblical tradition, *Enuma elish* is for the Babylonian-Assyrian.[101] This great work, which must have originated in Babylon and was recited every year on the fourth day of the Babylonian New Year festival, was recorded on seven clay tablets.[102] Some date it to the time of Hammurapi, when Babylon first flourished (ca. 1750 B.C.), but linguistic indications place it closer to ca. 1250 B.C. The hero of the work is the principal god of Babylon, Marduk. In the Assyrian copies, most of which come from the first half of the first millennium B.C., the god Ashur appears in place of Marduk. Not only its extent but also the fact that many older traditions, including Sumerian genealogies of gods, the *Lugal* Myth, an Old Canaanite myth of Baal and Yam, the creation of man from the Old Babylonian *Atra-hasis*, the building of the tower of Babel, etc., are reflected in its final edited form reinforce the importance of *Enuma elish*.

Principal topics contained in the work are the battle against Apsû, the fresh-water ocean, and Tiamat, the salt sea, as well as the achievement of kingship by Marduk. Like the *Lugal* Myth preceding it, *Enuma elish* is also easy to interpret

---

100. On Genesis 1 in the context of the Priestly primeval history, see Zenger 1983, Löning and Zenger 1997: 135–77; on the Sabbath, see the excursus in chap. III.7 above, pp. 56ff.

101. Translation by W. G. Lambert, *TUAT* III 565–602; see Smith 1876; Gunkel 2006; Labat 1935, 1959; Jacobsen 1976: 165–91.

102. On tablet VI, which reports the creation of man, see chap. VI.1 above, pp. 108ff.

historically, because it is the poem that promotes the exceptional character of Babylon (or Assur). A dramatic climax (Jacobsen 1976: 167–91) tells how the kingdom arose out of victory over mortal danger (cf. Saul and the Philistine threat). Stable kingship signifies the surmounting of cosmic crises.

Individual elements of the narrative of the cosmic battle in *Enuma elish*, such as the battle against Tiamat (see McBeath 1999), must come from Syria's traditions. The motif of the battle against chaos is found in iconography from this region as early as 2000 B.C. (cf. figs. 106–107 above). In the texts from Ugarit (Ras Shamra) dating to the thirteenth century B.C. the overthrow of chaos is portrayed in the myth of Baal's wrestling with the sea god Yam or Nahar (KTU 1.2 IV). Whether this myth should be understood cosmogonically, seasonally, or even politically has long been a matter of discussion.[103] But such distinctions do not apply to myth in general or to the myth of the battle against chaos in particular. The struggle on behalf of fertile land against any sort of body of water, the battle between cosmos and chaos, lives forever. Political powers always are making the claim that they are battling chaos.[104]

As many studies have shown,[105] the Bablyonian-Syrian myth of the battle against chaos is taken up many times in the First Testament and used in a wide variety of contexts. In two popular laments and prayers, Psalm 74 (the Temple, a cosmos-constructing place, is threatened) and Psalm 89 (the Davidic dynasty, a cosmos-constructing historical power, is threatened), in the face of the enemy YHWH is reminded that he did indeed act in creation in primeval times in order to defeat chaos in a mighty battle (Ps 74:12–17, 89:10–15).[106] Why does he now give chaos free rein? Why does he not show the "dragon" and his "kingdom of evil" to the door once again? A historicizing interpretation of the myth has been favored in this context. It was not a dragon, but historical powers, that threatened the Temple and the Davidic dynasty. But the historicizing of myth always incorporates the mythicizing of history. The dragon is Assur or Babylon, and Assur or Babylon is a dragon. The historical phenomenon turns into a mythical kingdom of absolute evil, which determines the ultimate limits of meaning. It is reported of the Assyrian or Babylonian opponents in Ps 74:8 that they said in their hearts: "Let us destroy them." But how does the praying community know what the opponents are thinking? It is intimated that they do not seek destruction. Assur and Babylon were expanding, aggressive powers, but their political goals were limited—and "man proposes, God disposes," as Isaiah, Jeremiah, and Ezekiel well knew. But in Ps 74:8 a desire for unlimited destruction is attributed to them. They are made into monsters, Leviathan and Rahab. The God who overcame these monsters at the beginning of creation is mobilized against them:

> You stirred up the sea by your might;
> you smashed the heads of the dragons in the waters.
> You crushed the heads of Leviathan,
> and made food of him for the dolphins.
> You released the springs and torrents;
> you brought dry land out of the primeval waters.

---

103. See M. Dietrich and O. Loretz, *TUAT* III, esp. 1094, 1129–34.

104. In contrast to the Baal–Yam myth, the Baal–Mot myth is explicitly cyclic-seasonal, and in this context Mot, the god of drought and death, is not cosmos-threatening in the same way that Yam is; and the victory over Mot is not cosmos-constructing in the same way that the victory over Yam is. The palace-building of Baal, which is both the foundation and declaration of his kingship, thus follows the victory over Yam and not the cyclically repeated victories over Mot (Grønbaeck 1985).

105. Gunkel 2006; Keel 1997); Wakeman 1973; Kubina 1979: 43–76; Day 1985; Grønbaeck 1985; Kloos 1986; Uehlinger 1991a, 1995; on the significance of the battle against chaos in the book of Job, see Fuchs 1993 and chap. VIII below.

106. For Psalm 74, see Keel 1991: 104–12, Weber 2000; for Psalm 89, see Veijola 1982; additional bibliography in Hossfeld and Zenger 2000: 355, 576f.

Yours is the day, and yours the night;
    you fashioned the moon and the sun.
You fixed all the limits of the land;
    summer and winter you made. (Ps 74:13–17)

In other contexts, the motif of battle against chaos is used to reinterpret the flood that YHWH used to assist a group of oppressed foreign workers through the marshes on the edge of the eastern Nile Delta (Exod 14:5) into a cosmos-constructing event. The liberation of Israel from the alien land and alienation is a victory over chaos, as YHWH is reminded in the Psalms (Norin 1977):

The waters saw you, O God;
    the waters saw you and shuddered;
    the very depths were troubled.
The clouds poured down water;
    the skies gave forth their voice;
    your arrows also spread abroad.
Your thunder resounded in the whirlwind;
    your lightning illumined the world;
    the earth quivered and quaked.
Through the sea was your way,
    and your path through the deep waters,
    though your footsteps were not seen. (Ps 77:17–21)[107]

In the time of Deutero-Isaiah, God is summoned:

Awake, awake, put on strength,
    O arm of YHWH!
Awake as in the days of old,
    in ages long ago!
Was it not you who crushed Rahab,
    you who pierced the dragon?
Was it not you who dried up the sea,
    the waters of the great deep,
Who made the depths of the sea into a way
    for the redeemed to pass over? (Isa 51:9f.; cf. 43:6)

Here, too, Israel recognizes not just a historicizing of myth, but—inextricably interwoven—a mythicization of history (Kloos 1986: 160–90). The accidental, contingent event of a successful escape becomes an "earthshaking" phenomenon.

Traces of the motif of the battle against chaos can be found in many Old Testament passages.[108] The motif of the battle against chaos has an especially interesting, adapted use in the Aramaic portion of Daniel, which is strongly marked by historical and political considerations (Keel 2000). The structure of Daniel 2–7 is chiastic—that is, chapters 2 and 7 (teachings of four kingdoms), 3 and 6 (fiery furnace, den of lions), and 4 and 5 (king open/closed to conversion) correspond to each other. In chapter 7, the four beasts that emerge from the roiling sea recall the monster that Tiamat sent from the sea (*Enuma elish* I 125–46). The sea in the book of Daniel is always a danger-harboring protagonist (cf. Ps 104:25f.), but here it no longer stands for "chaos" pure and simple. In Dan 7:2f., sea and wind are part of a God-created world that harbors the potential for life in addition to mortal threats.[109] The political powers that emerge from the sea are not *a priori* "chaos powers." In a perfectly Greek perspective, *the* man (biblically

---

107. Cf. Ps 66:6, 114, 136:13. On Psalm 77, see Weber 1995 and additional bibliography in Hossfeld and Zenger 2000: 401.
108. See Gen 1:2, 6f.; 9:14; Ps 104:6–8, 26; and in detail chap. V.3 above, pp. 97ff.
109. Cf. the proximity of *gwḥ* to birth events in Job 38:8, Ps 22:10, and the stormy revival by *rwḥ* in Ezek 37:9.

"Son of Man") is unconditionally set opposite the animals.[110] Because the humanizing of the monster's rule is already the main theme of the core chapters 4–5 (Dan 4:25–31, 5:17–23), so also is the God-enacted dissolution of the rule of the four beasts that emerge from the roiling sea by the Son of Man the main theme of chapter 7.

Without the mythological background of the motif of the battle against chaos, several New Testament texts are incomprehensible (e.g., Luke 21:25; Rev 13:3, 21:1). In particular, the great and central chapter 12 of the Revelation of St. John the Divine reaches back to ancient ideas.[111] The endangerment of the woman in childbirth and of her child by the seven-headed dragon can only be averted by a battle between the angel and the chaos-monster. Its cosmic power is broken completely, but thenceforth it spreads limited confusion across the earth. The dragon simply embodies evil, which for the author of Revelation exists especially in a historical form, the blasphemous Roman Empire, which is dangerous to the nascent church. Only belief in a "heavenly" victory over the dragon gives the community the strength to endure the tribulation of the end-times. By comparison with the Old Testament tradition of battles against dragons, the intensification of apocalyptic mythology consists in confidence that the "gentle" conquest of chaos and the maintenance of the existing creation is now shattered. The dragon cannot be banished to its lair, as is described so frequently in the First Testament. It must instead be destroyed so that new creation can arise.

Excursus:
Functions of Biblical Discourse on Creation
and Sustenance of the World as a Whole

Memory of the primordial creation of the world and the divine power that guaranteed the preservation of the order of creation was awakened in Israel in joy or sorrow or uncertainty but not, as is often suggested, in regard to or in the context of history and experiences of deliverance. In the surrounding civilizations, creation was invoked in times of rejoicing and trouble as well as in critical moments of transition. The course of the sun in the sky caused the people of Egypt to sing the praise of the solicitous creator god again and again. In ancient Mesopotamia, the creation myths were told even in order to counter a serious toothache with the certainty that such unnerving experiences have a regular place in the divine plan for the world. *Enuma elish* was used at the turn of the year. Births, New Year festivals, and other dangerous and critical transitional times called for creation narratives, which in a wider or narrower sense established and explained the existing world and its regular patterns, insofar as they refer back to their origins (etiology). Christians' liturgical reading of Genesis 1 at the Easter vigil is reminiscent of this tradition.

1. Israelites recall the creation and sustenance of the world in hymnic rejoicing (Psalm 104), and sometimes after being rescued (1 Sam 2:8, Jdt 16:14). But it is not only people who rejoice in the work of the creator God—every creature participates.[112]

2. Remembrance of the fundamental regulation of the world is awash with the assurance that God supports the prevailing of right and justice. Praise of creation and

---

110. The biblical tradition stresses the relationship between man and animal; the Greek defines humanity as non-animality (de Pury 1993a, 1993b; Keel 2000: esp. 18–29).
111. On Revelation 12, see Gollinger 1971, van Henten 1994, Paul 2000, Kalms 2001; for the motif of the woman in childbirth, see Sutter Rehmann 1995.
112. Job 38:7; Ps 19:1–4, 65:14; cf. the introduction to chap. III, pp. 22ff.

praise of God's law are closely intertwined in Psalm 19 (but cf. also Ps 8:3, 75:3f.). Yнwн's justice can be compared with the works of creation:

Your justice is like the mountains of God;
your judgments, like the mighty deep. (Ps 36:7)

God's wrath against injustice that befalls the one who worships him throws all creation into turmoil (Ps 18:7–16). The raging of the elements of chaos, the crisis, is interpreted as the beginning of salvation.

3. Israelites recall creation in times of personal trial, which represent the inbreaking of cosmic chaos into individual experience (Jonah 2:3–7). The book of Job places the speeches of God, with their portrait of a solicitous creator god who gives some rein to the powers of chaos without abandoning control over them, literarily into the story of a man on whom the most profound sorrow falls and who therefore calls into question the basic regulation of the world.[113] Memory of the creation of the world and the acceptance of responsibility for its regulation as well as God's intervention as the one who battles chaos are intended to draw Job out of the constriction of his sorrowful experience into the breadth of all creation. Here, too, the connection between righteousness and the fundamental regulation of the world is central. Not so common is a declaration of confidence such as that of the one who is deathly ill in Ps 102:25–29, who holds even heaven and earth to be an ephemeral work of creation but takes all the more comfort in the exalted greatness and trustworthiness of one who can manage to alter such works like a change of clothes:

Of old you established the earth,
and the heavens are the work of your hands.
They shall perish, but you remain
though all of them grow old like a garment.
Like clothing you change them, and they are changed,
but you are the same, and your years have no end. (Ps 102:26–28)

4. In addition to individual trial, communal trial also calls for reassurance concerning cosmic regulation. Just as the oppressed pray to Yнwн to recall that he had created them,[114] to bind him in an oath, so Israel reminds its God in the midst of catastrophe that he was able then and is able here and now to strike off dragons' heads and create a well-regulated cosmos.[115]

5. The history of Israel, the Exodus, fundamental regulations like the Sabbath, and also covenants and promises are frequently exalted in the creation structures. In the book of Jeremiah, confidence in the historical power of the creator is attributed to Yнwн as a self-obligation:

Thus says Yнwн,
He who gives the sun to light the day,
moon and stars to light the night;
Who stirs up the sea till its waves roar,
whose name is Yнwн of hosts:
If ever these natural laws give way
in spite of me, says Yнwн,
Then shall the race of Israel cease
as a nation before me forever.
Thus says Yнwн:
If the heavens on high can be measured,
or the foundations below the earth be sounded,

---

113. For Job, cf. further chap. VIII below.
114. See the excursus to chap. VI.1, pp. 122ff.
115. Cf. the recollection of the victory over Rahab in Isa 51:9f. and also in the context of Yнwн's obligation to the Davidic dynasty in Ps 89:11. For Psalm 74, see Keel 1991: 104–11.

> Then will I cast off the whole race of Israel
> because of all they have done, says Yʜᴡʜ. (Jer 31:35–37; cf. 32:17, 33:2)

Yʜᴡʜ would thus no sooner break the covenant with the line of David than he could break the covenant with day and night (Jer 33:19–26).

With the Exile, Israel came into closer and sharper contact with the profane world than ever before. Their own history became one history among many. In order to display it as a constitutive history, as a consequence of events that transcended the limited space and limited time of Israel in Egypt and Palestine, cosmic, permanent, and superior defining characteristics were bestowed on it. The history of Israel was made into a cosmic event and the God of Israel the sole God. God proves his superiority over other gods and through his role as creator justifies his claim to dominion encompassing the entire world (Jer 10:12ff.).[116]

In Deutero-Isaiah, the God who operates in history, liberating Israel from Egypt and from the Exile, presents himself again and again as creator of the heavens and the entire inhabited earth.[117] The mythicization of history and the historicization of myth arise from the idea of a God who as the creator of the world is also the mover and sovereign of history.

---

116. See especially H. Weippert 1981: 65–90.
117. See the introductory formulas in Isa 42:5; 44:24; 45:7, 18; 48:13; 51:13.

VII. The Destruction of Creation as a Result of Human Failure

The collapse of individual lands or of the entire creation into chaos was not an abstract notion for people in the ancient Near East but a persistent existential concern. The *creatio prima* gave hope for a *creatio continua* but did not grant certainty. Behind many creation texts and the rituals—mostly unknown to us—in which they were embedded stands anxiety over the threatening collapse (Auffahrt 1991). Just as the fate of the world could be depicted in various images, this descent into chaos could also be described in many ways. Central is the fearsome specter of annihilation by inundation and the onset of an inhospitable water wasteland. Devastation by desiccation could also be imagined, and sometimes both are even found side by side:

> What a horror has Babylon become among nations:
>> against Babylon the sea rises,
>> she is overwhelmed by the roaring waves!
> Her cities have become a desert,
>> parched and arid land
> Where no man lives,
>> and no one passes through. (Jer 51:41b–43)

Neither sort of wasteland, in the thought of that time, had anything "natural" about it; both are embodiments of "anti-creation" and "anti-nature." It was a painful and not all that rare experience for areas of human civilization that had been laboriously carved out of wilderness to turn back into wasteland at any time. Something sinister and demonic clung to the ruins of demolished cities, and the cities were quickly reconquered by plants (cf. fig. 145 above) and wild animals (Isa 13:19–22, 34:11–15; Jer 50:39f.; Mic 3:12; Zeph 2:12–15).

The Egyptian tradition has a more-or-less natural process of aging and death for the divine powers and the world that is guaranteed and regulated by them.[1] The ultimate timespan of the gods, which sets a limit on their eternal renewal, was rarely discussed, out of fear of conjuring something up. But in the Coffin Texts[2] Atum prophesies to the personnel in the sun's bark that after a million years creation will collapse back into chaos, in which only he and Osiris will remain in undifferentiated space and time. In the Book of the Dead (utterance 175:35–40) it is even clearer:

> But I [Atum] shall destroy all that I have created,
> This world will become primeval ocean (Nun),
> Primeval flood as at its beginning.
> It is I who will remain, together with Osiris,
> after I have transformed myself into another serpent,
> which men do not know and gods do not see.

The Egyptian "Book of the Cow of Heaven" tells in its first part (lines 1–100)[3] of an uprising of men against the aging sun god Re, who thereupon sends Hathor

---

1. For what follows, see Hornung 1996: 143–69, esp. pp. 151–65.
2. Spell 1130 of the Book of Two Ways, CT (Coffin Texts) VII 467f. [de Buck's ed., cf. Lichtheim 1.131]
3. Complete translation with commentary in Hornung 1997: 37–50; cf. the translation by H. Sternberg el-Hotabi, *TUAT* III 1021–27. [Lichtheim 2.198f.]

to kill mankind. At the last moment, Re takes pity on all creation and stops the goddess from her act of annihilation by plying her with alcohol to knock her out. But this text does not mention a great flood as the means of destruction.

1. The Great Flood: Crisis and Alteration of the Relationship between God(s) and Man

As early as the *Atra-hasis* poem, the Near Eastern tradition includes a Flood tradition (unknown in Egypt) as a counterpart to the creation of man.[4] Both in the older version, formerly called "Yahwist," and in the later, Priestly, version of the biblical Flood narrative in Genesis 5–9, the Flood is the counterpart, the alternative, to creation.[5] Nothing about the Flood is narrated for the sake of sensationalism but in order to assure the audience that there had been another salvation and that with this episode the last truly great crisis between gods and men was overcome. In the *Sumerian Flood Story*, the Old Babylonian *Atra-hasis* poem, and the *Gilgamesh* Epic, the conflict is described as a power struggle within the world of the gods, especially between the warlike Enlil, the wise Enki, and Nintu (the Lady of Birth) or Ishtar, and is resolved on this level.[6] A mighty flood wipes out life on earth. Nevertheless, in the end, the gods who advocate the perpetuation of humankind prevail. The mother goddess is seized with compassion for the children of men whom she herself had created and regretfully laments their annihilation:

> The goddess [Ishtar] cried out like a woman in childbirth,
> Belet-ili wailed, whose voice is so sweet:
> . . . "It is I who give birth, these people are mine!
> And now, like fish, they fill the ocean!" (XI 116f., 122f.) [trans. George 1999: 92]

The survival of a protagonist (Ziusudra, Atra-khasis, Utnapishtim) who secretly receives instructions to build an ark ultimately ensures the survival of the human race. In the *Gilgamesh* Epic, Ishtar swears at the end of the Flood that she will not forget what has happened—that is, that such a thing will never happen again:

> "O gods, let these great beads in this necklace of mine
>   make me remember these days, and never forget them!
> All the gods shall come to the incense,
>   but to the incense let Enlil not come,
> because he lacked counsel and brought on the Deluge,
>   and delivered my people into destruction." (XI 164–69) [trans. George 1999: 94]

The older of the two biblical versions of the Flood recasts the contrary opinions and emotions of different gods into a change of heart of the one God YHWH. The sympathy and regret of a mother goddess now seize YHWH, who had intended destruction (Keel 1989a; Baumgart 1999: esp. 419–559). The tradition-history thus takes on a psychological and ultimately theological cast: God alters himself in the course of history from one who would contemplate total annihilation to restore righteousness to one who has compassion for all living things and therefore enters into a unilateral vow (despite the baseness of man) never again under any circumstances to destroy all creation. The solemn self-avowal of YHWH upon

---

4. Cf. chap. VI.1 above, pp. 108ff. On Flood traditions among various peoples, see Usener 1899.
5. Zenger 1983; Löning and Zenger 1997: esp. 160–73; Baumgart 1999.
6. *Sumerian Flood Story* III 15 (translation by W. H. P. Römer, *TUAT* III 453); *Atra-hasis* III/III 32–38 (translation by W. von Soden, *TUAT* III 640); *Gilgamesh* XI 115–25 (translation by K. Hecker, *TUAT* III 732f.).

Noah's sweet sacrifice after the flood in Gen 8:20–22 recalls Ishtar's oath in the *Gilgamesh* Epic. The book of Deutero-Isaiah also is aware of an oath of YHWH's in the days of Noah:

> For a brief moment I abandoned you,
>   but with great tenderness I will take you back.
> In an outburst of wrath, for a moment
>   I hid my face from you;
> But with enduring love I take pity on you,
> ˙ says YHWH, your redeemer.
> This is for me like the days of Noah,
>   when I swore that the waters of Noah
>   should never again deluge the earth;
> So I have sworn not to be angry with you,
>   or to rebuke you.
> Though the mountains leave their place
>   and the hills be shaken,
> My love shall never leave you
>   nor my covenant of peace be shaken,
>   says YHWH, who has mercy on you. (Isa 54:7–10)

In the Priestly version of the Flood, composed about the same time (Gen 9:11, 13ff.), on the other hand, it is a matter of a *berit*, a covenant of God with man, land animals, and birds. God's covenant with Noah[7] and his descendants, including the post-Flood generation, in the Priestly mind renews basic confidence in the regulation of creation that had been breached. Although, or precisely because, animals after the Flood live under drastically more difficult circumstances than before (Gen 9:1–3), the Noachic covenant is struck explicitly with the animals as well (Janowski 1999); that is, the inviolable "never again" holds for them as well as for man:[8]

> God said to Noah and to his sons with him: "See, I am now establishing my covenant with you and your descendants after you and with every living creature that was with you: all the birds, and the various tame and wild animals that were with you and came out of the ark. I will establish my covenant with you, that never again shall all bodily creatures be destroyed by the waters of a flood; there shall not be another flood to devastate the earth." (Gen 9:8–11)

As already in the *Atra-hasis* poem, in the biblical Flood narrative the catastrophe is unleashed by human misbehavior. In *Atra-hasis*, Enlil takes umbrage especially at the unchecked multiplication of humanity and the resulting din. In the older biblical version (Gen 6:1–8), the ultimate cause is a transgression of the sons of God with the daughters of men (6:1–4)—the nature of the wrong is not completely understandable, and the direct cause is a vaguely defined general evil of humankind (6:5–8).[9] In the later version, the cause is the depravity and violence of humanity (Gen 6:11f.). In the Akkadian version of the flood story, found in the XIth tablet of the *Gilgamesh* Epic, in contrast to *Atra-hasis*, the question of guilt does not come up. It simply says (XI 14):

> The great gods decided to send down the Deluge. [trans. George 1999: 88]

7. See especially Rendtorff 1991: 108–12.
8. In YHWH's renewed covenant with Israel, the animals are also specifically mentioned (Hos 2:18, Ezek 34:25f.), but rather as significant entities to be kept in check (cf. Lev 26:6). The book of Jonah (3:3b–10) takes the domesticated animals fully into account in the fate of Nineveh.
9. Dexinger 1966; on Gen 6:1–4 see most recently, with detailed information on the content and bibliography of previous research, Zimmermann and Zimmermann 1999.

2. The Result of Human Guilt:
Destruction of the Habitable Living Space

The question of guilt remains similarly vague in another tradition of destruction, which actually deals not with the downfall of all creation but only with the destruction of a region: the destruction of Sodom (and Gomorrah) by the sungod in Genesis 19 (Keel 1979; cf. chap. III.7 above, pp. 56ff.). The reason for the devastation for which Sodom and Gomorrah became proverbial[10] is given in Genesis 19 as the violence of the inhabitants and their disregard for the sacred law of hospitality. On the other hand, Ezekiel says:

> And look at the guilt of your sister Sodom: she and her daughters were proud, sated with food, complacent in their prosperity, and they gave no help to the poor and needy. (Ezek 16:49)

Isaiah in turn stresses the impenitence of the people of Sodom. Obviously, the most disparate sins could be denounced as typical of Sodom (Keel and Küchler 1982: esp. 249f.), but all sources are unanimous that it was human failure that brought about the catastrophe. Ps 107:33f. too contains the idea of the devastation of a fertile region as divine punishment for the evil of its inhabitants.

In eschatological and apocalyptic texts, the destruction of miscreant cities and kingdoms, even the entire earth, is painted in broad strokes,[11] and creation can also appear as an ally, as a weapon of God, in the battle against the godlessness of its inhabitants (Wis 5:17–19). Annihilation in the sense of complete collapse into a "pre-world" condition obviously could not be conceived, although far-reaching devastation by earthquake, water, or lack of water (cf. Jer 4:27) could be invoked, even to the extent of convulsions of the cosmic regulation of light and darkness and the courses of the heavenly bodies:

> Lo, the day of YHWH comes
> cruel, with wrath and burning anger;
> To lay waste the land
> and destroy the sinners within it!
> The stars and constellations of the heavens
> send forth no light;
> The sun is dark when it rises,
> and the light of the moon does not shine. (Isa 13:9f.; cf. Isaiah 24)

Even for the city of Sodom, however, the possibility of averting its fate could be imagined (Ezek 16:53–58). God in his sovereignty as creator can devastate and annihilate (Ps 107:33f.; Isa 42:15, 50:2f.), yet revive the wasteland anew on each occasion (Ps 107:35–38). In the book of Deutero-Isaiah, YHWH proves himself master of history through acts of revivification of the desertified regions of Judah and Jerusalem (Isa 41:18f., 43:19f.).[12]

The connection between human guilt and the destruction of creation, on the one hand, and extirpation of the sinners or forgiveness of guilt and healing of creation, on the other, is encountered in some biblical passages. It is part of the greater cause-and-effect relationship, which presupposes the concomitant dependency of harmony between society and cosmos. This fusion of social and cosmic organization is more firmly established in Egyptian thought than in

---

10. The Southern Kingdom prophets, for example, referred to this event (Isa 1:7, 9f.; 13:9–22; Jer 50:40; Ezek 16:46–56; Amos 4:11; cf. Revelation 11).

11. Jer 4:23–28 (Judah); Isaiah 13–14 (Babylon), 24 (earth), 34 (Edom); Zephaniah 1 (earth).

12. This corresponds to the exiles' idea in Ezek 36:3, 13f. that the land has fallen to the wild animals. On the contemporary background, place of redaction, and intended audience of Deutero-Isaiah, see now Baltzer 1999: esp. 49–60.

the Israelite picture of the world (Assmann 1990), but genuine biblical reminiscences of it can be found.[13] According to Hosea, the evil of Israel corrupted creation, so that in a reabsorption of the works of creation the living things of the earth disappear:

> False swearing, lying, murder, stealing, adultery!
>   in their lawlessness, bloodshed follows bloodshed.
> Therefore the land mourns,
>   and everything that dwells in it languishes:
> The beasts of the field,
>   the birds of the air,
>   and even the fish of the sea perish. (Hos 4:2f.; cf. Jer 4:19–31, 12:4)

In Jer 5:24f. and Ps 107:33 also, the destruction of the order of creation is explained by human guilt. The only serious threat to creation appears, in the biblical perspective, to be represented by man (Ebach 1989: 120). Through evil, greed, and the corruption of the law, Israel breaks up God's blessing and draws the curse of drought or war down upon itself.[14] Successful, healthy creation will endure no evil or sin, so that the creation hymn in Psalm 104 ends with the desire that sinners disappear from the earth (cf. Job 38:12–15). Correspondingly, through the restoration of justice in the time of salvation, a new order of creation will be constituted that is no longer controlled by the pressure to plunder and to kill and in which every living thing, as before the Flood, will live on plants alone:

> Then the wolf shall be a guest of the lamb,
>   and the leopard shall lie down with the kid;
> The calf and the young lion shall browse together,
>   with a little child to lead them.
> The cow and the bear shall be neighbors,
>   together their young shall rest;
>   the lion shall eat hay like the ox.
> The baby shall play by the cobra's den,
>   and the child lay his hand on the adder's lair.
> There shall be no harm or ruin on all my holy mountain. (Isa 11:6–9a; cf. 65:25)

Rosemary Radford Ruether (1994: 16f., 73–96) has rightly raised the question as to whether it is not only that one could imagine the end of the world, which especially underlies the apocalyptic scenarios having their origins in Jewish and Christian thought, that has aided and abetted problematic developments in modern times. The Old Testament discourse of the destruction of creation and its becoming new again originally served mostly as a warning: just as a good anti-war film shows only the physical and moral destruction that results from war, so the Old Testament exhibits only the consequences of guilt. In apocalyptic, destruction is discussed in the context of a cosmic battle between good and evil, which is described so dramatically, in the style of a simplistic anti-war film, that its power induces not only fear but fascination.[15] Little today is left of the original concern for the fragility of creation and its permanent endangerment or of knowledge of the dependency of the order of creation on the ethical behavior

---

13. Cf. chap. IV above. The curse of Adad that is frequently mentioned in Babylonian and Assyrian texts also has climatic and ecological consequences (Grätz 1998: 7–90).

14. That human guilt brings a curse upon the land and its population is also the theme of Athenian tragedy. Sophocles' *Oedipus Rex* opens with a procession of supplicants and the description of a dramatic drought and sterility throughout the land. Remorselessly, the cause of the evil, the inadvertent incest of the king with his mother, is disclosed (cf., similarly, Pharaoh's inadvertent adultery as the cause of the plagues on the royal house in Gen 12:10–20).

15. Consider the seven trumpets of Rev 8:6–11:19.

of humanity. What remains today is the prospect of a God who destroys in order to exact revenge or to restore justice and the fatalistic or even fascinated expectation of an absolute catastrophe. Since from the beginning of the twentieth century humankind has effectively been capable of completely destroying the earth and all life on it, it is important to be careful in our use of the biblical discourse on the end of the world and the last judgment.

As a result, the biblical story of the Flood deserves special attention. People will not really change because of it (Gen 8:21)—in their sinfulness, they will continue to disrupt creation; but God will not permit its destruction:

> As long as the earth lasts,
>   seedtime and harvest,
>   cold and heat,
> Summer and winter,
>   and day and night
>   shall not cease. (Gen 8:22; cf. Hos 2:21f., Ezek 34:26f.)

VIII. The Threatening World as the Work of God in God's Speeches (Job 38–41)

Psalms such as 74 and 89, which vividly portray YHWH's capabilities as the opponent of chaos (cf. chaps. V.3, pp. 97ff., and VI.3, pp. 147ff.), at the same time contain serious accusations against God: that he had acquiesced in devastation and annihilation (of the Temple in Psalm 74, of the Davidic dynasty in Psalm 89) and so had not fulfilled his obligation as sustainer of the cosmos.

Central to the book of Job as well is God's success or lack thereof in his role as battler of chaos (Fuchs 1993). Here, however, the problem of the disrupted order is considered not in prayer form but in a greatly extended disputation (Job 3–42:6).[1] There is a long tradition of this sort of disputation, with rebukes of gods, in Egypt and Mesopotamia.[2] But the book of Job in various respects represents something new and unique.

Job's friends represent an untroubled world in which the good do well and the bad do poorly. Job's contradictory experiences (Job 1–2) prompt him to react to this picture of a perfectly ordered, transparent world with sharp attacks on the creator God (Job 3 and 9, esp. 9:24).[3] The friends, who at first reply compassionately, quickly evade this troublesome business by explaining that Job himself is responsible for his plight. More and more, Job turns away from them and directly toward God. In chapter 31, he rejects every reproach of his friends with a conditional curse upon himself of a sort that was greatly feared in ancient Israel (made explicit elsewhere only in Ps 7:4–6, 137:6).[4] This oath of purification is legally binding (cf. Exod 22:9f.), and Job must therefore be perceived as guiltless. The friends' solution has not been validated. Job challenges God to explain himself (31:35–40).

The author of the book has God answer the challenge of chapter 31 directly[5] in chapters 38ff. and contrasts the God of the friends—that is, the God of legitimate correspondence between cause and effect, but also the God of Job the accuser, a heavenly tyrant—with a God who pays heed to the breadth of his entire creation, free of human control. This last portion of the book clearly refers to the two positions in the disputation (Mettinger 1997).

---

1. For the book of Job, see Dhorme 1926, Fohrer 1989, Müller 1978, and for the mythical element, especially the battle with chaos, very comprehensively, Fuchs 1993; on God's speeches, see Keel 1978 (the 1993 French translation includes an ecological epilogue) and Ritter-Müller 2000; strictly limited to literary-critical problems are Kubina 1979 and van Oorschot 1987. For an attempt at a social-historical interpretation of Job, see Crüsemann 1980. The approach to the interpretation of God's speeches put forward here is also the basis of the feminist exegesis of the book of Job by Maier and Schroer 2012. For the liberation-theology reading, see most recently B. Weber 1999.
2. For this literature, see now the comprehensive treatment by Sitzler (1995). In Egypt after the fall of the Old Kingdom at the end of the third millennium B.C., the first writings describing the collapse of all order appear (*The Complaints of Khakheperre-sonb, The Eloquent Peasant, The Dispute between a Man and his Ba, The Admonitions of Ipuwer* [see Lichtheim 1.145–84]). In the Akkadian work *ludlul bel nemeqi* from the twelfth century B.C., a sick man desperately voices his distress and declares his piety, until he is saved by Marduk (translation by W. von Soden, *TUAT* III 110–35). In the *Babylonian Theodicy* (800–750 B.C.), a righteous sufferer bewails his misfortune to his friend and protests his innocence in several stanzas (translation by W. von Soden, *TUAT* III 143–57).
3. Cf. already the Babylonian Talmud (*Baba bathra* 16a = Goldschmidt 1933: 983). For Job 9–10, see now Egger-Wenzel 1998.
4. Usually it reads only "May God do thus and so to you if/if not . . ." (1 Sam 3:17, 2 Sam 3:35).
5. The *wayya'an* in 38:1 corresponds to the *ya'aneni* in 31:35 as a literal reference. The speeches of Elihu in Job 32–37 are an interpolation.

The argument between creator and creation confers a new prominence on a third party, namely wisdom (*ḥokmah*), the plan (*'eṣah*) of creation (cf. Job 38:2, 36f.; 42:3). In fact, those who pray Psalm 104 are already persuaded that YHWH had done the works of creation "in wisdom" (104:24), but in the psalm it was a rather incidental if not insignificant adverbial specification of the acts of God. In the Priestly report of creation in Genesis 1, to be sure, wisdom or plan is not explicitly mentioned, but the deliberate sequence of words and acts of creation insinuates that some sort of intelligence underlies the acts of God. The idea that history is based on a divine plan was introduced into theology by Isaiah.[6] Deutero-Isaiah then explicitly applies the idea to creation as well (Isa 40:12–14, 46:10f.; cf. Ps 33:11). That God created heaven and earth in wisdom and insight proves, according to Jer 10:12, his superiority to idols and images of gods.

In the book of Job, the plan of the world is mentioned only to be disputed. The central portion of the book, the poetry, begins with an unsparing inquisition into the entire order of creation (Job 3). Since the direct, positive relationship to the creator has been shattered, it can only be restored by proof of divine wisdom and insight (*binah*) in creation (cf. 38:36f., 39:26). God himself assumes the burden of proof when he gives Job the answer he had so stiff-neckedly demanded (31:35), immediately and unsparingly rebuking him harshly as a slanderer of the world's plan:

Then YHWH addressed Job out of the storm and said:
Who is this that obscures divine plans (*'eṣah*)
with words of ignorance? (Job 38:1f.)

In the first part of God's first speech (Job 38:1–38), the world is now celebrated as a cosmos that is indeed perpetually wrestling with chaos but is controlled by wisdom (vv. 36f.), whose full extent at any rate is concealed from man, and man therefore should be circumspect in his judgment.

In the second part of God's first speech (38:39–39:30), some ten animals are presented, at times in pairs: lion and raven, ibex and stag, wild ass (onager) and wild bull, ostrich and steed, hawk and vulture. What are we to make of these animals? Exegetes usually limit themselves to listing rudimentary zoological information about the individual animals. But the question of the function of these animals in context is important. By what criteria have they been gathered together, and what do they all have in common?

Two animals were already named in the first part of God's first speech: ibis and cock (38:36). They are introduced as bearers of special wisdom. On this basis, attempts have been made to see the ten following animals as additional bearers of divine wisdom. But of the ostrich hen it is explicitly said:

For God has withheld wisdom from her
and has given her no share in understanding. (Job 39:17)

Another objection is that the four animals praised in Prov 30:24–28 as particularly wise—ant, rock badger, locust, and lizard—do not appear in Job 39. So the point is not wisdom. The lion at the beginning of the list might suggest that the point is particularly dangerous animals. But then we would expect a mention of panther and bear, since they are named together with the lion in Hos 13:7f., or panther, bear, wolf, and serpent, which appear in company with the lion in Isa 11:6–8. But these animals are not listed, and several of the animals that are— ibex, stag, and ostrich—can hardly be considered dangerous.

---

6. See H. P. Stähli, "*y'ṣ*," *THAT* I, esp. 752f.

146 Ceremonial shield from the tomb of Tutankhamun (ca. 1325 B.C.). Beneath the protecting wings of the vulture goddess Nekhbet, Pharaoh Tutankhamun slays a lion. The
king is in full regalia; his behavior is intrinsic to the royal dominion of the land legitimated by the gods. The meaning of the lion hunt is very close to that of war against
human enemies: a chest from the same king's tomb, on which the king is represented
identically in a war chariot in two scenes, shows on one side a lion hunt and on the other
war against the Nubians (Keel 1996a: pl. XVI). (Keel 1974b: 185, fig. 49)

The common denominator of the list of animals in Job 39 is neither wisdom
nor dangerousness. A further insight is gained, instead, by the depictions of the
hunt by ancient Near Eastern rulers, which show that the preferred quarry in
the royal hunt are the animals named in Job 39. One of the essential duties of
these rulers was to keep human and animal enemies of their people far away,
to defend the cosmos of their own inhabited world from in-pressing chaos. War
and the hunt were in this sense closely parallel. The lion in particular, which
could threaten both man and domesticated animals, was the primary target of
the royal hunt. But the wild bull and onager, too, which could inflict serious **Fig. 146**
damage on the fields, turn up again and again in this context. Ibex, stag, and **Figs.**
ostrich were hunted by the king not because they represented a threat to human **147–148**
civilization but because they embodied realms that appeared to ancient Near
Eastern man as ungovernable if not inaccessible. North Syrian kings and princes
especially loved to show that they controlled these all but inaccessible regions.
They are hardly depicted realistically: they use light war chariots, suitable only

147 Carved ivory casket from a tomb in Enkomi, Cyprus (ca. 1200 B.C.). A hunting scene is shown in great detail on this casket, whose top may have been used as a game board. In an open chariot drawn by galloping horses and driven by a charioteer stands a bearded prince. He aims his bow and arrow at a wild bull and a variety of caprids that either have already been hit or are stampeding in panic. A hunting dog accompanies the chariot at a dead run. A warrior identified as a representative of the Sea Peoples assists the princely hunter. In a tassled loincloth and typical helmet, with hatchet in hand, he runs as an escort behind the chariot. The figure at the left in the tumult of the fray may represent the same man. He thrusts an arrow through a lion attempting to pounce on him. The front of the ivory casket shows two wild bulls lying down. (Drawing by Inés Haselbach after Orthmann 1975: no. 472)

148 Part of a relief from the outer wall of the temple of Ramses III in Medinet Habu (1204–1173 B.C.). The pharaoh from his war chariot with bow and arrow attacks herds of wild asses and antelopes that flee in panic. That they cannot save their lives is shown by the animals that are already downed and hit by arrows beneath and in front of the team. (Nelson 1932: pl. 116)

Figs. 149–150 for level ground, to chase ibexes and stags, which inhabit mountain forests and the rocky mountains. The steed, lion, and hawk represent an additional group of animals in Job 39. The horse was regarded quite unfavorably in Israel: as a costly, prestige weapon, it was typical of the great empires of the ancient Near East (Egypt, Assyria) whoe aggression Judah and Israel regularly had to suffer. **Fig. 151** The description of the steed in Job 39:20–25 appears to be positive at first glance, but when the parallel with the ostrich is considered and in light of Jer 8:6, the horse's unbridled charge takes on a questionable character. Finally, ravens and **Fig. 152** vultures are traditionally associated with corpses on battlefields, which represent the transition from the realm ruled by man to that of the animals.

149 Middle Assyrian cylinder seal (14th–11th centuries B.C.). Standing in a war chariot, an Assyrian prince shoots ibexes in the mountains. The image is rather unrealistic, since the light vehicle presumably was unsuitable for traveling in the mountains, but it does strikingly express the idea of the heroic hunt on inhospitable ground. (Keel 1978: 72, fig. 2)

150 Late Hittite relief from Malatya (10th–9th centuries B.C.). The ideal hunt, with horse and chariot, had especially high prestige for centuries. Here the archer aims at a fleeing stag while the driver controls the vehicle. (Keel 1978: 75, fig. 6)

151 Glazed vessel from the Northwest Palace of Assurbanipal II in Nineveh (883–859 B.C.). A mounted hunter drives ostriches to a river. (Mallowan 1966: fig. 61)

Various forms of counter-human worlds are the topic not only of hunt imagery but also of another motif that unlike the hunt is limited to Southwest Asia: the motif of "lord of the animals" or "lord of the wilderness."[7] A numinous **Fig. 153**

7. Cf. Keel 1978: esp. 86–125; B. Lang, "Tiere, Herr der," *NBL* 3 (2001): 858–71. Lang's article (p. 869) extends the concept "lord of the animals" so far with respect to biblical passages that every image of a god, other than those connected with history and the Exodus, can be included: "In the Bible two

152 Lower part of an Egyptian slate palette (ca. 3000 B.C.). The battle scene on the front has given this palette its name. Naked men with curly hair and beard lie on the ground, one of them fettered. A massively maned lion falls on an unarmed man lying on his back. The others, who appear to be already dead, are swarmed by vultures and ravens, which are about to snatch the limbs and heads of the dead. The disproportionately large lion stands for the king who defeats the enemy. That this is a war scene is also clarified by the scenes of prisoners on the upper part of the palette, which is fragmentary and not shown here. (Keel 1997a: 104, fig. 135)

153 Middle Assyrian cylinder seal (14th–11th centuries B.C.). A naked hero brandishes his spear at a stag, a rearing lion, and an ostrich. The three animals represent the threatening world directly hostile to man. (Keel 1978: 74, fig. 3)

154 Scaraboid from Phoenicia (6th/5th centuries B.C.). A bearded hero with a conical head-covering and a pleated skirt firmly grasps the foreleg of a prancing lion on each side of him. The lions' mouths are open. (Drawing by Ulrike Zurkinden after Keel-Leu 1991: no. 106)

155 Neo-Assyrian cylinder seal (8th century B.C.). A hero with six braids holds a stag under each arm and a gazelle in each hand by the hind legs as well. This mastery of the wilderness serves the culture and the "secure world," which is symbolized by the adjacent scene. Two scorpion-men support the (winged) sky, with the head of the sun-god and his servants, law and justice (cf. figs. 50–51). Beneath the plane of the sky is the symbol of the ordered world, a stylized tree or a standard in a sort of shrine. The sacredness of this secure cosmic order is emphasized by the flanking priests or worshipers. (Keel 1978: 89, fig. 13)

156 Middle Assyrian cylinder seal (14th–11th century B.C.). A "lord of the animals," whose face and upper body are shown frontally, takes two wild goats or ibexes (one on each side) by the horns, thus holding them back from the stylized world trees on which they are rearing to feed on the leaves. The world of the animals, the wilderness, is in this way held in check for the benefit of the ordered world. (Keel 1978: 91, fig. 16)

157 Neo-Assyrian cylinder seal (9th–7th centuries B.C.). A four-winged "lord of the animals" holds two rearing wild bulls by a foreleg. The wings highlight the potency of the divine hero. He also appears to be holding the wild animals back from a stylized palm tree, which would symbolize the ordered world. (Keel 1978: 98, fig. 28)
158 Cylinder seal impression from northeastern Syria (14th–13th centuries B.C.). A "lord of the animals" subdues an onager and an ibex or wild billy goat. The date palm appears as a major plant deserving protection. (Keel 1993c: 79, fig. 25a)
159 Neo-Assyrian cylinder seal (ca. 650 B.C.). A "lord of the animals" skillfully grips two ostriches by the neck, dominating them. Above are astral symbols (Pleiades, star, crescent moon) and a pomegranate. (Keel-Leu and Teissier 2004: no. 223)

Figs. 154–160 form, sometimes with two faces, frequently provided with wings, stands between two lions, stags, ibexes, wild bulls, onagers, ostriches, birds of prey, or composite beings, subduing them with his bare hands. In the Persian period,

images of God stand side by side, older and more recent in terms of history of religion. The older image portrays God as the "lord of the animals"; in the later, he is the God of the people Israel." The emphasis on the role of "lord of the animals" is acceptable, but this opposition is far too simplistic. For the religion of the Israelite people, for example, the Canaanite storm-god was very important. He is no "lord of the animals." An objection to the (in any case too simple) relative chronology is that the motif, which is indeed old in terms of history of religion and leaves many traces in the Bible, is in fact quite late in the iconography of Palestine/Israel, first found only in the Early Iron Age (12th–11th centuries B.C.).

160 Neo-Assyrian cylinder seal (8th/7th centuries B.C.). The "lord of the animals" some-times appears on Neo-Assyrian cylinder seals grasping birds of prey by the neck or claws. Here, too, a crescent moon and the Pleiades appear above the scene. (Keel 1978: 111, fig. 50)

161 Scarab from ancient Akko (Tell Fukhar) (1600–1500 B.C.). Already in the middle of the second millennium, the "lord of the caprids" has found a place in the stamp seal art of Palestine. (Keel 1997a: 537, Akko no. 18)
162 Scaraboid from Beth Shemesh (ca. 1000 B.C.). A highly schematized Judahite "lord of the animals" holds two ostriches. (Keel 1978: 103, fig. 36)

the Great King himself is portrayed in this role (cf. fig. 35 above). Often, the numinous figure or the royal hero is restraining the animals from attacking a world tree or some other symbol of the well-regulated world. The animals or composite beings stand for a chaotic world that is dangerous but held in check. The visual arts of Palestine/Israel were especially fond of the variants "lord of the caprids" and "lord of the ostriches."

Figs. 161–162

In Job 39, the iconic "lord of the animals" is translated into literary terms to be applied to YHWH. In contrast to the majority of the visual depictions, how-ever, YHWH does not appear as the lord who keeps the animals in the list within bounds and subdues them but as the one who initiated and protects this world that is felt to be anti-human. This is especially clear for the wild bull and the onager. According to Job 39, these varieties of ox and ass that do not draw the plow or patiently bear people's burdens are not unacceptable mistakes that are to be beaten into submission or even exterminated but major players placed on the scene by God. They might appear from an anthropocentric point of view to be purposeless, even harmful. But from their own point of view and God's, they have just as much right to live as do humans. God defends the right of the wilderness to its own life and thus throws the anthropocentrism of Job and his friends into question. In this world with many environments, it is not easy to

163 Scarab of the 12th Dynasty (before 1750 B.C.). Hippopotamus-hunting is very rarely depicted on Egyptian seal amulets (cf. Keel 1993d). An unusual scarab shows the king with the red crown in a papyrus boat. In his outstretched hand he holds a rope with a barb already stuck in the animal's neck. He holds the harpoon in his upraised right hand. It sticks in the hippo's back, whose chest and belly alone are visible. Its head is turned in a typical pose with jaws agape toward the attacker. Between pharaoh and hippo, a papyrus plant is shown. The heroic battle against the male (red) hippopotamus is an idealistic task assigned to the ruler. That it has mythic aspects is suggested by the size of the beast, which challenges the warlike determination of the pharaoh. (Keel 1993c: 109, fig. 73a)

164 Relief in the temple of Edfu from the time of Ptolemy IX or Alexander I (107–88 B.C.). In Egypt's late period, Horus exclusively took over the battle against the hippopotamus. Here he appears triumphantly before the assembled community of gods on the back of the defeated animal, which embodies the demonic and evil. (Keel 1978: 138, fig. 80)

see how the damage wreaked by the large on the small fits into the big picture. With these images, God calls into question the rigid, strictly anthropocentric order to which Job and his friends are oriented and sketches a much less transparent, much more complex world, in which not every form of suffering and injury is to be regarded as punishment for a transgression (so Job's friends) and which, if this balance is not struck, must be rejected as meaningless (so Job). It opens the world to a mysterious order that is susceptible to ambiguous interpretations; in it, what appears to humans as "wilderness" also has its own lord and its own order.

In God's second speech (40:9–41:26), it is conceded to Job that the world is in part controlled by criminals (40:9–14) and chaotic powers (40:15–41:26). Using the image of the Egyptian Horus, which struggles against hippopotamus (Behe-

165 Vignette from the Book of the Dead papyrus of Kha from the 18th Dynasty (1530–1292 B.C.). In Book of the Dead spell 31, the dangerous crocodile, which would rob the deceased of his magical powers, is banished by magic. The vignette shows him catching the crocodile with a cord and raising his knife against it (cf fig. 4). (Keel 1993c: 121, fig. 83d)
166 Roman-period relief in the temple of Dendera (A.D. 100). Horus appears triumphantly on the back of the conquered crocodile, which embodies the greatest enemy of the gods, the diabolical Seth. Horus takes revenge on Seth for the murder of his father Osiris, who is enthroned at the right of the triumphal scene, protected by the goddesses Isis (left) and Nephthys (right). (Keel 1978: 152, fig. 143)

moth) and crocodile (Leviathan), Yᴴᴡᴴ puts himself forth in the tradition of the battle with chaos as the one who alone struggles against these powers and is in a position to lord it over them (cf. fig. 4 above).[8]

To Job, who called into question the intelligibility of the world order and indicted God as a criminal, God's speeches contrast a world plan in which wild

**Figs.
163–166**

---

8. In apocalyptic, this mastery becomes a matter for the future or the end time, a master that God achieves only in a final victory.

animals and the mythic embodiments of the evil ecosystems—that is, chaos—are accorded a certain degree of freedom. The concept of creation in this wisdom literature is decidedly non-anthropocentric. In Job 38, the creation of man is not even mentioned at first, and in the following chapter Job must learn that the order of creation is not designed solely to satisfy human wants.

If this answer to the desperate question of one who has been tested by suffering appears at first sight cynical or brutal, on second view it is not. Suffering leads to fear and narrows the view. God himself would lead Job out of this tight spot by explaining to him the breadth of creation. The perspective is reversed. Look around you: "you are only a part of the whole" is the message of God's discourse. It is not intended to make Job and his problems small, as is commonly supposed to this day. It takes the sufferer very seriously but relativizes the "problematic" Job, who has slandered the order of creation because of his limited perspective. The message of God's discourse is properly one that unburdens man, because he does not need to be the pivot and cardinal point of the entire world, and so it is actually a message of consolation. Observing God's concern for creation is meant to bring Job courage and confidence. Within the same Israelite wisdom tradition, Jesus of Nazareth spoke of the animal world, which does not operate according to human rules—it does not work, produce, and accomplish—in order to inspire in his disciples more trust in the order of creation and God's solicitude:[9]

> Look at the birds in the sky. They do not sow or reap, they gather nothing into barns; yet your heavenly Father feeds them. Are not you more important than they? Which of you by worrying can add a moment to his life-span? As for clothes, why be concerned? Learn a lesson from the way the wild flowers grow. They do not work; they do not spin. Yet I assure you, not even Solomon in all his splendor was arrayed like one of these. . . . (Matt 6:26–29; parallel Luke 12:24–27)

Job's indictment of a God who permits injustice and suffering has received a new and sharper formulation in and after Auschwitz. God's plan for the world is opaque and threatening (Job 3), and the conclusion that God is a sadist (Job 9:22f.) is all but inescapable. In the face of so devastating a triumph of evil over six million human lives, how can Jewish or even Christian people still find assurance that God—as asserted in God's discourse in the book of Job—in the end holds in check and even wins out over the powers of chaos? Astonishingly, even in this deep darkness, for a few, such as the Jewish writer Margarete Susman, whose book *Job* was published in Zurich in 1946, the miracle of creation nonetheless shines a lone gleam of light from the horizon. God's power is revealed not in history, but in creation. The miracle of life is greater than man can comprehend—and the meaning of life is also beyond the grasp of man.

---

9. See Schroer 1994b: 86f.

IX. The Question of Origins in the Ionian Natural Philosophers

Early on, both biblical and Greek (Hesiod) creation texts placed the creator god or the cosmic gods at the center, but in the sixth century B.C. the question of the plan, the wisdom, the principle (Hebr. *re'šit*; Gk. *archē*) of the world pushes to the foreground. The God who stands above or behind creation loses significance. This new formulation of the question was obviously approached with especially vigorous consistency by the natural philosophers of Ionia,[1] or at least by the natural philosophers of Ionia as represented by Aristotle.[2] The *Whence* of things, their origin and cause, was investigated in the hope of explaining their *Why*.

The circumstances giving rise to this philosophy are to be sought in the position held by the industrious Greek trading cities in southwestern Asia Minor, with their wide-ranging colonization and their relations with the East and Egypt.[3] Greek philosophy arose not in the motherland but in the colonial regions, especially the coast of Asia Minor and lower Italy. Miletus on the southwest coast of Asia Minor, an important transshipment point for wares from the east that were sent by sea to Greece, was a particularly busy colony. Her *periegetes*, who were "scouts" for new markets, explored the Mediterranean coasts, exploring the feasibility of founding new settlements. The first half of the sixth century B.C., when Thales of Miletus lived, saw the replacement of Assyrian by Babylonian rule in the Near East (the destruction of Jerusalem took place in 587/586 B.C.), and in Asia Minor, Medes and Persians contested for sovereignty.

1. Thales of Miletus (ca. 580 B.C.)

Thales, as Diogenes Laertius (I 27) tells us in the second century A.D.:

> ... the beginning of everything was water (*hydōr*) and the cosmos was animated and full of gods.

Already Aristotle (*Met.* A3, 983 b6; *De anima* I 411a.7) knew Thales as the author of this thesis but seems to have misunderstood his watery *archē* ('origin') hylomorphically, as an original substance having material and form. At any rate, he conjectured that Thales as a result supposed that the earth would float on water like wood.[4] But Thales probably taught that the earth came out of the water

---

1. See Diels and Kranz 1951 (a Greek–German edition of Thales and the others with introduction in Mansfeld 1987); Capelle 1953; Gadamer 1968; Röd 1976; Graeser 1981; Kirk, Raven, and Schofield 1983; Keel 2001. On Greek imagery for the world, see Ekschmitt 1989: esp. 9–52.
2. As for sources, only fragments survive, principally within the works of Aristotle and his school, so retrojections of Aristotelian hylomorphism must be watched out for—that is, the opinion that all visible beings are composed of material (*hylē*) and form (*morphē*).
3. Ancient tradition attributed a Phoenician origin to Thales' family (Herodotus I 170). He may have been a *periegete*; but this cannot be proved. It is also said that Thales visited Egypt.
4. Aristotle *Cael.* B13.294a 28. Aristotle rightly objected to the floating-earth theory, noting that the water would in turn have to rest on something (and earth is heavier than water). Cf. Kirk, Raven, and

or—like Egypt from the Nile inundation, the *nun*—emerged (Kirk, Raven, and Schofield 1983: 88–98), without attaching to it the idea that all things are made out of water. Instead, his statement clearly belongs in a broader sense to the genealogical tradition about the origin of the world, like that propounded by Hesiod. Its content differs from all known Greek speculation, however, in that the earth is a prior, not a derived, great thing.[5]

The interpretation of the fragments of Thales in terms of ancient Near Eastern thought contradicts traditional philosophy, which since Antiquity has seen Thales as the father of metaphysics, since it has interpreted his water as original substance, foundation, and impersonal principle (Röd 1976: 33) and has seen numerous philosophical developments nestled there *in nuce*.[6] But it seems much more likely that underlying the water-as-origin idea is the concept of *nun* (Egyptian) or *tehom* (Hebrew; cf. Gen 1:2) or Tiamat and Apsû (Mesopotamian). The Greek Okeanos, whose waves merely encircle the earth rather than the earth resting on the waves, in the *Iliad* (14.200, 246) still is described as the father of the gods, which, mythologically interpreted, could mean that he was regarded as the origin of the world.[7]

Thales may not have sufficiently considered the distinction between Egyptian *nun*, the numinous water of creation, and Egyptian *mu*, ordinary drinking water. His description of the earth that floats on the water must have fallen prey to the same misunderstanding that befalls the modern so-called "ancient Near Eastern worldviews" that ignore the religious component (Keel 1985a, 2001). When biblical passages discuss the founding of the earth over the water (Ps 24:2, 136:6; Deut 33:13), the main focus of attention is on the divine power that brought about these miracles (Job 38:4–7; cf. figs. 81–85 above). Of course, in Thales, the numinous component in the thesis "all things are full of gods,"[8] as opposed to the modern "ancient Near Eastern worldview," is still tangible. Aristotle (*De anima* I 405a.19) reports that Thales considered the soul something capable of motion, so he said that magnets have a soul. This view, given the background of ancient Near Eastern thought—that life, action, and movement on the whole cannot be separated from each other—is also not totally revolutionary, even if it is an example of a universalistic exaggeration of things that are ensouled (such as the "living" magnet, instead of the traditional stars, rivers, and so on). "All is full of gods" in Thales is to be understood along the lines that the whole world, much more than had previously or generally been realized, is living or filled with life. So what is really real about reality is the presence of the divine powers in which it is grounded. Thales' perplexing fragments should then probably be seen as a bridge between myth and philosophy rather than as a victory over mythological concepts. In the ancient Near East, gods and their deeds were spoken of in the same way that people are spoken of (cf. Job). Thales, on the other hand, if the tradition is accurate, speaks of the gods in an entirely different, material way. They become objects that serve the explication of the

---

Schofield 1983: 76–108; and for Thales' imagery in the context of ancient Near Eastern imagery for the world as well as for more detail on what follows, see Keel 2001.

5. Hesiod *Theog.* 116–18.

6. (1) The notion of unity in multitude, (2) the notion of development as the alteration of something permanent, (3) the distinction of being and appearance, and (4) the notion of a prime mover. The fact that metaphysical unity would then have been specified as purely material already in Thales should make us skeptical in general.

7. W. Jaeger (1933: 207) recognized this connection, though his view has not generally been accepted: "It is really not easy to say how the teaching of the Homeric poet, that Okeanos is the origin of all things, differs from that of Thales."

8. Aristotle *De anima* I 411a.7.

world. On this point rests the novelty of philosophy vis-à-vis myth: it inquires expressly into the original and the divine, the deep structure of the world.

2. Anaximander of Miletus (ca. 560 B.C.)

Anaximander was probably born around 610 B.C., so he was only about fifteen years younger than Thales, and he is regarded as his student and possibly a relative. Just as scientific knowledge is ascribed to Thales, such as the explanation of the Nile inundation, so are glorious inventions ascribed to Anaximander, like the gnomon, a kind of sundial, which even Herodotus (II 109) already knew that the Greeks had pinched from the Babylonians. This sentence has been transmitted from Anaximander:

> The principle and element (*stoicheion*) of existing things was the *apeiron* [indefinite *or* infinite]. . . . And the source of coming-to-be for existing things is that into which destruction, too, happens according to necessity (*kata to chreōn*); for they pay penalty (*dikēn*) and retribution (*tisin*) to each other for their injustice according to the assessment of time (*kata tēn tou chronou taxin*)."[9] [trans. Kirk, Raven, and Schofield 1983: 107f.]

Anaximander is further reported to have said of *apeiron* that it is without age, without death, and is unchangeable (i.e., eternal, indestructible, divine) and from it there is no *archē*.[10] The Greek word *apeiron* must have had two connotations, "without (spatial) boundaries" and "without investigation." In Homer, Pindar, Empedocles, and other early Greek writers it is connected with the dark, the sea, the depths of the earth. Inasmuch as Anaximander does not identify the basic principle, the *archē*, with the empirical concept water (*hydōr*), like Thales, he has understood the Orient better than Thales, since the *tehom*, the *nun*, etc., are not simply water but primeval water characterized by dark (Eg. *kek/kuk*), endlessness (Eg. *heh/hehet*), and secrecy (Eg. *amun/amaunet*) (cf. figs. 91–95 above). It is spaceless (slumbering compass points) and timeless (Ouroboros). The return of all that has arisen into the *nun* is also a typically Egyptian concept.[11] But because of the fact that the formative principle is seen as abstract law and no longer as a god (Atum), Anaximander has distanced himself further from the ancient Near East than Thales, since the Near East did not consider myth and science to be different things and did not think of them differently. Necessities, justice, the regulation of time (*to chreōn, dikē, hē taxis tou chronou*) are impersonal principal actors, with some of which (*dikē, adikia*) an ethical impetus resonates. They recall the *moira* of Homeric religion[12] that stands independently alongside Zeus and the *heimarmenē* of the philosophers, especially the Stoics: both of these embodied a fateful, inescapable necessity as a basic principle of the world that stands beside or even above the gods. Not even the gods can liberate man from the fate of their mortality (Homer *Od.* 3.236ff., 24.29). It is not Zeus but the *moira* that decides whether Achilles or Hector will die (Homer *Il.* 22.209ff.). The philosophers of the time were much more interested in the *moira* than in Zeus.[13]

---

9. From Simplicius, *In Phys.* 24.13; Kirk, Raven, and Schofield 1983, esp. 105–17; for Anaximander, see Keel 2001.
10. Hippol. *Haer.* I 6.1; Arist. *Phys.* III 4.203b 6 and 13.
11. Coffin Text spell 1130 = CT (Coffin Texts) VII 467f.; Book of the Dead spell 175; see Hornung 1996: 163f.
12. Cf. *Od.* 3.236–38, *Il.* 22.209ff.
13. The Egyptian god Shai, who is comparable with the *moira*, is known since the 15th century B.C. as a protective good spirit but only later took on greater significance. Cf. I. Grumach-Shirun, "Schai," *LÄ* 5 (1984) 524–26.

3. Heraclitus of Ephesus (ca. 500 B.C.)

For Heraclitus,[14] the permanently operational origin was fire:

> This world-order [the same of all] did none of gods or men make but it always was and is and shall be: an ever-living fire, kindling in measures (*metra*) and going out in measures (*metra*). (frag. 30) [trans. Kirk, Raven, and Schofield 1983: 198]

The gods, represented by Zeus, retreat ever more into the background, but Heraclitus can still say:

> One thing, the only true wise (*hen to sophon mounon*), does not and does consent to be called by the name of Zeus. (frag. 32) [trans. Kirk, Raven, and Schofield 1983: 202]

Since it rules all, it will be called Zeus; but since it is impersonal in nature and man and gods are subordinate to it, it will not be called Zeus.

In Heraclitus, we find further concepts that were already encountered in Anaximander, such as justice and necessity (*dikē, chreōn*).[15] Alongside them he used many other expressions for the power that keeps the world in perpetual change (war, god, *nomos, metra, sophon*):

> It is necessary to know that war is common and right (*dikē*) is strife (*eris*), and that all things happen by strife and necessity (*kata erin kai chreōmena*). (frag. 80) [trans. Kirk, Raven, and Schofield 1983: 193]

> War is the father of all and king of all, and some he shows as gods, others as men; some he makes slaves, others free. (frag. 53) [trans. Kirk, Raven, and Schofield 1983: 193]

> Sun will not overstep his measures (*metra*); otherwise the Erinyes, ministers of Justice, will find him out. (frag. 94) [trans. Kirk, Raven, and Schofield 1983: 201]

The idea of war as father—that is, origin and principle—of all things recalls the ancient Near Eastern ideas of the origin of the world through battle.[16] The warlike, only-wise *logos*, the harmony of opposites, sets the boundary that the sun itself will not overstep. The *metra* of Heraclitus, especially fragment 94, recalls Egyptian ideas of Maat, since Maat likewise embodies a fundamental order that all the gods of the pantheon must obey, even the sun-god, who is regarded as Maat's father.[17]

In place of the gods (Thales) and order and necessity (Anaximander), Heraclitus sets the *logos*:

> Fire's turnings: first sea, and of sea the half is earth, the half "burner" [i.e., lightning or fire] . . . earth is dispersed as sea and is measured so as to form the same proportion (*logos*) as existed before it became earth. (frag. 31) [trans. Kirk, Raven, and Schofield 1983: 198]

> Listening not to me but to the Logos it is wise to agree that all things are one. (frag. 50) [trans. Kirk, Raven, and Schofield 1983: 187]

---

14. For the following, see Keel 2001; Kirk, Raven, and Schofield 1983: 181–212.

15. Heraclitus (frag. 90) also knew the idea of a reciprocal transformation, which Anaximander designated with the phrase *taxis tou chronou*.

16. See chap. III.3 above, pp. 35ff.

17. For Maat, see Assmann 1990. For the connection between Dike, the daughter of Zeus, and Maat, the daughter of the sun-god, see also Tobin 1987. There are quite a few conceptual similarities between Hesiod (*Works* 213–50) and some Old Testament passages on law and justice. Hesiod distinguishes— with respect to concrete justice in a city (cf. Gen 18:20–19:29)—between the observance of *dikē* and the doing of *dikaia* on the one hand and a personified divine *dikē* on the other. To this corresponds Hebrew *ṣedeq* and *ṣedaqah* (e.g., Ps 89:15), which is accomplished by the observance of concrete law (*mišpat*).

> You would not find out the boundaries of soul, even by traveling along every path: so deep a measure (*logos*) does it have. (frag. 45) [trans. Kirk, Raven, and Schofield 1983: 203]

Although the *logos* defines man most inwardly, it is—except for Heraclitus[18]—not known or accessible to man:

> With the *logos* with which they most constantly deal, the steward of the universe, with which they quarrel, and the things which they encounter daily, they appear to them strange. (frag. 72)

With his discourse on the *logos* and on the "wise" person, Heraclitus provided a crucial loosening of *archē*-speculations about the world of the gods. His thought may have left traces in the discourse on the hidden wisdom of Israel in Job 28 (Bircher 1980). Much later, Jewish scholars such as Philo of Alexandria, and the author of the prologue to John's Gospel as well, so thoroughly reformulated Israelite-Jewish speculation on the *archē* underlying the world—namely, divine wisdom, using this vocabulary—that it must have appeared familiar to Greek ears.

---

18. Heraclitus's attitude to the Logos recalls Akhenaton's perspective on Aton.

X. The Wisdom Immanent in the World as the Prime Beginning in the First Testament

Earlier, in older biblical passages (Ps 104:24), the wisdom indwelling the cosmos was expressed only adverbially, although in God's speeches in the book of Job it already took on greater significance (*ḥokmah* or the related concept *'eṣah*); but in a few post-exilic texts, it has become a central concept.[1]

1. The World Formula Hidden from Man (Job 28)

Almost without exception, in the history of research into Job 28, this beautiful poem or song about the inaccessible wisdom that is available only to God, which is inserted directly before Job's final long speech, has been considered a foreign body in the book of Job, a secondary intrusion, based on linguistic, stylistic, form-critical grounds, in addition to its variant content.[2] However, Ruben Zimmermann (1994: 80–100) has shown with many concrete arguments that there is no conclusive proof for treating this chapter as a distinct source. The songlike excursus of Job 28 is tightly bound to the rest of the book by the repetition of key words and especially references to the themes found in God's speeches. Quite aside from questions regarding sources, however, in God's speeches and in Job 28 two different traditions do come into play, which is why the passages are discussed in two separate chapters here. God's speeches center on the nature of the creator, who appears primarily as *deus faber* and is viewed as a court of justice that can clarify the relationship between chaos and cosmos and bring them into balance. In Job 28, on the other hand, the main interest is not in the divine creator but in the *archē* behind and in creation. Wisdom, if not yet entirely personified, becomes an independent protagonist.

The poem describes how she herself is not to be found in the most adventurous human undertakings. The grasping of *homo faber* who mines the earth's innards is described with near-blasphemous turns of phrase (Zimmermann 1994: esp. 89). Human beings do things that are properly reserved to God (rampaging with fire, overturning mountains, cleaving rocks). The spotlighting of these encroachments is critical of dominion and implicitly of patriarchy. *Homo faber* might successfully get to the root of many matters, but wisdom, the principle or concept of the whole, is not available to him. Wisdom can be neither manufactured nor bought; in his efforts to gain wisdom, man remains a *homo sapiens ignorans* and directed to God, who alone knows the way to her, for he used her as a sort of blueprint of the world:[3]

---

1. On personified wisdom in the post-exilic writings, see also Schroer 1986.
2. On Job 28, see von Rad 1972: 206–25, Keel 1974a: 10f., Zerafa 1978: 126–84, Bircher 1980 (for the connections with Heraclitus's thought and conceptualization), Geller 1987, van Oorschot 1994, Zimmermann 1994 (with further bibliography).
3. Blueprints (1 Chr 28:19) and models (2 Kgs 16:10; 1 Chr 28:11f., 18f.; Ps 144:22) were not unknown in Israel. For the model of a heavenly pattern for earthly things, see Exod 25:9, 40.

Whence, then, comes wisdom,
and where is the place of understanding?
. . .
God knows the way to it;
it is he who is familiar with its place.
For he beholds the ends of the earth
and sees all that is under the heavens.
He has weighed out the wind,
and fixed the scope of the waters;
When he made rules for the rain
and a path for the thunderbolts,
Then he saw wisdom and appraised it (*wayesaperah*),
gave it its setting, knew it through and through (*haqarah*). (Job 28:23–27)

Here, wisdom appears closely connected with weights and measures, with principles and parameters[4] and mysterious mathematics.[5] The text is silent about the origin of this wisdom used by God at creation, quite unlike Prov 8:22–31. The presence of wisdom in the created world and its simultaneous inaccessibility recall Heraclitus, who, however, unlike the poet of Job 28, excepted himself from this ignorance. The notion of a quantifiable "wisdom" also recalls Heraclitus's *metra*. But Heraclitus, unlike Job 28, fails to recognize a personal creator god. The *logos* is god and "wisdom" wrapped up in one.

The paean to hidden wisdom retained its vitality in Jewish tradition. Thus, in the book of Baruch (3:15–38), from the second century B.C., it is elaborated, and wisdom is reclaimed for Israel alone. The Septuagint, in translating Job 28, adopted theologically crucial textual omissions and alterations (Küchler 1992, esp. 125–33). In an alteration, the Greek text offers the (especially) wise of Israel a door to find a clue to the hidden wisdom. In an omission, pre-creation wisdom as an independent protagonist and God's inspiring encounter with this mysterious wisdom are both summarily eliminated. What remains is wisdom as part of God's creation. The monotheistic system of symbols is rigorously purged of all images and words that might lead to the conclusion that there is a counterpart to the One God. Using this same theological tendency, but on the whole rather less successfully, the Septuagint also sought to level the independence of wisdom in Prov 8:22–31 (Küchler 1992: 133–39).

2. An Erotic Wisdom as Principle of the Divine Desire to Create (Proverbs 1–9)

The oldest passage in the Bible in which divine wisdom appears in the very colorful image of a dynamic and self-aware woman is the post-exilic frame of the book of Proverbs (Proverbs 1–9 in connection with chapter 31).[6] In the poem Prov 1:20–33, in contrast to Job 28, Wisdom is openly available; indeed, she woos men.[7] Her words are full of reminiscences of the prophets.[8] As with the word of God, hearers and non-hearers decide for salvation or non-salvation. The

---

4. See Isa 40:12, 14; Wis 7:21, 8:1, 11:20.
5. For the impenetrability of the mathematical secrets of the world see Job 38:37; Bar 3:15, 31; Isa 40:12; Jer 31:37.
6. For Proverbs 1–9, see especially Keel 1974a, Lang 1986, Winter 1987: 508–29, Schroer 1991, Baumann 1996, Maier 2012, and Zimmermann and Zimmermann 2000. On the shape and topic of "wisdom" in feminist theologies, see the survey of research in Hailer 2001.
7. See von Rad's beautiful chapter, 1972: 226–37.
8. With v. 24: compare Isa 65:2, 12; v. 26: Deut 28:63; v. 27: Jer 23:19; v. 28: Jer 11:11, Hos 5:6; v. 32: Amos 6:1; v. 33: Jer 5:12f.

form of self-praise is suitable for a speaking, self-revealing goddess, since only she herself can reveal herself.[9]

In the long poem Prov 8:1–36, as well, in the first three verses as already in 1:20–33, the public nature of Wisdom's appearance is stressed. She is not hidden, she is not directed solely to Israel but to all humankind, not to an exclusive circle (a collegium of civil servants, etc.) but to all. In 8:4–21, she praises her qualities (insight, cleverness, righteousness, trustworthiness), by virtue of which are acquired justice, honor, and wealth. As in Job 28, her value is set higher than corals and gold. It is especially noteworthy that through her emperors and kings rule, as in Egypt Maat, the goddess of wisdom and correct order, stands behind the reigning king.[10]

The influence of ḥokmah is still more inclusive. In Proverbs 8 she describes how God created, acquired, or bore her as archē of his work of creation, before he called into existence all the mighty foundational works such as primeval sea, mountains, and rivers:

> YHWH created me (qanani), the firstborn of his ways (re'šit darko),
>   the forerunner of his prodigies of long ago;
> From of old I was formed (nisakti),
>   at the first, before the earth.
> When there were no depths I was brought forth (ḥolalti),
>   when there were no fountains or springs of water;
> Before the mountains were settled into place,
>   before the hills, I was brought forth (ḥolalti);
> While as yet the earth and the fields were not made,
>   nor the first clods of the world.
> When he established the heavens I was there (šam 'ani),
>   when he marked out the vault over the face of the deep;
> When he made firm the skies above,
>   when he fixed the foundations of the earth;
> When he set for the sea its limit,
>   so that the waters should not transgress his command;
> Then was I beside him as his expert craftswoman ('amon),
>   and I was his delight day by day,
> Bantering and joking before him (mesaḥeqet) all the while,
>   bantering (mesaḥeqet) on the surface of his earth;
> [and I found delight in humans.] (Prov 8:22–31)

During all of creation, she cooperated[11] and had a voice in the event of creation, in that by her jests (saḥaq) she kept the creator in an optimistic, lighthearted mood. In the Egyptian tale of the struggle between Horus and Seth, the goddess Hathor appears in a similar but not identical role in the presence of the father of the gods, Re, who is tired of creating; she entices Re back to his proper activity through her erotic and wanton entertainment.[12] The motif probably traces back to the goddess uncovering herself in the Old Syrian tradition (cf. figs. 89 and 112; Winter 1987: 523f.).

The closest parallel to an entertaining dance before YHWH is found in 2 Samuel 6, where David—modestly clad in a linen loincloth—performed his acrobatic dances before the ark of YHWH (Keel 1974a: 35–38; 1996). The famous 'amon in Prov 8:30 is applied to God in the sense "master craftsman," but even more so

Figs. 167–168

---

9. For the form of the revelation, see Kayatz 1966, Bergman 1968.

10. Assmann 1990; for the biblical reception, see Keel 1974a, Schroer 2000: 26–30; for the relationship between Egyptian Maat and Greek Dike, see Tobin 1987.

11. For "I was there," cf. Isa 48:16 and the paratactic nature of ancient Near Eastern representational art. Further particulars on the text are explicated in detail in Keel 1974a: 15–30.

12. TUAT III 938; Keel 1974a: 45.

167 Pectoral of King Shoshenq II from Tanis (10th century B.C.). Along with the goddess Hathor, Maat (at right with an ostrich feather) protects the sun disk in its bark. Simultaneously, she stands inside the sun disk, supplicating before the enthroned sun-god Amon-Re. (Winter 1987: fig. 515)

to wisdom (cf. the *technitis* in Wis 7:21, 8:6), and perhaps also in a different derivation in the sense "intimate"; but it cannot be translated "pampered child" or "spoiled child," as is unfortunately still the case in a large number of Bible translations.[13] The idea of a "suckling" contradicts the ancient Near Eastern tradition of the goddess of wisdom (Maat) and the other biblical sayings about wisdom and her part in creation. She also does not fit the unequivocal erotically colored cultic "jests" (cf. Gen 26:8).

Through her vitality and her cultic jests, Wisdom stimulated and encouraged YHWH in the creation of the world. Creation thus arose, quite differently from what is reported in Genesis 1–2, not according to the will and action of a One, but in a relationship, in any event: in the relationship between Two.[14] The

---

13. Cf. in detail Zimmermann and Zimmermann 2000: 78ff., esp. 85. The infantilization of the woman continues to be perpetuated, most recently in Bauks and Baumann 1994: 24–52 and Baumann 1996: 112, 131–38. The patriarchally and clerically inspired translations muffle or eliminate the erotic connotations.

14. Whether the *qanani* in v. 22 in the sense of "bride-price" can be taken to refer to a celestial bride metaphor (as cautiously considered by Zimmermann and Zimmermann 2000: 88–91) must remain

168 Relief from a tomb in Thebes West (ca. 1450 B.C.). A festival is depicted, showing the partygoers indulging not only at a bountiful table but also in musical and acrobatic presentations. (Keel 1974a: 52, fig. 12)

conspiratorial involvement of Wisdom lends a special quality to creation. Her happy jests in the face of the mighty works that ensue correspond to the spirited cries of the sons of God in Job 38:7 and the rejoicing of heaven in Ps 19:2. God in his creational aloneness does not need to conclude for himself that all his works are truly special. Because Wisdom herself is so invigorating, those who listen to her obtain the same outcome as wisdom-inspired creation—a prosperous, joyful life. Cheerful Wisdom, immanent in the world, which extends the invitation to a prosperous life, is imagined in Prov 9:1–6 as a landlady, and in Prov 3:17–20 as the ancient symbol of the tree of life.

3. Eroticism as an Individual Origin of Creation (Song 8:6f.)

At the end of the collection of love songs[15] that was admitted to the canon as the Song of Solomon, there is a text in which the world is presented as the battlefield of two powers, love and death:

---

open. There is no explicit formulation of a marriage-like relationship between God and Wisdom until the late book of Wisdom (see chap. XI.3 below, pp. 189ff.).

15. On the Song of Songs, see Keel 1984, 1986, 1997; M. V. Fox 1985; Walter 1985; Bühlmann 1997; for feminist aspects of the exegesis, see Brenner 2012. In recent years, there have been more and more attempts to understand the Song of Songs as an overarching composition and transfer it to the Hellenistic period. But even though the problem of the paths of transmission has not been unequivocally settled, no one can deny that in form and content the songs stand infinitely closer to the Egyptian love songs of the 13th/12th centuries B.C. than to the Hellenistic idylls of Theocritus (3rd century B.C.). The

169 Painted limestone relief in Sethos I's mortuary temple in Abydos (ca. 1280 B.C.). The dead Osiris lies on the lion bier. Isis mounts the (subsequently effaced) erect phallus as his falcon-mate, who subsequently conceives the avenger and heir of Osiris, Horus. The goddess in human form at the right extends her hands protectively over her dead brother. At the far left, the falcon-headed Horus attends his own conception. The falcon-mates at the head and foot of the bier represent Nephthys and yet again Isis. Below the bier are the Ibis-headed Thoth, two rearing serpents (uraei or serpent goddesses), and a long-tailed monkey. (Keel 1986a: 249, fig. 143)

> Set me as a seal on your heart,
>   as a seal on your arm;
> For stern as death is love,
>   relentless as the nether world is devotion;
>   its flames are a blazing fire.
> Deep waters cannot quench love,
>   nor floods sweep it away.
> Were one to offer all he owns to purchase love,
>   he would be roundly mocked. (Song 8:6f.)

Love (the Beloved) represents herself as an amulet against death. She assumes the mythic role of adversary to the power of death. Just as Anat and Isis achieve new life in the myths and rescue their lovers, Baal and Osiris, from the clutches of Mot and Seth,[16] so the loving woman takes on the greatest enemy of life and love: death. In the Hebrew Bible, the woman who opposes the interruption of the line of descent and death with her love is found in sayings and tales like those of Lot's daughters (Gen 19:30–38), Tamar (Genesis 38), Ruth, Michal (1 Sam 19:9–17), Abigail (1 Samuel 25), and the wise woman of Maacah (2 Sam 20:14–22). The cosmic dimension of this defiant love, which also resolutely opposes societal pressures (cf. the lifting of the curse of Gen 3:16 in Song 7:11), is clearly emphasized by its resonance with the motif of battle against chaos (compare Song 8:7 with Ps 18:6, 15, 17 and figs. 109–111 above).

Fig. 169

---

older and regularly renewed attempts to find in the Song of Songs not just a collection of songs but a single overarching concept have to this day (despite certain indications—refrains—in the text) led to no consensus and no convincing solution (see most recently Bosshard-Nepustil 1996).

16. The closest connection in time and place is to a myth indigenous to Phoenicia, the myth of Adonis, whose partner is the love goddess Aphrodite.

The role of the beloved as a principle of creation is also clear in what are known as the descriptive songs (4:1–7, 5:9–16, 7:2–6). The form of these songs ultimately goes back to the Old Kingdom Pyramid Texts, in which the attempt to make the pharaoh into god was implemented by identifying each of his members with a god, so that in the end he was the pantheon:

> Your head is Horus of the underworld, O immortal one. . . .
> Your ears are twin children of Atum, O immortal one.
> Your nose is Upuaut, O immortal one. . . . (Pyr 215 §148f.)

In the biblical love songs, each part of the beloved's body is equated with a splendor of creation. The beloved thus becomes the core, the "soul" of creation, in whom the creation finds its consistency and sense. Through the love of the beloved, the love of all creation becomes the beloved's portion.[17] The loss of the beloved signifies the loss of the world, because the beloved is the principle through which the world becomes existentially accessible. This connection is the reason why the metaphors of the Song of Songs lead over and over to ancient Near Eastern images and symbols of creation.

---

17. In order to understand fully the depths of these descriptions, one must in any case free oneself from the failed custom of understanding the metaphors as a realization of "forms" (Keel 1984: 27–30). The Hebrew names for body parts already point to activities and dynamic processes, not to forms. Thus the "eye" is related to twinkling, gleaming, bewitching; the "nose" to snorting, animosity, anger; the "neck" to haughtiness; the "breasts" to gifts of love, life, blessing, abundance, etc. (see most recently Schroer and Staubli 2001).

XI. The Theologization of Wisdom, a Post-Critical Naivete (Modesty), and the Desire for Eternity

1. Creation and Election (Ben Sira)

In God's speeches in the book of Job, Job 28, and Proverbs 1–9, life experience, all sorts of foreign influences, and indigenous folk tradition (cf. Prov 1:20–33) all work together, but in the Wisdom of Sira[1] folk tradition comes to the fore. The book documents an attempt, full of tension, to understand "wisdom" between creation and election, between universal and particular approaches to the divine. In the process, the earlier public understanding of wisdom is channeled into narrower paths on the one hand, but on the other an attempt is made to classify anew the specific history of Israel with respect to creation and the wisdom that is immanent in the world.

In the prologue to the Greek translation of the book, the writer's grandson announces that his grandfather was a scribe (one learned in the Scriptures). In the programmatic introduction, 1:1–10, he attempts to mediate between the contrasting positions of Job 28, where wisdom is conceived as operating in creation but inaccessible to man, and Proverbs 1–9, where the Wisdom immanent in the world offers herself to every hearer. Cosmic wisdom is available to all people as a gift of the creator who alone is wise (cf. Heraclitus, frag. 32, p. 174 above), but especially to Israel:

> All wisdom is from the Lord,
> and with him it remains forever.
> The sand of the sea, the drops of rain,
> and the days of eternity—who can count them?
> The height of heaven, the breadth of the earth,
> the abyss, and wisdom—who can search them out?
> Wisdom was created before all other things,
> and prudent understanding, from eternity.
> The root of wisdom—To whom has it been revealed?
> Her subtleties—who knows them?
> There is but one who is wise, greatly to be feared,
> seated upon his throne—the Lord.
> It is he who created her,
> he saw her and took her measure;
> he has poured her out upon all his works,
> upon all the living according to his gift;
> he lavished her upon those who love him. (Sir 1:1–10)

The scribe Ben Sira succeeded in making contact with the earlier speculation on wisdom, in the process defining it in his mind and fitting it into a patriarchal system of thought. Thus, unlike Prov 8:22–31, where the relation between YHWH

---

1. The Greek and what remains of the Hebrew text are found in Vattioni 1968; also important are Marböck 1971, 1995; Barthélemy and Rickenbacher 1973; Rickenbacher 1973; Schnabel 1985; Skehan and Di Lella 1987; Reiterer 1999; Wénin 1999; Sauer 2000; less of a contribution is Rogers 1996; on gender-specific aspects, see Botha 1996; Schroer 2000: 107–12; Strotmann 1998.

and *ḥokmah* remains in a flux filled with theological significance, he classifies wisdom as unequivocally subordinate to the God of Israel (1:14, 16, 18, 20). The exegetical, systematizing endeavor of the scribe can also be recognized in the great poem about wisdom in chapter 24. Wisdom enters with her self-praise (vv. 1–2) not into public places, as in Proverbs 1–9, but in the presence of the (earthly and heavenly) community of God. Divine Wisdom, who presents herself in Proverbs 8 (where a whiff of her mythic origin might hang in the air), becomes in Sir 24:3 the "word of God," her independence thereby sharply reduced. This word-of-God wisdom rules nature[2] and history (cf. Ps 147:15–19). In v. 7, the wandering is interpreted as her seeking a resting place. In older passages, YHWH finds "heritage" and "resting place" in Israel (Deut 32:8f., Ps 132:8). Locating the abode or tent of wisdom in Israel is astonishing after the background of Job 28. In order to dispel all doubts, v. 9 stresses that it is an absolute certainty that wisdom is eternal. Verse 10 transforms her cultic jests (cf. Prov. 8:30f.) into a solemn liturgical act. This wisdom is now operative in the Jerusalem cult.[3]

Verses 13–17 are prepared by v. 12 (roots). They incorporate the image of wisdom as the tree of life (Prov 3:18), in the process laying special weight on the localization of the tree in and around Israel. Wisdom's invitation in vv. 19–22 to this tree, with an allusion to and differentiation from the tree of knowledge in Gen 3:4, implies that eating of the fruit of wisdom would not make one like God.

In v. 23, wisdom is identified with the Torah (Gk. *nomos*) of Moses.[4] This prosaic equivalence may not come from Ben Sira himself but fits the wider context very well. The way for the identification of the cosmic wisdom immanent in the world with the Torah wisdom of Israel was prepared by the harmonization of wisdom to the concept "word of God."[5] What Ben Sira sees operating in creation is not so much "wisdom" as the "word of God" (cf. 42:15; 43:5, 10, 26). The goodness of creation, as in Heraclitus (frag. 102), is an assumption and a dogma—no longer an experience. The song of praise to the lord of creation in Sir 39:12–35 is framed by the decisive statement that his works are entirely good (39:16, 33), and a repeated refrain stresses that there is no a priori reason to doubt this:

> No one can say, "What is this?" or "Why is that?"—
> for everything has been created for its own purpose.
> No one can say, "This is not as good as that,"
> for everything proves good in its appointed time. (Sir 39:21, 34; cf. 17)

The dogmatic thread in this approach is also evident in the fact that wisdom is no longer seen as active in the management of history in general, as in Prov 8:15f., but only in the history of Israel, where the word of God takes the form of threats and promises and their fulfillment as well as in the revelation of laws and obedience or disobedience of those laws.[6]

Excursus:
Wisdom and Torah

Johannes Marböck (1971: 72, 76) stresses the demythologizing effect of the identification of wisdom with Torah. While wisdom diminished in mythic luster, the appeal

---

2. Cf. Isis as lady of the rivers, sea, and every land. For wandering about, cf. Gen 13:17.
3. For the *esterichthēn* in v. 10b, compare the translation of *'amon* in Prov 8:30 with *esterigmenē*!
4. Cf. Deut 4:5–6 and, for the formulation of this connection, Deut 33:4 and the Deuteronomistic identification of covenant and law in Deut 17:12, 28:7.
5. Compare the hypostasizing of this word in Isa 45:23, 55:11.
6. Sir 44:17, 22; 45:1–5, 17; 46:13f.; 47:9f., 22; 48:3, 7; 48:22; 49:4.

of Torah grew, as subsequent developments show. As with the battle against chaos, here too the historicizing of myth led to the mythologizing of history.[7] Hans Heinrich Schmid (1966: 196ff.) sees this development as a withering away of true wisdom, while Max Küchler (1979: esp. 18–20, 547–52) sees it as the wise entering into the concerns of the time. In the sixth century B.C., in the Greek sphere, a powerful struggle over the interpretation of the mean (*archē, sophia*) had set in, and after this, for the wise of Israel, formulating individual rules of experience could no longer suffice. By identifying wisdom with the law, it was possible for Ben Sira to keep Israel contemporary without surrendering its identity.

The question remains as to whether Ben Sira maintained that the goal of wisdom was always to keep open a path to interpret the world and question its regularity and intelligibility (Schmid) or whether he understood it differently, adapted to the exigencies of the time (Küchler)—no longer as a collection of rules for living but as a system that somehow remained subject to experience and reason. A look at Ben Sira's understanding of the law can take the discussion further.

It is noteworthy that in his "praises of famous men" Ben Sira devotes in all no more than five verses to Moses the lawgiver, in contrast to the high priests Aaron and Simon II (45:6–22, 50:1–21), who get many. A special role is played by the esthetic—that is, a universal—impulse. It is likewise striking that the author contrasts the law with nature (42:15–43:33) and with people's history (44:1–50:21) but does not make it a separate topic of his investigations. The pericope 32:14–33:2, which speaks of upholding the commandments, parallels concepts such as god-seeker, Torah-seeker, god-fearer, life-keeper, wise, and so on. These concepts mutually interpret one another. In 16:24–17:14, the Torah on Sinai appears as part of the creator's cosmic regulation that is immanent in the world (see Wénin 1999). The Torah is a "law of life and understanding" (17:11; cf. 45:5). To distinguish good and evil, man has his understanding (17:7) and can hone it, for instance, by observations during travels (Sir 39:4). The wisdom of the cosmos is rationally verifiable—for example, no star collides with its neighbor (*to plēsion*) (16:28). Similarly, defining the content of the Torah as shunning evil or not becoming faithless[8] or arranging one's relationship with one's neighbor (*plēsion*) as beneficially as possible (17:14; cf. Matt 22:34–40) make rational good sense.[9] Also, just as God revealed himself to Israel through the covenant at Sinai and the gift of the Torah, so too all revelation is already contained in the mysterious order of creation.

Ben Sira furthermore often conceives Torah as "Book of the Torah of Moses" (Sir 41:4, 44:20). But where the reference is concretely to the latter expression, it refers to relationships with one's neighbor.[10] By keeping the law understood in this way, love for God is realized (cf. Sir 2:16, 1 John 2:3–5). Ben Sira never names dietary commandments, ritual purity commandments, ritual regulations, etc., as the content of Torah. For him, Torah is a law of life and understanding.[11]

Even if the identification of wisdom and Torah in 24:23 does go back to Ben Sira himself, this connection is to be interpreted as incorporating Torah into wisdom, not wisdom into Torah. Specific experiences of salvation such as deliverance and

---

7. The Torah that was identified with wisdom by Ben Sira is endowed by the rabbis with preexistence (Strack and Billerbeck 1926: I 974, II 355). It is the product of creation (II 365f.): to study and maintain Torah is to participate in creation (I 833, 873; II 33). The Torah is eternally valid (I 245ff.; cf. Sir 24:9b; differently, however, Hebrews 7, Galatians 3, etc.).

8. The Greek and Syriac textual traditions diverge here.

9. The content that the cosmic law still has in Ben Sira and which in Ben Sira is accessible to reason becomes in PsSol 18:10–12, for example, a totally formalistic and legalistic attitude of obedience (Kautzsch 1962: 148).

10. Sir 19:13–17 (to put the question), 23:23 (adultery), 29:9–13 (almsgiving), 35:1–4 (spiritualizing of the offering).

11. It remains a law of life among the rabbis, but not a law of understanding; see Strack and Billerbeck 1926: IV 18, 1153f.

election, like their flip-sides doubt and suffering, have a tendency to become global perspectives and theories. (A good example is Job: because he experiences what seems to him to be injustice, he questions the entire world order—and is even aware of this, when he says "I also could talk as you do, if you were in my place" 16:4.) They extend themselves and of their own accord, as it were, look for a place in the cosmic, in the ordering of the world; they exert pressure in the direction of universalization. So the soteriological experience by which the Torah provided Israel with meaning and identity led Ben Sira to combine the concept "word of God" with the wisdom that is immanent in the world, the cosmic law. What is inconvenient in the Torah, such as the ritual laws, is passed over in silence.

The rabbis already had brought this unifying aspect to the fore but held on to the identification of wisdom and Torah. The law of understanding thereby became a law of obedience. The question regarding the foundations of Torah (ta'ame hattorah) was consciously avoided. For humankind, it must suffice that in it the will of God, the King of Kings, manifests itself. It is Israel's task to sustain the Torah, not to understand it, as Rabbi Aqiba puts it in the little religious conversation he is supposed to have had with the Roman governor Tinejus Rufus in A.D. 132:

> Rufus: Wherein does this day [the Sabbath] differ from any other?
> Aqiba: Wherein does one man [the governor] differ from any other?
> Rufus: Because my Lord [the Emperor] wishes it.
> Aqiba: The Sabbath too, then, is distinguished because the Lord wishes it so.[12]
> [trans. H. Freedman]

To inquire into the foundations of Torah is unnecessary, then; doing so is downright harmful:

> Rabbi Isḥaq (ca. A.D. 300) said: Why were the reasons of [some] Biblical laws not revealed? —Because in two verses reasons were revealed, and they cause the greatest in the world [Solomon] to stumble. Thus it is written: *He shall not multiply wives to himself, that his heart turn not away* (Deut 17:17), whereon Solomon said, "I will multiply wives yet not let my heart be perverted." [But it did happen.] (1 Kgs 11:4).[13] [trans. Jacob Schachter]

Only a Judaism that existed in close interaction with its environment—such as that of, say, Maimonides—could withdraw from obedience of this sort and renew a systematic inquiry into the foundations of Torah.

For the Christian communities, the experience of salvation and rescue, of coming into existence through the Christ event, of coming from darkness to light (a creation event), led to the praise of Christ as the beginning, as the principle of all of God's activities, even that of creation (John 1:1–18; Col 1:13–23; Rev 3:14, 21:6). As in Ben Sira and in orthodox rabbinic Judaism, the establishment of soteriological power leads to praise of cosmic relevance.

2. Contentedness in Place of Enthusiasm (Qohelet)

The book of Qohelet,[14] in contrast to Ben Sira, is decidedly anthropocentric (see 1:3, 2:3), but like Ben Sira, is impressed with patriarchal modes of thought.

---

12. Talmud *Sanhedrin* 65b; Strack and Billerbeck 1926: I 861.
13. Talmud *Sanhedrin* 21b; Strack and Billerbeck 1926: I 660.
14. See Zimmerli 1967; Loretz 1964; Müller 1968: 507–21; Klopfenstein 1972; Braun 1973; Lauha 1978; Crüsemann 1979: 80–104; Lohfink 1980; Michel 1988, 1989; Schubert 1989; Schwienhorst-Schönberger 1997, especially Uehlinger's article; Rose ed. 1999; for a feminist interpretation, Kato 2012; for a liberation theology rereading, see Tamez 2001. Comprehensive bibliographies are in Michel 1989: 290–322 (by R. G. Lehmann) and Rose 1999b: 557–612 (by B. Perregaux Allisson); see also Krüger 2000: 2–9.

The suspicion that, when Qohelet speaks universally of "man," in androcentric narrowness, he really means only his own kind—that is, well-to-do, educated men—is not to be lightly dismissed. Qohelet's problem is that man has a nagging need to understand the whole, the cosmos in its fullest extent,[15] but because of his limitations, especially his mortality, his forgetfulness, and his ordained forgottenness (1:11), he is forbidden access to this knowledge. The pessimistic refrain "All is vanity and a chasing after wind" again and again recalls the finitude of human life. The inability to grasp the whole and his deadly fate affect not just the foolish, as in traditional wisdom,[16] but every man, in his affinity to the animals, even beasts of burden (3:18–22; cf. Ps 49:11). Man must limit himself to and concentrate only on the portion that is allotted to him (*passivum divinum*). He should grasp tightly what he can reach and what is possible for him, act on it, and be happy[17] and not attempt to be any too wise (2:15, 7:16f.). The fear of God means to be aware of the distance between God and man (3:14, 4:17–5:6) and to accept from God what he gives (7:13f.).

The "crisis of wisdom" that is reflected in the book of Qohelet was the reflex of a deep-seated economic and political crisis with far-reaching societal consequences. The cause-and-effect connection that had been postulated on the basis of experience was shattered. The result, however, was not a break with the methods of recognizing wisdom (Rose 1999). Qohelet wrestles with a new formulation of wisdom on the basis of new premises. How, if the old regularities of life have become uncertain, can one nonetheless lead a good life? How can one nonetheless be wise?

With the renunciation of knowledge of *archē* and acknowledgment of being delivered to the giving, sharing creator God, we are once more among narrative texts like Genesis 2 (Adam and Eve). But, in Qohelet, this realization is no longer the result of a fascinated intuition but of a resigned instruction. Behind Qohelet lies an intensive effort to comprehend what maintains the world in the most basic sense, what the sparking intuition, its *archē*, was. The place of the transcendent and acting-with-precision God who cooperates with wisdom in Job 28 and the joyfully creating creator of Prov 8:22–31 has been taken by the rather wan "making" and "giving" God. The abundant, vibrantly colorful gifts that man discovers with excitement have turned into the "portion" or "share" of mankind, a concept that, alongside the gift, also makes its limitations precisely clear.

This visionless and perspectiveless view of the world is typical of a life context suffused with prosperity (Crüsemann 1979). Of course, we must not forget that life expectancy even in the most prosperous circles was about forty years on average for men, considerably less for women. Death always loomed, and much less accountably than now, in life. Christoph Uehlinger (1997) and Kumiko Kato (2012) convincingly interpret Qohelet according to the tradition of festival songs, as attested, for instance, in the Egyptian harpers' songs that were widespread from the middle of the fourteenth century B.C. on and in Hellenistic

---

Martin Rose (1999a) considers the book the result of a rewriting process in which the basic text of a Persian-period author of the 5th century B.C. was expanded in two phases, the last at the end of the 3rd century B.C., with conceptual content that may be distinguished. Diachronically, for Rose, a philosophy of clinging to joy in life is followed by a philosophy of total senselessness, and this ultimately is then followed by an allotment of negative experiences to the world and humanity, while all that is positive is expected only from God and eternity. What we have to say about the book of Qohelet below, independent of diachronic considerations, concerns the final redaction of the text and interpretation of what has been transmitted.

15. Especially Qoh 3:10f.; cf. also 1:8, 13; 7:23f.; 8:17. The *'olam* in 3:11 means not just a very long time, but as the "everything" at the start and the "from the beginning to the end" at the close of the sequence shows, the entirety of the "world."

16. Ps 73:22; Prov 12:1, 30:2.

17. Qoh 2:24–26; 3:12f., 22; 5:17–19; 9:7–10.

culture as well, and as it has lived on in the appeal to *carpe diem*. Like Qohelet, in view of the shortness of life and the threat of death, these songs issue an invitation to enjoy the day, food and drink, and the coupling of man and woman.[18] To treat life as a gift and hang onto joy in life despite everything is Qohelet's final advice. It is clear that Qohelet's worldview and perspective is completely directed toward the present world and concrete earthly life—utterly unlike the Wisdom of Solomon, which is oriented toward the next world (see chap. XI.3).

For Qohelet, as for Heraclitus (frag. 102) and Ben Sira (39:16–21), God has made everything suitable for its time (3:11). Man, too, he had made "fitting," but Qohelet can think of a thousand things that make life difficult for him (7:29). Qohelet does not think fundamental changes are necessary. Man should strive, as in the time of Solomon, to eat, drink, and be happy (1 Kgs 4:20). This is not godless enjoyment of life. Whenever Qohelet says that happiness under this sun consists of eating and drinking, he also says that this is the fate, the portion, that God allotted to man (2:24, 3:13, 5:17, 8:15, 9:7). Naturally, the question immediately arises as to why God's gift of creation has not been bestowed equally on all. Qohelet at least entertains the suspicion that the gifts of God turn into a privilege for wealthy men. This attitude, with its respect for what God allots and sends (*miqreh*) to man, appears, to contemporary groups who held a different opinion, to be worshiping the god Fortune (*gad*) or the god Destiny (*meni*) (Isa 65:11). The faithless are threatened:

> My servants shall eat,
>   but you shall be hungry;
> my servants shall drink,
>   but you shall be thirsty;
> my servants shall rejoice,
>   but you shall be put to shame. (Isa 65:13)

To this dualistic view, Qohelet's advice not to be too righteous or act too wisely (7:15f.) must have appeared blasphemous. In fact, in Qohelet's mindset of making what *is* into the norm there lurks a certain cynicism, as when he extends an invitation to accept injustices:

> If you see in a province the oppression of the poor and the violation of justice and right, do not be amazed at the matter; for the high official is watched by a higher, and there are yet higher ones over them. But all things considered, this is an advantage for a land: a king for a plowed field. (Qoh 5:7f.)[19]

But this advice must be contrasted with the horror that a kingless, anarchic period[20] can actually bring.

For Qohelet, taking into consideration that the time for any event is determined (3:1–8) and the fact that trouble and sin come into the world through man, the world is fundamentally in order. More oppressed and more strongly religious or ideological groups in the second century B.C., in contrast to Qohelet, relied more and more on schemes in which the world becomes God's world, becomes creation in the full meaning of the word, only in the future (apocalyptic), while in the present they were largely under the control of chaotic powers and writhed in the pains that precede the birth of a better world. In these writings,

---

18. Translation by J. Assmann, *TUAT* II 905–8 [Lichtheim I 193–97] For the combination of wisdom and philosophical reflections with drinking songs, see Sir 31:27–32:4 and the *Gaudeamus igitur* of academic festivals.

19. For a variety of interpretations of this passage, see Krüger 2000: 216–20.

20. Compare the uprising against Roman dominion inspired by the Zealots in A.D. 66–70, 132, and 135.

wisdom is correspondingly either ultimately hidden (in heaven) (Bar 3:15–38) or else discarded by man and accursed in heaven (Enoch 42:1–3).[21]

3. The Appointment of All Beings for Life (Wisdom of Solomon)

The "Wisdom of Solomon" or "Book of Wisdom" (henceforth *Sapientia*),[22] which cultivates and vivifies wisdom in the person of Solomon the Wise and thus promotes Solomonic wisdom (cf. Platonic or Aristotelian philosophy), was written in Greek in the second half of the first century B.C. in Alexandria. The composition is an extremely interesting product of intercultural contact, with a clearly antiparticularistic tenor. Jewish tradition and Greek philosophy flow together here, and the Egyptian and Hellenistic worship of Isis is constructively assimilated into personified Sophia.

The *first part* (1:1–6:11)[23] comes to very critical engagement with the position represented by Qohelet. The people whose philosophy emerges from the fact that life is short and sorrowful (2:1–5) and one must therefore "seize the day" (2:6–8) because that is man's lot[24] (compare 2:9c with Qoh 3:22) are called impious (*asebeis*) and ungodly. Of course, *Sapientia* does not precisely criticize Qohelet's position but an (obvious?) caricature or interpretation of it: it overlooks the condition that these people thankfully regard the enjoyment of life (eating and drinking) as a (limited) gift of God. She insinuates that her adversaries would maintain the right of the strong to oppress the poor, consider the wise (in the sense of *Sapientia*) a lasting reproach, and accordingly hate them (2:10–21). The blindness and bestiality of man, which Qohelet (3:18f.) takes as the basic condition of human existence, leads *Sapientia* back to the corresponding evilness of a particular group of people (2:21) who, on the basis of their evilness, are blind to the secrets of God (*mystēria theou*; 2:22) and live on impassively as beasts of burden.

Sapientia replaces Qohelet's empiricism[25] with ideas—that is, God's secrets. Since ideas are not visible but must be believed, and since most people are not at all prepared to believe them, the book develops a fierce polemic against those who are not prepared to trade the bird in the hand for two in the bush.

The secrets of *Sapientia* can be reduced to a single secret into which Wisdom is initiated (*mystis*; 8:4). This is the insight that God did not make death but created all that *is* for ongoing existence (Zenger 1989). All that God has made and makes is just, but incorruption (*aphtharsia*) belongs to justice and immortality (*athanasia*).[26] God specially created man to be incorruptible, which constitutes

---

21. We thank Prof. S. Vollenweider (Zurich) for the information that in the 3rd century B.C. Aratus (*Phainomena* 130) says that Dike wanted to stay among men but was driven away by their wickedness and returned to heaven. In the Greek tradition as well, the version in which Dike is carried away is distinct from an earlier variant of the myth, transmitted by Hesiod (*Works* 221–23), in which Dike, because she was expelled, weeping and wandering throughout the earth, complained to her father Zeus about the injustice.

22. See Reese 1970; Winston 1979; Kloppenborg 1982; Larcher 1983–85; Gilbert 1986 (review article with comprehensive bibliography); Schmitt 1986, 1989; Hentschel and Zenger 1991; Schroer 1994c: 543–58 (= 1996a: 110–26, 1998); Engel 1998; H. Hübner 1999.

23. The division between the first two main parts is usually placed at Wis 6:21/22, but the praise of accessible wisdom can also be seen as the introduction to the encomium of wisdom. The personified Sophia of *Sapientia* is less hidden than the one in Job 28, less particular than the one in Sira 24, and clearly more individual and psychological than the one in Proverbs 8.

24. Gk. *meris* very often renders Hebr. *ḥeleq*.

25. Cf. his "I saw" in Qoh 2:3, 24; 3:16, 18, 22; 7:16; 8:9; 9:1.

26. *Aphtharsia* Wis 2:23, 6:19; *athanasia* Wis 1:13–15; 3:4; 4:1, 8; 8:17; 15:3; 16:13. Neither word has an equivalent in Hebrew.

humanity's being in the image of God (2:23). *Sapientia*, of course—in the best Old Testament tradition—does not say that man or his soul is immortal. To the extent that man opens himself to the wisdom, the spirit, and the justice of God, he becomes incorruptible and immortal.

In Wisdom 3–6, in the traditional fashion of proverbial wisdom (e.g., Proverbs 10–22; some psalms), the righteous (*dikaioi*) and impious (*asebeis*) are contrasted. What is new is that, in judging their fate, their earthly condition (painful or painless, children or no children) is unimportant, for fate is decided no longer in this world but in a hope, an idea, or a mystery that reaches far beyond this life, namely, to be ultimately taken up by God. This turn of events, which in the First Testament affects only two outstanding persons[27] and is longed for by the one who prays Psalm 73 (Irsigler 1984), in *Sapientia* becomes a prospect for all of the "pious." Since one's true life is seen in one's relationship with God, the value of concrete life is relativized before death.[28] The contrast to Qohelet is obvious. Qohelet is largely oriented to this world, *Sapientia* much more strongly to ideas and hopes beyond this world.

The *second part* (6:12–8:18) shows that this Wisdom is accessible (6:12–21) and that her mystery is not limited to Israel. In contrast to Ben Sira, who has wisdom dwell in Jerusalem (Sir 24:10), *Sapientia* has Wisdom and her mysteries, which ever since their origin (*ap' archēs geneseōs*, 6:22) she wants to understand and understands "without envy," enlighten everyone, since the multitude of the wise is the salvation of the world (*sōtēria kosmou*; 6:22–25). The putative Solomon speaking in 7:1–6 bases this universalist position on the fact that, along with the broadly realized topos of the tradition of man's creation,[29] he declares himself to be a human like any other. Here and hereafter, *Sapientia*, no matter how clear the allusions to biblical characters in the text, never names a name, thus turning the wise of Israel into examples of transcultural wisdom. Thus, in the case of Solomon's prayer for wisdom (1 Kgs 3:6–9), the speaking *I* in 7:7–16 explains that he implored God for nothing but wisdom, which is more valuable than all the splendors of the world (cf. Job 28); and that he received this wisdom from God and in its train all the splendors of the world as well, since Wisdom is the source and birth-mother of everything (*genetin*, 7:12; cf. Prov 8:12–21). The science-like character of the subsequent exposition on wisdom (7:17–21) is startling. Perhaps the occasion for it was Solomon's traditional talk of plants and animals (1 Kgs 5:12f.). In *Sapientia*, he is exclusively concerned with the fact that Wisdom is the master-builder, the fashioner of all things (*hē gar pantōn technitis*). This is probably a reflection of the *'amon* "master worker" of Prov 8:30.

In 7:22–8:1, Wisdom is first described with a long series of (3 × 7) adjectives with which Stoic philosophers, especially Cleanthes (head of the Stoa 262–232 B.C.), had conceptualized the good or the Logos that permeates and shapes matter. According to 7:26, Wisdom is a reflection (cf. Heb 1:3) of eternal light (*apaugasma phōtos aidiou*), an image (cf. 2 Cor 4:4) of God's goodness (*eikōn tēs agathotētos autou*). She continually renews all things, like the spirit of God in Ps 104:30. In 7:29, she is described like the beloved in Song 6:10, anticipating the love affair between the speaking *I* and Wisdom that is the theme of 8:2–18.

In 8:2–18, the choice of Wisdom as a bride is grounded first in her good breeding, which she exhibits in her symbiosis with God (8:3), whose work of creation she defined and defines (8:4). She also defines human companionship. In accordance with her honorable heritage, on those who strive for her

---

27. Enoch in Gen 5:24, Sir 44:16; Elijah in 2 Kgs 2:1–18.
28. Not unrelated is the positive interpretation of an early death in a verse of Menander's translated by Plautus (*Bacch.* 4.7.18): *Quem di diligunt, adolescens moritur* 'Whom the gods love dies young'.
29. Cf. Job 31:13–15, 33:6, 34:19; Prov 17:5, 22:2.

she bestows the cardinal virtues (*temperantia, prudentia, justitia, fortitudo*; 8:6f.). Above and beyond economic, social, and political success, the speaking *I* expects of this marriage, first of all, immortality (8:13, 17). But through all this, Wisdom remains the delightful playmate as in Prov 8:30b–31 (8:16).

The *third part* (8:19–19:22) comprises a great prayer for Wisdom. Her saving power in history is the broad topic. It can barely be considered history any more, of course. Reminiscences of the narrative traditions of the First Testament are in fact impossible to hide, but the personal names are consistently omitted and the biblical content is turned into paradigms for the direct operation of Wisdom in human life.[30] A dismantling of the boundaries[31] of Israelite traditions, making them universal, thus took place. After brief allusions to Genesis 1 (9:2ff.), in the resumed prayer for Wisdom in 9:4, she is apostrophized with the title of a goddess—literally, "the possessor of thy (God's) throne" (*tēn tōn sōn thronōn parhedron*). Her role as God's throne-companion is grounded once again in her participation in the creation of the world (9:9). In 11:20b, borrowing from Job 28:25f., a mathematical formula underlies the world. The most varied Old Testament wisdom traditions are thus taken up, combined, and overhauled in *Sapientia*.

What appeared briefly in 5:17 and 20—namely, that all creation (*ktisis*) or the entire cosmos serves to promote the pious and punish the impious—is greatly expanded in the third part. While the prophets viewed history as directed by God and the rulers (Assyrians, Nebuchadnezzar, Cyrus) as God's tools, in *Sapientia*, it is above all the powers of nature, its elements guided by Wisdom, that serve to carry out God's plans. In the process, the "law" that the punishment should fit any sinner is observed. The traditional plagues of Egypt (frogs, gnats, locusts) were regarded as an appropriate response to Egyptian worship of animals.[32] Wisdom plays creation like a harp (19:18) and works tirelessly to punish the impious and to save the pious. Traditions of creation and history flow together in *Sapientia* into a single unified cosmos, whose leader and director is Wisdom. Her titles and the sayings about her have left a great impression on New Testament Christology. Christ as the firstborn of all creation (Col 1:15) is unimaginable (see Schroer 2000: 132–48) without Wisdom.

---

30. From this perspective, the Exodus looks like a creation event, liberation as new creation.
31. The same tendency is found in the not specifically Israelite expressions for "God" in Wisdom 1.
32. Wis 11:15–20, 12:23–27, 15:18–16:1.

Epilogue

Our overview of Israel's traditions of creation and their relationship with those of its neighbors has shown how strongly Israel's experiences and reflections on the world resembled those of its time and place. But alongside this horizontal factor is a vertical factor specific to its own experience. The former empowers it not to become rigid or sectarian. The latter helps it to preserve its identity and not lose house and home.

The impending modern ecological catastrophe challenges everyone to become involved constructively in their own domain. Dockworker or doctor, engineer or farmer, it represents a challenge. Whoever accepts this challenge cannot lose. It summons theologians, who along with others comprise the memory of the community, to search the ancient traditions for source, direction, and encouragement for today's pressing task. Theologians are the scribes trained for the kingdom of heaven who, challenged by the new, bring out from the treasure of their religious tradition what is old (Matt 13:52). The highly anthropocentric and power-oriented creation narrative of Genesis 1 must be relieved of its monopoly by this opportunity and replaced, or at least supplemented, by less aggressive texts such as Genesis 2, Psalm 104, Job 38–39, Proverbs 8, and so on, which entitle those who share the world with humankind to their own law and their own place. The unexamined idea that Israelite monotheism deprives Creation of its sanctity must be corrected at least in part. Those who are patient, who look, and who see (Matt 6:25–34 and parallels) can still encounter mysterious regularity (Job 28) and vitality (Proverbs 8) and give meaning to life. Israel's God is not merely a God of History but also always a God of Creation, whose "acts" in this realm are just as great, powerful, beautiful, comforting (Psalms 135f., Qoh 3:11, Wis 8:9), frightening, and incomprehensible as are those in the realm of History.

Bertolt Brecht—who in questions of ecology generally did not display an exemplary consciousness—in his poem "The Doubter" ("Der Zweifler," 1937) attempts to offer a structural-skeptical encounter with answers to big questions. If we remain in the stream of existence, we must connect with what has already been said—perhaps to refute it, to engage new thought with experience, recognize dangerous ambiguities, but at the same time not to remove the contradictions from things; and above all, we must always establish the vital relevance of our ideas (our theology): How does one act if one believes what you say?

Brecht's poem closes soberly, but energetically, with the necessity to make a fresh start again. To be able to make a fresh start is a blessing, since in every new beginning there is hidden *in nuce* that to which we owe our existence: the power of Creation.

THE DOUBTER

Whenever we seemed
to have found the answer to a question
One of us untied the string of the old rolled-up
Chinese scroll on the wall, so that it fell down and
Revealed to us the man on the bench who
Doubted so much.

I, he said to us
Am the doubter. I am doubtful whether
The work was well done that devoured your days.
Whether what you said would still have value for anyone if it were less well said.
Whether you said it well but perhaps
Were not convinced of the truth of what you said.
Whether it is not ambiguous; each possible misunderstanding
Is your responsibility. Or it can be unambiguous
And take the contradictions out of things; is it too unambiguous?
If so, what you say is useless. Your thing has no life in it.
Are you truly in the stream of happening? Do you accept
All that develops? Are *you* developing? Who are you? To whom
Do you speak? Who finds what you say useful? And, by the way:
Is it sobering? Can it be read in the morning?
Is it also linked to what is already there? Are the sentences that were
Spoken before you made use of, or at least refuted? Is everything verifiable?
By experience? By which one? But above all
Always above all else: how does one act
If one believes what you say? Above all: how does one act?

Reflectively, curiously, we studied the doubting
Blue man on the scroll, looked at each other and
Made a fresh start.

Bertolt Brecht

Translated by Lee Baxendall, from *Bertolt Brecht: Poems 1913–1956*, edited by John Willett and Ralph Manheim with the cooperation of Erich Fried (New York: Routledge, 1987 [orig. Methuen, 1979]), pp. 270f.

A Selection of Nonbiblical Texts

Text 1
Enki and Ninmaḫ 4–37

Information on the text: Pettinato 1971: 69–73; Römer, *TUAT* III 386–401; Sauren 1993.

As the gods of heaven came to life,
as the mother goddesses were married,
as the gods dispersed throughout heaven and earth,
as the mother goddesses [. . .] in Aha gave birth,
then the gods had to worry about their food and drink through forced labor,
    which they were bound to:
the upper gods supervised the work, the lower gods bore the carrying basket;
the gods piled up ground in Ḫarali, to dig canals;
the gods hastened there, therefore they complained.
Then lay Enki, the extremely wise one, the creator who had caused many gods
    to be,
in the Engur, the trough, from which the water flows, the place
    whose inwards no other god can penetrate (with his eye),
in his bedchamber (and) did not arise from his sleep.
The gods wept and complained: "He created misery";
but they did not dare, against the sleeping one, against the one lying there,
    to intrude into his bedchamber.
(But) Nammu, the mother who precedes all, the bearer of the many gods,
brought to her son the tears of the gods:
"My son, you are lying there, truly, you are sleeping!
[. . .] the upper gods strike the body of your creatures;
My son, arise from your bedchamber, you who from the fullness of your wisdom
    understand every art;
make a replacement for the gods, so that they can throw away their carrying basket!
Enki, by the word of his mother Nammu, stood up from his bedchamber;
the god went around in the holy room, reasoning, struck himself on the thigh,
the wise, the knowing, the insightful, who knows all that is necessary and
    ingenious,
    the creator and he who forms all things, causes the *Sigensigšar* to emerge;
Enki fixes his arms and forms his chest.
Enki, the creator, causes his wisdom to enter the inwards of his own creature.
He says to his mother Nammu:
"My mother, on the creatures you cause to exist,
    bind on the forced labor of the gods;
after you have mixed the inwards of the clay over the Apsû,
you will form the *Sigensigšar* and the clay; let the creature be present,
and Ninmaḫ be your helper,
Ninimma, Egiziana, Ninmada, Ninbara,

– 194 –

Ninmug, Sarsardu, and Ninniginna, whom you bore, may they stand in
   your service.
My mother, determine his destiny; may Ninmaḫ bind (on him) the forced labor.

Text 2
Enki and Ninmaḫ 4–47

Translation: Sauren 1993

As Nammu, Enki, came to life,
as the goddess was taken in entrance-marriage,
as the goddess was devised in heaven and earth,
as this goddess b.c.me pregnant and gave birth,
as heaven and food supply were formally arranged,
all the myriads of gods stood by,
even the minor gods held the tankard.
The gods were digging canals,
they piled up the ground on the reed,
the gods were grumbling at their work,
they had words about their life,
[and they poured their tears before Nammu:]

On this day, the wise one,
the creator of all myriads in existence,
Enki, (lay) inside the deep well,
at the place where no god is,
where no worship takes place,
he lay in his bed, and
he did not arise from his sleep.
To the sleeping one, to the lying one,
to the one who did not arise from his bed,
Nammu, the primeval mother,
(brought) the tears of the gods,
she brought (them) to her boy.

Woe! You are lying there.
Woe! you are sleeping there.
My son, from your bed,
woe! you don't arise!
The gods, your creatures,
are destroying their work.
My son, arise from your bed!
In your great wisdom
let work your sacredness!
The family of the gods,—
my son, create them,
so that they shall hold the tankard!

Enki, (obedient) to the word of his mother,
to Nammu, arose from his bed,
he cut the holy lamb,
(the lamb) of appeasement,
the intelligent, the thoughtful, the researcher,
the god, the omniscient of sacredness, the creator,
the universal, brought forth from the womb,

Enki put his hand therein,
he moved and moved his thoughts.
The god, Enki, the creator,
from his own, from his thinking,
from his intelligence, really stamps it.

He answered his mother Nammu:
"My mother, the creature you propose will exist,
put on the carrying basket of the gods,
multiply what is in the waters of your belly,
and you will give form to the limbs,
Ninmaḫ will act at your head,
Ninimma, Šuziana, Ninmada,
Ninbara, (the other) Ninbara, Ninmuga,
Sarsardu, and Ninguna are your birth-goddesses.
My mother, you will determine the destiny,
Ninmaḫ will tie up this basket (the difficulties of birth),
they all will do the work: (creating) mankind.

Nammu gave birth to mankind,
the being, out of the waters the head came out:
"he has our limbs, will be his omen."
Nammu held her flesh to the sperm,
a second time, a woman, was the being.
She (Nammu) stamped her for the carrying basket of birth, for the sperm.
"She is a woman, birth shall be her counsel."
Enki stopped all the works going on,
he looked at it, his heart was joyful,
he prepared a feast for Nammu,
he ate at the side of the womb together with the new-born princes,
the bread and (he drank) from the main reed-tube.

Text 3
Atraḫasis I 189–248

Translation: Lambert and Millard 1969: 55ff.
Information on the text: Pettinato 1971: 101–4; von Soden, TUAT III 612–45

While [Bēlet-ilī, the birth-goddess], is present,
"Let the birth-goddess create offspring(?),
And let man bear the toil of the gods."
They summoned and asked the godess,
The midwife of the gods, wise Mami,
'You are the birth-goddess, creatress of mankind,
Create Lullû that he may bear the yoke,
Let him bear the yoke assigned by Enlil,
Let man carry the toil of the gods.'
Nintu opened her mouth
And addressed the great gods,
"It is not possible for me to make things,
Skill lies with Enki.
Since he can cleanse everything
Let him give me the clay so that I can make it."
Enki opened his mouth
And addressed the great gods,

'On the first, seventh, and fifteenth day of the month
I will make a purifying bath.
Let one god be slaughtered
So that all the gods may be cleansed in a dipping.
From his flesh and blood
Let Nintu mix clay,
That god and man
May be thoroughly mixed in the clay,
So that we may hear the drum for the rest of time
Let there be a spirit from the god's flesh.
Let it proclaim living (man) as a sign,
So that this be not forgotten let there be a spirit.'
In the assembly answered 'Yes'
The great Anunnaki, who administer destinies.
On the first, seventh, and fifteenth day of the month
He made a purifying bath.
Wê-ila, who had personality,
They slaughtered in their assembly.
From his flesh and blood
Nintu mixed clay.
For the rest [of time they heard the drum],
From the flesh of the god [there was] a spirit.
It proclaimed living (man) as its sign,
And so that this was not forgotten [there was] a spirit.

After she had mixed that clay
She summoned the Anunnaki, the great gods.
The Igigi, the great gods,
Spat upon the clay.
Mami opened her mouth
And addressed the great gods,
'You commanded me a task, I have completed it;
You have slaughtered a god together with his personality.
I have removed your heavy work,
I have imposed your toil on man.
You raised a cry for mankind,
I have loosed the yoke, I have established freedom.'
They heard this speech of hers,
They ran together and kissed her feet, (saying,)
'Formerly we used to call you Mami,
Now let your name be Mistress-of-All-the-Gods (Bēlet-kāla-ilī).'

Text 4
KAR 4

Translation after Pettinato 1971: 74–81, esp. 77–79 (lines 1–73)

After heaven was separated from earth—they were both solidly founded—
and the mother goddesses had sprung up,
after the earth was set, the earth was founded,
after (the gods) had set the rules of heaven and earth,
after they, in order to arrange the dikes and canals,
had set the banks of the Tigris and Euphrates,
then An, Enlil, Utu, and Enki,

the great gods,
and the Anunna, the great gods,
at the prominent high place, which is clothed with fear, took their places
and talked among themselves;
after the gods had set the rules of heaven and earth,
and in order to arrange the dikes and canals,
the banks of the Tigris and Euphrates
had set, then Enlil spoke to them:
"What will you do now,
what will you now create?"
The great gods who stood there,
and the Anunna who decide fate,
both answered Enlil:
"In Uzuma of Duranki
we want to slaughter the Lamga gods,
so that their blood will cause humanity to gush forth;
let the workload of the gods be their workload:
that they set the boundary ditches forever,
take the pickax and carrying basket in their hands,
for the temple of the great gods,
which is intended for a prominent high place,
floor on floor [or: slab on slab] align,
forever the boundary ditches
set,
arrange the dike,
set the boundary ditches,
[. . .] plants of every kind
cause to thrive,
rain, rain [. . .]
set the boundary ditches,
pile up grain heaps;
[. . .]
[. . .]
[. . .]
That they cause the grainfield of the Anunna prosper,
multiply the surplus in the land,
celebrate the festivals of the gods suitably,
gush forth cold water,
in the great dwelling place of the gods, which is suited for a prominent high place,
Ullegarra and Annegarra
you will name them.
That they cattle, sheep, beasts, fish, and birds,
the surplus of the land, multiply,
Enul and Ninul
have resolved with their pure mouth.
Aruru, who is suited for the ladyship,
has drafted the great rules from herself.
That experienced on experienced, inexperienced on inexperienced
spring up from themselves, like barley from the earth,
is a thing that will not be altered, like the eternals star of heaven.
That the festivals of the gods, day and night,
they celebrate suitably:
the great rules for which from themselves
drafted
An, Enlil,

Enki and Ninmaḫ,
the great gods.
In the place at which they created mankind,

Nisaba was truly installed as lady.
Mystery. The knowing shall show it to the knowing. End. Collated. Old forerunner.
Hand of Kiddin-Sîn, the young scribe, son of Sutu, the royal scribe.

Text 5
Enuma elish VI 1–34

Translation: Dalley 1991: 260f.
Information on the text: Smith 1876, King 1902, Jacobsen 1976: 165–91

When Marduk heard the speech of the gods,
He made up his mind to perform miracles.
He spoke his utterance to Ea,
And communicated to him the plan that he was considering.
    Let me put blood together, and make bones too.
    Let me set up primeval man: Man shall be his name.
    Let me create aprimeval man.
    The work of the gods shall be imposed (on him), and so they shall be at leisure.
    Let me change the ways of the gods miraculously,
    So they are gathered as one yet divided in two.'
Ea answered him and spoke a word to him,
Told him his plan for the leisure of the gods.
    'Let one who is hostile to them be surrendered (up),
    Let him be destroyed, and let people be created (from him).
    Let the great gods assemble,
    Let the culprit be given up, and let them convict him.'
Marduk assembled the great gods,
Gave (them) instructions pleasantly, gave orders.
The gods paid attention to what he said.
The king addressed his words to the Anunnaki,
    'Your election of me shall be firm and foremost.
    I shall declare the laws, the edicts within my power.
    Whosoever started the war,
    And incited Tiamat, and gathered an army,
    Let the one who started the war be given up to me,
    And he shall bear the penalty for his crime, that you may dwell in peace.'
The Igigi, the great gods, answered him,
Their lord Lugal-dimmer-ankia, counsellor of gods,
    'It was Qingu who started the war,
    He who incited Tiamat and gathered an army!'
They bound him and held him in front of Ea,
Imposed the penalty on him and cut off his blood.
He created mankind from his blood,
Imposed the toil of the gods (on man) and released the gods from it.

Text 6
Childbirth Incantation

Translation after the French translation by van Dijk 1973: 504f.

In the seminal fluids
the skeleton formed,
in the web of musculature
the offspring formed.
In the wild and fearsome waters of the ocean,
where the arms of the fetus are bound,
at the place whose deeps the eye of the sun does not illuminate,
there the son of Enki, Asarluḫi,
could direct his gaze upon it.
He untied the bonds
that held it bound.
The way for him,
he prepared his way for him.
Now the ways are open for you,
your ways are [. . .]
She stands for you at [. . .]
she who was there at the formation of the [. . .],
who assisted at the origin of all of us,
so that we bear the yoke of service.
She said: "You are free.
The bars are unbarred,
the gates are open,
that [. . .] may strike.
Like the beloved child
make that you go out."
Incantation for a woman giving birth.

Text 7
Gilgamesh I iii 25 – iv 29

Translation: George 1999: 6ff.
Information on the text: Schott 1969, Tigay 1982

[*Paying heed*] to the advice of his father,
   the hunter went off, [*set out on the journey.*]
He took the road, set [his face] toward Uruk,
   before Gilgamesh *the king* [*he spoke these words:*]

'There was a man [came *by the water-hole,*]
   mightiest in the land, strength [he possesses,]
[his strength] is as mighty as a rock from the sky.

'Over the hills he roams *all* [*day,*]
   always with the herd [*he grazes on grasses,*]
always his tracks [*are found*] by the water-[hole,]
   I am afraid and I dare not approach [him.]

'He fills in the pits that I [myself] dig,
   he pulls up the snares [that I lay.]

He sets free from my grasp all the beasts of the field,
  he stops me doing the work of the wild.'

Said Gilgamesh to him, to the hunter:
  'Go, hunter, take with you Shamhat the harlot!

'When the herd comes down to the water-hole,
  she should strip off her raiment to reveal her charms.
He will see her, and will approach her,
  his herd will spurn him, though he grew up amongst it.'

Off went the hunter, taking Shamhat the harlot,
  they set out on the road, they started the journey.
On the third day they came to their destination,
  hunter and harlot sat down there *to wait.*

One day and a second they waited by the water-hole,
  then the herd came down to drink the water.
The game arrived, their hearts *delighting in* water,
  and Enkidu also, born in the uplands.

With the gazelles he grazed on grasses,
  joining the throng with the game at the water-hole,
his heart *delighting* with the beasts in the water:
  then Shamhat saw him, the child of nature,
the savage man from the midst of the wild.

'This is he, Shamhat! Uncradle your bosom,
  bare your sex, let him take in your charms!
Do not recoil, but take in his scent:
  he will see you, and will approach you.

'Spread your clothing so he may lie on you,
  do for the man the work of a woman!
Let his passion caress and embrace you,
  his herd will spirn him, though he grew up amongst it.'

Shamhat unfastened the cloth of her loins,
  she bared her sex and he took in her charms.
She did not recoil, she took in his scent:
  she spread her clothing and he lay upon her.

She did for the man the work of a woman,
  his passion caressed and embraced her.
For six days and seven nights
  Enkidu was erect, as he coupled with Shamhat.

When with her delights he was fully sated,
  he turned his gaze to his herd.
The gazelles saw Enkidu, they started to run,
  the beasts of the field shied away from his presence.

Enkidu had defiled his body so pure,
  his legs stood still, though his herd was in motion.
Enkidu was weakened, could not run as before,
  but now he had *reason*, and wide understanding.

Text 8
Instruction of Merikare 312–34

Translation: Lichtheim 1973: 106
Information on the text: Eliade et al. 1964: 96; Brunner 1988: 137–54, 442–49;
Assmann, *TUAT* II 835f.

Well tended is mankind—god's cattle,
He made sky and earth for their sake,
He subdued the water monster,
He made breath for their noses to live.
They are his images, who came from his body,
He shines in the sky for their sake;
He made for them plants and cattle,
Fowl and fish to feed them.
He slew his foes, reduced his children,
When they thought of making rebellion.
He makes daylight for their sake,
He sails by to see them.
He has built his shrine around them,
When they weep he hears.
He made for them rulers in the egg,
Leaders to raise the B.C. of the weak.
He made for them magic as weapons
To ward off the blow of events,
Guarding them by day and by night.
He has slain the traitors among them,
As a man beats his son for his brother's sake,
For god knows every name.

Text 9
Hymn to Amun-Ra

Translation: John A. Wilson, *ANET* 366b

Thou art the sole one, who made [all] that is,
[The] solitary sole [one], who made what exists,
From whose eyes mankind came forth,
And upon whose mouth the gods came into being.
He who made herbage [for] the cattle,
And the fruit tree for mankind,
Who made that (on which) the fish in the river may live,
And the birds *soaring in* the sky.
He who gives breath to that which is in the egg,
Gives life to the son of the slug,
And makes that on which gnats may live,
And worms and flies in like manner;
Who supplies the needs of the mice in their holes,
And gives life to flying things in every tree.
Hail to thee, who did all this!
solitary sole one, with many hands,
Who spends the night wakeful, while all men are asleep,
Seeking benefit for his creatures.

Amon, enduring in all things, Atum and Har-akhti—
Praises are thine, when they all say:
"Jubilation to thee, b.c.use thou weariest thyself with us!
Salaams to thee, b.c.use thou didst create us!"
Hail to thee for all beasts!
jubilation to thee for every foreign country—
To the height of heaven, to the width of earth,
To the depth of the Great Green Sea!
The gods are bowing down to thy majesty
And exalting the might of him who created them,
Rejoicing at the approach of him who begot them.
They say to thee: "Welcome in peace!
Father of the fathers of all the gods,
Who raised the heavens and laid down the ground,
Who made what is and created what exists;
sovereign—life, prosperity, health!—and chief of the gods!
We praise thy might, according as thou didst make us.
Let (us) act for thee, b.c.use thou brought us forth.
We give thee thanksgiving b.c.use thou hast wearied thyself with us!"
Hail to thee, who made all that is!

Text 10
The Great Aton Hymn from Amarna

Translation: Lichtheim 1976: 96–99
Information on the text: Assmann, *TUAT* II 848–53

Adoration of *Re-Harakhti-who-rejoices-in-lightland In-his-name-Shu-who-is-Aten*,
living forever; the great living Aten who is in jubilee, the lord of all that the Disk
encircles, lord of sky, lord of earth, lord of the house-of-Aten in Akhet-Aten; (and)
of) the King of Upper and Lower Egypt, who lives by Maat, the Lord of the Two
Lands, *Neferkheprure, Sole-one-of-Re*; the Son of Re who lives by Maat, the Lord of
Crowns, Akhenaten, great in his lifetime; (and) his beloved great Queen, the Lady
of the Two Lands, *Nefer-nefru-Aten Nefertiti*, who lives in health and youth forever.
The Vizier, the Fanbearer on the right of the King, ———[Ay]; he says:

Splendid you rise in heaven's lightland,
O living Aten, creator of life!
When you have dawned in eastern lightland,
You fill every land with your beauty,
You are beauteous, great, radiant,
High over every land;
Your rays embrace the lands,
To the limit of all that you made.
Being Re, you reach their limits,
You bend them ‹for› the son whom you love;
Though you are far, your rays are on earth,
Though one sees you, your strides are unseen.

When you set in western lightland,
Earth is in darkness as if in death;
One sleeps in chambers, heads covered,
One eye does not see another.
Were they robbed of their goods,

That are under their heads,
People would not remark it.
Every lion comes from its den,
All the serpents bite;
Darkness hovers, earth is silent,
As their maker rests in lightland.

Earth brightens when you dawn in lightland,
When you shine as Aten of daytime;
As you dispel the dark,
As you cast your rays,
The Two Lands are in festivity.
Awake they stand on their feet,
You have roused them;
Bodies cleansed, clothed,
Their arms adore your appearance.
The entire land sets out to work,
All beasts browse on their herbs;
Trees, herbs are sprouting,
Birds fly from their nests,
Their wings greeting your *ka*.
All flocks frisk on their feet,
All that fly up and alight,
They live when you dawn for them.
Ships fare north, fare south as well,
Roads lie open when you rise;
The fish in the river dart before you,
Your rays are in the midst of the sea.

Who makes seed grow in women,
Who creates people from sperm;
Who feeds the son in his mother's womb,
Who soothes him to still his tears.
Nurse in the womb,
Giver of breath,
To nourish all that he made.
When he comes from the womb to breathe,
On the day of his birth,
You open wide his mouth,
You supply his needs.
When the chick in the egg speaks in the shell,
You give him breath within to sustain him;
When you have made him complete,
To break out from the egg,
He comes out from the egg,
To announce his completion,
Walking on his legs he comes from it.

How many are your deeds,
Though hidden from sight,
O Sole God beside whom there is none!
You made the earth as you wished, you alone,
All peoples, herds, and flocks;
All upon earth that walk on legs,
All on high that fly on wings,
The lands of Khor and Kush,
The land of Egypt.

You set every man in his place,
You supply their needs;
Everyone has his food,
His lifetime is counted.
Their tongues differ in speech,
Their characters likewise;
Their skins are distinct,
For you distinguished the peoples.

You made the Nile in the netherworld,
You bring him when you will,
To nourish the people,
For you made them for yourself.
Lord of all who toils for them,
Lord of all lands who shines for them,
Aten of daytime, great in glory!
All distant lands, you make them live,
You made a heavenly Nile descend for them;
He makes waves on the mountains like the sea,
To drench their fields and their towns.
How excellent are your ways, O Lord of eternity!
A Nile from heaven for foreign peoples,
And all lands' creatures that walk on legs,
For Egypt the Nile who comes from the netherworld.

Your rays nurse all fields,
When you shine they live, they grow for you;
You made the seasons to foster all that you made,
Winter to cool them, heat that they taste you.
You made the far sky to shine therein,
To behold all that you made;
You alone, shining in your form of living Aten,
Risen, radiant, distant, near.
You made millions of forms from yourself alone,
Towns, villages, fields, the river's course;
All eyes observe you upon them,
For you are the Aten of daytime on high.

When you are gone, your eye is no longer there,
which you created for the purpose that you not be the only one
to see what you created(?); [these three lines after Assmann's restoration –trans.]
you are in my heart,
There is no other who knows you,
Only your son, *Neferkheprure, Sole-one-of-Re,*
Whom you have taught your ways and your might.
‹Those on› earth come from your hand as you made them,
When you have dawned they live,
When you set they die;
You yourself are lifetime, one lives by you.
All eyes are on ‹your› beauty until you set,
All labor ceases when you rest in the west;
When you rise you stir [everyone] for the King,
Every leg is on the move since you founded the earth.
You rouse them for your son who came from your body,
The King who lives by Maat, the Lord of the Two Lands,
Neferkheprure, Sole-one-of-Re,
The Son of Re who lives by Maat, the Lord of crowns,

Akhenaten, great in his lifetime;
(And) the great Queen whom he loves, the Lady of the Two Lands,
Nefer-nefru-Aten Nefertiti, living forever.

Text 11
The Monument of the Memphite Theology 48–61

Translation: Lichtheim 1973: 54f.
Information on the text: Junker 1940, Koch 1965
New translation with comments: Peust and Sternberg el-Hotabi, *TUAT Ergänzungs-lieferung* 2001: 166–75.

The gods who came into being in Ptah:
Ptah-on-the-great-throne ———.
Ptah-Nun, the father who [made] Atum.
Ptah-Naunet, the mother who bore Atum.
Ptah-the-Great is heart and tongue of the Nine [Gods].
[Ptah] ——— who bore the gods.
[Ptah] ——— who bore the gods.
[Ptah] ———.
[Ptah] ——— Nefertem at the nose of Re every day.

There took shape in the heart, there took shape on the tongue the form of Atum. For the very great one is Ptah, who gave [life] to all the gods and their *kas* through this heart and through this tongue, in which Horus had taken shape as Ptah, in which Thoth had taken shape as Ptah.

Thus heart and tongue rule over all the limbs in accordance with the teaching that it (the heart) is in every body and it (the tongue) is in every mouth of all gods, all men, all cattle, all creeping things, whatever lives, thinking whatever it wishes and commanding whatever it wishes.

His (Ptah's) Ennead is before him as teeth and lips. They are the semen and hands of Atum. For the Ennead of Atum came into being through his semen and his fingers. But the Ennead is the teeth and lips in this mouth which pronounced the name of every thing, from which Shu and Tefnut came forth, and which gave birth to the Ennead.

Sight, hearing, breathing—they report to the heart, and it makes every understanding come forth. As to the tongue, it repeats what the heart has devised. Thus all the gods were born and his Ennead was completed. For every word of the god came about through what the heart devised and the tongue commanded.

Thus all the faculties were made and all the qualities determined, they that make all foods and all provisions, through this word. ‹Thus justice is done› to him who does what is loved, ‹and punishment› to him who does what is hated. Thus life is given to the peaceful, death is given to the criminal. Thus all labor, all crafts are made, the action of the hands, the motion of the legs, the movements of all the limbs, according to this command which is devised by the heart and comes forth on the tongue and creates the performance of everything.

Thus it is said of Ptah: "He who made all and created the gods." And he is Ta-tenen, who gave birth to the gods, and from whom every thing came forth, foods, provisions, divine offerings, all good things. Thus it is recognized and understood that he is the mightiest of the gods. Thus Ptah was satisfied after he had made all things and all divine words.

He gave birth to the gods,
He made the towns,
He established the names,
He placed the gods in their shrines,
He settled their offerings,
He established their shrines,
He made their bodies according to their wishes.
Thus the gods entered into their bodies,
Of every wood, every stone, every clay,
Every thing that grows upon him
In which they came to be.
Thus were gathered to him all the gods and their *kas*,
Content, united with the Lord of the Two Lands.

Text 12
Lugal Myth VIII 5–38

Translation after Pettinato 1971: 93f.
Information on the text: van Dijk 1983; Römer, *TUAT* III 444–48

At that time no lucky water that comes from the ground gushed forth on the meadow;
ice-cold water that flooded all like the breaking day brought from the mountains devastation;
the gods of the lands set in,
bore the pickax and carrying basket:
this was their workload.
The people in their [. . .]; mankind was called.
The Tigris in its greatness did not bring its floodwaters to heaven,
its mouth did not end in the sea; it did not gush sweet water;
no one entered the sanctuary on the quai;
no bread soothed severe hunger;
no one cleared the small canals; no one dredged the sediment;
no one watered the good field; one to dig the irrigation ditches was nowhere to be found.
In the lands the seed furrows were not dug; the grain grew wild.
The lord directed his broad mind there,
Ninurta, the son of Enlil, undertook great things:
He erected a pile of stones in the mountains;
like clouds drawing hither he dug thither,
like a great battlement he stretched out before the land of Sumer,
he set a barrier on the horizon;
the hero bowed, he [. . .] the cities all together.
With the mighty waters, the stones competed;
now the waters of the mountains forever will no longer come down to the valley (= the earth);
the waters that were scattered, he gathered,
the waters that were lost in the mountain range
he gathered, threw them into the Tigris,
early floods he poured over the fields.
Now until all future time:
The kings of the land of Sumer rejoiced forever about the lord Ninurta.
In the grainfields he (= Ninurta) created the mottled barley,

he caused the orchards to bear fruit at the harvest,
he piled up grain heaps as high as tells;
the lord [. . .]ed a quai from the land of Sumer.
He made the minds of the gods gay:
Ninurta, their father, they (= the gods) praise.

Bibliography

The bibliography includes all works referred to except for articles in dictionaries (*HALAT*, *THAT*, *ThWAT*), encyclopedias (*BNP*, *LÄ*, *LIMC*, *NBL*, *RlA*, *RGG*, *TRE*), and the anthologies *ANET* and *TUAT*. These are cited in the text, where possible, by author, title, and date.

The abbreviations follow Siegfried Schwertner, *Internationales Abkürzungsverzeichnis für Theologie und Grenzgebiete* (IATG²), *Supplementband zur Theologischen Realenzyklopädie* (TRE) (Berlin 1992). Add: BNP – Christine F. Salazar, Francis G. Gentry, et al., eds., *Brill's New Pauly: Encyclopedia of the Ancient World* (Leiden/ Boston, 2002–2010).

A supplementary bibliography of publications that have appeared since the first edition of this book may be found on pp. 232ff.

Abou Assaf, Ali; Bordreuil, Pierre; and Millard, Alan R.
1982   *La statue de Tell Fekherye et son inscription bilingue assyro-araméenne*. Etudes assyriologiques 7. Paris.
Ahuis, Ferdinand
2011   Behemot, Leviatan und der Mensch in Hiob 38–42. *ZAW* 123: 72–91.
Albertz, Rainer
1974   *Weltschöpfung und Menschenschöpfung. Untersucht bei Deuterojesaja, Hiob und in den Psalmen*. Stuttgart.
1992   *Religionsgeschichte Israels in alttestamentlicher Zeit*, Teil 1: *Von den Anfängen bis zum Ende der Königszeit*. Göttingen.
Allen, James Peter
1988   *Genesis in Egypt: The Philosophy of Ancient Egyptian Creation Accounts*. Yale Egyptological Studies 2. New Haven.
Alster, Bendt
1978   Enki and Ninhursag: The Creation of the First Woman. *UF* 10: 15–28.
Alt, Albrecht
1951   Die Weisheit Salomos. *ThL* 76: 139–44 = idem, *Kleine Schriften zur Geschichte des Volkes Israel II*, 90–99. Munich, 1959.
Altermatt, Urs
1996   *Das Fanal von Sarajewo: Ethnonationalismus in Europa*. Zürich.
Altner, Günter, ed.
1989   *Ökologische Theologie. Perspektiven zur Orientierung*. Stuttgart.
Amery, Carl
1974   *Das Ende der Vorsehung: Die gnadenlosen Folgen des Christentums*. Reinbek, 1972; 2nd ed., 1974.
Amiran, Ruth
1962   Myths of Creation of Man and the Jericho Statues. *BASOR* 167: 23–25.
1969   *Ancient Pottery of the Holy Land: From Its Beginnings in the Neolithic Period to the End of the Iron Age*. Jerusalem.
Arneth, Martin
2000   *Sonne der Gerechtigkeites: Studien zur Solarisierung der Jahwe-Religion im Lichte von Psalm 72*. Beiheft zur Zeitschrift für Altorientalische und Biblische Rechtsgeschichte 1. Wiesbaden.
Assmann, Jan
1982   Die Zeugung des Sohnes: Bild, Spiel, Erzählung und das Problem des ägyptischen Mythos. Pp. 13–61 in Jan Assmann, Walter Burkert, and Fritz Stolz, eds., *Funktionen und Leistungen des Mythos: Drei altorientalische Beispiele*. OBO 48. Freiburg, Switzerland/ Göttingen.
1983   *Re und Amun: Die Krise des polytheistischen Weltbilds im Ägypten der 18.–20. Dynastie*. OBO 51. Freiburg, Switzerland/Göttingen.

1990   *Ma'at: Gerechtigkeit und Unsterblichkeit im Alten Ägypten.* Munich.

1903   *Monotheismus und Kosmotheismus: Ägyptische Formen eines „Denken des Einen' und ihre europäische Rezeptionsgeschichte.* Heidelberg.

1996   *Ägypten: Ein Sinngeschichte.* Darmstadt.

1997a   Rezeption und Auslegung in Ägypten: Das «Denkmal memphitischer Theologie» als Auslegung der heliopolitanischen Kosmogonie. Pp. 125–39 in Reinhard Gregor Kratz and Thomas Krüger, eds., *Rezeption und Auslegung im Alten Testament und in seinem Umfeld: Ein Symposion aus Anlass des 60. Geburtstags von Odil Hannes Steck.* OBO 153. Freiburg, Switzerland/ Göttingen.

1997b   *Moses the Egyptian: The Memory of Egypt in Western Monotheism.* Cambridge, 1997a.

1998   Mono-, Pan-, and Cosmotheism: Thinking the "One" in Egyptian Theology. *Orient* 33: 130–49.

1999   *Ägyptische Hymnen und Gebete: Übersetzt, kommentiert und eingeleitet.* 2nd edition.OBO. Freiburg, Switzerland/Göttingen.

Assmann, Jan; Burkert, Walter; and Stolz, Fritz

1982   *Funktionen und Leistungen des Mythos: Drei altorientalische Beispiele.* OBO 48. Freiburg, Switzerland/Göttingen.

Attinger, Pascal

1984   Enki et Ninḫursaga. *ZA* 74: 1–52.

Auffahrt, Christoph

1991   *Der drohende Untergang. „Schöpfung" in Mythos und Ritual im Alten Orient und in Griechenland am Beispiel der Odyssee und des Ezechielbuches.* RVV 39. Berlin/New York.

Auffret, Pierre

1981   *Hymnes d'Égypte et d'Israël.* OBO 34. Freiburg, Switzerland/Göttingen.

Avigad, Naḥman

1972   Excavations in the Jewish Quarter of the Old City of Jerusalem, 1971. *IEJ* 22: 193–200.

Avigad, Nahman, and Benjamin Sass

1997   *Corpus of West Semitic Stamp Seals.* Jerusalem: Israel Academy of Sciences and Humanities; Israel Exploration Society; and Hebrew University, Institute of Archaeology.

Bailey, John A.

1970   Initiation and the Primal Woman in Gilgamesh and Genesis 2–3. *JBL* 89: 137–50.

Baltzer, Klaus

1999   *Deutero-Jesaja.* Kommentar zum Alten Testament X,2. Gütersloh.

Barach, John

2011   The Glory of the Son of Man: An Exposition of Psalm 8. Pp. 3–33 in P. Leithart et al., eds., *The Glory of Kings: A Festschrift in Honor of James B. Jordan.* Portland: Pickwick.

Barthélemy, Dominique, and Rickenbacher, Otto

1973   *Konkordanz zum hebräischen Sirach: Mit syrisch-hebräischem Index.* Göttingen.

Baumgart, Norbert Clemens

1999   *Die Umkehr des Schöpfergottes: Zu Komposition und religionsgeschichtlichem Hintergrund von Gen 5–9.* HBS 22. Freiburg i. Breisgau.

Bauks, Michaela

1997a   *Die Welt am Anfang: Zum Verhältnis von Vorwelt und Weltentstehung in Gen 1 und in der altorientalischen Literatur.* WMANT 74. Neukirchen-Vluyn.

1997b   Präfigurationen der hermopolitanischen Achtheit in den Sargtexten? *BN* 88: 5–8.

Bauks, Michaela, and Baumann, Gerlinde

1994   Im Anfang war. . . ? Gen 1,1ff und Prov 8,22–31 im Vergleich. *BN* 71: 24–52.

Baumann, Gerlinde

1996   *Die Weisheitsgestalt in Proverbien 1–9: Traditionsgeschichtliche und theologische Studien.* FAT 16. Tübingen.

Beaux, Nathalie N.

1990   *Le cabinet de curiosités de Thoutmosis III: Plantes et animaux du Jardin botanique de Karnak.* OLA 36. Leuven.

Bechmann, Ulrike

2011   Chaos am Anfang und Ende der Welt: das biblische Weltbild. Pp. 31–55 in U. Bechmann and C. Friedl, eds., *Chaos: Beiträge von Vortragenden der Montagsakademie 2010/11.* Graz.

Beckerath, Jürgen von

1984   *Handbuch des ägyptischen Königsnamen.* MÄS 20. Munich and Berlin.

Ben-Dov, Jonathan

2011   Psalm 104:19: Ben-Sirah and the History of Calendars in Ancient Israel. *JJS* 62/1: 7–20.

Benz, Arnold

2009   *Das geschenkte Universum: Astrophysik und Schöpfung.* Düsseldorf.

Bergman, Jan
1968   *Ich bin Isis.* Uppsala.
Berlejung, Angelika
1998   *Die Theologie der Bilder: Herstellung und Einweihung von Kultbildern in Mesopotamien und die alttestamentliche Bilderpolemik.* OBO 162. Freiburg, Switzerland/Göttingen.
Bernett, Monika, and Keel, Othmar
1998   *Mond, Stier und Kult am Stadttor: Die Stele von Betsaida (et-Tell).* OBO 161. Freiburg, Switzerland/Göttingen.
Bickel, Susanne
1994   *La cosmogonie égyptienne avant le Nouvel Empire.* OBO 134. Freiburg, Switzerland/Göttingen.
1996   Changes in the Image of the Creator God During the Middle and New Kingdoms. Pp. 165–72 in Christopher J. Eyre, ed., *Proceedings of the Seventh International Congress of Egyptologists, Cambridge, 3–9 September 1995.* OLA 82. Leuven.
Bickel, Susanne, et al.
2007   *Bilder als Quellen/Images as Sources: Studies on Ancient Near Eastern Artefacts and the Bible Inspired by the Work of Othmar Keel.* OBO Sonderband. Freiburg, Switzerland / Göttingen.
Bircher, Andreas
1980   *Ijob 28—Heraklit: Einige Ausführungen zu einem Vergleich des Verhältnisses von Weisheit— Logos und Schöpfung.* Unveröffentlichte Vorexamensarbeit, Freiburg, Switzerland.
Black, Jeremy, and Green, Anthony
1992   *Gods, Demons and Symbols of Ancient Mesopotamia: An Illustrated Dictionary.* London.
Blacker, Carmen, and Loewe, Michael
1975   *Ancient Cosmologies.* London.
Bleibtreu, Erika
1989   Zerstörung der Umwelt durch Bäumefällen und Dezimierung des Löwenbestandes in Mesopotamien. Pp. 219–33 in Bernhard Scholz, ed., *Der Orientalische Mensch und seine Beziehungen zur Umwelt.* Beiträge zum 2. Grazer Morgenländischen Symposium (2.–5. März 1989). Graz.
Blum, Erhard
2004   Von Gottesunmittelbarkeit zu Gottesähnlichkeit: Überlegungen zur theologischen Anthropologie der Paradieserzählung. Pp. 9–29 in G. Eberhard and K. Liess, eds., *Gottes Nähe im Alten Testament.* SBS 202. Stuttgart, 2004. = Blum, Erhard. Von Gottesunmittelbarkeit zu Gottähnlichkeit: Überlegungen zur theologischen Anthropologie der Paradieserzählung. Pp. 1–19 in idem, *Textgestalt und Komposition: Exegetische Beiträge zu Tora und Vordere Propheten.* FAT 69. Tübingen, 2010.
Boessneck, Joachim
1988   *Die Tierwelt des Alten Ägypten untersucht anhand kulturgeschichtlicher und zoologischer Quellen.* Munich.
Böhm, Manfred
1988   *Gottes Reich und Gesellschaftsveränderung: Traditionen einer befreienden Theologie im Spätwerk von Leonhard Ragaz.* Münster.
Böhme, Hartmut, and Böhme, Gernot
1985   *Das Andere der Vernunft: Zur Entwicklung von Rationalitätsstrukturen am Beispiel Kants* (stw 542). Frankfurt a.M.
Bonnafé, Annie
1996   *Die Ordnung der Welt nach griechischer Vorstellung.* WUB 1/2: 16–19.
Bormann, Lukas, ed.
2008   *Schöpfung, Monotheismus und fremde Religionen.* BThSt 95. Neukirchen-Vluyn.
Borowski, Oded
1998   *Every Living Thing: Daily Use of Animals in Ancient Israel.* Walnut Creek, CA.
Bosshard-Nepustil, Erich
1996   Zu Struktur und Sprachprofil des Hohenliedes. *BN* 81: 45–71.
Botha, P. J.
1996   Through the Figure of a Woman Many Have Perished: Ben Sira's View of Women. *Old Testament Essays* 9/1: 20–34.
Bottéro, Jean, and Kramer, Samuel Noah
1989   *Lorsque les dieux faisaient l'homme: Mythologie mésopotamienne.* Paris.
Brandon, Samuel George Frederick
1963   *Creation Legends of the Ancient Near East.* London.
Braun, Rainer
1973   *Kohelet und frühhellenistische Popularphilosophie.* BZAW 130. Berlin.

Bravmann, Meir Max
1977   *Studies in Semitic Philology.* Leiden.
Breasted, James Henry
1901   The Philosophy of a Memphite Priest. *ZÄS* 39: 39–54.
Brecht, Bertolt
1987   *Poems 1913–1956,* ed. John Willett and Ralph Manheim with the cooperation of Erich Fried. New York: Routledge [orig. Methuen, 1979].
Brenner, Athalya
2012   Song of Songs: Polyphony of Love. Pp. 288–302 in Luise Schottroff and Marie-Theres Wacker, eds., *Feminist Biblical Interpretation.* Grand Rapids/Cambridge.
Brown, John Pairman
1969   *The Lebanon and Phoenicia: Ancient Texts Illustrating Their Physical Geography and Native Industries,* Vol. 1: *The Physical Setting and the Forest.* Beirut.
Brunner, Hellmut
1988   *Altägyptische Weisheit: Lehren für das Leben: Eingeleitet, übersetzt und erläutert.* Zürich.
Brünenberg, Esther
2009   *Der Mensch in Gottes Herrlichkeit: Psalm 8 und seine Rezeption im Neuen Testament.* Würzburg.
Brunner-Traut, Emma
1990   *Altägyptische Märchen, Mythen und andere volkstümliche Erzählungen.* 9th edition. Düsseldorf/Cologne.
Bühlmann, Walter
1997   *Das Hohelied.* NSK-AT 15. Stuttgart.
Budd, Philip J.
1984   *Numbers.* World Biblical Commentary 5. Waco, TX.
Bührer, Walter
2014   *Am Anfang. . . : Untersuchungen zur Textgenese und zur relativ-chronologischen Einordnung von Gen 1–3.* Göttingen.
Capelle, Wilhelm
1953   *Die Vorsokratiker. Die Fragmente und Quellenberichte übersetzt und eingeleitet.* 4th ed. Stuttgart. Reprinted, 1968.
Chapman, George
1875   *The Works of George Chapman: Homer's Iliad and Odyssey,* ed. Richard Herne Shepherd. London: Chatto and Windus.
Clifford, Richard J.
1994   *Creation Accounts in the Ancient Near East and the Bible.* CBQMS 26. Washington.
Clifford, Richard J., and Collins, John J., eds.
1992   *Creation in the Biblical Traditions.* CBQMS 24. Washington.
Collon, Dominique
1987   *First Impressions: Cylinder Seals in the Ancient Near East.* Chicago/London.
Cross, Frank Moore
1999   King Hezekiah's Seal Bears Phoenician Imagery. *BAR* 25/2: 42–45, 60f.
Crüsemann, Frank
1979   Die unveränderte Welt. Überlegungen zur „Krisis der Weisheit" beim Prediger (Kohelet). Pp. 80–104 in Willy Schottroff and Wolfgang Stegemann, eds. *Der Gott der kleinen Leute: Sozialgeschichtliche Auslegungen, Altes Testament.* Munich.
1980   Hiob und Kohelet. Ein Beitrag zum Verständnis des Hiobbuches. Pp. 373–93 in Rainer Albertz et al., eds. *Werden und Wirken des Alten Testaments: Festschrift für Claus Westermann zum 70. Geburtstag.* Göttingen and Neukirchen.
1989   Tendenzen der alttestamentlichen Wissenschaft zwischen 1933 und 1945. Pp. 79–103 in Hans-Peter Stähli, ed. *Wort und Dienst.* Jahrbuch der Kirchlichen Hochschule Bethel, NF 20. Bethel.
Daecke, Sigurd
1981   Gott als Faktor der Evolution? Zum Gespräch der Theologie mit den Naturwissenschaften. *EK* 14: 624–26.
1989   Anthropozentrik oder Eigenwert der Natur? Pp. 277–99 in Günter Altner, ed. *Ökologische Theologie: Perspektiven zur Orientierung.* Stuttgart.
Dalley, Stephanie
1991   *Myths from Mesopotamia: Creation, the Flood, Gilgamesh, and Others.* The World's Classics. Oxford: Oxford University Press.

Daniels, Peter T.
1994   Edward Hincks's Decipherment of Mesopotamian Cuneiform. Pp. 30–57 in *The Edward Hincks Bicentenary Lectures*, ed. Kevin J. Cathcart. Dublin: University College Dublin, Department of Near Eastern Studies.
1995   The Decipherment of Near Eastern Scripts. Pp. 81–93 in *Civilizations of the Ancient Near East*, ed. Jack M. Sasson et al. New York: Scribners.
Daum, Ahron
1994   *Die Feiertage Israels, vol. 2: Die jüdischen Feiertage in der Sicht der Tradition*. Frankfurt a.M.
Daumas, François
1959   *Les Mammisis de Dendera*. Cairo.
Day, John
1985   *God's Conflict with the Dragon and the Sea: Echoes of Canaanite Myth in the OT*. Cambridge.
Deissler, Alfons
1972   *Die Grundbotschaft des Alten Testaments*. Freiburg i.Br.
Deist, Ferdinand E.
1994   The Dangers of Deuteronomy: A Page from the Reception History of the Book. Pp. 13–29 in Florentin Garcia Martinez et al., eds. *Studies in Deuteronomy in Honour of Caspaer J. Labuschagne on the Occasion of His 65th Birthday*. Leiden.
Delcor, Marcel
1974   Astarté et la fécondité des troupeaux en Deut. 7,13 et parallèles. *UF* 6: 7–14.
Delgado, Mariano
1991   *Gott in Lateinamerika: Texte aus fünf Jahrhunderten. Ein Lesebuch zur Geschichte*. Unter Mitarbeit von Bruno Pockrandt und Horst Goldstein. Düsseldorf.
Derchain, Philippe, and von Recklinghausen, Daniel
2004   *La création – Die Schöpfung. Poème pariétal – ein Wandgedicht. La façade ptolémaique du temple d'Esna. Pour une poétique ptolémaique*. Rites Egyptiens X. Turnhout.
Deutsch, Robert
1999   *Messages from the Past: Hebrew Bullae from the Time of Isaiah, through the Destruction of the First Temple: The Shlomo Moussaieff Collection and an Up to Date Corpus*. Tel Aviv.
Deutsch, Robert, and Lemaire, André.
2000   *Biblical Period Personal Seals in the Shlomo Moussaieff Collection*. Jerusalem.
Dexinger, Ferdinand E.
1966   *Sturz der Göttersöhne oder Engel vor der Sintflut? Versuch eines Neuverständnisses von Gen 6,2–4, unter Berücksichtigung der religionsvergleichenden und exegesegeschichtlichen Methode*. WBTh 13. Vienna.
Dhorme, Paul
1926   *Le Livre de Job*. EtB. Paris.
Dick, Michael Brennan.
1999   *Born in Heaven, Made on Earth: The Making of the Cult Image in the Ancient Near East*. Winona Lake, IN.
Diels, Hermann, and Kranz, Walther, eds.
1951   *Die Fragmente der Vorsokratiker. Griechisch und Deutsch (außer Thales)*. 3 volumes. 6th ed. Berlin.
Dijk, Jan van
1973   Une incantation accompagnant la naissance de l'homme. *Or.* 42: 502–7.
1983   *LUGAL UD ME-LÁM-bi NIR-GÁL Tome I. Introduction, texte composite, traduction*. Leiden.
Dohmen, Christoph
1988   *Schöpfung und Tod: Die Entfaltung theologischer und anthropologischer Konzeptionen in Gen 2/3*. SBB 17. Stuttgart.
2000   "Der siebte Tag soll ein Sabbat sein." *WUB* 17/3: 43–47.
Doll, Peter
1985   *Menschenschöpfung und Weltschöpfung in der alttestamentlichen Weisheit*. SBS 117. Stuttgart.
Drewermann, Eugen
1981   *Der tödliche Fortschritt. Von der Zerstörung der Erde und des Menschen im Erbe des Christentums*. Regensburg; 6th ed., 1991, Freiburg im Breisgau.
Duchrow, Ulrich, and Liedke, Gerhard
1989   *Biblical Perspectives on Creation, Justice, and Peace*. WCC Publications. Geneva.
Ebach, Jürgen
1989   Schöpfung in der hebräischen Bibel. Pp. 98–129 in Altner Günter, ed., *Ökologische Theologie: Perspektiven zur Orientierung*. Stuttgart.

Edel, Elmar, and Wenig, Steffen
1974   Die Jahreszeitenreliefs aus dem Sonnenheiligtum des Königs Ne-User-Re: Tafelband und Text-
        beilage. Berlin.
Egger-Wenzel, Renate
1998   Von der Freiheit Gottes anders zu sein: Die zentrale Rolle der Kapitel 9 und 10 für das Ijob-
        buch. FB 83. Würzburg.
Eisen, Gustavus A.
1940   Ancient Oriental Cylinder and Other Seals with a Description of the Collection of Mrs. Wil-
        liam H. Moore. OIP 47. Chicago.
Ekschmitt, Werner
1989   Weltmodelle: Griechische Weltbilder von Thales bis Ptolemäus. Kulturgeschichte der An-
        tike 43. Mainz.
Elan, Shlomo
1979   Der Heilige Baum: ein Hinweis auf das Bild ursprünglicher Landschaft in Palästina.
        MDOG 111: 89–101.
Elayi, Josette
1988   L'exploitation des cèdres du Mont Liban par les rois assyriens et néo-babyloniens.
        Journal for the Economic and Social History of the Orient 31: 14–41.
El Hawary, Amr
2010   Wortschöpfung: Die Memphitische Theologie und die Siegesstele des Pije – zwei Zeugen kul-
        tureller Repräsentation in der 25. Dynastie. OBO 243. Freiburg, Switzerland / Göttingen.
Eliade, Mircea, et al.
1964   La naissance du monde. Paris, 1959. German edition: Die Schöpfungsmythen. Ägypter,
        Sumerer, Hurriter, Hethiter, Kanaaniter und Israeliten. Einsiedeln, 1964.
Elliger, Karl
1966   Leviticus. HAT 4. Tübingen.
Engel, Helmut
1998   Das Buch der Weisheit. NSK-AT 16. Stuttgart.
Erman, Adolf
1911a   Denksteine aus der thebanischen Gräberstadt. SPAW 49: 1096–1110. Berlin.
1911b   Ein ägyptische Quelle der "Sprüche Salomos." SPAW.PH 15: 86–93. Berlin.
Esterbauer, Reinhold
1996   Verlorene Zeit — wider eine Einheitswissenschaft von Natur und Gott. Stuttgart.
Felber, Peter, and Pfister, Xaver, eds.
1989   Gerechtigkeit und Frieden umarmen sich: Europäische Ökumenische Versammlung Basel
        1989. Basel/Zürich.
Fetz, Reto Luzius, and Oser, Fritz
1985   Weltbildentwicklung und religiöses Urteil. Berichte zur Erziehungswissenschaft 47. Frei-
        burg, Switzerland.
Fieger, Michael, and Lanckau, Jörg
2010   Erschaffung und Zerstörung der Schöpfung: Ein Beitrag zum Thema Mythos. Berne.
Fohrer, Georg
1989   Das Buch Hiob. KAT 16. 2nd ed. Gütersloh.
Forrester, Jay Wright
1972   Der teuflische Regelkreis: Das Globalmodell der Menschheitskrise. Stuttgart.
Fox, Matthew
1983   Original Blessing: A Primer in Creation Spirituality. Rochester, 1983; revised edition,
        1996.
1988   The Coming of the Cosmic Christ. San Francisco.
1991   Creation Spirituality: Liberating Gifts for the Peoples of the Earth. San Fransisco.
Fox, Michael V.
1986   Egyptian Onomastica and Biblical Wisdom. VT 36: 302–10.
1985   The Song of Songs and the Ancient Egyptian Love Songs. London.
Frankfort, Henri
1939   Cylinder Seals. London.
1955   Stratified Cylinder Seals from the Diyala Region. OIP 72. Chicago.
1969   The Art and Architecture of the Ancient Orient. Harmondsworth.
Frettlöh, Magdalene L.
1998   Theologie des Segens: Biblische und dogmatische Wahrnehmungen. Gütersloh.
Frevel, Christian
2000   Mit Blick auf das Land die Schöpfung erinnern: Zum Ende der Priestergrundschrift. Freiburg
        i.Br./Basel/Vienna.

Fritsch, Charles T.
1943   *The Anti-Anthropomorphisms of the Greek Pentateuch.* Princeton.
Fuchs, Gisela
1993   *Mythos und Hiobdichtung: Aufnahme und Umdeutung altorientalischer Vorstellungen.* Stuttgart.
Fuchs, Gisela, and Knörzer, Guido, eds.
1998   *Tier, Gott, Mensch: Beschädigte Beziehungen.* Frankfurt a.M.
Fünfsinn, Bärbel, and Zinn, Christa
1998   *Das Seufzen der Schöpfung: Ökofeministische Beiträge aus Lateinamerika.* Hamburg.
Gadamer, Hans Georg, ed.
1968   *Um die Begriffswelt der Vorsokratiker.* WdF 9. Darmstadt.
Galling, Kurt, ed.
1977   *Biblisches Reallexikon.* Second, revised edition. HAT I/1. Tübingen.
Gard, Donald H.
1952   *The Exegetical Method of the Greek Translator of the Book of Job.* JBL Monograph Series 8. Ann Arbor, MI.
Gardiner, Alan H.
1947   *Ancient Egyptian Onomastica.* Oxford.
1968   *Ancient Egyptian Onomastica I.* 2nd ed. Oxford.
Garr, W. Randall.
2003   *In His Own Image and Likeness: Humanity, Divinity, and Monotheism.* Culture and History of the Ancient Near East 15. Leiden and Boston.
Geisen, Richard
1992   *Anthroposophie und Gnostizismus: Darstellung, Vergleich und theologische Kritik,* Paderborn.
Geller, Stephen A.
1987   "Where is Wisdom?" A Literary Study of Job 28 in its Settings. Pp. 155–88 in Jacob Neusner et al., eds., *Judaic Perspectives on Ancient Israel.* Philadelphia.
George, Andrew.
1999   *The Epic of Gilgamesh: A New Translation.* Penguin Classics. Harmondsworth.
Gerber, Peter R.
1988   Der Indianer: ein homo oekologicus? Pp. 221–44 in Fritz Stolz, ed., *Religiöse Wahrnehmung der Welt.* Zürich.
Gerstenberger, Erhard S.
2001   *Theologien im Alten Testament: Pluralität und Synkretismus alttestamentlichen Gottesglaubens.* Stuttgart.
Gertz, Jan Christian
2006   Beobachtungen zum literarischen Charakter und zum geistesgeschichtlichen Ort der nichtpriesterschriftlichen Sintfluterzählung. Pp. 41–58 in U. Schorn and M. Beck, eds., *Auf dem Weg zur Endgestalt von Genesis bis II Regum: Festschrift Schmitt.* BZAW 370. Berlin/New York.
Gilbert, Maurice.
1973   *La critique des dieux dans le Livre de la Sagesse (Sg 13–15).* Rome.
1986   Art. »Sagesse de Salomon (ou Livre de la Sagesse)«. Pp. 58–119 in volume 9 of *Dictionnaire de la Bible. Supplément,* ed. Louis Pirot. Paris.
Goethe, Johann Wolfgang von
1983   *Selected Poems,* ed. Christopher Middleton. Goethe's Collected Works, 1. Boston: Suhrkamp/Insel. Repr. Princeton: Princeton University Press, 1994.
2009   Antibabylonische Polemik im priesterlichen Schöpfungsbericht? *ZThK* 106: 137–55.
Goldschmidt, Lazarus
1933   *Der babylonische Talmud VI.* The Hague.
Gollinger, Hildegard
1971   *Das "Große Zeichen" von Apokalypse 12.* Stuttgart.
Görg, Manfred
1993   Die "Astarte des Kleinviehs." *BN* 69: 9–11.
1997   *Nilgans und Heiliger Geist: Bilder der Schöpfung in Israel und Ägypten.* Düsseldorf.
Gorelick, Leonard, and Elizabeth Williams-Forte, eds.
1983   *Ancient Seals and the Bible.* Malibu.
Gorges-Braunwarth, Susanne
2002   *"Frauenbilder – Weisheitsbilder – Gottesbilder" in Spr 1–9: Die personifizierte Weisheit im Gottesbild der nachexilischen Zeit.* Münster.
Graeser, Andreas
1981   Die Vorsokratiker. Pp. 13–47 in Ottfried Höffe, ed., *Klassiker der Philosophie I.* Munich.

Gräb, Wilhelm, ed.
1995   *Urknall oder Schöpfung? Zum Dialog von Naturwissenschaft und Theologie.* Gütersloh.
Granqvist, Hilma
1950   *Child Problems among the Arabs.* Helsinki/Copenhagen.
Grätz, Sebastian
1998   *Der strafende Wettergott: Erwägungen zur Traditionsgeschichte des Adad-Fluchs im Alten Orient und im Alten Testament.* BBB 114. Bodenheim.
Gray, George Buchanan
1903   *A Critical and Exegetical Commentary on Numbers.* International Critical Commentary. Edinburgh.
Green, Elizabeth, and Grey, Mary, eds.
1994   *Ökofeminismus und Theologie.* Jahrbuch der Europäischen Gesellschaft für die Theologische Forschung von Frauen 2. Kampen/Main.
Greiner, Dorothea
1998   *Segen und Segnen: Ein systematisch-theologische Grundlegung.* Stuttgart.
Gressmann, Hugo
1909   *Altorientalische Texte und Bilder zum Alten Testamente.* 2 volumes. Tübingen.
1926   *Altorientalische Texte zum Alten Testament.* 2nd edition. Berlin/Leipzig.
Grey, Mary, ed.
1996   *Ecotheology.* Sheffield.
Grønbaeck, Jakob H.
1985   Baal's Battle with Jam: A Canaanite Creation Fight. *JSOT* 33: 27–44.
Gross, Walter
1993   Die Gottebenbildlichkeit des Menschen nach Gen 1,26–27 in der Diskussion des letzten Jahrzehnts. *BN* 68: 35–48.
Grossmann, Sigrid
1989   Schöpfer und Schöpfung in der feministischen Theologie. Pp. 213–33   in Altner Günter, ed., *Ökologische Theologie: Perspektiven zur Orientierung.* Stuttgart.
Grueber, Herbert Appold
1970   *Coins of the Roman Republic in the British Museum.* 3 volumes. London, 1910; reprint.
Gunkel, Hermann
1997   *Genesis: Translated and Explained.* 3rd edition. Macon.
2006   *Creation and Chaos in the Primeval Era and the Eschaton.* Grand Rapids.
Haag, Herbert
1962   *Homer, Ugarit und das Alte Testament.* BiBe NF 2. Freiburg, Switzerland.
Habel, Norman C.
2000   *Readings from the Perspective of the Earth.* The Earth Bible 1. Sheffield.
Hailer, Martin
2001   *Figur und Thema der Weisheit in feministischen Theologien. Ein kommentierender Forschungsbericht.* Frankfurt a.M.
Halbe, Jörn
1979   "Altorientalisches Weisheitsdenken" und alttestamentliche Theologie: Zur Kritik eines Ideologems am Beispiel des israelitischen Rechts. *ZThK* 76: 381–418.
Halkes, Catharina J. M.
1990   *Das Antlitz der Erde erneuern. Mensch, Kultur, Schöpfung.* Gütersloh.
Hallmann, David G., ed.
1994   *Ecotheology: Voices from South and North.* Geneva.
Hangartner, Li, and Brigitte Vielhaus, eds.
2006   *Segnen und gesegnet werden.* Düsseldorf.
Hannig, Rainer
1995   *Die Sprache der Pharaonen: Großes Handwörterbuch Ägyptisch-Deutsch (2800–950 v.Chr.).* Mainz.
Hannig, Rainer, and Vomberg, Petra
1999   *Wortschatz der Pharaonen in Sachgruppen.* Mainz.
Hartenstein, Friedhelm
2009   Wettergott – Schöpfergott – Einziger. Kosmologie und Monotheismus in den Psalmen. Pp. 77–97 in F. Hartenstein and M. Rösel, eds., *JHWH und die Götter der Völker. Symposium zum 80. Geburtstag von Klaus Koch.* Neukirchen-Vluyn.
2009   Zur Bedeutung der Schöpfung in den Geschichtspsalmen. Pp. 335–49 in R. Achenbach and M. Arneth, eds., "Gerechtigkeit und Recht zu üben" (Gen 18,19). *Studien zur altorientalischen und biblischen Rechtsgeschichte, zur Religionsgeschichte Israels und zur Religionssoziologie.* BZAR 13. Wiesbaden.

2013   JHWH, Erschaffer des Himmels: Zu Herkunft und Bedeutung eines monotheistischen Kernarguments. *ZThK* 110/4: 383–409.

Heidemanns, Katja, and Hollmann, Nikola
1996   Bibliographie Ökofeminismus. *Schlangenbrut* 14/No. 52: 33f.

Helbling, Dominik
2001   *Transzendierung der Geschichte. LXX Dan 3,57–90 als hymnische Exegese.* Unpublished Lizentiatsarbeit. Lucerne.

Hendin, David
1996   *Guide to Biblical Coins.* 3rd edition. New York.

Henten, Jan Willem van
1994   Dragon Myth and Imperial Ideology in Revelation 12–13. Pp. 496–515 in Eugene H. Lovering ed., *Society of Biblical Literature 1994 Seminar Papers.* SBL Seminar Paper Series 33. Atlanta.

Hentschel, Georg, and Zenger, Erich, eds.
1991   *Lehrerin der Gerechtigkeit.* EThS 19. Leipzig.

Hilpert, Karl
1987   Aufmerksamkeit und Sorge für die Schöpfung: Zur ökologisch reformulierten Schöpfungslehre und Schöpfungsethik. *Orien.* 51: 170–73, 182–85.

Hösle, Vittorio
1991   *Philosophie der ökologischen Krise.* Moskauer Vorträge. Munich; revised and enlarged edition, 2005.

Holzinger, Heinrich
1903   *Numeri.* Tübingen/Leipzig.

Hoping, Helmut
2005   Gottes Ebenbild: Theologische Anthropologie und säkulare Vernunft. *ThQ* 185: 127–49.

Hornung, Erik
1996   *Conceptions of God in Ancient Egypt: The One and the Many.* Ithaca, NY.
1997   *Der ägyptische Mythos von der Himmelskuh: Ein Ätiologie des Unvollkommenen.* In collaboration with Andreas Brodbeck, Hermann Schlögl, and Elisabeth Stähelin, and with a supplement by Gerhard Fecht. OBO 46. 3rd edition. Freiburg, Switzerland/Göttingen.
1999   *Akhenaten and the Religion of Light.* Ithaca, NY.
1999   *The Ancient Egyptian Books of the Afterlife.* Ithaca, NY.

Hossfeld, Frank-Lothar, and Zenger, Erich
2000   *Psalmen 51–100.* HThKAT. Freiburg i.Br.
2003   Schöpfungsfrömmigkeit in Ps 104 und bei Jesus Sirach. Pp. 129–38 in I. Fischer, U. Rapp, and J. Schiller, eds., *Auf den Spuren der schriftgelehrten Weisen: Festschrift für Johannes Marböck.* BZAW 331. Berlin and Vienna.

Houtman, Cornelis
1993   *Der Himmel im Alten Testament: Israels Weltbild & Weltanschauung.* Leiden.

Hubbard, Ruth
1989   Hat die Evolution die Frauen übersehen? Pp. 301–33 in Elisabeth List and Herlinde Studer, eds., *Denkverhältnisse: Feminismus und Kritik.* Hamburg.
1990   *The Politics of Women's Biology.* London.

Hübner, Hans
1999   *Die Weisheit Salomos.* ATD Apokryphen 4. Göttingen.

Hübner, Jürgen, ed.
1987   *Der Dialog zwischen Theologie und Naturwissenschaft: Ein bibliographischer Bericht.* FBESG 41. Munich.

Hübner, Kurt
1985   *Die Wahrheit des Mythos.* Munich.

Humbert, Paul
1940   Etudes sur le récit du paradis et de la chute dans la Genèse, in *Mémoires de l'Université de Neuchâtel* 14. Neuchâtel.

Ibrahim, Moawiyah M., ed.
1988   *Museum of Jordanian Heritage.* Amman: Yarmouk University, Institute of Archaeology and Anthropology.

Irsigler, Hubert
1984   *Psalm 73: Monolog eines Weisen.* ATSAT 20. St. Ottilien.

Jacobsen, Thorkild
1976   *The Treasures of Darkness: A History of Mesopotamian Religion.* New Haven/London.

Jaeger, Werner
1933   *Paideia: Die Formung des griechischen Menschen, Bd. I.* Berlin.

Janowski, Bernd
1989   *Rettungsgewißheit und Epiphanie des Heils: Das Motiv der Hilfe Gottes "am Morgen" im Alten Orient und im Alten Testament, I Alter Orient.* WMANT 59. Neukirchen-Vluyn.
1993a   Herrschaft über die Tiere. Gen 1,26–28 und die Semantik von רדה. Pp. 183–98 in Georg Braulik, ed., *Biblische Theologie und gesellschaftlicher Wandel: Für Norbert Lohfink SJ.* Freiburg i.Br.
1993b   Tempel und Schöpfung. Schöpfungstheologische Aspekte der priesterschriftlichen Heiligtumskonzeption. Pp. 214–46 in Bernd Janowski, ed., *Gottes Gegenwart in Israel: Beiträge zur Theologie des Alten Testaments.* Neukirchen-Vluyn.
1999   Auch die Tiere gehören zum Gottesbund. Gott, Mensch und Tier im alten Israel, in ders., *Die rettende Gerechtigkeit.* Pp. 3–32 in *Beiträge zur Theologie des Alten Testamens 2.* Neukirchen-Vluyn.
Janowski, Bernd, ed.
1993   *Gottes Gegenwart in Israel: Beiträge zur Theologie des Alten Testaments.* Neukirchen- Vluyn.
Janowski, Bernd, and Riede, Peter, eds.
1999   *Die Zukunft der Tiere: Theologische, ethische und naturwissenschaftliche Perspektiven.* Stuttgart.
Janowski, Bernd, Neumann-Gorsolke, Ute, and Gleßmer, Uwe, eds.
1993   *Gefährten und Feinde des Menschen: Das Tier in der Lebenswelt des alten Israel.* Neukirchen-Vluyn.
Jaroš, Karl
1982   *Die Stellung des Elohisten zur kanaanäischen Religion.* OBO 4. 2nd edition. Freiburg, Switzerland/Göttingen.
Jeremias, Alfred
1906   *Das Alte Testament im Lichte des Alten Orient.* 2nd edition. Leipzig.
Jeremias, Jörg
1983   *Der Prophet Hosea.* ATD 24/1. Göttingen.
Jeremias, Jörg, and Hartenstein, Friedhelm
1999   "JHWH und seine Aschera": "Offizielle Religion" und "Volksreligion" zur Zeit der klassischen Propheten. Pp. 79–138 in Bernd Janowski and Matthias Köckert, eds., *Religionsgeschichte Israels: Formale und materiale Aspekte.* Gütersloh.
Jericke, Detlef
2001   Königsgarten und Gottes Garten. Aspekte der Königstheologie in Genesis 2 und 3. Pp. 161–76 in Christl Maier et al., eds., *Exegese vor Ort: Festschrift für Peter Welten zum 65. Geburtstag.* Leipzig.
Jörns, Klaus-Peter
2001   Zur Notwendigkeit, von Erwählungsvorstellungen in der Theologie Aschied zu nehmen. Pp. 177–98 in Christl Maier et al., eds., *Exegese vor Ort: Festschrift für Peter Welten zum 65. Geburtstag.* Leipzig.
Johanning, Klaus
1988   *Der Bibel-Babel-Streit. Ein forschungsgeschichtliche Studie.* Frankfurt a.M.
Junge, Friedrich
1974   Zur Frühdatierung des sogenannten "Denkmals memphitischer Theologie." *MDAIK* 29/2 (1973) 195–204. Mainz.
Junker, Hermann
1940   *Die Götterlehre von Memphis.* ADAW 1939. Berlin.
Kaiser, Otto
1998   *Der Gott des Alten Testaments: Wesen und Wirken. Theologie des Alten Testaments Teil 2: Jahwe, der Gott Israels, Schöpfer der Welt und des Menschen.* Göttingen.
Kalms, Jürgen U.
2001   *Der Sturz des Gottesfeindes: Tradtionsgeschichtliche Studien zur Apokalypse 12.* WMANT 93. Neukirchen-Vluyn.
Kapelrud, Arvid
1979   Die Theologie der Schöpfung im Alten Testament. *ZAW* 91: 159–70.
Kato, Kumiko
2012   Qoheleth (Ecclesiastes): Man Alone, without Woman. Pp. 273–87 in Luise Schottroff and Marie-Theres Wacker, eds., *Feminist Biblical Interpretation.* Grand Rapids/Cambridge.
Kautzsch, Emil
1962   *Die Apokryphen und Pseudepigraphen des AT II.* 2nd edition. Darmstadt.
Kayatz, Christa
1966   *Studien zu Prov 1–9: Eine form- und motivgeschichtliche Untersuchung unter Einbeziehung ägyptischen Vergleichsmaterials.* WMANT 22. Neukirchen-Vluyn.

Keel, Othmar
1972   Erwägungen zum Sitz im Leben des vormosaischen Pascha und die Etymologie von
       פסח. ZAW 84: 414–34.
1974a Die Weisheit spielt vor Gott. Freiburg, Switzerland.
1974b Wirkmächtige Siegeszeichen im Alten Testament. Ikonographische Studien zu Jos 8,18.26; Ex
       17,8–13; 2 Kön 13,14–19 und 1 Kön 22,11. OBO 5. Freiburg, Switzerland / Göttingen.
1975   Die Stellung der Frau in Genesis 2 und 3. Orien. 39: 74–76.
1977a Jahwevisionen und Siegelkunst: Ein neue Deutung der Majestätsschilderungen in Jes 6, Ez 1
       und 10 und Sach 4. SBS 84/85. Stuttgart.
1977b Vögel als Boten. OBO 14. Freiburg, Switzerland/Göttingen.
1977c Der Bogen als Herrschaftssymbol: Einige unveröffentlichte Skarabäen aus Ägypten
       und Israel zum Thema "Jagd und Krieg." ZDPV 93: 141–77.
1978   Jahwes Entgegnung an Ijob. Eine Deutung von Ijob 38–41 vor dem Hintergrund der zeitgenös-
       sischen Bildkunst. FRLANT 121. Göttingen. English edition, 1997.
1979   Wer zerstörte Sodom? ThZ 35: 10–17.
1980   Das Böcklein in der Milch seiner Mutter und Verwandtes. OBO 33. Freiburg, Switzerland /
       Göttingen.
1981   Zwei kleine Beiträge zum Verständnis der Gottesreden im Buch Ijob (38,36f; 40,25).
       VT 31: 220–25.
1984   Deine Blicke sind Tauben: Zur Metaphorik des Hohen Liedes. SBS 114/115. Stuttgart.
1985a Das Tier in der Bibel, in Mensch und Tier. Pp. 33–54 in Collegium generale der Universi-
       tät Bern. Kulturhistorische Vorlesungen 1984/85. Berne.
1985b Das sogenannte altorientalische Weltbild. BiKi 40 (1985) 157–61.
1986a Das Hohelied. ZBK.AT 18. Zürich.
1986b Vernachlässigte Aspekte biblischer Schöpfungstheologie. KatBi 111: 168–79.
1987   Sind die biblischen Schöpfungsüberlieferungen anthropozentrisch? Orien. 51/20:
       221f.
1989a Jahwe in der Rolle der Muttergottheit. Orien. 53: 89–92.
1989b Die Ω-Gruppe: Ein mittelbronzezeitlicher Stempelsiegel-Typ mit erhabenem Relief aus
       Anatolien-Nordsyrien und Palästina. Pp. 39–98 in Othmar Keel et al., Studien zu den
       Stempelsiegeln aus Palästina/Israel, vol. 2. OBO 88. Freiburg, Switzerland / Göttingen.
1989c Zur Identifikation der Falkenköpfigen auf den Skarabäen der ausgehenden 13. und
       der 15. Dynastie. Pp. 243–80 in Othmar Keel et al., Studien zu den Stempelsiegeln aus
       Palästina/Israel, vol. 2. OBO 88. Freiburg, Switzerland/Göttingen.
1991   Schöne, schwierige Welt—Leben mit Klagen und Loben: Ausgewählte Psalmen. Berlin.
1992   Das Recht der Bilder gesehen zu werden: Drei Fallstudien zur Methode der Interpretation
       altorientalischer Bilder. OBO 122. Freiburg, Switzerland / Göttingen.
1993a Allgegenwärtige Tiere: Einige Weisen ihrer Wahrnehmung in der hebräischen Bibel.
       Pp. 155–93 in Bernd Janowski, Ute Neumann-Gorsolke, and Uwe Gleßmer, eds. Ge-
       fährten und Feinde des Menschen: Das Tier in der Lebenswelt des alten Israel. Neukirchen-
       Vluyn.
1993b Der Wald als Menschenfresser, Baumgarten und Teil der Schöpfung in der Bibel und
       im Alten Orient. Pp. 47–71 in Daphinoff Dimiter, ed. Der Wald: Beiträge zu einem inter-
       disziplinären Gespräch. Seges NF 13. Freiburg, Switzerland / Göttingen.
1993c Dieu répond à Job: Une interprétation de Job 38–41 à la lumière de l'iconographie du
       Proche-Orient ancien. Paris.
1993d Königliche Nilpferdjagd: Eine ungewöhnliche Darstellung auf einem Skarabäus des
       Mittleren Reiches. GM 134: 63–68.
1994a Das Mondemblem von Harran auf Stelen und Siegelamuletten und der Kult der nächt-
       lichen Gestirne bei den Aramäern. Pp. 135–202 in idem, Studien zu den Stempelsiegeln
       aus Palästina/Israel IV. OBO 135. Freiburg, Switzerland/Göttingen,.
1994b Sturmgott – Sonnengott – Einziger: Ein neuer Versuch, die Entstehung des judäischen
       Monotheismus historisch zu verstehen. BiKi 49: 82–92.
1995   Corpus der Stempelsiegel-Amulette aus Palästina/Israel: Von den Anfängen bis zur Perserzeit.
       Einleitung. OBOSA 10. Freiburg, Switzerland/Göttingen.
1996a Die Welt der altorientalischen Bildsymbolik und das Alte Testament am Beispiel der Psal-
       men. 5th edition. Neukirchen-Vluyn.
1996b Davids "Tanz" vor der Lade. BiKi 51 (1996) 11–14.
1997a The Symbolism of the Biblical World: Ancient Near Eastern Iconography and the Book of
       Psalms. 2nd edition. Winona Lake, IN: 1997.
1997b Corpus der Stempelsiegel-Amulette aus Palästina/Israel, Von den Anfängen bis zur Perserzeit.
       Katalog Bd. 1. OBOSA 13. Freiburg, Switzerland/Göttingen.
1997c Le cantique des cantiques. Lectio Divina 6. Paris.

1998   *Goddesses and Trees. New Moon and Yahweh. Two Natural Phenomena in Ancient Near Eastern Art and in the Hebrew Bible.* JSOTSup. Sheffield.

2000   Die Tiere und der Mensch in Daniel 7. Pp. 1–35 in Othmar Keel and Urs Staub, *Hellenismus und Judentum: Vier Studien zu Daniel 7 und zur Religionsnot unter Antiochus IV.* OBO 178. Freiburg, Switzerland / Göttingen.

2001a   Altägyptische und biblische Weltbilder, die Anfänge der vorsokratischen Philosophie und das ἀρχή-Problem in späten biblischen Schriften. Pp. 27–63 in Beate Ego and Bernd Janowski, eds. *Das biblische Weltbild und seine altorientalischen Kontexte.* FAT 32. Tübingen, 2001.

2001b   Drachenkämpfe noch und noch im Alten Orient und in der Bibel. Pp. 14–26 in Sylvia Hahn et al., *Sanct Georg: Der Ritter mit dem Drachen (Ausstellungskatalog).* Freising.

2002   Der salomonische Tempelweihspruch: Beobachtungen zum religionsgeschichtlichen Kontext des Erstens Jerusalemer Tempels. Pp. 9–23 in Keel and Zenger 2002.

2003   Schwache alttestamentliche Ansätze zur Konstruktion einer stark dualistisch getönten Welt. Pp. 211–36 in *Die Dämonen / Demons: The Demonology of Israelite, Jewish, and Early Christian Literature,* ed. Armin Lange, Hermann Lichtenberger, and K. F. Diethard Römheld. Tübingen.

Keel, Othmar, ed.

1980   *Monotheismus im alten Israel und in seiner Umwelt.* Freiburg, Switzerland.

Keel, Othmar, and Küchler, Max

1982   *Orte und Landschaften der Bibel. Ein Handbuch und Studienreiseführer zum Heiligen Land,* Bd. 2: *Der Süden.* Zürich/Göttingen.

1983   *Synoptische Texte aus der Genesis.* BiBe NF 8,2. 3rd edition. Einsiedeln, 1983.

Keel, Othmar; Küchler, Max; and Uehlinger, Christoph

1998   *Orte und Landschaften der Bibel: Ein Handbuch und Studienreiseführer zum Heiligen Land,* Bd. 1: *Geographisch-geschichtliche Landeskunde.* Zürich/Göttingen, 1984.

Keel, Othmar, and Schroer, Silvia

1998   Darstellungen des Sonnenlaufs und Totenbuchvignetten auf Skarabäen. *ZÄS* 125: 13–29.

2010   *Eva: Mutter alles Lebendigen—Frauen—und Göttinnenidole aus dem Alten Orient.* Third edition. Freiburg, Switzerland.

Keel, Othmar, and Staub, Urs

2000   *Hellenismus und Judentum: Vier Studien zu Daniel 7 und zur Religionsnot unter Antiochus IV.* OBO 178. Freiburg Schweiz / Göttingen.

Keel, Othmar, and Uehlinger, Christoph

1994   Jahwe und die Sonnengottheit von Jerusalem, Pp. 269–306 in W. Dietrich and M. Klopfenstein, eds., *Ein Gott allein: JHWH-Verehrung und biblischer Monotheismus im Kontext der israelitischen und altorientalischen Religionsgeschichte.* OBO 139. Freiburg, Switzerland / Göttingen.

1996   *Altorientalische Miniaturkunst: Die ältesten visuellen Massenkommunikationsmittel.* 2nd edition. Freiburg, Switzerland / Göttingen.

1998   *Gods, Goddesses, and Images of God.* Minneapolis.

Keel, Othmar, and Zenger, Erich, eds.

2002   *Gottesstadt und Gottesgarten: Zu Geschichte und Theologie des Jerusalemer Tempels.* QD 191. Freiburg i.Br.

Keel-Leu, Hildi

1991   *Vorderasiatische Stempelsiegel: Die Sammlung des Biblischen Instituts der Universität Freiburg Schweiz.* OBO 110. Freiburg, Switzerland/Göttingen.

Keel-Leu, Hildi, and Teissier, Beatrice

2004   *Die Rollsiegel der Sammlungen BIBEL + ORIENT der Universität Freiburg/Schweiz.* OBO 200. Freiburg, Switzerland/Göttingen.

Kenyon, Kathleen M., and Holland, Thomas A.

1983   *Excavations at Jericho, Vol. V.* Jerusalem/London.

Kikawada, Isaac M.

1983   The Double Creation of Mankind in Enki and Ninmah, Atrahasis I 1–351, and Genesis 1–2. *Iraq* 45: 43–45.

King, L. W.

1902   *The Seven Tablets of Creation or the Babylonian and Assyrian Legends Concerning the Creation of the World and of Mankind.* London.

Kirk, Geoffrey S., John E. Raven, and Malcolm Schofield

1983   *The Pre-Socratic Philosophers.* 2nd edition. Cambridge.

Klatt, Werner
1969   Hermann Gunkel: Zu seiner Theologie der Religionsgeschichte und zur Entstehung der form-
        geschichtlichen Methode. FRLANT 100. Göttingen.
Klinger, Cornelia
1993   Was ist und zu welchem Ende betreibt man feministische Philosophie? Pp. 7–22 in
        Lynn Blattmann et al., eds. Feministische Perspektiven in der Wissenschaft. Zürcher
        Hochschulforum Band 21. Zürich.
Kloos, Claudia
1986   Yhwh´s Combat with the Sea: A Canaanite Tradition in the Religion of Israel. Leiden.
Klopfenstein Martin A.
1972   Die Skepsis des Qohelet. TZ 28: 97–109.
1997   Wenn der Schöpfer die Chaosmächte "anherrscht" (גער) und so das Leben schützt: Zu
        einem wenig beachteten Aspekt des Zorns Gottes im Alten Testament. ThZ 53: 33–43.
1998   "Und siehe, es war sehr gut!" (Genesis 1,31): Worin besteht die Güte der Schöpfung
        nach dem ersten Kapitel der hebräischen Bibel? Pp. 56–74 in Hans-Peter Mathys, ed.,
        Ebenbild Gottes: Herrscher über die Welt. Studien zu Würde und Auftrag des Menschen.
        BThSt 33. Neukirchen.
Kloppenborg, John S.
1982   Isis and Sophia in the Book of Wisdom. HThR 75: 57–84.
Klüger, Hermann
1912   Friedrich Delitzsch der Apostel der neubabylonischen Religion: Ein Mahnruf an das deutsche
        Volk. Leipzig.
Knauf, Ernst Axel
1999   Schadday. Pp. 749–53 in Karel van der Toorn et al., eds., Dictionary of Deities and De-
        mons in the Bible. 2nd edition. Leiden.
Koch, Klaus
1955   Gibt es ein Vergeltungsdogma im Alten Testament? ZThK 52: 1–42.
1965   Wort und Einheit des Schöpfergottes in Memphis und Jerusalem: Zur Einzigartigkeit
        Israels. ZThK 62: 251–93.
1983   Gestaltet die Erde, doch hegt das Leben! Pp. 23–36 in Hans-Georg Geyer et al., eds.
        Wenn nicht jetzt, wann dann? Festschrift für Hans-Joachim Kraus. Neukirchen-Vluyn.
2000   Imago Dei: Die Würde des Menschen im biblischen Text. Berichte aus den Sitzungen der
        Joachim Jungius-Gesellschaft der Wissenschaften e.V., Hamburg, Jg. 18/Heft 4. Göt-
        tingen.
Köckert, Matthias
2000   Literaturgeschichtliche und religionsgeschichtliche Beobachtungen zu Ps 104.
        Pp. 259–79 in Reinhard G. Kratz, Thomas Krüger, and Konrad Schmid, eds., Schriftaus-
        legung in der Schrift: Festschrift für Odil Hannes Steck zu seinem 65. Geburtstag. BZAW 300.
        Berlin.
Körting, Corinna
1999   Der Schall des Schofar: Israels Feste im Herbst. Berlin.
Kohlmeyer, Kay
2000   Der Tempel des Wettergottes von Aleppo. Münster.
Kopp, Clemens
1959   Die heiligen Stätten der Evangelien. Regensburg.
Kramer, Samuel Noah
1997   Sumerian Mythology. New York; revised edition, Philadelphia.
Kraus, Hans-Joachim
1982   Geschichte der historisch-kritischen Erforschung des Alten Testaments, 2nd edition. Neu-
        kirchen-Vluyn, 1969; expanded 3rd edition, 1982.
Krolzik, Udo
1989   Die Wirkungsgeschichte von Genesis 1,28. Pp. 149–63 in Günter Altner, ed. Ökolo-
        gische Theologie: Perspektiven zur Orientierung. Stuttgart.
Krüger, Thomas
1990   Theologische Gegenwartsdeutung im Kohelet-Buch. Munich (unpublished Habilitations-
        schrift).
1993   "Kosmo-theologie" zwischen Mythos und Erfahrung. Psalm 104 im Horizont alt-
        orientalischer und alttestamentlicher "Schöpfungs"-Konzepte. BN 68: 49–74.
2000   Kohelet (Prediger). BKAT XIX. Neukirchen-Vluyn.
Kubina, Veronika
1979   Die Gottesreden im Buch Hiob. Freiburg i.Br.

Küchler, Max
1979   *Frühjüdische Weisheitstraditionen. Zum Fortgang weisheitlichen Denkens im Bereich des frühjüdischen Jahweglaubens.* OBO 26. Freiburg, Switzerland / Göttingen.
1992   Gott und seine Weisheit in der Septuaginta (Ijob 28; Spr 8). Pp. 118–43 in Hans-Josef Klauck, ed. *Monotheismus und Christologie: Zur Gottesfrage im hellenistischen Judentum und im Urchristentum.* QD 138. Freiburg/Basel/Vienna.
Labat, René
1935   *Le poème babylonien de la création.* Paris.
1959   Les origines et la formation de la terre dans le poème babylonien de la création. *AnBib* 12: 205–15.
Lambert, Wilfred G.
1960   *Babylonian Wisdom Literature.* Oxford; reprinted, Winona Lake, IN, 1996.
1965   A New Look at the Babylonian Background of Genesis. *JThS* N.S. 16: 287–300.
Lambert, Wilfred G., and Millard, Alan Ralph
1959   *Atraḥasis.* Oxford; reprinted, Winona Lake, IN, 1999.
Landsberger, Benno
1976   Die Eigenbegrifflichkeit der babylonischen Welt. *Islamica* 2: 355–72. Translated by Thorkild Jacobsen, Ben Foster, and H. von Siebenthal under the title *The Conceptual Autonomy of the Babylonian World.* Monographs on the Ancient Near East 1.4. Malibu, CA.
Lang, Bernhard
1986   *Wisdom and the Book of Proverbs: An Israelite Goddess Redefined.* Cleveland.
Larcher, Chrysostome
1983–85 *Le livre de la Sagesse ou la Sagesse de Salomon.* 3 volumes. EtB.NS 1,3 und 5. Paris.
Lauha, Aarre
1978   *Kohelet.* BK 19. Neukirchen-Vluyn.
Layard, Austen Henry
1949   *The Monuments of Nineveh: From Drawings Made on the Spot I.* London.
Lewis, Theodore J.
1998   Divine Images and Aniconism in Ancient Israel. *JAOS* 118: 36–53.
Lehmann, Reinhard G.
1994   *Friedrich Delitzsch und der Babel-Bibel-Streit.* OBO 133. Freiburg, Switzerland / Göttingen.
Lemaire, André
1977   *Inscriptions hébraiques,* vol. 1: *Les ostraca.* Paris.
Lichtheim, Miriam
1973–76 *Ancient Egyptian Literature.* 3 volumes. Berkeley.
Liedke, Gerhard
1979   *Im Bauch des Fisches: Ökologische Theologie.* Stuttgart/Berlin.
Lindt, Andreas
1956   *Leonhard Ragaz: Ein Studie zur Geschichte und Theologie des religiösen Sozialismus.* Zürich.
Loewenstamm, Samuel Ephraim
1992   Ostracon 7 from Arad Attesting the Observance of the New-Moon Day. Pp. 131–35 in idem, *From Babylon to Canaan: Studies in the Bible and its Oriental Background.* Jerusalem.
Lohfink, Norbert
1974   "Macht euch die Erde untertan"? in *Or.* 38: 137–42.
1980   *Kohelet.* Die Neue Echter Bibel. 2nd edition. Würzburg.
Löning, Karl, and Zenger, Erich
1997   *Als Anfang schuf Gott: Biblische Schöpfungstheologien.* Düsseldorf.
Loretz, Oswald
1964   *Kohelet und der alte Orient.* Freiburg i. Br.
1967   *Die Gottebenbildlichkeit des Menschen.* With a contribution by Erik Hornung: Der Mensch als "Bild Gottes" in Ägypten. Munich.
1988   Ugarit-Texte und Thronbesteigungspsalmen: Die Metamorphose des Regenspenders Baal-Jahwe. *UBL* 7: 232–48. Münster.
Lorton, David
1993   God's Beneficient Creation: Coffin Texts Spell 1130, The Instructions for Merikare, and the Great Hymn to Aton. *SAK* 20: 125–55.
1999   The Theology of Cult Statues in Ancient Egypt. Pp. 123–210 in Michael B. Dick, ed., *Born in Heaven, Made on Earth: The Making of the Cult Image in the Ancient Near East.* Winona Lake, IN, 1999.

Lüdemann, Gerd, ed.
1996   "Die Religionsgeschichtliche Schule." Facetten eines theologischen Umbruchs. Studien und Texte zur Religionsgeschichtlichen Schule 1. Frankfurt a.M.

Maag, Victor
1954   Sumerische und babylonische Mythen von der Erschaffung der Menschen. AS 1–4: 85–106.
1955   Alttestamentliche Anthropogonie in ihrem Verhältnis zur altorientalischen Mythologie. AS 9: 15–44.

Madden, Frederic W.
1881   Coins of the Jews. The International Numismata Vol. II. London.

Maier, Christl
2012   Proverbs: How Feminine Wisdom Comes into Being. Pp. 255–72 in Luise Schottroff and Marie-Theres Wacker, eds., Feminist Biblical Interpretation. Grand Rapids, MI/Cambridge.

Maier, Christl, and Schroer, Silvia.
2012   Job: Questioning the Book of the Righteous Sufferer. Pp. 221–39 in Luise Schottroff and Marie-Theres Wacker, eds., Feminist Biblical Interpretation. Grand Rapids, MI/Cambridge, 2012.

Mallowan, Max E. L.
1966   Nimrud and Its Remains. Vol. I. London.

Mansfeld, Jaap
1987   Die Vorsokratiker. Reclams Universalbibliothek Nr. 10344. Stuttgart.

Marböck, Johannes
1971   Weisheit im Wandel: Untersuchungen zur Weisheitstheologie bei Ben Sira. BBB 37. Bonn.
1995   Gottes Weisheit unter uns: Studien zur Theologie des Buches Sirach. HBS 6. Freiburg i.Br.

Marti, Karl
1906   Die Religion des alten Testaments unter den Religionen des Vorderen Orients. Tübingen.

Mathys, Hans-Peter, ed.
1998   Ebenbild Gottes: Herrscher über die Welt. Studien zu Würde und Auftrag des Menschen. BThSt 33. Neukirchener-Vluyn.

Matthews, Donald M.
1990   Principles of Composition in Near Eastern Glyptic of the Later Second Millenium B.C. OBO.SA 8. Freiburg, Switzerland/Göttingen.

Mattmüller, Markus
1957, 1968   Leonhard Ragaz und der religiöse Sozialismus: Ein Biographie in 2 Bänden. Zürich.

McBeath, Alastair
1999   Tiamat's Brood: An Investigation into the Dragons of Ancient Mesopotamia. London,.

Meadows, Dorothea H.
1972   The Limits to Growth. New York.

Meiggs, Russell
1982   Trees and Timber in the Ancient Mediterranean World. Oxford; reprinted, 1985.

Merchant, Carolyn
1980   Der Tod der Natur: Ökologie, Frauen und neuzeitliche Naturwissenschaft. 2nd edition. Munich, 1994 (English original: 1980).

Mettinger, Tryggve N. D.
1995   No Graven Image? Israelite Aniconism in Its Ancient Near Eastern Context. Stockholm.
1997   The Enigma of Job. The Deconstruction of God in Intertextual Perspective. JNWSL 23/2: 1–19.

Metz, Johann Baptist
1962   Christliche Anthropozentrik: Über die Denkform des Thomas von Aquin. Munich.

Michel, Diethelm
1988   Qohelet. Erträge der Forschung 258. Darmstadt.
1989   Untersuchungen zur Eigenart des Buches Qohelet. BZAW 183. Berlin.

Miller Jr., George Tyler
2000   Living in the Environment: Principles, Connections and Solutions. 11th edition. Pacific Grove, CA.

Mies, Maria, and Shiva, Vandana
1995   Ökofeminismus: Beiträge zur Praxis und Theorie. Zürich.

Moltmann, Jürgen
1994   Gott in der Schöpfung: Ökologische Schöpfungslehre. 4th edition. Munich.

Morenz, Siegfried
1957   Ein Naturlehre in den Sargtexten. WZKM 54: 119f.

Morenz, Siegfried, and Schubert, Johannes
1954   Der Gott auf der Blume: Ein ägyptische Kosmogonie und ihre weltweite Bedeutung. Ascona.
Mortensen, Viggo
1995   Theologie und Naturwissenschaft. Gütersloh.
Moser, Tilmann
1976   Gottesvergiftung. Frankfurt a.M.
Müller, Hans-Peter
1968   Wie sprach Qohälät von Gott? VT 18: 507–21.
1978   Das Hiobproblem. Erträge der Forschung 84. Darmstadt.
Münch, Paul, and Walz, Rainer
1998   Tiere und Menschen: Geschichte und Aktualität eines prekären Verhältnisses. Paderborn.
Mysliwiec, Karol
1978   Studien zum Gott Atum, vol. 1. Hildesheimer Ägyptologische Beiträge 5. Hildesheim.
Nelson, Harold Hayden
1932   Later Historical Records of Ramses III: Medinet Habu II. OIP 9. Chicago.
Niwiński Andrzej
1988   21st Dynasty Coffin from Thebes: Chronological and Typological Studies. Theben 5. Mainz.
1989   Studies on the Illustrated Theban Funerary Papyri of the 11th and 10th Centuries B.C. OBO
        86. Freiburg, Switzerland/Göttingen.
Norin Stig I. L.
1977   Er spaltete das Meer: Die Auszugsüberlieferung in Psalmen und Kult des alten Israel. Lund.
Noth, Martin
1966   Das vierte Buch Mose: Numeri. ATD 7. Göttingen.
Noth, Martin, and Thomas, D. Winton
1955   Wisdom in Israel and in the Ancient Near East: Presented to Harold Henry Rowley in Cele-
        bration of His Sixty-Fifth Birthday, 24 March 1955. VTSup 3. Leiden.
O'Brien, Joan, and Wilfred, Major
1982   In the Beginning: Creation Myths from Ancient Mesopotamia, Israel and Greece. Aids for the
        Study of Religions Series 11. Chico, CA.
Ockinga, Boyo.
1984   Die Gottebenbildlichkeit im alten Ägypten und im Alten Testament. ÄAT 7. Wiesbaden.
Oorschot, Jürgen von
1987   Gott als Grenze: Ein literar- und redaktionsgeschichtliche Studie zu den Gottesreden des
        Hiobbuches. BZAW 170. Berlin.
1994   Hiob 28: Die verborgene Weisheit und die Furcht Gottes als Überwindung einer ge-
        neralisierten חכמה. Pp. 183–201 in W. A. Beuken, ed., The Book of Job. Leuven.
Orland, Barbara, and Scheich, Elvira, eds.
1995   Das Geschlecht der Natur. Feministische Beiträge zur Geschichte und Theorie der Natur-
        wissenschaften. Hamburg.
Orlinsky, Harry Meyer
1959   Studies in the LXX of Job III: On the Matter of Anthropomorphisms, Anthropopa-
        thisms, and Euphemisms. HUCA 30: 153–67.
1961   Studies in the LXX of Job III: On the Matter of Anthropomorphisms, Anthropopa-
        thisms, and Euphemisms. HUCA 32: 239–68.
Orthmann, Winfried
1975   Der alte Orient. PK 14. Berlin.
Osten-Sacken, Peter von der
1978   Rückzug ins Wesen und aus der Geschichte: Antijudaismus bei Adolf von Harnack
        und Rudolf Bultmann. WuPKG 67: 108–12.
Otto, Eberhard
1971   Der Mensch als Geschöpf und Bild Gottes in Ägypten. Pp. 335–45 in Hans Walter
        Wolff, ed., Probleme biblischer Theologie: Festschrift Gerhard von Rad. Munich.
Otto, Eckart
1996   Die Paradieserzählung Genesis 2–3: Ein nachpriesterschriftliche Lehrerzählung in
        ihrem religionshistorischen Kontext. Pp. 167–92 in Anja A. Diesel et al., eds., "Jedes
        Ding hat seine Zeit . . ." Studien zur israelitischen und altorientalischen Weisheit: Diethelm
        Michel zum 65. Geburtstag. BZAW 241. Berlin.
Page Gasser, Madeleine
2001   Götter bewohnten Ägypten: Bronzefiguren der Sammlungen BIBEL + ORIENT der Universität
        Freiburg/Schweiz. Freiburg, Switzerland.
Paterson, Archibald
1915   Assyrian Sculptures. Palace of Senacherib. Plates and Ground-Plan of the Palace. The Hague.

Paul, Ian
2000   The Use of the Old Testament in Revelation 12. Pp. 256–76 in Steve Moyise, ed., *The Old Testament in the New Testament: Essays in Honour of J. L. North.* JSNTSup 189. Sheffield.
Perler, Dominik
1998   *René Descartes.* Munich.
Pettinato, Giovanni
1971   *Das altorientalische Menschenbild und die sumerischen und akkadischen Schöpfungsmythen.* Heidelberg.
Petrie, W. M. Flinders
1930   *Beth-Pelet I (Tell Fara).* London.
Piaget, Jean
1926   *The Child's Conception of the World.* Trans. Joan and Andrew Tomlinson. London: Routledge and Kegan Paul [numerous reprints]. (French original, 1926.)
1978   *La représentation du monde chez l'enfant.* Paris, 1926; dt. Ausgabe Stuttgart, 1978.
Piankoff, Alexandre, and Rambova, N.
1957   *Mythological Papyri.* 2 volumes. Egyptian Religious Texts and Representations III. New York.
Plaskow, Judith
1990   *Standing Again at Sinai: Judaism from a Feminist Perspective.* San Francisco: Harper & Row.
Podella, Thomas
1993   Der "Chaoskampfmythos" im Alten Testament. Pp. 283–329 in Manfred Dietrich and Oswald Loretz, eds., *Mesopotamica – Ugaritica – Biblica: Festschrift Kurt Bergerhof.* AOAT 232. Neukirchen-Vluyn/Kevelaer.
Porada, Edith
1983   Cylinder Seal From Jericho. Pp. 774–76 in Kathleen M. Kenyon and T. A. Holland, *Excavations at Jericho,* Vol. V. Jerusalem/London.
Praetorius, Ina
1991   "Schöpfung/Ökologie." Pp. 354–60 in Elisabeth Gößmann et al., eds. *Wörterbuch der Feministischen Theologie.* Gütersloh.
2000   Die Würde der Kreatur. Ein Kommentar zu einem neuen Grundwert. Pp. 97–137 in eadem, *Zum Ende des Patriachats: Theologisch-politische Texte im Übergang.* Mainz.
Precht, Richard David
1997   *Noahs Erbe: Vom Recht der Tiere und den Grenzen des Menschen.* Hamburg.
Preuß, Horst Dietrich
1970   Erwägungen zum theologischen Ort alttestamentlicher Weisheitsliteratur. *EvTh* 30: 393–417.
1991   *Theologie des Alten Testaments,* vol. 1: *JHWHs erwählendes und verpflichtendes Handeln.* Stuttgart.
Pritchard, James B., ed.
1969   *Ancient Near Eastern Texts Relating to the Old Testament.* 3rd edition. Princeton.
Pury, Albert de
1993a   *Homme et animal Dieu les créa. L'ancien Testament et les animaux.* Essais Bibliques 25. Geneva.
1993b   Gemeinschaft und Differenz. Aspekte der Mensch-Tier-Beziehung im alten Israel. Pp. 112–49 in Bernd Janowski, Ute Neumann-Gorsolke, and Uwe Gleßmer, eds. *Gefährten und Feinde des Menschen: Das Tier in der Lebenswelt des alten Israel.* Neukirchen-Vluyn.
Rad, Gerhard von
1955   Hiob xxxviii und die altägyptische Weisheit. Pp. 293–301 in Martin Noth and D. Winton Thomas, eds., *Wisdom in Israel and in the Ancient Near East: Presented to Harold Henry Rowley in Celebration of His Sixty-Fifth Birthday, 24 March 1955.* VTSup 3. Leiden, 1955 = idem, *Gesammelte Studien zum AT,* pp. 262–71. ThB 8. Munich, 1961.
1961   *Genesis: A Commentary.* Old Testament Library. Philadelphia.
1962   *Old Testament Theology,* vol. 1: *The Theology of Israel's Historical Traditions.* New York, 1962; reprinted, 2001.
1966   The Theological Problem of the Old Testament Doctrine of Creation. Pp. 131–43 in idem, *The Problem of the Hexateuch and Other Essays.* New York, 1966.
1971   Christliche Weisheit? *EvTh* 31: 150–55.
1972   *Wisdom in Israel.* London, 1972; 7th printing, 1993.

Radford Ruether, Rosemarie
1994   *Gaia and God: An Ecofeminist Theology of Earth History*. San Francisco, 1992; 2nd edition, 1994.
Ragaz, Leonhard
1990   *Die Bibel: Eine Deutung*. Erster Band: Die Urgeschichte, Moses. Originally published, Zürich; new edition, Freiburg, Switzerland/Brig.
Rambova, N., ed.
1954   *The Tomb of Ramesses VI. Texts*. Bollingen Series XL,1. New York.
Rappel, Simone
1996   *"Macht euch die Erden untertan": Die ökologische Krise als Folge des Christentums?* Paderborn.
Reese, James M.
1970   *Hellenistic Influence on the Book of Wisdom and its Consequences*. AnBib 41. Rome.
Reich, K. Helmut
1987   *Children and Adolescents between Religious and Scientific World Views: The Role of Thinking in Terms of Complementarity*. Berichte zur Erziehungswissenschaft 63. Freiburg, Switzerland.
Reicke, Bo, and Rost, Leonhard
1964   *Biblisch-Historisches Handwörterbuch*, vol. 2. Göttingen.
Reinke, Otfried
1995   *Tiere: Begleiter des Menschen in Tradition und Gegenwart*. Neukirchen-Vluyn.
Reiterer, Friedrich Vinzenz
1999   Die immateriellen Ebenen der Schöpfung bei Ben Sira. Pp. 91–127 in Nuria Calduch-Benages and Jacques Vermeylen, eds., *Treasures of Wisdom: Studies in Ben Sira and the Book of Wisdom: Festschrift M. Gilbert*. Leuven.
Renckens, Henricus
1957   *Urgeschichte und Heilsgeschichte: Israels Schau in die Vergangenheit nach Gen.1–3*. Mainz, 1959 (English edition, 1957); 4th edition, 1972.
Rendtorff, Rolf
1991   "Wo warst du, als ich die Erde gründete?" Schöpfung und Heilsgeschichte. Pp. 94–112 in idem, *Kanon und Theologie*. Neukirchen-Vluyn.
Richards, Robert John
1987   *Darwin and the Emergence of Evolutionary Theories of Mind and Behavior*. Chicago.
Rickenbacher, Otto
1973   *Weisheitsperikopen bei Ben Sira*. OBO 1. Freiburg, Switzerland/Göttingen.
Riede, Peter
1993   "Denn wie der Mensch jedes Tier nennen würde, so sollte es heißen": Hebräische Tiernamen und was sie uns verraten. *UF* 25: 331–78.
1995   David und der Floh: Tiere und Tiervergleiche in den Samuelbüchern. *BN* 77: 86–117.
1997   "Doch frag' nur die Tiere, sie werden dich lehren" (Hiob 12,7): Tiere als "Lehrer" des Menschen. *Beiträge Pädagogischer Arbeit* 40/2: 19–38.
2000   Im Spiegel der Tiere: Überlegungen zum Verhältnis von Mensch und Tier in der christlich-jüdischen Tradition. Pp. 9–41 in *Lammfromm oder saudumm? Das Tier in unserer Kultur*, ed. Evangelische Akademie Baden. Karlsruhe.
Ritter-Müller, Petra
2000   *Kennst du die Welt? Gottes Antwort an Ijob: Ein sprachwissenschaftliche und exegetische Studie zur ersten Gottesrede Ijob 38 und 39*. Münster.
Röd, Wolfgang
1976   *Die Philosophie der Antike I: Von Thales bis Demokrit*. Munich.
Rogers, Jessie F.
1996   Wisdom and Creation in Sirach 24. *JNWSL* 22: 141–56.
Rose, Martin
1999   De la "crise de la sagesse" à l'"sagesse de la crise." Pp. 27–46 in Martin Rose, ed., *Situer Qohélet: Regards croisés sur un livre biblique*. Revue de Théologie et de Philosophie. Genf.
Rose, Martin, ed.
1999a   *Situer Qohélet: Regards croisés sur un livre biblique. Revue de Théologie et de Philosophie*. Genf.
1999b   *Rien de nouveau: Nouvelles approches du livre de Qohéleth. Avec une bibliographie (1988–1998) élaborée par Béatrice Perregaux Allisson*. OBO 168. Freiburg, Switzerland/Göttingen.
Rosenzweig, Franz
1976   *Der Stern der Erlösung*. Den Haag. 4th edition,1976 (= Frankfurt a.M., 1988).

Rowe, Alan
1936   *A Catalogue of Egyptian Scarabs, Scaraboids, Seals and Amulets in the Palestine Archaeological Museum.* Cairo.
Rudolph, Wilhelm
1966   *Hosea.* KAT 13,1. Gütersloh.
Rüterswörden, Udo
1993   *Dominium terrae: Studien zur Genese einer atl Vorstellung.* BZAW 215. Berlin.
Ryhiner, Marie-Louise
1986   *L'offrande du Lotus dans les temples égyptiens de l'époque tardive.* Rites égyptiens 6. Brussels.
Saladin, Peter
1992   Das Recht der Natur in unserer Kultur. Pp. 201–22 in M. Svilar, ed., *Kultur und Natur.* Kulturhistorische Vorlesungen der Universität Bern. Berne.
Sass, Benjamin, and Uehlinger, Christoph, eds.
1993   *Studies in the Iconography of Northwest Semitic Inscribed Seals.* OBO 125. Freiburg, Switzerland/Göttingen.
Sauer, Georg
2000   *Jesus Sirach/Ben Sira.* ATD Apokryphen 1. Göttingen.
Sauer-Gaertner, Martin
2001   Drachenkämpfer in der Antike. Pp. 27–31 in Sylvia Hahn et al., *Sanct Georg: Der Ritter mit dem Drachen* (Ausstellungskatalog). Freising.
Sauren, Herbert
1993   Nammu and Enki. Pp. 198–208 in M. E. Cohen et al., eds., *The Tablet and the Scroll: Near Eastern Studies in Honor of William W. Hallo.* Bethesda, MD.
Scannone, Juan Carlos
1992   *Weisheit und Befreiung: Volkstheologie in Lateinamerika.* Theologie interkulturell 5. Düsseldorf.
Schenker, Adrian
1998   Der Boden und sein Produktivität im Sabbat- und Jubeljahr. Das dominium terrae in Ex 23,10f und Lev 25,2–12. Pp. 94–106 in H.-P. Mathys, ed., *Ebenbild Gottes: Herrscher über die Welt. Studien zu Würde und Auftrag des Menschen.* BThSt 33. Neukirchen-Vluyn.
Schiebinger, Londa
1995   *Am Busen der Natur. Erkenntnis und Geschlecht in den Anfängen der Wissenschaft.* Stuttgart.
Schiller, Friedrich
1852   *The Poems and Ballads of Schiller.* Trans. by Sir Edward Bulwer Lytton. 2nd edition. Edinburgh: Blackwood.
Schlögl, Hermann A.
1977   *Der Sonnengott auf der Blüte: Ein ägyptische Kosmogonie des neuen Reiches.* Aegyptiaca Helvetica 5. Genf.
1980   *Der Gott Tatenen.* OBO 29. Freiburg, Switzerland/Göttingen.
1986   *Amenophis IV: Echnaton.* Reinbek bei Hamburg.
1993   *Echnaton – Tutanchamun: Daten, Fakten, Literatur.* 4th edition. Wiesbaden.
Schmid, Hans Heinrich
1966   *Wesen und Geschichte der Weisheit.* BZAW 101. Berlin.
1968   *Gerechtigkeit als Weltordnung: Hintergrund und Geschichte des alttestamentlichen Gerechtigkeitsbegriffs.* BHTh 40. Tübingen.
1974   *Altorientalische Welt in der alttestamentlichen Theologie.* Zürich.
Schmidt, Wolf-Rüdiger, et al.
1996   *Geliebte und andere Tiere im Judentum, Christentum und Islam: Vom Elend der Kreatur in unserer Zivilisation.* Gütersloh.
Schmitt, Armin
1986   *Das Buch der Weisheit: Ein Kommentar.* Würzburg.
1989   *Weisheit.* NEB.AT 23. Würzburg.
Schmitz-Kahmen, Florian
1997   *Geschöpfe Gottes unter der Obhut des Menschen: Die Wertung der Tiere im Alten Testament.* NThDH 10. Neukirchen-Vluyn.
Schmitz-Moormann, Karl
1997   *Materie – Leben – Geist. Evolution als Schöpfung Gottes.* Mainz.
Schmökel, Hartmut
1974   *Das Gilgameschepos.* 3rd edition. Stuttgart.

Schnabel, Eckhard J.
1985   *Law and Wisdom from Ben Sira to Paul: A Tradition Historical Enquiry into the Relation of Law, Wisdom and Ethics.* Tübingen.
Schoske, Sylvia, and Wildung, Dietrich
1992   *Gott und Götter im Alten Ägypten.* Mainz.
Schott, Albert
1969   *Das Gilgameschepos.* Ergänzt und teilweise neu gestaltet von Wolfram von Soden. Stuttgart (first edition, 1934).
Schottroff, Willy
1969   *Der altisraelitische Fluchspruch.* WMANT 30. Neukirchen-Vluyn.
Schroer, Silvia
1986   Der Geist, die Weisheit und die Taube: Feministisch-kritische Exegese eines neutestamentlichen Symbols auf dem Hintergrund seiner altorientalischen und hellenistisch-frühjüdischen Traditionsgeschichte. *FZPhTH* 33: 197–225.
1987a   *In Israel gab es Bilder: Nachrichten von darstellender Kunst im Alten Testament.* OBO 74. Freiburg, Switzerland/Göttingen.
1987b   Die Zweiggöttin in Palästina/Israel. Von der Mittelbronze IIB-Zeit bis zu Jesus Sirach. Pp. 201–25 in Max Küchler and Christoph Uehlinger, eds., *Jerusalem: Texte – Bilder – Steine: FS Hildi und Othmar Keel-Leu.* NTOA 6. Freiburg, Switzerland/Göttingen.
1989   Die Göttin auf den Stempelsiegeln aus Palästina/Israel. Pp. 89–207 in Othmar Keel et al., *Studien zu den Stempelsiegeln aus Palästin,* vol. 2. OBO 88. Freiburg, Switzerland/Göttingen.
1990   Psalm 65: Zeugnis eines integrativen JHWH-Glaubens? *UF* 22: 285–301.
1991   Die göttliche Weisheit und der nachexilische Monotheismus. Pp. 151–82 in Marie-Theres Wacker and Erich Zenger, eds., *Der eine Gott und die Göttin: Gottesvorstellungen im Horizont feministischer Theologie.* QD 135. Freiburg i.Br.
1994a   Die Aschera. Kein abgeschlossenes Kapitel. *Schlangenbrut* 44: 17–22.
1994b   "Die Eselin sah den Engel JHWHs": Ein biblische Theologie der Tiere—für Menschen. Pp. 83–87 in Dorothee Sölle, ed., *Für Gerechtigkeit streiten: Theologie im Alltag einer bedrohten Welt. Festschrift für Luise Schottroff.* Gütersloh. [1994a]
1994c   Die personifizierte Sophia im Buch der Weisheit. Pp. 543–58 in Walter Dietrich and Martin A. Klopfenstein, eds., *Ein Gott allein: JHWH-Verehrung und biblischer Monotheismus im Kontext der israelitischen und altorientalischen Religionsgeschichte.* OBO 139. Freiburg, Switzerland/Göttingen.
1996   Der israelitische Monotheismus als Synkretismus: Einblicke in die Religionsgeschichte Israels/Palästinas auf der Basis der neueren Forschung. Pp. 268–87 in Peter Anton, ed., *Christlicher Glaube in multireligiöser Gesellschaft: Erfahrungen – Theologische Reflexionen – Missionarische Perspektiven.* Immensee.
1998a   "Under the Shadow of Your Wings": The Metaphor of God's Wings in the Psalms, Exodus 19:4, Deuteronomy 32:11, and Malachi 3:20, as Seen through the Perspectives of Feminism and the History of Religion. Pp. 264–82 in Athalya Brenner and Carole R. Fontaine, eds., *Wisdom and Psalms.* The Feminist Companion to the Bible, Second Series 2. Sheffield, 1998.
1998b   Das Buch der Weisheit. Pp. 352–62 in Zenger Erich et al., *Einleitung in das Alte Testament.* 3rd edition. Stuttgart, 1998.
2000   *Wisdom Has Built Her House: Studies on the Figure of Sophia in the Bible.* Minneapolis.
2002   Griechische Heiligtümer im Spiegel alttestamentlicher Kosmologien und Theologien. Pp. 231–88 in Keel and Zenger 2002.
Schroer, Silvia, and Thomas Staubli
2001   *Body Symbolism in the Bible.* Collegeville, MN.
Schubert, Mathias
1989   *Schöpfungstheologie bei Kohelet.* BEAT 15. Frankfurt a.M./Berne.
Schüngel-Straumann, Helen
1997   *Die Frau am Anfang: Eva und die Folgen.* 2nd edition. Münster.
Schüssler Fiorenza, Elisabeth
1994   *Jesus—Miriam's Child, Sophia's Prophet: Critical Issues in Feminist Christology.* New York.
Schwienhorst-Schönberger, Ludger, ed.
1997   *Das Buch Kohelet: Studien zur Struktur, Geschichte, Rezeption und Theologie.* BZAW 254. Berlin.
Seidel, Hans
1969   *Das Erlebnis der Einsamkeit im Alten Testament: Ein Untersuchung zum Menschenbild des AT.* Berlin.

Seidl, Ursula
1989   *Die babylonischen Kudurru-Reliefs. Symbole mesopotamischer Gottheiten.* OBO 87. Freiburg Switzerland/Göttingen.
2000   Babylonische und assyrische Kultbilder in den Massenmedien des 1. Jahrtausends v.Chr. Pp. 89–114 in Christoph Uehlinger, ed., *Images as Media: Sources for the Cultural History of the Near East and the Eastern Mediterranean (1st millenium BCE).* OBO 175. Freiburg, Switzerland/Göttingen.

Seifert, Elke
1997   *Tochter und Vater im Alten Testament: Ein ideologiekritische Untersuchung zur Verfügungsgewalt von Vätern über ihre Töchter.* Neukirchener Theologische Dissertationen und Habilitationen 9. Neukirchener-Vluyn.

Shekan, Patrick W., and Di Lella, Alexander A.
1987   *The Wisdom of Ben Sira.* AB 39. New York.

Sitzler, Dorothea
1995   *Vorwurf gegen Gott. Ein religiöses Motiv im Alten Orient (Ägypten und Mesopotamien).* StOR 32. Wiesbaden.

Smith, George
1876   *The Chaldean Account of Genesis Containing the Description of the Creation etc.* London.

Soden, Wolfram von
1965   *Leistung und Grenze sumerischer und babylonischer Wissenschaft.* Darmstadt.
1979   Konflikte und ihre Bewältigung in babylonischen Schöpfungs- und Fluterzählungen. *MDOG* 111: 1–33.

Sölle, Dorothee
1985   *Lieben und arbeiten: Ein Theologie der Schöpfung.* Stuttgart.
1990   *Gott denken: Einführung in die Theologie.* Stuttgart.

Sölle, Dorothee, and Schottroff, Luise
1996   *Den Himmel erden: Ein ökofeministische Annäherung an die Bibel.* Munich.

Stähli, Hans-Peter
1985   *Solare Elemente im Jahweglauben des Alten Testaments.* OBO 66. Freiburg, Switzerland/Göttingen.

Stamm, Johann Jakob
1956   Die Imago-Lehre von Karl Barth und die alttestamentliche Wissenschaft. Pp. 84–98 in F. Winter, ed., *Antwort: Festschrift Karl Barth.* Zürich-Zollikon.
1959   Die Gottebenbildlichkeit des Menschen im Alten Testament. *ThSt* 54: 81–90.

Staub, Urs
1985   Das älteste Bild des Pharao. Vom Ursprung des göttlichen Königtums. *BiKi* 40: 162–64.

Staubli, Thomas
1991   *Das Image der Nomaden im Alten Israel und in der Ikonographie seiner sesshaften Nachbarn.* OBO 107. Freiburg, Switzerland/Göttingen.
1996   *Die Bücher Levitikus und Numeri.* NSK-AT 3. Stuttgart.
2001   Schöpfungsdämmerung. *NW* 95: 197–206.

Staudacher, Willibald
1942   *Die Trennung von Himmel und Erde: Ein vorgriechischer Schöpfungsmythus bei Hesiod und den Orphikern.* Tübingen.

Steck, Odil Hannes
1970   *Die Paradieserzählung: Ein Auslegung von Genesis 2,4b–3,24.* Neukirchen-Vluyn, 1970 = idem, *Wahrnehmungen Gottes im AT: Gesammelte Studien,* pp. 9–116. ThB 70. Munich, 1982.
1975   *Der Schöpfungsbericht der Priesterschrift.* FRLANT 115. Göttingen.
1978a   Alttestamentliche Impulse für ein Theologie der Natur. *ThZ* 34: 202–11.
1978b   Der Wein unter den Schöpfungsgaben. *TThZ* 87: 173–91.
1978c   *Welt und Umwelt: Biblische Konfrontationen.* Stuttgart.

Steymans, Hans Ulrich
1995   *Deuteronomium 28 und die adê zur Thronfolgeregelung Asarhaddons: Segen und Fluch im Alten Orient und in Israel.* OBO 145. Freiburg, Switzerland/Göttingen.

Stolz, Fritz
1972   Die Bäume des Gottesgartens auf dem Libanon. *ZAW* 84: 141–56.
1992   Natur und Kultur: Diesseits und Jenseits. Orientierungslinien in den Weltreligionen. Pp. 29–52 in Maja Svilar, ed., *Kultur und Natur.* Kulturhistorische Vorlesungen der Universität Bern. Berne.

Strack, Hermann L., and Paul Billerback
1926   *Kommentar zum Neuen Testament aus Talmud und Midrasch.* 4 volumes. 3rd edition. Munich.

Strahm, Doris.
1999   Ökofeminismus: eine Spiritualität des Lebens. Zur Theologie von Ivone Gebara. *Neue Wege* 93: 134–43.

Strotmann, Angelika
1998   Das Buch Jesus Sirach: Über die schwierige Beziehung zwischen göttlicher Weisheit und konkreten Frauen in einer androzentrischen Schrift. Pp. 428–40 in Luise Schottroff and Marie-Theres Wacker, eds., *Kompendium Feministische Bibelauslegung.* Gütersloh.

Susman, Margarete
1946   *Das Buch Hiob und das Schicksal des jüdischen Volkes.* Zürich.

Sutter Rehmann, Luzia
1995   *Geh, frage die Gebärerin! Feministisch-befreiungstheologische Untersuchungen zum Gebärmotiv in der Apokalyptik.* Gütersloh.

Talmud. *Sanhedrin.* Trans. by Jacob Schachter and H. Freedman (Hebrew–English Edition of the Babylonian Talmud, ed. I. Epstein, vol. 4, pt. 4). London: Soncino, 1987.

Tamez, Elsa
2000   *When the Horizons Close: Rereading Ecclesiastes.* New York.

Teissier, Beatrice
1984   *Ancient Near Eastern Cylinder Seals from the Marcopoli Collection.* Berkeley.

Teutsch, Gotthard Martin
1995   *Die "Würde der Kreatur": Erläuterungen zu einem neuen Verfassungsbegriff am Beispiel des Tieres.* Berne.

Theuer, Gabriele
2000   *Der Mondgott in den Religionen Syrien-Palästinas: Unter besonderer Berücksichtigung von KTU 1.24.* OBO 173. Freiburg, Switzerland/Göttingen.

Thomson, James G. S. S.
1955   Sleep: An Aspect of Jewish Anthropology. *VT* 5: 421–33.

Tigay, Jeffrey H.
1982   *The Evolution of the Gilgamesh Epic.* Philadelphia.

Tobin, Vincent Arieh
1987   Maʿat und DIKH: Some Comparative Considerations of Egyptian and Greek Thought. *JARCE* 24: 113–21.

Toorn, Karel van der
1997   Ein verborgenes Erbe. Totenkult im frühen Israel. *ThQ* 177: 105–20.

Toorn, Karel van der, ed.
1997   *The Image and the Book: Iconic Cults, Aniconism, and the Rise of Book Religion in Israel and the Ancient Near East.* Contributions to Biblical Exegesis & Theology 21. Leuven.

Tosi, Mario, and Roccati, Alessandro
1972   *Stele e Altre Epigrafi di Deir el Medina: Catalogo del Museo Egizio di Torino,* Ser. 2, vol. 1. Turin.

Trigo, Pedro
1991   *Creation and History.* Maryknoll, NY.

Tromp, Nicholas J.
1969   *Primitive Conceptions of Death and the Nether World in the Old Testament.* BibOr 21. Rome.

Tropper, Josef
1987   "Seele" oder "Totengeist"? Erwägungen zum Begriff *eṭemmu* in Atramḫasīs I 215–217. *UF* 19: 301–8.

Troy, Lana
1997   Engendering Creation in Ancient Egypt. Still and Flowing Waters. Pp. 238–68 in Athalya Brenner and Carol Fontaine, eds., *A Feminist Companion to Reading the Bible: Approaches, Methods and Strategies.* Sheffield.

Tufnell, Olga et al.
1958   *Lachish IV (Tell ed-Duweir): The Bronze Age.* 2 volumes. London.

Uehlinger, Christoph
1988   Eva als "lebendiges Kunstwerk": Traditionsgeschichtliches zu Gen 2,21–22(23.24) und 3,20. *BN* 43: 90–99.

1990   Leviathan und die Schiffe in Ps 104,25–26. *Bib.* 71: 499–526.

1991a   Der Mythos vom Drachenkampf: Von Sumer nach Nicaragua—Ein biblisches Feindbild und sein Geschichte. *BiKi* 46: 66–77.

1991b   Vom dominium terrae zu einem Ethos der Selbstbeschränkung? Alttestamentliche Einsprüche gegen einen tyrannischen Umgang mit der Schöpfung. *BiLi* 64: 59–74.

1995a Drachen und Drachenkämpfe im alten Vorderen Orient und in der Bibel. Pp. 55–101 in Bernd Schmelz and Rüdiger Vossen, *Auf Drachenspuren: Ein Buch zum Drachenprojekt des Hamburgischen Museums für Völkerkunde*. Bonn.

1995b Gab es eine joschijanische Reform? Plädoyer für ein begründetes Minimum. Pp. 57–89 in Walter Groß, ed., *Jeremia und die "deuteronomistische Bewegung."* BBB 98. Bonn.

1996 Astralkultpriester und Fremdgekleidete, Kanaanvolk und Silberwäger. Zur Verknüpfung von Kult- und Sozialkritik in Zef 1. Pp. 49–83 in Walter Dietrich and Milton Schwantes, eds., *Der Tag wird kommen: Ein interkulturelles Gespräch über das Buch des Propheten Zefanja*. SBS 170. Stuttgart.

1997 Qohelet im Horizont der mesopotamischen, levantinischen und ägyptischen Weisheit der persischen und hellenistischen Zeit. Pp. 155–247 in Ludger Schwienhorst-Schönberger, ed., *Das Buch Kohelet: Studien zur Struktur, Geschichte, Rezeption und Theologie*. BZAW 254. Berlin.

1998 Nicht nur Knochenfrau: Zu einem wenig beachteten Aspekt der zweiten Schöpfungserzählung. *BiKi* 53: 31–34.

Usener, Hermann
1899 *Die Sintflutsagen*. Bonn.

Vattioni, Francesco
1968 *Ecclesiastico: Testo ebraico con apparato critico e versioni greca, latin e sirica*. Naples.

Veijola, Timo
1982 *Verheißung in der Krise: Studien zur Literatur und Theologie der Exilszeit anhand des 89. Psalms*. AASF SerB 220. Helsinki.

Wacker, Marie-Theres
1996 *Figurationen des Weiblichen im Hosea-Buch*. HBS 8. Freiburg i.Br.

Wakeman, Mary K.
1973 *God's Battle with the Monster: A Study in Biblical Imagery*. Leiden.

Walker, Christopher, and Michael B. Dick
1999 The Induction of the Cult Image in Ancient Mesopotamia: The Mesopotamian *mīs pî* Ritual. Pp. 55–121 in M. B. Dick, ed., *Born in Heaven, Made on Earth: The Making of the Cult Image in the Ancient Near East*. Winona Lake, IN.

Walter, Hans-Ulrich
1985 Das Hohelied: Ein alttestamentliche Sprengung der alttestamentlichen Diskriminierung der Frauen. DBAT 22: 140–74.

Webb, George Ernest
1994 *The Evolution Controversy in America*. Lexington, KY.

Weber, Burkhard
1999 *Ijob in Lateinamerika: Deutung und Bewältigung von Leid in der Theologie der Befreiung, Mit einem Vorwort von Leonardo Boff*. Mainz.

Weber, Beat
1995 *Psalm 77 und sein Umfeld: Ein poetologische Studie*. BBB 103. Weinheim.
2000 Zur Datierung der Asaph-Psalmen 74 und 79. *Bib* 8: 521–32.

Weber, Cornelia
2000 *Altes Testament und völkische Frage: Der biblische Volksbegriff in der alttestamentlichen Wissenschaft der nationalsozialistischen Zeit, dargestellt am Beispiel von Johannes Hempel*. FAT 28. Tübingen.

Wehmeier, Gerhard
1970 *Der Segen im Alten Testament: Ein semasiologische Untersuchung der Wurzel* brk. ThDiss 6. Basel.

Weidner, Stephan
1985 *Lotos im alten Ägypten*. Pfaffenweiler.

Weippert, Helga
1981 *Schöpfer des Himmels und der Erde: Ein Beitrag zur Theologie des Jeremiabuches*. SBS 102. Stuttgart.

Weippert, Manfred
1998 Tier und Mensch in der menschenarmen Welt. Zum sog. dominium terrae in Gen 1. Pp. 35–55 in Hans-Peter Mathys, ed., *Ebenbild Gottes – Herrscher über die Welt: Studien zu Würde und Auftrag des Menschen*. BThSt 33. Neukirchener-Vluyn.

Welker, Michael
1995 *Schöpfung und Wirklichkeit*. NBST 13. Neukirchen-Vluyn.

Wénin André
1999 De la création à l'alliance sinaïtique: La logique de Si 16,26–17,14. Pp. 147–58 in Nuria Calduch-Benages and Jacques Vermeylen, eds., *Treasures of Wisdom: Studies in Ben Sira and the Book of Wisdom. Festschrift M. Gilbert*. Leuven.

Westermann, Claus
1984   Schöpfung und Evolution. Pp. 27–38 in idem, *Erträge der Forschung am Alten Testament: Gesammelte Studien III*. Munich.
1994   *Genesis*. Minneapolis.
1992   *Der Segen in der Bibel und im Handeln der Kirche*. 2nd edition. Munich.
White Jr., Lynn
1970   Die historischen Ursachen unserer ökologischen Krise. Pp. 20–29 in Michael Lohmann, ed., *Gefährdete Zukunft: Prognosen anglo-amerikanischer Wissenschaftler*. Munich.
Wildung, Dietrich
1984   *Ni-User-Rê: Sonnenkönig – Sonnengott*. SAS Heft 1. Munich.
1984a   *Sesostris und Amenemhet: Ägypten im Mittleren Reich*. Freiburg, Switzerland/Munich.
Winston, David
1979   *The Wisdom of Solomon*. AB 43. New York.
Winter, Urs
1987   *Frau und Göttin Exegetische und ikonographische Studien zum weiblichen Gottesbild im Alten Israel und in dessen Umwelt*. OBO 53. 2nd edition. Freiburg, Switzerland/Göttingen.
1986a   Der stilisierte Baum: Zu einem auffälligen Aspekt altorientalischer Baumsymbolik und seiner Rezeption im Alten Testament. *BiKi* 41: 171–77.
1986b   Der "Lebensbaum" in der altorientalischen Bildsymbolik. Pp. 57–88 in H. Schweizer, ed. *". . . Bäume braucht man doch": Das Symbol des Baumes zwischen Hoffnung und Zerstörung*. Sigmaringen.
Wolff, Hans Walter
1974   *Hosea*. Old Testament Library. Philadelphia.
Wreszinski, Walter
1923–38 *Atlas zur altägyptischen Kulturgeschichte*. 3 volumes. Leipzig.
Wuketits, Franz M.
1998   *Naturkatastrophe Mensch*. Düsseldorf.
Wyss, Stephan
1984   *Fluchen: Ohnmächtige und mächtige Rede der Ohnmacht*. Freiburg, Switzerland.
Yoyotte, Jean
1996   Ägyptische Vorstellungen von der Entstehung der Welt. *WUB* 1/2: 12–15.
Zenger, Erich
1983   *Gottes Bogen in den Wolken: Untersuchungen zu Komposition und Theologie der priesterschriftlichen Urgeschichte*. SBS 112. Stuttgart.
1989   "Du liebst alles, was ist" (Weish 11,24): Biblische Perspektiven für einen erneuerten Umgang mit der Schöpfung. *BiKi* 44: 38–47.
Zerafa, Pietro Paolo
1978   *The Wisdom of God in the Book of Job*. Rome.
Zimmerli, Walther
1967   *Das Buch des Predigers Salomo*. ATD 16. 2nd edition. Göttingen.
1999   *Grundriß der alttestamentlichen Theologie*. 7th edition. Stuttgart.
Zimmermann, Mirjam, and Zimmermann, Ruben
1999   "Heilige Hochzeit" der Göttersöhne und Menschentöchter? Spuren des Mythos in Gen 6,1–4. *ZAW* 111: 327–52.
2000   Vom "Hätschelkind" zur "Himmelsbraut": Eine "relecture" zum Weisheitsverständnis in Spr 8,22–31. *BZ* 44: 77–91.
Zimmermann, Ruben
1994   Homo Sapiens Ignorans: Hiob 28 als Bestandteil der ursprünglichen Hiobdichtung. *BN* 74: 80–100.
2001   *Geschlechtermetaphorik und Gottesverhältnis: Traditionsgeschichte und Theologie eines Bildfelds in Urchristentum und antiker Umwelt*. WUNT 2, Reihe 122. Tübingen.

Supplementary Literature

Ahuis, Ferdinand
2011   Behemot, Leviatan und der Mensch in Hiob 38–42. *ZAW* 123: 72–91.
Barach, John
2011   The glory of the Son of Man. An exposition of Psalm 8. Pp. 3–33 in P. Leithart et al., eds., *The Glory of Kings: A Festschrift in Honor of James B. Jordan*. Pickwick.

Bechmann, Ulrike
2011   Chaos am Anfang und Ende der Welt: das biblische Weltbild. Pp. 31–55 in U. Bech-
        mann and C. Friedl, eds., *Chaos: Beiträge von Vortragenden der Montagsakademie* 2010/11.
        Graz.
Ben-Dov, Jonathan
2011   Psalm 104:19: Ben-Sirah and the History of Calendars in Ancient Israel. *JJS* 62/1: 7–20.
Benz, Arnold
2009   *Das geschenkte Universum: Astrophysik und Schöpfung.* Düsseldorf.
Brünenberg, Esther
2009   *Der Mensch in Gottes Herrlichkeit: Psalm 8 und seine Rezeption im Neuen Testament.* Würz-
        burg.
Blum, Erhard
2004   Von Gottesunmittelbarkeit zu Gottesähnlichkeit. Überlegungen zur theologischen
        Anthropologie der Paradieserzählung. Pp. 9–29 in G. Eberhard and K. Liess, eds.,
        Gottes Nähe im Alten Testament. SBS 202. Stuttgart. = Blum, Erhard, Von Gottesun-
        mittelbarkeit zu Gottähnlichkeit: Überlegungen zur theologischen Anthropologie der
        Paradieserzählung. Pp. 1–19 in idem, *Textgestalt und Komposition: Exegetische Beiträge zu
        Tora und Vordere Propheten.* FAT 69. Tübingen.
Bormann, Lukas (ed.)
2008   *Schöpfung, Monotheismus und fremde Religionen.* BThSt 95. Neukirchen-Vluyn.
Bührer, Walter
2014   *Am Anfang. . . : Untersuchungen zur Textgenese und zur relativ-chronologischen Einordnung
        von Gen 1–3.* Göttingen.
Derchain, Philippe, and Daniel von Recklinghausen
2004   *La création – Die Schöpfung: Poème pariétal – ein Wandgedicht. La façade ptolémaique du
        temple d'Esna. Pour une poétique ptolémaique.* Rites Egyptiens X. Turnhout.
El Hawary, Amr
2010   *Wortschöpfung: Die Memphitische Theologie und die Siegesstele des Pije – zwei Zeugen kul-
        tureller Repräsentation in der 25. Dynastie.* OBO 243. Freiburg, Switzerland, and Göttin-
        gen.
Fieger, Michael, and Lanckau, Jörg
2010   *Erschaffung und Zerstörung der Schöpfung: Ein Beitrag zum Thema Mythos.* Berne.
Garr, W. Randall
2003   *In His Own Image and Likeness: Humanity, Divinity, and Monotheism.* Culture and History
        of the Ancient Near East 15. Leiden.
Gertz, Jan Christian
2006   Beobachtungen zum literarischen Charakter und zum geistesgeschichtlichen Ort der
        nichtpriesterschriftlichen Sintfluterzählung. Pp. 41–58 in U. Schorn and M. Beck, eds.,
        Auf dem Weg zur Endgestalt von Genesis bis II Regum. FS Schmitt. BZAW 370. Berlin.
Gertz, Jan Christian
2009   Antibabylonische Polemik im priesterlichen Schöpfungsbericht? *ZThK* 106: 137–55.
Gorges-Braunwarth, Susanne
2002   *«Frauenbilder – Weisheitsbilder – Gottesbilder» in Spr 1–9: Die personifizierte Weisheit im
        Gottesbild der nachexilischen Zeit.* Münster.
Hangartner, Li, and Brigitte Vielhaus (eds.)
2006   *Segnen und gesegnet werden.* Düsseldorf.
Hartenstein, Friedhelm
2009a   Wettergott – Schöpfergott – Einziger. Kosmologie und Monotheismus in den Psalmen,
        Pp. 77–97 in F. Hartenstein and M. Rösel, eds., *JHWH und die Götter der Völker: Sympo-
        sium zum 80. Geburtstag von Klaus Koch.* Neukirchen-Vluyn.
2009b   Zur Bedeutung der Schöpfung in den Geschichtspsalmen. Pp. 335–349 in R. Achen-
        bach and M. Arneth, eds., *«Gerechtigkeit und Recht zu üben» (Gen 18,19). Studien zur
        altorientalischen und biblischen Rechtsgeschichte, zur Religionsgeschichte Israels und zur Re-
        ligionssoziologie.* BZAR 13. Wiesbaden.
2013   JHWH, Erschaffer des Himmels: Zu Herkunft und Bedeutung eines monotheistischen
        Kernarguments. *ZThK* 110/4: 383–409.
Hoping, Helmut
2005   Gottes Ebenbild. Theologische Anthropologie und säkulare Vernunft. *ThQ* 185: 127–
        49.
Hossfeld, Frank-Lothar
2003   Schöpfungsfrömmigkeit in Ps 104 und bei Jesus Sirach. Pp. 129–38 in I. Fischer,
        U. Rapp, and J. Schiller, eds., *Auf den Spuren der schriftgelehrten Weisen: FS für Johannes
        Marböck.* BZAW 331. Berlin.

Janowski, Bernd
2004   Die lebendige Statue Gottes. Zur Anthropologie der priesterlichen Urgeschichte. Pp. 183–214 in M. Witte, ed., *Gott und Mensch im Dialog: FS für Otto Kaiser zum 80. Geburtstag*, Band 1. BZAW 345. Berlin.
2008   *Die Welt als Schöpfung. Beiträge zur Theologie des Alten Testaments 4.* Neukirchen-Vluyn.
2011   Gottes Sturm und Gottes Atem. Zum Verständnis von רוח אלוהים in Gen 1,2 und Ps 104,29f. Pp. 3–29 in M. Ebner, et al., eds. *Heiliger Geist. JBTh* 24. Neukirchen-Vluyn.
Kämmerer, Thomas R
2012   *Das babylonische Weltschöpfungsepos "Enūma Elîš."* AOAT 375. Münster.
Kraut, Judah
2010   The Birds and the Babes: The Structure and Meaning of Psalm 8. *JQR* 100/1: 10–24.
Knigge, Carsten
2006   *Das Lob der Schöpfung: Die Entwicklung ägyptischer Sonnen- und Schöpfungshymnen nach dem Neuen Reich.* OBO 219. Freiburg, Switzerland / Göttingen.
Krüger, Annette
2010a *Das Lob des Schöpfers. Studien zur Sprache, Motivik und Theologie von Psalm 104.* WMANT 124. Neukirchen-Vluyn.
2010b Psalm 104 und der Grosse Amarnahymnus. Eine neue Perspektive. Pp. 609–21 in E. Zenger, ed., *The Composition of the Book of Psalms.* Leuven, 2010.
Krüger, Thomas
2009   Schöpfung und Sabbat in Genesis 2,1–3. Pp. 155–69 in C. Karrer-Grube et al., eds., *Sprachen – Bilder – Klänge: Dimensionen der Theologie im Alten Testament und in seinem Umfeld. Festschrift für Rüdiger Bartelmus zu seinem 65. Geburtstag.* AOAT 359. Münster.
Leuenberger, Martin
2008   *Segen und Segenstheologien im alten Israel: Untersuchungen zu ihren religions- und theologiegeschichtlichen Konstellationen und Transformationen.* AThANT 90. Zürich.
MacDonald, Nathan et al., eds.
2012   *Genesis and Christian Theology.* Grand Rapids.
Mettinger, Tryggve N. D.
2007   *The Eden Narrative: A Literary and Religio-Historical Study of Genesis 2–3.* Winona Lake, IN.
Müller, Hans-Peter
2004   Schöpfungsmythen – literarisch und theologisch – mit Anschlusserörterungen. *ZThK* 101: 506–25.
Münk, Hans J., and Durst, Michael (eds.)
2006   *Schöpfung, Theologie und Wissenschaft.* Freiburg, Switzerland.
Neumann-Gorsolke, Ute
2004   *Herrschen in den Grenzen der Schöpfung: Ein Beitrag zur alttestamentlichen Anthropologie am Beispiel von Psalm 8, Genesis 1 und verwandten Texten.* Neukirchen-Vluyn.
Oberforcher, Robert
2003a Was ist der Mensch? Antwortangebote im Horizont des biblischen Schöpfungsglaubens. Pp. 9–44 in K. Breitsching and W. Guggenberger, eds., *Der Mensch – Ebenbild Gottes: Vorträge der dritten Innsbrucker Theologischen Sommertage 2002.* Thaur.
2003b Biblische Lesarten zur Anthropologie des Ebenbildmotivs. Pp. 131–68 in A. Vonach and G. Fischer Georg, eds., *Horizonte biblischer Texte: FS für Josef M. Oesch zum 60. Geburtstag.* OBO 196. Freiburg, Switzerland / Göttingen.
Rechenmacher, Hans
2002   Gott und das Chaos. Ein Beitrag zum Verständnis von Gen 1,1-3. *ZAW* 114: 1–20.
Reichmann, Sirje
2009   Psalm 104 und der Grosse Sonnenhymnus des Echnaton. Erwägungen zu ihrem literarischen Verhältnis. Pp. 257–288 in M. Pietsch et al., eds., *Israel zwischen den Mächten: Festschrift für Stefan Timm zum 65. Geburtstag.* Münster.
Riede, Peter
2002   *Im Spiegel der Tiere: Studien zum Verhältnis von Mensch und Tier im alten Israel.* OBO 187. Freiburg, Switzerland / Göttingen.
Schmid, Konrad
2002   Die Unteilbarkeit der Weisheit: Überlegungen zur sogenannten Paradieserzählung Gen 2f. und ihrer theologischen Tendenz. *ZAW* 114: 21–39.
2011   Neue Schöpfung als Überbietung des neuen Exodus: Die tritojesajanische Aktualisierung der deuterojesajanischen Theologie und der Tora. Pp. 185–205 in idem, *Schriftgelehrte Traditionsliteratur: Fallstudien zur innerbiblischen Schriftauslegung im Alten Testament.* FAT 77. Tübingen.

Schmid, Konrad (ed.)
2012   *Schöpfung.* Tübingen.
Schmid, Konrad, and Riedweg, Christoph (eds.)
2008   *Beyond Eden: The Biblical Story of Paradise and its Reception History.* FAT II/34. Tübingen.
Schmidt, Wolf-Rüdiger
2003   *Der Schimpanse im Menschen – das gottebenbildliche Tier: Menschenaffen, Evolution, Schöpfung.* Gütersloh.
Schroer, Silvia
2009   Die numinose Wertung der Umwelt in der Hebräischen Bibel. Pp. 537–590 in B. Janowski and K. Liess, eds., *Der Mensch im Alten Israel: Neue Forschungen zur alttestamentlichen Anthropologie.* HBS 59. Freiburg i. Br. (in collaboration with Othmar Keel).
2010   "Du sollst dem Rind beim Dreschen das Maul nicht zubinden" (Dtn 25,4): Alttestamentliche Tierethik als Grundlage einer theologischen Zoologie. Pp. 38–56 in R. Hagencord, ed., *Wenn sich Tiere in der Theologie tummeln: Ansätze einer theologischen Zoologie.* Regensburg.
2013   *Tiere in der Bibel.* Freiburg i. Br.
Schroer, Silvia, and Staubli, Thomas
2006   "Wie man sagt, wenn Saft in der Traube sich findet: Verdirb sie nicht, es ist ein Segen darin." Bedenkenswertes zum Segen aus biblischer Sicht. Pp. 30–42 in L. Hangartner and B. Vielhaus, eds., *Segnen und gesegnet werden: Reflexionen, Impulse, Materialien.* Düsseldorf.
Schüle, Andreas
2005   Made in the "Image of God": The Concepts of Divine Images in Gen 1-3. ZAW 117: 1–20.
2006   *Der Prolog der Hebräischen Bibel: Der literar- und theologiegeschichtliche Diskurs der Urgeschichte (Genesis 1–11).* AThANT 86. Zürich.
2009   *Die Urgeschichte (Genesis 1–11).* ZBK 1.1. Zürich.
Scoralick, Ruth
2006   Biblische Schöpfungstheologie in Gen 1–9. Pp. 58–93 in H. J. Münk, ed., *Schöpfung, Theologie und Wissenschaft.* Theologische Berichte 29. Freiburg, Switzerland.
Shaviv, Shaya
2004   The Polytheistic Origins of the Biblical Flood Narrative. *VT* 54: 527–48.
Smith, Mark
2010   *The Priestly Vision of Genesis 1.* Minneapolis, 2010.
Staubli, Thomas, and Silvia Schroer
2014   *Menschenbilder der Bibel.* Ostfildern.
Stingelhammer, Hermann
2011   *Einführung in die Schöpfungstheologie.* Darmstadt.
Van Kooten, George H. (ed.).
2005   *The Creation of Heaven and Earth. Re-interpretations of Genesis 1 in the Context of Judaism, Ancient Philosophy, Christianity, and Modern Physics.* Leiden, 2005.
Waschke, Ernst-Joachim
2009   Die Bedeutung der Königstheologie für die Vorstellung der Gottesebenbildlichkeit des Menschen. Pp. 235–52 in A. Wagner, ed. *Anthropologische Aufbrüche. Alttestamentliche und interdisziplinäre Zugänge zur historischen Anthropologie.* Göttingen.
Weippert, Manfred
2004   Schöpfung am Anfang oder Anfang der Schöpfung? Noch einmal zu Syntax und Semantik von Gen 1,1-3. *ThZ* 60: 5–22.
Whitekettler, Richard
2011   A Communion of Subjects: Zoological Classification and Human/Animal Relations in Psalm 104. *BBR* 21/2: 173–87.
Wilcke, Claus
2010   Altmesopotamische Weltbilder. Die Welt mit altbabylonischen Augen sehen. Pp. 1–27 in P. Gemeinhardt and A. Zgoll, eds., *Weltkonstruktionen. Religiöse Weltdeutung zwischen Chaos und Kosmos vom Alten Orient bis zum Islam.* ORA 5. Tübingen.
Wöhrle, Jakob
2009   Dominium Terrae: Exegetische und religionsgeschichtliche Überlegungen zum Herrschaftsauftrag in Gen 1,26–28. *ZAW* 121: 171–88.

Index of Authors

Index of Scripture

New Testament

Deuterocanonical Works